The Last Passage

The Last
Passage

Recovering a Death of Our Own

Donald Heinz

New York   Oxford
OXFORD UNIVERSITY PRESS
1999

Oxford University Press

Oxford   New York
Athens   Auckland   Bangkok   Bogotá   Buenos Aires   Calcutta   Cape Town
Chennai   Dar es Salaam   Delhi   Florence   Hong Kong   Istanbul
Karachi   Kuala Lumpur   Madrid   Melbourne   Mexico City   Mumbai
Nairobi   Paris   São Paulo   Singapore   Taipei   Tokyo   Toronto   Warsaw

and associated companies in
Berlin   Ibadan

Published by Oxford University Press, Inc.
198 Madison Avenue, New York, New York 10016

Oxford is a registered trademark of Oxford University Press, Inc.

Library of Congress Cataloging-in-Publication Data
Heinz, Donald.
       The last passage : recovering a death of our own / Donald Heinz.
          p.   cm.
       Includes bibliographical references and index.
       ISBN 0–19–511643–7
       1. Death—Psychological aspects—United States.   2. Death—Social
aspects—United States.   3. Funeral rites and ceremonies.   I. Title.
BF789.D4H423   1998
306.9'0973—dc21   98–10378

Since this page cannot legibly accomodate all the permissions, page vi constitutes
an extension of the copyright page.

1 3 5 7 9 8 6 4 2

Printed in the United States of America on acid-free paper

To the memory of my father and mother,
who taught me the most important lines of the Story

William Vincent Heinz 1909–1987
Stella Lona Heinz 1911–1994

The author gratefully acknowledges permission to reprint the following:

"Margaret, are you grieving," by Gerard Manley Hopkins. From *The poetical works of Gerard Manley Hopkins,* ed. Norman H. Mackenzie. Oxford: Clarendon Press, 1990. Used with permission of the Society of Jesus.

"The Envelope," copyright 1978 by Maxine Kumin, from *Selected Poems 1960–1990,* by Maxine Kumin. Reprinted by permission of W. W. Norton & Company, Inc.

"Belief," from *New Selected Poems,* by Philip Levine, copyright 1991 by Philip Levine. Reprinted by permission of Alfred A. Knopf, Inc.

Four lines from "Little Gidding," from *Four Quartets,* by T. S. Eliot. Reprinted by permission of Faber and Faber Ltd.

"By the waters of the woodland," by Kim Chernin, copyright 1978 by Kim Chernin. Permission to reprint is gratefully acknowledged.

"Tarry a while," by Sarojini Naidu, in Lisl Goodman, *Death and the Creative Life,* copyright 1981. Used by permission of Springer Publishing Company, Inc.

Three lines from "Paterson," from *Paterson,* by William Carlos Williams, copyright 1949 by William Carlos Williams. Reprinted by permission of New Directions Publishing Corp.

"Descent," by William Carlos Williams, from *Collected Poems 1939–1962,* Volume II. Copyright 1951 by William Carlos Williams. Reprinted by permission of New Directions Publishing Corp.

Four lines from "Sailing to Byzantium" and four lines from "The Tower." Reprinted with the permission of Simon & Schuster from *The Collected Works of W. B. Yeats,* Volume I: *The Poems,* revised and edited by Richard J. Finneran. Copyright 1928 by Macmillan Publishing Company, renewed 1956 by Georgie Yeats.

Eight lines from "Death and the Maiden," by Matthias Claudius and twelve lines from "To the Parcae," by Holderlin, translated by Walter Kaufman, *25 German Poets,* copyright 1975. Used by permission of W. W. Norton.

"The Passing Storm," from *Poems,* by Boris Pasternak, copyright 1959, University of Michigan Press. Used by permission.

Contents

Preface

MASTERING MY MOTHER'S TAPES, HURRYING IN MY FATHER'S STEPS

I remember my parents coming to visit me in California one spring. My mother brought from Dubuque precious family tapes she wanted me to turn into cassettes she could play on the small machine I had given her the Christmas before. These were the family stories, reel-to-reel, she had packed in her suitcase. Mostly they were rites of passage: a memorial service for my brother who had died in Vietnam, family weddings, my brother's and my ordination services, a first sermon.

My parents had only three days to spend with me before taking the Greyhound on to see my sister in Texas. There was much to talk about, especially the coming celebration of their fiftieth wedding anniversary. But it was the tapes that preoccupied my mother. When the transcribing was over, she rested like God on the seventh day. Creation was done, and the words that called us all to life could be listened to over and over again.

I supposed the tapes would be my mother's companions while she sewed quilts and baby clothes for Lutheran World Relief. Even my father might stay awake one evening, listening to the tapes after a long day at the store, grieving again his elder boy's death, celebrating his daughter's wedding, nodding through initiation sermons.

I look back on how I struggled, grudgingly, with aging tape machines and obsolete hookups, how the taping project seemed such an insignificant task. But my mother was insistent in her special way. She was the guardian of family memories, she kept our stories close to her heart. I remember the time when I sat, as a little boy, watching her crying as she threw away old treasures after spring cleaning the attic. This was now her autumn, and she was storing up our futures.[1] It was no accident that I, the surviving son, was asked to preside over this handing down from tape to tape. In India, the sacred texts were written on palm leaf sheets tied together with a string. Dharma, the moral order of the universe, is as fragile and vulnerable to disintegration as these texts on palm leaves. Every generation must copy them anew if dharma is to be kept alive in the world. It pleases me to think of myself as such a copyist. My mother is a biblical woman. She knows the directive to "tell these things in the ears of your children and your children's children." My mother was beginning to arrange for her last passage, and I was invited to assist in the long rowing toward God.

I have learned about passages from her. Indeed, my mother kept my own passages closer to her heart than I myself do. It was her midwestern gift to an expatriate in California lest he lose his hold on the story he carried across the Rockies years ago. The congratulation cards and crisp five-dollar bills—my father was scrupulous about crisp money for special occasions, it's what banks are for—arrived from Iowa to mark my milestones. The last passage had already come for my brother, an army chaplain in Vietnam, and even a funeral at Arlington could not requite an unobserved death under unknowable circumstances. When the last passage would come for my parents, the family would know what to do, how to keep faith with each other, how to tell the story. My parents taught us well to guard our own history, to hold it as a treasure.

Over the years I have found time to practice the lesser passage of going home to Iowa. After I flew to a meeting in Chicago close to Thanksgiving one year, I rented a car and drove home to Dubuque. Halfway there it started to snow, and the driving instincts of my youth returned. Crawling at fifteen miles per hour in second gear, sometimes sliding helplessly down the hills by Galena, I thought of promises to keep while finding the way home.

We ritualized this time together, as we did on the other occasions we got together. We talked about the death of my brother, still laboring over unfinished business. We studied scrapbooks, counted anniversaries, traded recent news on the relatives, worried over the state of the church. Underneath it all, with diligence but unknowingly, they were teaching me my lines, so that when they exited the stage, their voices would keep speaking through mine. Relinquished to me, the family story would remain intact. Someday I would have mastered all the tapes and prepared for my own passage.

The second day home, I set out in exploration of the landscape of my childhood. I reported back how I had lingered in front of the old house and walked the back alley behind it, naming each child who had ever lived in those houses. I did not mention glimpsing again in a doorway the first girl I ever tried to kiss, or how my cheek burned again where she had slapped me. I prowled my old elementary school and startled a kindergarten teacher working late. I remembered junior-high baloney sandwiches and escaping it all to enter prep school in Milwaukee. My parents secretly hoped some child of theirs would return to live in Dubuque, but we would continue as a diaspora. Only our story remains.

These days I think about the responsibility to get one's lines down. I try to pass it on to the students in my Death and Dying class at the university. They suspect I am more ready to take a look at death than they because death is more ready to take a look at me. But in the season when the light diminishes, when the fall semester's relationship is coming to an end, they arrive on the last day to give an account of themselves.

One December I faced a final of my own. My father had died suddenly, and I had to hurry home to trace his steps and to join my mother and sisters in finishing the story.

It's not as if I was unprepared. Two years earlier I had stood before a heavy woolen overcoat, made in Poland, the kind no one in California ever wears. I went back twice to admire that coat, to sample its weight. I invested, and I knew why. One day I would wear this to my father's funeral. I would not shiver in the final drive from O'Hare over the icy roads to Dubuque. I would not go unprepared for stormy weather, for I had invested in a great overcoat for my father's funeral. My father would die in winter, I knew. Snow would lie hard on the ground and the winds would blow a powerful chill on our party as we stood in the cemetery up on the bluffs overlooking the Mississippi and mourned his passing. But inside this greatcoat, I knew, I could take my time to remember. I would not need to hurry from that cold cemetery before I rehearsed the story I'd mastered from my mother's tapes.

Standing still in the snow that December day in Iowa, I felt I was already hurrying ahead in my father's steps. He ran everywhere. When his children scattered, he ran so he would not lose us. He ran so we would not forget. He ran to the mailbox to look for news from us. Every fall and spring he ran to visit us, traveling east or west or south to visit my sisters and me. Every December he ran to the post office to send packages to Pennsylvania and California and Texas, sacramentalizing our story in ways we could taste and see. That one December, as a great snowstorm closed the schools and the midwestern light was darkening, my father ran down. In front of the post office, where he had run to mail us Christmas packages, one of our relatives found him slumped over the wheel of his car. My father's race was over.

There had been rests in the race. The rhythm of life story requires them. He rested to dry between my toes after my Saturday night bath. He stopped to hug us morning and night and to tell us good-bye at least twice every day before he left the house. Each night he waited patiently by our bedroom door to assure himself we were breathing—sometimes we held our breath out of perversity, or to bring him nearer. He never failed to rest with God every Sunday morning, nor for prayer before and after every meal we ever ate, even in restaurants.

I have come to see that he ran and rested because his legs were short and his pride was great. This is the human condition. I understand that he ran so his children would hold their heads high and honor their name. Now I am running in his steps.

A few years later the time came for the final mastering of my mother's tapes. In her last months, as we struggled to sum the story, I tried to become mother to my mother in her time of frailty, not nearly successfully, sometimes resentfully. Is the parent's last passage the time when children try to repay the great debts they owe? I was not good enough to play my mother's tapes. I had not yet mastered the dispositions necessary to mother my mother in her old age. She would again have to teach her child, now in her need and his strength, as once in her strength and his weakness.

When my sisters and I pilgrimaged home to Dubuque for my mother's funeral, I found myself once again in the cemetery on the bluffs above the Mississippi. I tried to absorb the gravestone message my mother had already had engraved at my father's death: "William V. Heinz and Stella N. Heinz / Parents of Beverly, Roger, Donald, and Sandra." She saw her vocation as taking pride in her children. I stood there, about to leave Dubuque a last time, probably never to return. I felt like a motherless child, a long way from home, the only place in the world where they still called me Donny.

Are we learning lines that will ring true when our last passage requires them? Do we teach our children to play the tapes, to run in the steps of their story? How many will not know the words or the way? In this culture heading toward the third millennium, could we learn again to tell a story in public—who we tried to be, what meanings we acknowledged, what calls we heard? We must uncover the language, improvise the circumstances, rediscover the rituals that can carry us through to a proper end. Every well-done death is a version of life. But we have to find our way again, turning the lost passage of death into a last passage that returns meaning to life and pays dividends of hope. At the beginning of this century the German poet Rilke wrote: "Who cares anything today for a finely-finished death? The wish to have a death of one's own is growing ever rarer. A while yet, and it will be just as rare as a life of one's own."[2] He thought death a gift mostly passed on unopened. But poets and artists must be the seers of this lost agenda. "In this terror before mass-produced death there is the sadness of the artist who honors well-wrought things, who wants to make a work and make of death his work. Death is thus from the start linked to the movement, so difficult to bring to light, of the artistic experience."[3]

Much is against such an attempt. It is pilgrimage I have in mind, not tourism. A magic flute is required for dangerous journeys. The task we share in common is to learn again how to offer consent, to proffer the yes that rites of passage require. Offering consent to the last passage is a considered act, a wager with meaning, a completion of the story. Stories offered to the future tie two worlds together, the living and the dead. They sediment into the common wealth of human culture the struggles and celebrations expressed in our passages, repentance and grace, grief and hope. In offering our stories we lift the level of spirit in the world and invite the young to remark on mystery. This is a promise to keep.

Once women stitched grief quilts from the characteristic fabrics of family lives. Patches from here and there brought the family's purposes to life on the mother's lap. It is time again to take up this women's work. In all our recoveries of a death of our own, we create the great quilt for the human family, full of dreams and sewn with unutterable yearnings.

We have thought it prudent in our time to repress the line from the old prayer, "If I should die before I wake," in order to hide children from darkness. In fact, we must awaken before we die. This book is about an awakening through ritual from a death-denying cultural slumber. I am making a call to ordinary people to take up the possibility of ritualizing their living and their dying as completions of the human story and gifts to the future. This book is a plea not to scorn ritual and so leave no path for survivors to follow, no traveler's rest for those still on pilgrimage. Since death is as much human construction as biological given, can we not re-create a death of our own?

Introduction

AN INVITATION TO
EXPERIMENTAL THEATER

Death has returned to the American stage, having outlived an interdiction that lay over it for most of this century in Europe and North America. French, British, and American critics, in particular, had traced death's demise to causes several centuries old in the Western tradition. Philippe Ariès saw death moving from tamed to untamed and, with a brief romantic interlude in the nineteenth century, to invisible and even forbidden. The Enlightenment bequest of the triumph of reason was to render death an outmoded theme in the drama of the human condition. The English had come to fear death even more than sex, Geoffrey Gorer thought. Even in the late 1960s Elisabeth Kübler-Ross could find no hospitals in Chicago willing to acknowledge it.

But now innumerable books, films, and media events have billed death's restoration to the theater of public view. Critics describe a new age of death since 1960. Initial reviews are cautious. At the end of his great tome *The Hour of Our Death*, Philippe Ariès acknowledges that the silence has been broken and the attempt to evacuate death from public consciousness has mostly ended. But the new plays lack depth.

> They acknowledge the necessity of death, but they want it to be accepted and no longer shameful. Although they may consult the ancient wisdom, there is no question of turning back or of rediscovering the evil that has been abolished. They propose to reconcile death with happiness. Death must simply become the discreet but dignified exit of a peaceful person from a helpful society that is not torn, not even overly upset by the idea of a biological transition without significance, without pain or suffering, and ultimately without fear.[1]

Whether the entrance of AIDS will deepen this drama remains to be seen. Ariès feared that neither the individual nor the community is strong enough to recognize the existence of death.

This book is an invitation to readers to enter the experimental theater in which death is being restaged.[2] As recent scripts are critiqued, new ones attempted and old ones reprised, and tentative lines uttered, ritual improvisation unites audience and stage. The pervasive mood is the recovery of *death as opportunity*—including opportunity for improvisation—and not just death as a neglected problem that still nags. The opportunity is not only religious, but social and cultural as well.

I have thought long about who the readers might be, the ones I would like to coax into the theater and onto the stage. It is to thoughtful, literate people who are shaped by the Western tradition, who are the heirs of our present culture, yet who are willing to reflect on their mortality, that I write. I write to people in the agony of mourning, people in the early stages of anticipatory grief, people who carry in their bodies the wounds of death. I also write to those whose brows are unclouded, whose generation is still untouched, but who are willing to think of death as a mystery or a challenge or a companion or an evil yet to be confronted.

Who are we, those of us in this theater? We have been shaped by the public deaths of Martin Luther King Jr. and John and Robert Kennedy. We have agonized over Vietnam and omnicide in nuclear war. We live with the temptations of postmodern ironic detachment and the ideologies that justify it. We have experimented with private retreats from a depressing macrocosm. We are curious about the quickening of spirituality in the environmental movement. We have tried our hand at reforming politics and at condemning it. We are liberals anxious about the intolerant stridency of neoconservatism, and we are conservatives lamenting lost values. Some of us deeply cherish traditions; some are pioneering away from familiar structures of meaning. Many of us have lived in religious communities that historically were custodians of the language of transcendence and practitioners of ritual life. Some of us are finding new hope in ethnic ways or are paving feminist approaches.

In a corner of the theater, assembled with some satisfaction at being members of the choir, sit many professing members of religious communities. Even we (I count myself among them) must acknowledge the collapse of the sacred canopy once erected over American culture, and we rue the fact that religious symbols often fail to instruct, much less govern, the consciousness and behavior of society. Indeed, our influence is least in the media, higher education, and corporate America. Nor have the individual members of churches and synagogues been able to resist the steady encroachments of a "death system" that denies, evades, trivializes, commercializes, romanticizes, sublets, and reduces death. Our liturgies are often lifeless and stilted; even the latest products of our worship committees, though long on the recovery of historical text, are short on imagination, embodiment, movement, and gesture. Where the faithful do participate meaningfully in ritual life, we worry that nearly every part of the cultural system that lies outside these brief religious exercises has lost its way with death, and that this death system exercises a symbolic power greater than anything warranted by a minimal exposure to our most powerful symbols and our finest theological convictions and expectations.

Though we are a diverse lot, though the argument of the book does not assume a homogeneous audience, I think we bear enough in common that we, in all our particularities, might accept a common invitation to an experimental theater of opportunity: improvising diverse works in progress for the last passage we all confront. We share, even in our diversity, a powerful, common context that we cannot escape. We all face death in a culture where a crass commercialism, a utilitarian individualism, and a dominating statism are in triumph, where biblical values, the social contract, and religious, educational, and civic mediating institutions are all in eclipse. These provide the milieu for the "fall of public man" and the decline of community, civic virtue, and the public good. Rituals that can connect us to communities of meaning have fallen on hard times; indeed, what passes as sophistication seems to require ritual detachment. Even in the locations where ritual still plays, marginalized groups suffer exclusion from communities of power, and boredom with ritual is typical. Religious communities have lost power, and secular culture has grown disenchanted with Enlightenment disenchantment. More and more, people die alone, off the stage—or they die hurried deaths, only half costumed with stock rituals by careless crews.

Lacking the resources to see death large, our culture has chosen to see it small. We, in turn, have become small. Taming and domesticating the great mystery, the insistent challenge, the perennial wound through which the soul might see, we shrink our own humanity as well. Despairing of religious resources weakened from within—the churches, for example, have been unable to convert the liberating power of the death of Christ into a pervasive symbol, even in their own life—severely circumscribed by a dominating secular culture, and chronically forgetful of the cultural knowledge we once possessed, we elect a practical death, one we can still cope with. In a culture specializing in the rights of the individual, our best choice is a managed exit, legalized by the recently enacted federal Patient Self-Determination Act.

The resources we have need of, I am convinced, must be found in communities of faith, communities of mutual consolation where we learn the rhythms of grief and hope, communities of the living that interpenetrate the community of the dead. Once clergy accepted a continuing obligation to maintain contacts between the living and the dead. Once the negotiation of two worlds was an important part of our intellectual geography. To conceive of purgatory, for example, meant "to change the geography of the other world and hence of the universe, to alter time in the afterlife and hence the link between earthly, historical time and eschatological time, between the time of existence and the time of anticipation."[3] Such a mapping produced an intellectual revolution that changed life itself. Should we succeed in creating powerful new ritualizations of death, reuniting two worlds, two times, two dimensions of meaning, we shall once again have produced a revolution. In doing so, we shall coincidentally grow into communities adequate to death and to the human condition.

This is the social drama, I think, in which we find ourselves, one that challenges us to new ritual plots and scripts.[4] In some other time the work of culture eventuated in death systems more or less adequate to the human condition. Times changed, and society moved in response to new cultural needs. The meanings previously constructed became moot, and the attendant death systems lost their power and atrophied. We now need to recognize and overcome our loss. We need to perform new cultural work that will retrieve or create anew a meaningful relation to death and to the world of the dead. New "cultural performances" may be differently conceived, but they must deliver to us effective ritualized connections to death.

A parallel example: The constructions of culture that produced Native American spirituality have become obsolete to us. But our own lack of spirituality with respect to nature has proved disastrous to ourselves and to our environment. Whether or not we can ever again reproduce that prototypical (native) cultural work that produced such a spirituality, we must recover or discover a spiritually meaningful connection to the environment. Without it we remain sick unto death.

This is the audience, the subtext, the social drama, the missing plot, the stage of experimental theater. What plays can be expected? What improvisations and collaborations? What retrievals and what creations?

In chapter 1, "The Dying and Reviving of Death," I describe how death has been revived in our time both by the violent explosion of AIDS and by the insidious fear that modern medical bureaucracies will rob us of self-determination in our old age. The failures of religion and the successes of secularism, preoccupations with individualism, and the dominance of a medical model produced a death system that truncated dying and rendered Western culture incapable of developing fully human responses to death and mortality. We lacked the resources to give death its due. The return of death to the public stage promises to move us beyond the death system of the sidelong glance. But psychological models dominate the death awareness movement, and AIDS deaths, so convoluted in the public consciousness, have made only a small, if promising, beginning in challenging us to develop new rites of last passage. The revival of death now requires a cultural and religious grounding sufficient to the needs of the human condition.

In chapter 2, "Imagining Death," I pause first for a graveyard meditation. What interactions with our mortality can we allow ourselves and what do they portend? Could we recover a connection between the communities of the living and of the dead? Lacking the resources to risk seeing death large, we have shrunk our imagination of it. But death is large. Could we again find ways to risk seeing it so? Since death systems are humanly constructed, we might ransack imaginations more vivid and ample than our own. In the mythological, the psychological, the anthropological, and the religious imaginations, across time and space, we glimpse how humans have tried to give death its due. Renewed and replenished by a tour of the human imagination, we acknowledge how far we have fallen short, how truncated are our responses to death, how impoverished is our death system. The death we had succeeded in managing turns out to be of much smaller proportions than the death of cultural memory—and so are we.

In chapter 3, "The Lost Art of Dying," I imagine the *ars moriendi* as the blue found in the stained-glass windows of Chartres Cathedral, a depth of color we no longer know how to produce. Thus we have lost our way in dying. I call for new scripts in which some few, by imagining and constructing great deaths, pioneer a dying that resolves the crises of our age. The way is thicketed with a psychologized, privatized, and bureaucratized death system, and new cultural constructions are difficult. But there are promising trends: the recent calls for dying as the last quest for responsibility and the opportunity for self-determination; the imaginings of poets and storytellers who see where new ground must be broken; the vision by Kübler-Ross and others of death as a final stage of human growth; and the still fertile ground of existentialism.

In chapter 4 I reenvision the time preceding death as "The Last Career." Death invites us to accept new images, expectations, roles, and norms. The cultural work of reimagining death and developing appropriate responses to it, of positioning ourselves between life and death, of negotiating travel between two worlds, is the assignment for this last career, a time, as I will show, for "gero-transcendence." Such a career begins with life review and ends with the completion of a story. In chapter 5, "Finishing the Story," I suggest an approach that runs through archaeological digs and eschatalogical reaches, climaxing in poetry and myth, perhaps even religious quest.

In chapter 6 I travel "Along the Ritual Way" and carry toward completion the argument of the book and the cultural process it enjoins. In order to emphasize death as our cultural construction, subject to change and evolution, I pause first to reflect on the changing history of the American funeral. Observing present ambiguities and weaknesses, I look to the power of ritual to change and to cause change. Carrying us beyond the biological moment and its attendant reductionisms, appropriate ritualizations of death could solidify, articulate, and display the recovery of a death of our own and bequeath it to culture and society. Through ritual, death works itself out. The fusion of our own dying and death (and life) as ultimate meaning is rehearsed and exemplified. To clarify these goals and the means to their achievement, I set forth the definitions, meaning, and power of rituals, and above all their ability to constitute our humanity. As rituals negotiate the human passage through the world, the world passes through our humanity. There are powerful impediments to ritual in the modern age, which I analyze. But the evolution of rituals and of culture and of our humanity can proceed together. From the pregnant liminality of death, new rituals, new cultural meanings, new life can be born. A fully ritualized death of our own becomes our bequest to the next generation.

The rituals to be retrieved or created must happen in real time and space, with physical bodies and within flesh-and-blood communities, using human words and texts and symbols and the arts, often drawing on the ingredients of "material culture." I proceed, then, to unearth the ingredients we need for rituals adequate to our human condition. In chapter 7, "Ritual Quarrying: Bodies in Motion," I focus on ritual embodiment in the concentric circles of body/community/site. Thence I attend to the loss of movement that too often freezes modern ritual and renders it stultifying. In chapter 8, "Ritual Quarrying: The Arts and Letters of Hope," I look to music, the visual arts, dance and theater, and creative words to enrich ritual. I come to rest in the ritual posture of hope.

This is the argument of the book. I have staged it before readers-become-audience in a setting of experimental theater, in order to mirror the larger arena in which the work of culture happens. My persistent theme is our contemporary truncation of death scripts because of imaginal resources too limited to risk larger plots. The missing resources add up to an empowered community—a community of meaning adequate to the human condition, a community with symbols sufficiently inclusive to unite the worlds of the dead and of the living. A community that empowers life, I allow myself to hope, will be the unexpected gift vouchsafed to the future as we join together to create cultural scripts sufficient to encounter death. This becomes the contribution of the audience, who respond to calls from the stage.

Thus I envision the audience of readers becoming a congregation. I alluded earlier to the possibility that religious readers might pose as the choir with a special sympathy to the rituals under way on stage. My own view is that a ritual community adequate to the human condition is ultimately one grounded in religious symbols, which alone are sufficiently expansive. It may be that all of our humanly constructed resources fall short of the human dilemma in which we struggle with limit, mortality, and moral failure. Whether, in fact, we discover or create religious symbols is a question I leave in the wings. Christopher Lasch raised the question whether the secular world can constitute an enduring structure in which late-life meaning can be sustained.[5] Does this mean that the solution, if not the diagnosis, requires religious resources? Even if so, it is hardly the case that orthodoxy has triumphed. If the "great tradition" and the folk tradition often come together to create rites of last passage, sometimes the latter's ear will be closer to the ground. These days alternative spiritualities and rival paths to transcendence bloom, and new light breaks from the East. Nor can the great intellectual and theological traditions escape the mandate to come to new completions in every age.

I have thought constantly about the role of religion while writing this book. I have not wanted to claim any epistemological privilege for my own Christian theology or indeed for any religious traditions.[6] I note, however, that Paul Ramsey, a Protestant ethicist who pioneered in the field of bioethics, sometimes prefaced his books by declaring that he wrote as a Christian ethicist and that "religious warrants need not be silenced in order to engage in fruitful moral discourse."[7] Nor did he avoid proposing normative obligations. I have wanted to remain sensitive to the kind of cynicism voiced by the anticlerical pharmacist in Flaubert's *Madame Bovary* who "compared priests to ravens attracted by the odor of death."[8] I allude below to the great cultural battles between believers and unbelievers fought over death rituals and systems. In postrevolutionary France, for example, "the most important battles with the Church were fought . . . on the front of death ceremonial."[9]

If, in our present context, we collectively find ourselves with a cultural problem—the inability to ritualize death in meaningful, empowering, and fully adequate ways—and if we all together are to respond to this problem on the widest possible stage, I have thought it necessary to avoid pressing any specific religious claims. There are indeed claims to be made on behalf of religious systems of meaning, as there are confessions to be made about the failures of religious communities to embody themselves culturally in ways close to the adequacy of their symbols. I think, for example, that Christian symbols of life and death as refined in contemporary theologies are very powerful resources for the task I have set, but they are not yet producing religious communities capable of believing, embodying, living, and sustaining them, nor have they been able persuasively to offer them to the wider culture as the answers to its best and deepest questions.[10] But it is also true that comfortable secularists returning from God's funeral in the 1960s have had second thoughts; much in the secular city turned out to be less than promising.[11]

If I carried my argument to its conclusion by calling for the renewal of Christian communities and their empowering symbols as the primary solution to the loss of a death of our own, would I lose the rest of the audience who had been willing to engage the tasks of the experimental theater of death?[12] If only the choir, and a Christian choir at that, finally comes onstage for collaborating on the still-unfinished improvisational tasks, won't the book have failed? I have preferred to cast my lot with inclusiveness. I have tried to frame my argument in a public language while not concealing my own Christian sources and biases.[13] If, well along in the cultural task and with the imagination newly stimulated by the serendipity of improvisational theater, the audience becomes a spiritual congregation, I shall certainly be glad. If they travel still further along to conclude that ultimately the recovery of a death of our own is a religious task, I shall rejoice. If some find in the Christian story the most promising resource for the recovery of a death of our own, I will recognize in them my sisters and brothers, while celebrating all our near and distant cousins as well.

The Last Passage

Chapter 1

The Dying and Reviving of Death

It is the blight man was born for,
It is Margaret you mourn for.
—GERARD MANLEY HOPKINS

La mort est à la mode.
—MICHEL VOVELLE

And what the dead had no speech for, when living,
They can tell you, being dead: the communication
Of the dead is tongued with fire beyond the language of the living.
—T. S. ELIOT MEMORIAL IN WESTMINSTER ABBEY

INTRODUCTION

Until yesterday we died in medical Latin. A forgotten language obscured our passing. The primal scene was airbrushed by professionals who uttered words that could not be understood. Sterile gauze concealed the soul's departure, so that we did not remark on the passing of the light. Medicine did not measure metaphysics.

Death had become a biological infection. It was not to be permitted to escape control centers. Failures at living were sent to the hospital's private places, hidden from public view and knowledge. In a postmodern society direct disposal was to be arranged, so that no one would be shamed by the excrement of death. The living could continue their tour with only the faint odor of disinfectant. We had decided not to know or even to sniff. Professionals scrubbed death's signifiers clean and quarantined its discourse. The wound of death was debrided, its lacerated metaphysics neatly removed. We consented to dramaturgically passive roles because compensations were promised. Honey-coated words such as *casket* (coffin) and *coach* (hearse) and *park* (cemetery) were used, and the undertaker's art promised as our souvenir a beautiful memory picture. No fear and trembling would be required.

All this was necessary because of mortality's hair-trigger response to death words and dying people, which, unless good isolation techniques were practiced, could summon the malaise of finitude. If we voided death, if we abandoned the dying, we would escape facing the emptiness toward which we were heading. We eliminated intimations of mortality. But still they ran, as in great underground sewers, beneath our consciousness.

Those who were mourning only dimly perceived the cruel trick played on them. We coaxed them out of their terrible sadness so that we could buy happiness. Bother not the living, we admonished. Modesty and good manners forbid public displays. Cry privately. Wear your despair at home. Widows' weeds intrude on public space. We congratulated ourselves for liberating grieving from vestigial mourning customs. Thoughtlessly celebrating the demise of such traditions, we sent the bereaved away, disinherited of cultural or religious bequests. Bewildered, they retreated to private pain and unaccompanied mourning. As soon as they mastered their grief through whatever private rituals they could scavenge, they emerged from confinement to invite compliments for their rapid recovery. We applauded premature closure and rejoiced that the voice of grief was so quickly stilled. If some few protested, they were muffled by a social contract in which grief is disallowed public expression in exchange for a triumphalist, death-free status quo.[1]

Children had to be shielded from death. They were educated in the American way of happiness. We taught them to avert their eyes from sorrow like monks averting their eyes from females; we turned their experiences away from tragedy; we expurgated mortality from their primers. Each morning they pledged allegiance to the untroubled pursuit of pleasantness. Learning to avoid death became a developmental task of the young. Death would wound their innocence and wither their pubescent bloom. Choosing to tell only stories that fence off the darkness, we kept innocent the child on our lap and the child inside us, protecting ourselves from both's unanswerable tears. We saved adolescence from such poetry as Gerard Manley Hopkins's:

> *Margaret, are you grieving*
> *Over Goldengrove unleaving?*

Leaves, like the things of man, you
With your fresh thoughts care for, can you?
Ah! as the heart grows older
It will come to such sights colder
By and by, nor spare a sigh
Though worlds of wanwood leafmeal lie;
And yet you will *weep and know why.*
Now no matter, child, the name:
Sorrow's springs are the same.
Nor mouth had, no nor mind, expressed
What heart heard of, ghost guessed:
It is the blight man was born for,
It is Margaret you mourn for.[2]

It was we, of course, who had to be protected. If we had chosen to address the claims of death and grief, they would have turned to confront us in our neediness. As unwelcome strangers, they would come to our cupboards and find them bare. Mortality was always threatening to engulf us; it slept with one eye open, watching us. So we decreed that no bells should toll, that mourning should be brief, private, and discreet, for the American way of not dying was our desperate prophylactic.[3]

Our blessing for the dead was the same as Russian Jewry's for the tsars: "May God keep them . . . far away from us." Cemeteries were distanced or disguised. It was not always so. Marginalized in modern society, a convenient landscape for horror films, or a mostly unrequested ritual pause, the cemetery was once the noisiest, busiest, most animated, most commercial place in the rural or urban center. You could dance there, and not just with death. Sacred and profane came together, and so did the living and the dead.[4]

But unwelcome reminders shadowed the cultural repression of death. Nuclear holocaust was nearly beyond imagining, and we did our best to ignore those who insisted on visualizing it. We dressed the bomb in necessity or masculine posturing and looked away from its possible effects—or projected them onto distant lands and peoples. The collapse of the Soviet Union and the end of the cold war fortuitously healed over the wound of megadeath. Then we discovered that mortality is as unbound as terrorist threats, and as hard to protect against.

Then the AIDS epidemic threatened us anew with brightly colored horror. AIDS was not the unimaginable, unrepresentable death of atomic vaporization. We were forced to look instead at countless individual deaths. AIDS provoked "a resurgence of the Middle Ages in our memory, our conscience, and our imagination."⁵ Beginning about 1983, we were dragged through a bazaar of deaths, as if in a bad dream in which sluggish feet try to escape but fail. The unexpected arrival of AIDS in a postmodern landscape that thought itself also postepidemic occasioned cultural reconstructions, altering public attitudes toward sex, disease, death, medicine, and politics. Apocalyptic and moralistic labelings about AIDS matched many misbegotten past attempts to make sense of death and disease, and were equally unsuccessful.

Whether AIDS gets its cure or is willfully isolated from public consciousness, one reminder of mortality always remains. No one can look straight at the sun or at death, it is said. Death is an intensity that casts a dense shadow. The aging are these shadows. Today, they move through society not as those who have achieved fullness of life, but as dangerous reminders of the repressed trajectories of those younger than they. The aged have steadily lost place in the imaginal life of society. Entranced with limitlessness and youth, as many people as possible cling to an American exceptionalism that leaves old-world customs, ancient institutions, and the aged themselves behind.

Society sees the aged, when it must, as perpetual mourners, carriers of mortality. Intercourse with them is shunned. All who can claim not to be aging must be protected, for the aging know good and evil; they have seen too much; they have forbidden knowledge. Like shamans who enter a trance state to recover the secret language they alone know, the aged, it is supposed, must speak among themselves a language of discovered death. But in public they are required to revert to a safer tongue, so as not to offend or to implicate others in unwelcome mysteries. "Being a widow is like living in a country where nobody speaks your language."⁶

Yet society finds a purpose for the elderly. They are assigned to do dying for the whole culture. Commissioning them, as it were, to go to war in its stead, society hopes to abolish universal conscription. Given a heavy assignment, the elderly carry the mortality of all outside the gate. Allotted low-grief deaths and commissioned to do most of the dying, they endure unremarked departures. Atrophied rites of passage and unelaborated rituals are their simple memorials. Better, they are encouraged to advertise "No services" in their obituaries, so that everyone else will suffer no obligations.

Do the aging dimly perceive themselves victims of a cruel hoax played by a death-denying culture? No inquiries are made. They are contagious with death, and their one remaining social obligation is to disappear without questions. The benediction we ask of them is not to cast a shadow over the living. From hoary heads one last promise is extracted, that they not filter the sunlight. Unwelcome reminders of a common repressed destiny, they are cleaned from the attics of public consciousness and set by the curb for collection, or stored in warehouses at the edge of town, away from common premises, until it is reported they have died. Society has come to expect from them an early social death, in case their biological dying should tarry. It is thought that those who look into their eyes see darkness. Their eyes must not be allowed to call to the darkness within all. They depress the culture. The culture represses them. Convenient theodicies are purchased by removing from view those whose existence challenges easy meanings. With careful magic, a cultural facelift is accomplished. The aging were mirrors in which all glimpsed their mortality. Now it has been arranged that they should live in unreflective and unreflected communities. Nothing remains to mirror the deep lines of cultural anxieties.

How has the dying of death come to pass? How did we come to think we could slay the dragon of mortality so easily? What made us think simply not pronouncing it would accomplish our end? "Just as the Jew, out of respect for the awesomeness of God, would not pronounce the name of Jahweh, so we find it difficult to bring the word death to our lips in the presence of its power. This is so because we are at a loss as to how to proceed on the far side of this word."[7] Was the repression of death an adaptive response to changing cultural conditions, the best deal we could make in bad times?

RECENT HISTORY

It is said we live in the first death-free generation in history. (It is not clear what it means that today's children do, however, see over twenty thousand violent deaths on television by the time they are eighteen.) A typical family may go twenty years without suffering any death. Death has disappeared as an ingredient of primary socialization. Today a fifty-year-old has seen as much death as a twenty-year-old had in 1820. In former times one got to know nature and death early as childhood companions; the family could not intervene to protect a child from a profound and rapid socialization to death and dying. Between 1920 and 1973, the death rate for those age one to twenty-five decreased by 83 percent. For those age twenty-six to sixty-five, the death rate decreased by 40 percent.

Premodern societies had to organize themselves around death's recurrent presence. In a small village, the sudden death of ten people in a flood, epidemic, or war was a public disaster. Death always creates a vacuum, but modern societies have learned how to insure against loss. If mostly the elderly die, the crisis is less acute. It is possible to mute the effect of death by reducing the importance of those who die. By disengaging the aged from the social system and locating them in a transition period on the way to death, modern societies enhance the continuity of institutional functions via the changeover of personnel. Permanent, autonomous social institutions that are effectively independent of the individuals who carry out roles within them are invulnerable to the depletion of personnel by death, for their bureaucratic functions are impersonal and transferable. In early societies, deaths that struck the family reverberated through the entire social structure. Now there are dikes against such tidal waves. Across the social system death has been transformed from a hovering menace into a remote prospect, insulated from everyday contact and sight, technologized into a system that seeks environmental mastery, and decontextualized from tradition.[8]

Yet while modern societies seem to have contained death, the individual is left more vulnerable than ever. "We have created systems which protect us in the aggregate from facing up to the very things that as individuals we most need to know."[9] It may be that the greater the emphasis on individual distinctness and separateness, the more intense the anguish when the individual dies.[10] Death's power is unabated for the individual, who faces it without significant mediating structures. The decline of churches, neighborhoods, and other forms of community has left individuals bereft of resources for constructing meaning and culture. Isolated individuals labor after meaning without a context of mutual endeavor and with little relation to living traditions. They stand alone against a world of powerful economic forces and bureaucratic institutions. Government, mass media, and business have taken control of the center, where life in community once flourished, and sucked it dry. The realm of rooted systems of meaning has been ceded to the powerful and the professional.

A number of major shifts in Western cultural and religious traditions have contributed to the new situation in which the isolated individual faces death with scarce resources. The Enlightenment's hope for human improvement included a bias against tradition and history and a devout trust in science. But death did not lend itself to the Enlightenment agenda, nor did it fit the Enlightenment's mode of analysis. The "de-Christianization" of death in eighteenth-century France left a heritage still much with us among intellectual elites.[11] At the dawn of that century elaborate means for death preparation were still in place. There were manuals on the art of dying, popular books, tracts, and catechisms that balanced fear and confidence. The practice of early contrition as a dying to self could lead to such a disengagement that actual death held little terror. It was a cultural expectation that toward the end of an active life, one began preparing for death. Some prayed the Office of the Dead as a penitential exercise. There was, of course, also continuing ritual participation in the death of others in the community of faith.

But during the course of the eighteenth century there developed a truncation of religious phraseology in wills, a reduction of the number of masses for the testator's soul, a decline in the number of books of devotional preparation for the dying, the rise of lay confessors who specialized in a new, humanistic dying, and an accompanying moralization of funeral sculpture and epitaphs. Somber and demanding Catholic deathbed rituals were rejected, ideas of eternal punishment were ridiculed, and the cemetery was removed from proximity to the church. Usurping the emotions aroused by Christian liturgy were the sentimental and literary fashions of lonely grief. A cult of tombs became a substitute religion and nature the ideal environment.

The dying of death in the United States between 1830 and 1920 can be traced to the impact of scientific naturalism, religious liberalism, and new death-related institutions such as life insurance, natural-looking cemeteries, and professionalized funerals.[12] Because it was contrary to nineteenth-century progressivism, death had to be redefined, assigned to specialists, and liberated from gruesomeness, thereby sparing society the public expression of incapacitating fears. Mourning was curtailed in duration and formality to prevent death from overshadowing life.

Scientific naturalism provided the cosmology within which the dying of death could proceed. Scientific plausibilities were selected to meet social needs and presuppositions. Nature was called upon to replace religion as the locus of causality and the engenderer of interpretations of the meaning of life and death. When death became a natural process, attention shifted from the individual to the species. Life insurance replaced religion as the new (social) guarantor of the immortality of the human race. In the last half of the nineteenth century supernaturalist and vitalist definitions of death's meaning gave way to disease studies. In a speech to the National Funeral Directors Association, an enthusiastic physician heralded the new day when science, unencumbered by expressions of divine will and unshrouded by mystery, could look the causes of death squarely in the face. Two trends emerged: Death was merely natural and therefore acceptable, and death was merely a disease and therefore curable. As anesthesia removed pain and the necessity to discover therein punishment or compensation, death promised to become an easy sleep, like the falling of a leaf.

All this gave modernity what Reinhold Niebuhr called an "easy conscience." We escape death's pathos by turning "from the daemonic chaos" of our spiritual lives "to the harmony, serenity and harmless unity of nature." Salvation lies in the descent "from the chaos of spirit to the harmony of nature."[13] Such language is reminiscent of Buddhist spirituality. In the absence of that tradition's depth and cultural location, however, it more likely represents an overeager escapism.

The religious liberalism of the day wedded romanticism to scientific naturalism. Death became a romantic prelude to immortality, heaven a natural human progression. Death was the lawful act of an immanent God, not a curse or divine judgment. Clergy came to console, not admonish. Memento mori gave way to the soothing of survivors. Between 1836 and 1916 the Methodist funeral order, for example, maintained a delicate balance between fear and hope. After 1916, hope triumphed. The mercy of God and the assurance of everlasting life replaced God's power and wrath. Judgment, fear, and pain of death were eliminated in the 1920 reforms. With the triumph of religious tolerance, rationality, and universalism, hell declined in importance. One of death's bibliographers notes that the overtones of death stopped sounding.[14]

SECULARISM AND THE DECLINE OF THE SACRED

The characteristic of modernity that has contributed most to the dying of death is the withering or repression of the symbols that could mediate the sacred.[15] The modern person stands before death as Jung's famous patient stood before her existence: With no mythological language in her possession, she had no resources to tell her story. Today our primal myths are threadbare and powerless. Biblical cosmogony is replaced with hardheaded science. The royal pageantry that once bespoke mythic underpinnings is reduced to commemorative plates or mint editions. Our minds can no longer take in the whole picture. "A wanderer in search of mythological sources of power has to roam the world 'like a dog sniffing out old bones.'"[16] This intimates a crisis of secularity, that triumphant worldview epitomized by empirical observation, technical mastery, and scientific knowledge, in which the ascent of rationalism parallels the "disenchantment" of the world—the voguish term for a world set free of any religious or symbolic underpinnings. Conversation lags among the pallbearers who laid religion to rest. "Called or uncalled, God will be there" goes the old proverb Jung had engraved above his door.

Formerly it was said that humans generated or discovered symbols as they sought bridges to another world. As they beheld such symbols, the sacred broke in. Through symbols they groped for the nature of things and encountered an overflow of Being. Symbols opened eyes wider, pushed the horizon back, affiliated the dead with the living. Symbols called to other worlds and fixed everyday life.

But in recent times whole orbs of society and culture and personality broke loose from the gravity of sacred symbols. Symbol-generated meaning receded as secularization advanced. Unable to locate and name their being-in-the-world, moderns experienced a loss of direction in their living and in their dying. As the echoes of the sacred died out, they sensed themselves homeless in the cosmos.

Many intellectuals, of course, profess no sense of loss, but rather self-congratulation at having rid themselves of dogmatism and religious mystifications. An anthology on religion and aging offers a wry comment on those who are well educated but undeveloped in their religious ideas and beliefs: "These persons appear to maintain a stylized stupidity, primitivity, naivete, or dull-wittedness in religious matters." For such intellectuals, religion is a "favorite and socially sanctioned area of stagnation, fixation, or regression."[17] In the center of their civilized, cultured, sophisticated lives, there lies a deliberate wasteland of underdevelopment.[18]

Once rituals enacted sacred order, and myth told our stories. Now the irrelevance of rituals is announced; they are debunked as empty and meaningless. The emperor has no clothes, the cynics smirk. Sophomores are suddenly wise. Liberation means freedom from ritual's constricting bonds, escape from the weight of uncongenial tradition. As ceremonies lost social space and public truths to tell, humans began to die private, culturally naked deaths.

Ritual and symbol had marked a space where one could look upon darkness, address evil, confess sin, face death. It was possible to name the secret without being engulfed by it. Now death and darkness are not addressed, but banished. Fluorescent lights burn all night in safe houses where the darkness cannot seep in. With little ballast left, people bear their finitude unsteadily and notice mortality only in passing glances. In their grief, for which the words are lost, the new homeless ransack nearly effaced symbols and look for meaning in seagulls or oceanic consciousness. Society and culture come to be disenchanted with a disenchanted world. The new surrogates for religion—language purified of metaphysical alloy, ersatz symbols disconnected from sacred power, commercial distractions, vain promises from the sciences, cultural remnants from which all traces of the Other are effaced—all these were no match for battles fought by night. Death itself would have to die to ensure peace in our time.

The religiosity that survived was often tended by uncertain acolytes. Post-Reformation clergy found their role increasingly secularized. The sacred symbols centered in rites of passage were in ruins. With the great system of sacred symbols broken or their power largely removed, the authority inherent in the cloth disappeared: "God's vicars need his signs to make manifest what it is that they and He are." Protestant reform purged the vivid and sensuous ceremonies that could capture the imagination of individuals and society. "The Protestant minister, weakly arrived with an anemic liturgical apparatus and devitalized spiritual imagery, has had his spiritual power reduced; the reinforcement of visual drama often needed to make his words significant to his congregation has been taken from him. He is often reduced to the use of verbal symbols, now impoverished by the debilitating effect of two centuries of science."[19]

INDIVIDUALISM AND THE LOSS
OF A SOCIAL WORLD

Once, as the Christian lay dying, church bells tolled and last prayers were promptly said. People who saw a priest carrying the viaticum, the last sacrament, through the streets immediately fell in step in a procession to the house of the dying. At the deathbed, the dying person held forth and last farewells were said. It was a public death, and the corpse kept its social engagements. Clocks were stopped, mirrors turned to the wall, black cloth thrown over pictures. Three blows were given to each wine barrel in the cellar. If the deceased lived near a windmill, the sails might be stopped in the form of a cross. A vigil was kept around the corpse that night, candles lit, holy water sprinkled, news sent around by bellman or placards. Finally came a procession from the house to the church, sometimes touring the town on the way, and finally to the cemetery.

Today the symbols found in such a social world have atrophied; the capacity to imagine such connections is gone; the truth of such a public life is unavailable. In today's social world religion, family, and work are projects for the expression of self rather than activities of objective social and ethical value.[20] Well-being and happiness are defined in individualized and abstract terms and not in relation to cultural and religious practices. When ancient Romans or medieval Christians took time off from work, it was not to go away by themselves or with their families, but to participate in communal celebrations. Such holidays might have taken up a third of the year, including civil commemorations, religious festivals, and saints' days.

The loss of a social world also means the end of the interpenetration between the worlds of the dead and of the living. Today, the world the dead enter is not a world in which the living participate. Communion between the two has been severed. A larger reality that includes both worlds and holds them together is lost from sight. Formerly, meaning flowed freely between the living and the dead. Now even the dying—to say nothing of the dead—are often isolated from contact with the living. Once the sacred hung low over the world of the dying, giving special poignancy to their destination. Now no sacred world beckons.

This is my argument: Individualism and the loss of a social world incapacitate us because they leave us isolated and without the resources to confront great mythologized issues such as death. We lose our ability to ritualize, which is a communal activity. This leads us to repress death, because we lack communities of meaning adequate to face and embrace it. Thus we lose a death of our own, but death remains, erupting in rearguard actions in our obsessions and compulsions and in cultural neuroses.

In a climate of individualism we lose both the capacity to symbolize society and the meaningfulness of action in the public sphere.[21] We have to fight for urban public space to "be in." We lose the insight that our bodies are "natural symbols" that carry larger social meanings and are transparent to communal meanings.[22] Our ability to posit reality in unseen things declines in a capitalist, secular, urban culture. The public self, set in webs of cultural meanings and social roles, becomes inferior to the authentic private self. Hence, private wealth and public squalor. Meaning is measured psychologically. The barriers of custom, manners, and gesture are stripped away because they stand in the way of frankness and openness. People author their own character, and the self is the sole social principle. Celebrities such as Elizabeth Taylor argue in court for the exclusive rights to their own lives, which they have turned into movies.

Living a healthy existence in community requires just the "habits of the heart" we have come to lack.[23] We are losing the social capacity for commitment to one another. Once family life, religious traditions, and participation in local endeavors such as politics or education were the glory of the American experiment. One of the keys to the survival of free institutions is the relationship between private and public life, and the ability of citizens to find meaning in both spheres. An older "social realism," common to biblical and republican traditions, saw society as real as individuals, produced a moral ecology of shared meanings and commitments, kept alive a language of public moral discourse, and produced a public good that exceeded the sum of private benefits.

In the face of cynicism about all institutions, from government to schools to churches to unions, we lose the knowledge that life is lived in and through social entities. Better institutions are essential if we are to lead better lives. But we do not even recognize the value—and certainly not the indispensability—of institutions. We forget that the common good is the pursuit of the good in common. Instead, we have made independence and self-reliance the stellar virtues. "American individualism demands personal effort and stimulates great energy to achieve, yet it provides little encouragement for nurturance, taking a sink-or-swim approach to moral development as well as to economic success."[24] A misconceived independence becomes an adolescent virtue that crowds out adult virtues such as care and generativity. Yet "real freedom lies not in rejecting our social nature but in fulfilling it in a critical and adult loyalty, as we acknowledge our common responsibility to contribute to the wider fellowship of life."[25]

How does this rampant individualism rob us of a death of our own? After individualism replaced religion as an all-embracing principle of meaning, after religion in the United States was banned from telling public truths and the commons cleared of religious symbols, after public life lost its grounding in transcendent systems of meaning, we lost death itself.[26] When it becomes impossible to visualize a good society in which people join together to face the great questions, the ritual union of the living and of the dead surely seems out of reach. Facing death should be an invitation to encounter a common mortality, to discover a mutual dependence that encourages the pursuit of qualitative and not merely quantitative goals. The harrowing questions about life and death are everyone's questions. The supposition that all are interested only in outdoing each other in wealth and fame is hollow. "Such competition is a derivative from rather than a cause of a sense of desperation and meaninglessness in a culture that isolates and abandons people in dealing with the enigma of death."[27] Death invites a move beyond the competitive individualism that requires the denial of death. "The portrait of the individual as a definitive whole who creates his own wealth and welfare through his own initiative and industry dissolves in the recognition, in the face of death, of how fragile is our existence and how much it is by the ministrations of others that we both live and die."[28] But contemporary culture discourages this awareness. The pursuit of wealth beyond necessity requires a flight from limits and community. Individual economic health is purchased at the price of social, psychological, and spiritual health.[29]

If we cannot reclaim a sense of community, if public truths are dead, if modernization has left in its wake only powerful bureaucratic structures that depersonalize and no mediating institutions that humanize, if the individual and the nuclear family do in fact stand alone without recourse to public meaning or sacred space, the repression of death may seem adaptive rather than maladaptive, the only course available.

New cultural definitions of death and dying had to arise. Death is first desocialized and then domesticated, because private and isolated selves face it alone. Professionals are hired to tame its power. Rituals can no longer mediate death if they lose their sacred power and context. The understanding that ritual is participation in expressive social action that connects to larger truths is lost. Public life once was a kind of ritual. But the claim of individual personality intruded on that of the public domain, and ritual became mere self-expression. When ritual still claims to mediate a public world, a sacred sphere —the world of the dead, a "calling" to public life, a genuine university or medical "community," marriage as a sacrament larger than two self-actualizing individuals—its promises appear incomprehensible. Where alienation from the public commons is strong, nothing further is expected or deemed possible. Unable to believe in larger meanings, society sidelines ritual.

And faces death alone. Grief becomes an embarrassing private trauma.[30] Other private selves join in the conspiracy to deny its reality or isolate its impact. The nuclear family stands alone, bearing asocial grief and seeking speedy disposals of the body and of mourning. Death rites are held only if the family requests them. If so, they are purchased from and provided by professionals. Isolated from the sacred, adrift from community and ritual, the family faces death hiding its pain and seeking little solace in others.

Could we overcome our captivity to individualism and recover a social world? The French humanist André Malraux in his writings beautifully portrayed individuals in vital contact with one another. An isolated prisoner keeps hearing knocks, which he is eventually able to decipher as saying, "Comrade, take courage." At a dangerous moment in their civil war, Spanish peasants come together, shining lights to illuminate a landing strip. Malraux believed that humans who join together in a common quest have access to regions they could never reach if left to themselves. Nobility lies in the ensemble.[31]

Death will resist denying. Its sacral power and its terrifying mystery will haunt us. We must seek new institutions, cultural forms, and religious symbols that allow and encourage us as individuals to come together to respond to death and mortality. Some imaginative entry into public space, some recovery of the sacred through ritual might be able to form in individuals a world of connections, of the spirit, of larger meaning capable of encompassing death.

Whether religious communities could contribute to a revival of public life is a question neglected until recently.[32] Whether some religious worldview could ever again undergird a common public life is still another question, and one unlikely to be answered in the affirmative. The efforts of Hindu and Islamic fundamentalisms to do just that by equating public life with politics do not look promising. Public life cannot be created by government. The religious symbol of covenant is, in fact, a master symbol for public life.[33] It is a life tested by the treatment of strangers, one in which intimacy cannot be the only prevailing value, and where the spiritual quest must take on social dimensions. Public life has been replaced by life subject to the state or to colonization by neocapitalism, and by an obsessive and fearful private life. The triumph of the therapeutic, the apotheosis of psychological man, reflects an aspiration to a completed identity independent of any public life. What society needs, however, is a therapy of public life, rather than balm for private pain. Feminism offers a promising example and suggests that there can be educations for public life that socialize us to be supportive of and accountable for one another. But the road ahead is clouded with false alternatives and the deceptive promises of science.

THE MEDICAL MODEL OF DEATH

The radical individualism I have lamented has, it must be admitted, provided resources to counteract the medical model of death I am about to decry.[34] For the last three decades the trend in bioethics has been to argue for individual rights against the hegemony of scientific medicine and the all-knowing paternalism of doctors. So the federal Patient Self-Determination Act requires hospitals to inform patients of their rights. Bioethics became a thicket for "our last quest for responsibility."[35] By the end of the millennium a medical right to physician-assisted suicide will probably have been established, primarily as a hedge against a runaway high-tech medical model and in continuity with a prevailing legal and philosophical mentality that privileges the rights of individuals.[36] The Hemlock Society and other groups have fought for such a right, and Hemlock's founder, Derek Humphry, has provided a best-selling self-help manual, *Final Exit.*

Good reasons are easily found for the continuing domination of death by a medical model. New medical abilities and accomplishments keep arriving at a bewildering rate. The great technological capacities to deny death its moment or significantly postpone its arrival have awakened the tantalizing idea that death might not be inevitable, or at least that it could be tamed by subsuming it under the paradigms of science.

Beginning in the eighteenth century, an objectivizing practice of pathology has achieved success in locating death precisely, sited death in the body, and taken the first significant steps toward somaticizing and clinicalizing death. Medicine, science, and modernity came together in a way that focused on bodily, anatomical space, readily manipulable, to the detriment of social space.[37] Social and cultural meaning was displaced by biology—itself, of course, a cultural product.

The recent evolution of the sociology of medical knowledge is telling. Over the last two centuries technical, scientific understandings of death have replaced magical, moral, and religious understandings. In Foucault's words, the empirical gaze has succeeded in objectifying the patient. As a subject for scientific investigation, death became intelligible, uniform, predictable. "How?" replaced "Why?" as the leading question, and death became an impersonal, technical matter or a failure of technology. While massively redirecting the course of human and social behavior, medicine pretended to be morally neutral.

Recall the story of the drunk who was discovered looking for his lost key under the streetlight. He had actually dropped it a block away, but, he reasoned, the light was better where he was looking. Unlike death, sickness can be defined, managed, and cured under the streetlight of science. Therefore cultural attention is shifted to sickness. Tamed sickness substitutes for untamed death. When Elisabeth Kübler-Ross began her research into death and dying, the large hospitals she approached always told her that they had no dying patients. But repressed death images are inevitably assigned to the sick anyway, and they are no gift. Societies in the nineteenth and twentieth centuries loaded tuberculosis and cancer with entire syndromes of negative images which then came to define the bearers of these diseases.[38] AIDS is the new vehicle for such off-loading. Society displaces or projects onto the gay community the repressed and frightening images of death it lacks the resources to face head on.

Redefining death as sickness allows a professionalized death system. The mystery of death is handed over to medical science, which offers to demystify it by turning it into something controllable. The advice comes down: Trust your doctor. But studies often suggest that physicians are more anxious about death than the general population. Perhaps they enter medicine to control death and lessen their own fears; the choice of medicine may be a reaction formation, a response to an unconquerable childhood anxiety. All the more, then, does the dying patient represent a loss of power and control for the physician, who may withdraw or become hostile or impersonal. The scientific ethos of medical school desensitizes future physicians to the symbolic fullness of death and dying in order to equip them for heroic battles they can win.

As the nemesis of medicine, death is greeted with "therapeutic passion," and the patient is overlooked in the physician's "clinical gaze." Formerly, mythical language about immortality or finitude hovered over the exchange between physician and patient. Now the scientific mind-set prevails. Or does it? Godlike, the physician hurls thunderbolts at the advancing enemy. The charisma granted the physician is not merely the self-aggrandizement of the medical community. A secular society finds in the physician the new priest it longs for. Garbed in the divine privileges of scientific medicine and not averse to Promethean posturing, the physician comes to patient and family, who weakly protest such privilege but inwardly call for and ascribe unbounded power. Enter the shaman and the dance of death performed for extravagant fees. "The religious use of medical technique has come to prevail over its technical purpose, and the line separating the physician from the mortician has been blurred. Beds are filled with bodies neither dead nor alive. The conjuring doctor perceives himself as a manager of crises. . . . He plans self-defeating strategies and commandeers resources which in their uselessness and futility seem all the more grotesque."[39] The modern person has lost the ability to recognize when death's time has come and must wait for the priest-physician to will it. Expenditures once lavished on tombs are now expended on terminal care. No one is to die without extensive medical assistance, the new rite of passage. For those who do not want such interventions, state ballot initiatives promote the right to be terminated professionally, and hospices offer mitigation. Meanwhile, few call into question the medicalization of dying, which creates this modern problem.

The sacred space for these rituals is the modern hospital. Dying has moved from a moral to a technical domain. Death in an intensive care unit is ubiquitous, yet somehow concealed. Of course, "lost" patients can only dwindle. This is not the place for a last stage of growth. The passing of a person, the possibility of self-transcendence, cannot be measured with sophisticated equipment. Nor can nurses tethered to technology cross the line into such territory. Technical competency replaces fear and trembling.

Added to the shortcomings of a scientific paradigm is the corporation-driven character of modern medicine.[40] How many hospital admissions did the doctor generate? How many of the available beds were used every day? How many tests and procedures were ordered? It is a world in which only doctors can order the admissions that fill the hospital beds and use the hospital as a highly profitable second office to generate fees. It is a world in which health maintenance organizations increasingly dominate physicians, patients, and hospitals. It does not bode well for the dying patient that the coming decades will see turbulent conflict—among physicians, between physicians and hospitals, between medical care providers and insurers, between all of them and government. There is a struggle over dying, but it will be a corporate and political struggle over the allocation of resources.

THE PRESENT DILEMMA

Death reduced to disease may be producing a contagion of public sickness and private malaise. Death repressed in the service of happiness returns to shadow human pursuits. To quote Simone Weil's enigmatic phrase, "The absence of the dead is their way of appearing." The interdiction of death does not promise peace in our time. The connection is broken between life and death, between the present and the continuity of life, between people. "Death equivalents" keep returning to haunt a culture that turns its face away from the perennial questions of death and continuity. Psychic numbing, death-denying stunts, and gangland bravado are behaviors invulnerable to death. The violence of popular culture has the (repressed) voice of death. Depression in the face of a death that will not die is a curious organismic imitation of death. Desperately seizing penultimate values is the distraction and denial chosen as a final detour before entering the inescapable tunnel. Suppressed death imagery breaks out and threatens to overwhelm life's projects. The suppression of death occasions the suppression of life.

Humans have been losing their own dying, giving their death away to empty lives. With no definitive form, *the last passage becomes a lost passage.* A life heading nowhere loses its depth dimension. Yet mementos of the repressed consciousness keep appearing like dead birds on the doorstep, a disgusting transgression of our suburban yard. The undisguisable debris of death litters our paths and, more, our nights. Carl Jung wrote: "But when one is alone and it is night and so dark and still that one hears nothing and sees nothing but the thoughts which add and subtract the years, and the long row of disagreeable facts which remorselessly indicate how far the hand of the clock has moved forward, and the slow, irresistible approach of the wall of darkness which will eventually engulf everything you love, possess, wish, strive, and hope for—then all our profundities about life slink off to some undiscoverable hiding place, and fear envelops the sleepless one like a smothering blanket."[41]

Writers and poets come as *nuntii mortis,* messengers of finitude. We look to poets to name the gods and to deconceal reality—to see what we are looking away from. Some beckon to other ways of being in the world than isolated individualism. Maxine Kumin's is a poetry of attachment, preservation. She envisions a living and a dying that are reconnected to the dead, to the not yet born, to every neighbor. In "The Envelope" she writes:

> *It is true, Martin Heidegger, as you have written,*
> *I fear to cease, even knowing that at the hour*
> *of my death my daughters will absorb me, even*
> *knowing they will carry me about forever*
> *inside them, an arrested fetus, even as I carry*
> *the ghost of my mother under my navel, a nervy*
> *little androgynous person, a miracle*
> *folded in lotus position.*
>
> *Like those old pear-shaped Russian dolls that open*
> *at the middle to reveal another and another, down*
> *to the pea-sized, irreducible minim,*
> *may we carry our mothers forth in our bellies.*
> *May we, borne onward by our daughters, ride*
> *in the Envelope of Almost-Infinity,*
> *that chain letter good for the next twenty-five*
> *thousand days of their lives.*[42]

In his poem "Belief," Philip Levine captures our honest ambivalence as we struggle between what we want to believe and what we fear we know. Through the recurring motif "No one believes" he manages to assert by denying:

No one believes that to die
is beautiful, that after the hard pain
of the last unsaid word I am swept
in a calm out from shore
and hang in the silence of millions
for the first time among all my family
and that the magic of water
which has filled me becomes me
and I flow into every crack and crevice
where light can enter.[43]

There are heartrending connections between moving toward death and the larger ebb and flow of meaning. In "Spindrift" Galway Kinnell sees an old man's ambivalence about the elapsing time that brings his end, because "everything he loved was made of it."[44]

The pastor of a church in northern California suggested the Easter sunrise service be held in a cemetery one year, instead of at the usual tawdry drive-in theater. The church members were horrified and refused. But in Los Angeles a Moravian trombone choir marches through a cemetery on Easter morning playing old hymns. Those who are attentive may find ways to improvise new cultural scripts.

THE CONTEMPORARY REVIVAL OF DEATH

In August 1970 *Psychology Today* invited its readers to participate in a survey on death and dying. Thirty thousand responded. A survey on sex had drawn the previous highest response, twenty thousand readers. Was this a sign of the reviving of death, an urge to speak out on a forbidden topic?

Books on death and dying began to appear in the mid-1960s. The great bestseller was Elisabeth Kübler-Ross's *On Death and Dying*, which appeared in 1969 and has continued to sell hundreds of thousands of copies. Kübler-Ross soon became the patron saint of the death awareness movement. In her book she recorded her work with dying patients and described the resistance of the medical community to her work. Her most famous contribution was her stage theory. From her experiences with the dying she concluded that the dying person typically moves through five stages, from denial to anger to bargaining to depression to acceptance. Acceptance, and the potential growth connected to it, became a well-known goal, which Kübler-Ross thought appropriate for every dying patient. She began calling for the rejection of a lonely, mechanical, dehumanized environment for the dying and for recovery of a cultural willingness to listen to them, humanize their surroundings, and become students of their teaching. In this way, humans could develop a proper response to the dying and to their own mortality. The work of Kübler-Ross has been enormously influential, especially within the nursing profession, in the hospice movement, and among advocates of alternative spiritual approaches to death and dying.

Already in 1979, a bibliographer concluded that death was a very badly kept secret, that 750 books were already asserting that we were ignoring it.[45] Another bibliographer, in 1991, strove to identify, classify, and evaluate a bewildering variety of death analyses and to provide an introduction to death's past before seeking wisdom about its future—lest readers assume it was a new discovery in the late twentieth century.[46] Did this proliferation of literature constitute a return to the good old days? Consider: "A narrative poem on death, *The Day of Doom*, was the first best-seller in America. First printed in 1662, it was a broadside of over 200 doggerel verses on death, doom, and judgment. The pamphlet was literally read to pieces in Puritan New England."[47]

A French historian in 1976 believed he was observing, in the sudden flurry of publications, nothing less than the displacement of a deeply held taboo on a subject that had stayed hidden since sometime in the nineteenth century.[48] The work of Gorer, Feifel, and Ariès in the 1950s and 1960s signified a turning point in Western sensibility to death comparable to that which occurred during the twilight of the Enlightenment. The literature appearing after the 1950s marks "the outer boundary of an era in which death was hidden in a veil of silence and secrecy, banished to the darker regions of everyday consciousness and repressed in a deliberate act of denial."[49] The deconcealment of death was under way: "*La mort est à la mode.*"

The revival of death was unanticipated, and its impact on American culture is even now unmeasured. Factors underlying this shift can be identified. Mass death in recent history and unthinkable death on a nuclear horizon that threatened the species with a common epitaph had sedimented into a fin de siècle consciousness. The evolution of modern medical science and technology, especially the pronounced accomplishments of recent decades, also contributed. The shifting of the location of dying to health care institutions for nearly 80 percent of those who die in the United States attracted public attention to that locale, as have transplant capabilities and the technology of life support. Out of the miracle and the coercion of modern medicine came patients' bills of rights, living wills, durable powers of attorney for health care, renewed interest in euthanasia societies, and public scrutiny of the veil of privilege and mystery that medical associations had successfully drawn around the practice of medicine. A demographic evolution, chiefly indebted to accomplishments in public health and nutrition, made the presence of the elderly in ever larger numbers a pressing social fact. Nursing homes nagged at the public conscience, and the politically active elderly, above all through the American Association of Retired Persons, demanded public attention.

A "new consumerism" led to devastating critiques of the funeral industry. Jessica Mitford bitingly attacked the American funeral industry for profiteering on the grief-stricken by marketing expensive goods and services to a captive audience under great stress. She ridiculed the elaborate treatment and display of the corpse and questioned much of the funeral ritual itself. She found the normal American funeral irrational. Above all she lampooned embalming:

> The corpse is in short order sprayed, sliced, pierced, pickled, trussed, trimmed, creamed, waxed, painted, rouged and neatly dressed . . . transformed from a common corpse into a Beautiful Memory Picture. This process is known in the trade as embalming and restorative art, and is so universally employed in the United States and Canada that the funeral director does it routinely without consulting corpse or kin. He regards as eccentric those few who are hardy enough to suggest that it might be dispensed with. Yet no law requires it, no religious doctrine commends it, nor is it dictated by considerations of health, sanitation, or even personal daintiness. In no part of the world but in North America is it widely used. The purpose of embalming is to make the corpse presentable for viewing in a suitably costly container; and here too the funeral director routinely, without first consulting the family, prepares the body for public display.[50]

College and then high-school classes began making field trips to mortuaries, consumers came to look over physicians' shoulders, new journals devoted to thanatology appeared, books flooded the market, courses were developed, grants funded. Certainly by 1970 a death awareness movement began to establish itself. There followed concerns for doing it right, moving beyond a "We covered death today" approach. Twelve goals were proclaimed in an article entitled "Death Education":

1. Gently remove the taboo aspect of death language so students can read and discourse upon death rationally without becoming anxious.
2. Promote comfortable and intelligent interaction with the dying as human beings who are living until they are dead.
3. Educate children about death so they grow up with a minimum of

death-related anxieties. Anxieties are too often based upon irrationality and myth rather than fact.

4. Assist the individual in developing a personal eschatology by specifying the relationship between life and death.

5. Perceive the health-care giver as a professional and human being, neither omnipotent nor omniscient, who has an obligation to give competent and humane service, attention, and information without mendacity to the dying and their families.

6. Understand the dynamics of grief and the reactions of differing age groups to the death of a "significant other."

7. Understand and be able to interact with the suicidal person.

8. Understand the role of those involved in what Kastenbaum and Aisenberg call the "death system" and the assets and liabilities of that system.

9. Educate consumers to the commercial death market.

10. Recognize that war and other holocausts are related to feelings of personal immortality and omnipotence. War might be avoided if we realize that it may be ourselves or our children who would be killed or mutilated as well as an amorphous "enemy."

11. Recognize the variations involved in aspects of death both within and between cultures. Death means different things to different people.

12. Know the false idols and mythology existing in the growing field of thanatology, the salient heuristic questions, and the great need for research.[51]

College courses in the early 1970s tended in three directions: death as a personal phenomenon; examination of the sociocultural aspects and effects of death; and a limited study of singular aspects of death, such as self-destructive behavior, religion, and funeral practices.

Undoubtedly, the hospice movement became the best-known institutional manifestation of the reviving of death. Dr. Cicely Saunders's St. Christopher's Hospice in England, founded in 1967, is everywhere seen as the mother of the modern movement. The first American hospice was established in 1973 in New Haven, Connecticut. By the early 1990s there were hundreds of hospices throughout the United States. The movement embodies central concerns of the death and dying movement. A rigid medical model of dying is challenged; caring replaces curing as a fundamental treatment modality. Pain management medications that preserve alertness for a death of one's own but end the cycle of fear and acute pain are pioneered. Holistic approaches to patient and family dominate. The hospice has become a multidisciplinary community of care, with strong reliance on volunteers, thus recovering some of the social support and sense of community so conspicuously absent in much American dying. The movement has been called "high-person and low-tech." Hospices offer bereavement counseling during dying and also after the death of the patient. In a relaxed, cheerful, and homey atmosphere the patient is encouraged to "own" death and dying. "Dying badly" because of inappropriate medical interventions or lonely terror is eliminated. Often the hospice workers can assist the dying person to return home and die there amidst family support.

Following widespread celebration of the arrival of a death awareness movement, there came cautions. There were warnings about death voyeurism in intrusive field trips and interviews; death exhibitionism by caregivers who like to display their patients; stage theories of dying that become prescriptive; hospices becoming death ghettos of fragmentation, overspecialization, and discontinuity in health care; smothering dying patients into overdependency; personality cults surrounding movement leaders.[52] Inevitably, one of the proliferating textbooks on death and dying asked already in 1982 whether all this was the result of reformation or reaction formation.[53]

If death was to enjoy more than a modest revival, it would need staging from within traditions richer than many close at hand. What would they be? The muckraking of Jessica Mitford and others wanted to eliminate guilt-ridden extravagance, but apparently only by reducing human passages to discount rituals and dead-in-the-morning-and-gone-by-noon bargains. A far richer approach is seen in the Jewish Talmud:

> Formerly, they used to bring food to the house of mourning, the rich in baskets of gold and silver, the poor in baskets of willow twigs; and the poor felt ashamed. Therefore, a law was instituted that all should use baskets of willow twigs. . . .
>
> Formerly they used to bring out the deceased for burial, the rich on a tall state bed, ornamented and covered with rich coverlets, the poor on a plain bier; and the poor felt ashamed. Therefore, a law was instituted that all should be brought out on a plain bier. . . .
>
> Formerly the expense of the burial was harder to bear by the family than the death itself, so that sometimes they fled to escape the expense. This was so until Rabban Gamaliel insisted that he be buried in a plain linen shroud instead of costly garments. And since then we follow the principle of burial in a simple manner.[54]

At its most idealistic, Judaism enfolds "a plain pine box" and a simple burial with a rich tradition of communal ritual, prayer, and nurture. A Christian example is seen in the funeral of Catholic social activist Dorothy Day, of whose coffin it was said: "The beautiful pine casket in which Dorothy Day's body lay . . . was so strikingly apt that it shocked one into consciousness of the incongruity of most coffins. It served so aptly the plain simplicity, grace, discernment, insight, honesty, directness, dignity of that great woman's remarkable life and ministry. The body was the sign, not the casket, and yet the casket communicated a craft and showed a care befitting its servant role."[55]

Fortunately, the revival of death was accompanied by the unlooked-for reawakening of religion. The eclipse of the sacred that had seemed an assured legacy of secular societies was coming under reexamination during the 1960s. In the early decades of the twentieth century many leading sociologists expected that by the year 2000 religion would have disappeared, replaced by a secular, scientific worldview. That expectation and the two centuries of Enlightenment thought that led up to it continued to have a profound effect on the denial of death, or on the tamed death permitted to arise. It remained an open question whether discoveries of death as a new peak experience, the retrieval of historic religious traditions, or the emergence of new alternatives would come to prevail.

A CALL FOR MORE

We began with death concealed in a forgotten language. It may now be asked whether death is again allowed to speak in the vernacular. But that question must be sharpened. Does the turn from an evasive, secularized, individualized, and medicalized language to the coinage of contemporary culture promise a more authentic mediation of death and dying? It is not certain that the lingua franca of the late twentieth century—beautiful, therapeutic, romantic, spiritual, banal, and above all psychological—gives death its due. If so, our humanity and our living and dying will remain slighted. The cultivation, again, of the awareness of death may require difficult spiritual disciplines, not just psychological uncoverings. What death awareness will mean may depend on what visions of the good life such spiritual disciplines proffer.

We have clearly entered a second phase of our recovery of death. First, death was deconcealed and rediscovered. Then we began reappropriating it. But we have remained "largely unaware of the degree to which captivating trends of popular cultural images determine our attitudes toward death."[56] The thus far unfulfilled second phase could be the one in which we move beyond the twin responses of concealment and obsession. The problem began to change as we became conscious of it. We now have the chance to move beyond institutional reflexes and responses and generate prescriptive moves.[57] They should include a rediscovery of the moral component in questions about death and dying—and not a morality limited to the uncritical enthusiasms of recent psychology.

The translation from obscurantist Latin to the human-potential language of a good death, for example, may facilitate progressive attempts to avoid psychological maladjustment and still, with determined optimism, refuse to look death in the face. Behind contemporary enthusiasms may lurk new commercializations and professionalizations to replace the physician's and the undertaker's profit making. The continuing inattention to the funeral, except in the form of consumerist critique, and the almost complete lack of interest in reimagining rites of last passage do not bode well.[58] "Funerals are custommade only in the same sense that automobiles are, and the price we pay for paying our last respects in the American way of death is the price of our personality, which we have purposely withheld from the funeral. By our passive role in directing our funerals, we have transformed an important rite of personal passage into an impersonal rite of impassivity."[59] As attention to the funeral lags, so even more does any rediscovery of a community of the living in an encounter with the dying, of death as a public event, of the need for symbolically rich religious and cultural resources. The revival of death remains largely in the hands of psychologists, therapists, and death awareness enthusiasts—not necessarily an inspiring cast. Many current approaches promise at best a new orthodoxy of the good death and at worst "terminal chic."

Therapeutic approaches that seek to confront the reality the dying person faces often succumb to romanticizing, beautifying, "dignifying," and rationalizing death. This constitutes an impoverishment both of the power and mystery of death and of the meaning of the human prospect. What if mortality *is* a terrible wound to the soul? An old etymology thought "death (*mort*) was so called because it bites (*mord*) horribly."[60] In Eugène Ionesco's play *Exit the King,* we learn of the king's discovery: that in youthful love one feels eternal, beyond contingency, but the day comes when we realize we are infected with mortality and there is no place to run. Marie speaks to him: "Love is mad. And if you're mad with love, if you love blindly, completely, death will steal away. If you love me, if you love everything, love will consume your fear. . . . The universe is one, everything lives again and the cup that was drained is full." The king will have none of it: "I'm full all right, but full of holes. I'm a honeycomb of cavities that are widening, deepening into bottomless pits. It makes me dizzy to peer into the gaping gulfs inside me."[61] Death does not readily yield to the power of positive thinking.

Patients' rights ideologies, although to be applauded, can produce a hypertrophy of individual responsibility and autonomy, an unexamined right to absolute control of the form and timing of one's last passage, which, in the contemporary cultural context, is subject to trivialization. Newly won bills of rights for patients cannot strip death of ambiguity. Hopeful bystanders may see in this new self-actualization a substitute for a confrontation with mortality. But deathbed control and effective pain management are only beginning responses to human dying.

Nor are mass-marketed self-help "deathings" and new variations on peak experiences sufficient responses to the wound of death. We must be wary of an ecstatic transcendence so readily embraced by a contemporary culture that no longer remembers that such transcendence requires a reservoir of shared religious imagery, which must be evoked ritually. In such traditional symbolizations, the sought-for ecstatic moment is grounded in a context that connects with prior and subsequent experiences.[62] But the modern seeker lacks a cultural reservoir of such imagery and must improvise or ignore the missing communal and ritual elements. "That absence of content—of images of symbolic immortality—is the key to the fallacy of spiritual cure via experiential transcendence alone. The pervasive tendency is a very American form of technicizing the spiritual—of converting quest into technique, transcendence into 'feeling good.'"[63]

Death was not discovered by the twentieth-century human-potential movement. Its revival will require continuities with the cultural and religious past, including a reacquaintance with the darker sides of human consciousness. "In attempting to restore his dignity to man, this psychology idealizes him, sweeping his pathologies under the carpet. . . . This kind of humanism promotes an ennobled one-sidedness, a sentimentalism which William James would have recognized as tender-mindedness."[64] Nor should Eastern imports too quickly be celebrated. "Once uprooted and imported to the West it arrives debrided of its imaginal ground, dirt-free and smelling of sandalwood, another upward vision that offers a way to bypass our Western psychopathologies."[65]

Elisabeth Kübler-Ross's worthy attempt to make of death a final stage of growth can too easily become trivialized in death as yet another peak experience.[66] What are the reasons for her enormous popularity? While she is to be applauded for opening up the subject of death to all and encouraging them to step over the threshold, her stage theory may have gained such widespread acceptance because it offers a clear structure that reduces anxiety. "Death becomes subsumed under dying, and dying transformed from a vague, overpowering, and terrifying mass to a delimited, coherent, orderly sequence."[67] What was once beyond the boundaries is now governed by rules. Secure knowledge replaces the anxiety of cognitive bewilderment.

Stages of death can be as exact as any positivist could wish and as tantaliz-ing as "coming to Christ" at summer camp. Thanatologists, like many church-men, can talk as if they know a great deal more than they do. "By establishing a *science* of thanatology, they imply that death remains within the realm of human comprehension and control."[68] The vaunted revival of death turns out to be a new mutation of the dying of death disguised as therapeutic mastery by means of talking about it. Kübler-Ross's earlier moral vision falls in line with the humanistic psychologies of Abraham Maslow, Carl Rogers, Fritz Perls, and William Shutz.[69] Death is an "ordinary fact of nature to be accepted as an occasion for the unfolding of innate potentialities."[70]

The dissatisfaction with psychology-based approaches mounts, and it is by no means limited to the offerings of humanistic psychology.[71] Psychology has come to define death's meaning for the public and usurped the role theology once played. Outstripping from its strictly scientific aspirations, the newest social science becomes a normative culture filled with images of what we are and should be. Personal fulfillment is the moral norm. "Psychology, narrowly conceived, easily becomes a broadly conceived project which shapes culture and projects an ideology based upon its own metaphors, myths and norms. This is particularly true when psychologists take up existential questions of death as the subject of their investigation."[72]

It is claimed that the clash of Freud with Calvin is the major cultural confl-ict of contemporary society.[73] Freud's psychological man competes with Calvin's religious man as the dominant symbolic character of the modern age. But the battle is over, and Freud has won. Modern persons construct their worlds with psychological imagery as second nature. It was only a question of time before psychologists became the new priestly caste and psychology the major new source of guidance, replacing antiquated religion. A brief tour of any urban bookstore confirms this. The psychology and self-help sections burgeon; the religion section, if there is one, offers eclectic and trendy repre-sentations from the East, and a few editions of the Bible for any fundamental-ists who may wander in.

What if death *is* an indignity and our attempts to "die with dignity" pre-tentious and dehumanizing? Protestant ethicist Paul Ramsey argued that to be fully human is to have some dread of death, to know its sting.[74] But a culture without religious resources is unable to deal with ultimates. It responds by sterilizing, reifying, naturalizing, or beautifying death. Death becomes a dis-sectible object, subject to therapeutic manipulation, not a mighty power that calls its seekers to give an account of themselves. Owning death is a task yet to be accomplished, not an already given. Death arrives as finis. It remains to be seen whether it can be translated into telos. A true humanism and the dread of death seem to be dependent variables.

Anthropology, too, has been charged with parochializing death through approaches that repress any transcendental and universal conception of the problem of death. *Death itself* is not a problem worthy of social scientific response, only deaths and forms of death-related behavior. Already the early anthropologists Tylor and Frazer steered anthropology away from universal problems of human existence to concern with particular products of evolution. Frazer produced a tour de force on death customs around the world, and concluded that, by comparison, his own culture was at a peak of intellectual and evolutionary development. But the problem continued. When culture as any kind of universal was renounced, it became clear that the discipline had no theoretical plane on which to face a challenge such as the problem of death. "Anthropologists had ceased to answer for humanity. . . . Having lost a universal frame of inquiry, questions having to do with the nature and meaning of death had to be implanted in various parochial units of research which came to replace that frame."[75] Because death could be seen as an event that terminated individual behavior, the anthropologists were relieved from proposing an anthropology of death and could limit themselves to behavior toward death as it affects those who survive. Such death-related behavior could then be placed at a safe distance from the core of one's own society, and the anthropologist becomes a spectator of, rather than a participant in, social reality.[76]

Having relegated death customs to folklore, anthropology then, as part of the secularization and religious devolution that anthropologists associated with modernity, located primitive and folkloric death customs in a nostalgic past.[77] The most that the anthropology of death produces is an exotic other to the anthropologists' "we." The remedy to this impasse in the anthropological imagination is clear. Death must be freed from its encapsulation in folklore and restored to its full problematic status. "This would call for an anthropology for which social reality and subjective participation in that reality are irreducible conceptual poles of inquiry."[78]

It is no return to nineteenth-century deathbed pain or terror before a capricious God that I am calling for, but a realization that anesthetics have not solved the mystery of the human condition and disease studies have not rendered unnecessary or irrelevant the shouldering of mortality. Easy psychological talk and anthropological distancing do not obviate the need for resacralization if death and humanity are to be given their due. It is time to move beyond the social sciences to philosophy and theology.[79] The foreword to *Aging and the Religious Dimension* claims that the intellectual elite still doesn't get it, that gerontologists are engaged in a fantastic effort not to face up to religion. "Gerontology has been colossally blind to the religious dimension of human aging."[80]

The trauma of dying exposes not just the individual, but also a whole contemporary culture. Suddenly the dying see their culture as a stranger, in the oppressiveness and hypocrisy of its social forms. "An apparently life-centered culture that systematically relegates the dying to indignity, humiliation, and oblivion because it cannot stand to be reminded of its own poverty of resources before death is vastly more morbid on the subject than the philosopher who reckons with dying as a human possibility."[81]

Much larger visions, then, are called for if the revival of death is to restore lost dimensions to humanity and, through cultural and religious outpourings, enrich the human prospect. In *Who Is Man?* Abraham Heschel decried escapes from ultimate questions and tried to raise images sufficient to the human condition. Establishing human identity in the equation "I am commanded—therefore I am," Heschel called for wonder, embarrassment, and awe. The proper response to transcendent meaning is radical amazement; finite pleasantries are easily uttered instead. Such wonder is not mist in the eyes or fog in speech, but an ascent beyond what is given. The human vocation is to pronounce a great amen to Being. For that we lack not information but appreciation. Awe precedes faith, and faith attaches to transcendence, to meanings beyond mystery. "Forfeit your sense of awe, let your conceit diminish your ability to revere, and the universe becomes a market place for you. The loss of awe is the avoidance of insight. A return to reverence is the first prerequisite for a revival of wisdom, for the discovery of the world as an allusion to God."[82]

But surrogates promise easier approaches. "Man is hard of inner hearing, but he has sharp, avid eyes. The power he unlocks surpasses the power that he is, dazzling him."[83] Avoiding death as cross-examination, running from being called upon to answer, we are determined to miss the experience of something forcing itself upon us. It was in being asked who we are and what we amount to that religion was born. In religious rituals we struggle with our ultimate embarrassment—that we were created in the likeness of God and yet unable to recognize God's presence. Death prompts the self-discovery that we are messengers who cannot recall the message, said Heschel. We are left like the angel Gabriel in Rilke's poem who, enchanted by the Virgin Mary's beauty, cannot recall the message he has been sent to announce.

The modern revival of death has taken us over a threshold of fear, avoidance, and denial. Fascination and striving for competencies mark the progress. Approaching that ultimate mystery, which calls us beyond self-actualization to self-transcendence, is the cultural and religious work still waiting to be accomplished. Religious institutions, which still know these truths, must reassert them eloquently and persuasively, and—above all—embody them in their own countercultural communities. Religious agendas change, of course, in response to changing needs. Fate and death confronted ancient civilizations, guilt and condemnation dominated the Middle Ages, emptiness and meaninglessness threaten to overwhelm the modern world.[84]

Since we cannot avoid, when we see darkly, the assault of finitude or meaninglessness and the wounding of consciousness, self-transcendence must be born in the call of the Other that comes to us as we stand naked on the boundary. The revival of death must take us beyond tourism to pilgrimage, where the great quest and the grandeur of surprise come together in earthen vessels.

In "Little Gidding," T. S. Eliot described a pilgrimage to an ancient chapel. Some pilgrims come with only moderate curiosity, asking small questions. But to some a larger understanding is vouchsafed.

> *You are not here to verify,*
> *Instruct yourself, to inform curiosity*
> *Or carry report. You are here to kneel*
> *Where prayer has been valid.*[85]

Seeking resources sufficient for the task ahead, we journey backward into the lives of many generations. There we find wellsprings, as the words on Eliot's own memorial in Westminster Abbey testify:

> *And what the dead had no speech for, when living,*
> *They can tell you, being dead: the communication*
> *Of the dead is tongued with fire beyond the language of the living.*[86]

Chapter 2

Imagining Death

Cry woe, destruction, ruin, loss, decay;
The worst is death, and death will have his day.
—SHAKESPEARE

Come lovely and soothing death,
Undulate round the world, serenely arriving, arriving.
—WALT WHITMAN

Because I could not stop for Death,
He kindly stopped for me;
The carriage held but just ourselves
And immortality.
—EMILY DICKINSON

OVERTURE TO IMAGINATION

I was what now thou art
And thou shalt be what I am now.

The memento mori theme haunts every graveyard. Lest we forget, tombstones of more obsessive epochs trail such epitaphs as the above into our consciousness. I am sitting in a small, not well kept park in the London borough of Camden. A handwritten plea on the gate requests community volunteers see to the welfare of the premises. Gradually, this somewhat seedy park gives evidence that it once was a cemetery. Or still is. Against the walls that run along its borders stand darkened tombstones, respectfully removed to the side to make way for winding tarmac paths for the living who walk unhurriedly through. Dotting the grassy areas are larger sarcophagi, with dates going back to the seventeenth century, left standing just where they had been, many sloping, some sticking out into the paths paved around them.

In the Middle Ages "the dead were a community that lived close by and shared space with the living."[1] Is this the mission of cemeteries? This little park fills my head with musings about the world of the dead, but I do not feel uneasy, and certainly not morbid. I am wondering about my connections to these dead, imagining some common world we both might inhabit, even now. I am curious whether their dreams and failures and the color of their daily lives were much like mine. The distance between the contemporary pensive observer and those long dead may not be as great as we are determined to believe.[2]

One can keep one's cemetery even closer to home. In Appalachia women created quilts with cloth coffins sewn on the borders, one for each member of the family. When someone died, the coffin with that name was unstitched from the border and resewn in the cemetery at the center of the quilt. Such a continuing and graceful interaction between the two worlds of the living and the dead is a long way from the twentieth-century attempt to outwit death by freezing the dead until they could be thawed, revived, and cured.

Dead are we all, and dying. "In the midst of earthly life / Snares of death surround us; Who shall help us in the strife / Lest the Foe confound us," a forgotten hymn by Martin Luther reminded us. Whatever our situation, death comes to press its claims upon us, to demand its due. We may enlarge death by the size of our wonder. We cannot extinguish it by strenuous denial. Against it we sometimes hurl epithets. Befriending it, we name it beautiful and natural. We may drive it off our daytime horizon and imagine we have escaped its power. But at night, death is "the secret agent dogging every alley way of my dreams."[3]

From the fear of death comes conscience. From efforts to avoid its violence comes law. We may, like Marx, erect against its inexorability an inexorable historical movement. We may answer it with radical assertions of self or by bending others to our will, as romantic fascism does. But it waits inescapably to confront us, as Captain Ahab came to know of the great whale in Herman Melville's *Moby Dick*. History becomes the record of what we do with death. Schopenhauer called death the muse of philosophy. Death demands meaningful reply. With our culture we shape it, even construct it, but never fully answer it. It is always only represented, never experienced and reported on. When we try to represent it, is it a presence or an absence, a terror or a sleep? Shakespeare wrote:

> *Cry woe, destruction, ruin, loss, decay;*
> *The worst is death, and death will have his day.*[4]

But in "When Lilacs Last in the Dooryard Bloomed" Walt Whitman offered an alternative reading:

> *Come lovely and soothing death,*
> *Undulate round the world, serenely arriving, arriving*
> *In the day, in the night, to all, to each,*
> *Sooner or later, delicate death.*

We fill the craters that are the wounds of death with outpourings of the heart. Religion blossoms. We are ground down by death, and we rise to visions beyond it. Which is it? Falling leaves and hurricane, friend of the old and assassin of the young, tamed and wondrous, wall and window, slayer of dreams and whisper of another world. We struggle to name the whirlwind, as everywhere around us lies its gentle and terrifying debris.

For Socrates, death is something alien, beyond which he expects to return to himself, situated in immortality. For the tragic hero death is familiar, personal, inherent. His life unfolds from death, which is not life's end but life's form—as tragic existence. Death is somehow both self and limiting Other.[5]

The Irish landscape is known for giving place to both the dead and the living, replete as it is with images of death and sad decay, yet possessing a haunting, almost unbearable beauty. The dead are buried in and around the sites of ancient abbeys and churches. "The combination of crumbling architecture (usually overgrown with ivy and mistletoe), graveyards and monuments, yew trees and silence, could hardly fail to have a profound and indelible effect on the sensibilities. . . . In Ireland it is likely that a Celtic sense of gloom and of desolation may have been strengthened in the presence of so many awesome structures from an ancient past, for the cult of death is still a powerful force in Irish life throughout the whole of that island."[6] The sad beauty of a past crumbling back into nature can become a permanent fixture in the landscape of consciousness.

But death can also be a drag on the mind, a contaminant from which we want to be purified. The idea of the vampire illustrates the power of the corpse to destabilize us. To mobilize against vampires ensures the finality of death and contains its contagion.[7] Pubs at the corner of the park-as-cemetery offer the opportunity to get our life and breath back.

Today we are jerked back and forth between the living and the dead because we no longer succeed in imagining a world both inhabit. Sometimes the dead reach out from their world and intrusively force us to do their bidding. Sometimes the living manipulate the dead to enlist them for work on our side.

In death the bodies of kings have been put through their paces—organs were disbursed to multiple resting places—to serve the body politic. The journey of their remains became public theater, a miniature reproduction of death and life in the cosmos and the kingdom. Or is it the other way around, the body politic serving the king? Did the requirements of the pyramids as receptacles for kings' bodies call for a social system that made such grand ventures possible? (Do we fight wars to ward off presidential mortality?) The king's body and the body politic were sometimes at odds. Charles I of England was beheaded in order to reenliven the body politic. The funeral that followed his execution provided a social inversion: The body natural disappeared so the body politic could again become visible. Sometimes certain death does uncertain life's bidding. In the Sudan, kings were secretly suffocated at the first sign of the lessening of their powers, because that suggested *social* decay.

Rites of passage sometimes become jousts. Once, just before a funeral, as the casket was about to be wheeled from the narthex down the aisle of the church, I began to spread a Christian funeral pall over the casket, upon which an American flag already lay. The funeral director, a stalwart in the Veterans of Foreign Wars, forcefully intervened. "Nothing can go over the American flag," he protested. "Nothing can go over a Christian funeral pall," I countered. "Then I'll remove the flag until after the funeral," he said. I knew this meant he would win, because the pall does not accompany a casket to the cemetery. This was a contest between two clashing symbols, religious and patriotic, a clash over which community of meaning the deceased most decisively belonged to. More crassly, it was a clash over which living community would get to use the dead for its own purposes. Patriotism won in the end. The twenty-one-gun salute for the deceased veteran was the last word at the cemetery, more dramatic than any benediction I could offer.

Places of burial can also be public contests. In England, Bunhill Fields had by the eighteenth century become a dissenters' Westminster Abbey, a rival sacred ground to receive the honored bodies of those who sought to disestablish the system symbolized at Westminster Abbey.

Sometimes death evokes reluctant assertions from the living. Death is a distant peak we gaze at when reflecting on the meaning of life. The death of a parent can be a telescope bringing that peak suddenly near. With the barrier of first resistance down, mortality breaks through in an urgent invitation to get on with who we will become. Meanwhile, the romantic ruins of graves and monuments spread across the landscape are signs of unattained dreams and of the eroding ruins we ourselves may become.

So the presence of death, sometimes benign, sometimes sharply questioning, beckons us to tasks—unfinished mourning and new creations. When we ignore death, it haunts us in various disguises. Even the appearance of the moon can invite unfinished grief work. All our watchings have filled it with tears. Death sometimes spills out of repressed consciousness and leaves its stains in unwelcome places, red blood on a white wedding dress.

Seeing that illness is the night side of life, Susan Sontag wants to scrape it clean of the metaphors and fantasies that attach to it like barnacles.[8] She wants illness to stay biological, physical, natural. But illness cannot escape bumping against death in the night, and will carry out into the daylight mortal mystifications. Can we teach ourselves not to pile up punitive metaphors of cancer—ruthless, implacable, predatory? Or of AIDS—homosexual terrorism? Can we pledge not to visualize illness as an invasion of pleasant neighborhoods, as urban blight? If we cannot learn to name death, it will project itself onto every terrifying disease and shadow every vulnerability with grotesque fantasies. After each disease, such as smallpox, is vanquished and buried, death returns and dresses new proxies in the costumes of frantic imagination. In the late 1990s it became the Ebola virus out of Africa.

Speaking of metaphors, is death male or female? The Latin *mors* and the French *mort* are feminine nouns. St. Jerome described death as *domina*. On the west front of Notre Dame in Paris she is an apocalyptic rider, and in some Roman images she was a Fury-like female. Medieval illuminators could picture "death entering through the eyes" in the form of the fascinating female body, which led men to sin. In the fourteenth-century manuscript illuminations of Pierre Remiet, Death steps up between her victim's legs onto the bed, the shaft of her scythe pointing at his genitals. This is death/sex with the woman on top.[9] Death, like the female body, is multiply coded. "As the mother, 'woman' is the original prenatal dwelling place; as the beloved, she draws fantasies of desire and otherness; and as Mother Earth, she is the anticipated final resting place. Freud has made this much clear: femininity and death are Western culture's two major tropes for the enigma."[10] The powers attributed to death are not unlike those associated with woman, both confounding. Woman *is* the body, and she is also the body's caretaker and the one who lays out the corpse. "If death is a kind of return to her care, then she is also contaminated by it, so that rituals must be found first to enable her care and then to dissociate her from the corpse. Like the decaying body, the feminine is unstable, liminal, disturbing. Both mourning rituals and representations of death may seek strategies to stabilize the body, which entails removing it from the feminine and transforming it into a monument, an enduring stone."[11]

All mausoleums are named after the great tomb built by Queen Artemisia for her husband, Mausolos, at Halicarnassas in the fourth century B.C. By contrast, the twentieth century is the first in history in which humans dispose of the dead as unceremoniously as possible. Will mortality irresistibly break out in unwitting self-disposals, aboveground but beneath consciousness?

Individuals and social systems collaborate in their response to death, producing over time a culture of death, a death system, which is the network of symbols, rituals, and meanings by which a society mediates and expresses what death is—or what they want it to be. A close look at death systems reveals death to be a cultural product that can be made and remade.

The evolution of the medieval Catholic doctrine of purgatory, for example, led to new ways of envisioning death. This, in turn, led to the elaboration of responses to this new vision, among which were chantries attached to monasteries, where endless masses for the dead could be prayed. This required unending numbers of priests to say such masses, which led to a system of endowments for churches, not unlike endowments today for perpetual-care cemeteries. Then in England Henry VIII saw in Protestantism his chance to pillage the monasteries, leaving only "bare ruined choirs," and to confiscate all the chantry endowments. Thus, through matrimonial politics, the greed of state, and the reform of Christianity did one dimension of one death system come to an inglorious end.

Death systems can be high-tech (cryonics) or low-tech. In America before the twentieth century, death occasioned the following homely scenario: A board was placed between two kitchen chairs and draped with a sheet. The body was laid out on it and washed. A forked stick between the breastbone and chin, fastened with string around the neck, closed the mouth. Coins closed the eyelids. In warm weather, a large block of ice was placed in a tub beneath the board and smaller chunks encircled the body.

In ancient China the death of an important person called for an entire retinue to be buried alive with him, but ceramic figures came to substitute for the living sacrifices—worthy art indeed. Until modern American military expenditures, Egypt saw the greatest percentage of gross national product devoted to death. Because death radically unsettles us, every death system is a pattern of responses intended to restore balance in the cultural system.

A death system is a complex of cultural performances. In such performances, if we enter them imaginatively, we can see individuals and society at work, constructing meanings, revealing their values, acting out, not always fully consciously, what they think they are about. Some death systems are dense with symbols and replete with elaborate rituals, demanding the investment of great time and meaning in response to death. As a cultural construction, death remains irreversible but not immutable.[12]

The American death system appears anemic by comparison. If it were a dream, it would be quite forgettable. Is there little we wish to say, to or through the dead? Perhaps a reimagination of death is appropriate if we are to inquire whether our death system is adequate to its tasks. After this overture, I play out an opera in which the mythological, the psychological, the anthropological, and the religious imagination sing all the notes of death and stage its plots. Just before the curtain rises, I pause for Emily Dickinson's procession, her calm notice of death and its notice of her:

> *Because I could not stop for Death,*
> *He kindly stopped for me;*
> *The carriage held but just ourselves*
> *And immortality.*
>
> *We slowly drove, he knew no haste,*
> *and I had put away*
> *My labor, and my leisure too,*
> *For his civility.*
>
> *We passed the school where children played*
> *Their lessons scarcely done;*
> *We passed the fields of grazing grain,*
> *we passed the setting sun.*
>
> *We paused before a house that seemed*
> *A swelling of the ground;*
> *The roof was scarcely visible,*
> *The cornice but a mound.*
>
> *Since then 'tis centuries; but each*
> *Feels shorter than the day*
> *I first surmised the horses' heads*
> *Were toward eternity.*[13]

THE MYTHOLOGICAL IMAGINATION

To treat death as a new discovery is ludicrous. The recovery of myth saves us from modernist delusions.[14] We cannot hope to create an alternative future until we have rehearsed death's past. So we must ransack the imagination, searching across times and cultures. In forgotten quarries we find materials to construct alternatives to our own truncated responses to death. Pilgrimages across time and space defamiliarize death and allow us to learn what we thought we already knew.

These days, we tend to miss the point of mythology.[15] Night-blind to images in the darkness on the road ahead, we confine ourselves to the world of the daytime ego, "in a state of constant overstimulation of historical consciousness."[16] To learn to see in the dark again, we need to recover mythological language. In the archaic past lay a way of seeing the unseen, of negotiating our way through the underworld. That mythological way gave form to our own most recent past and left us the rich legacy we struggle now to interpret.

To mythologize ourselves or death is to discover "in that other time" the larger context of the stories we find ourselves struggling to live out. Even now the underworld that fed the mythological imagination erupts in our night dreams. There is much to discover there. "Hades-vision relativizes the historical psyche and sets it on a path of psychologizing itself as an image of the *anima mundi* hiding in us, the *anima abscondita:* the reversal of psychological order in mythological thinking allows our earthly lives and personalities to become reflected in more universal, primordial images and dreams."[17] Our deeds and passages come to be seen in their fuller dignity within the unfolding of the eternal cosmos.

Taking the mythological cue, we decenter our stable egos in order to relearn troubling truth, unlearning what we have decided to call life in order to remember death. We call on Hermes to guide our journey to Hades. In an imaginal pilgrimage we rediscover that we who lie embedded in mortality might reach toward an eternalizing element in our experience and find ourselves live actors in a drama "with angels and archangels and all the company of heaven," as the Christian liturgy sings. This insight is overdue. "Being honest with oneself coincides with grasping a universal drama."[18] A call from primordial time turns around our gaze and direction and, if we heed it, lets us see many things we have missed. Long ago Heraclitus wrote: "Immortals become mortals, mortals become immortals; they live in each other's death and die in each other's life."

The mythological imagination will not render us immortal, but it can set our mortal journeys on a larger stage and excite us with the ancient archetypes that our struggles echo. Like Gilgamesh, we too have traveled to strange lands and found the flower of eternal life, then lost it while crossing a river on the way home.

The mythological imagination can be literalized, of course, and trivialized. We can reduce the special speech that is myth to a means to veil rational propositions, verbalize inner desires, explain the origins of events, justify social structures. But myths do not argue, they present. Myth is not a story told but a reality lived. In myths we see what societies and cultures have found it necessary to point to and preserve as centrally valid for their existence. Myths give an account of another time in order to help us find meaning in our time. It is the relation of the two times to each other and of the myth to the hearer that stretches the mythological imagination and gives it creative power.

We miss the power of mythological imagination when we reduce it to the spinning of outrageous tales. "Myth is the imagination beholding its own reality and plumbing the sources of its own creativity. . . . Myth reveals the sacred foundations and religious character of the imagination. Mythic symbols signify the possibility, variety, and meaning of cultural imagination."[19] Through myth we render ourselves intelligible. To discover how to proceed on the pilgrimage of life, how to fashion ourselves for the journey, we encircle the evidences around us with myth.

Death is *the* problem that stimulates the mythological imagination. In an Ivory Coast myth everyone flees into the bush as unknown Death approaches, except one old man who can no longer walk. He asks his grandson to make him a mat to lie upon. When Death arrives, the child is still busy working on the mat and so both die. We cannot escape death; neither do we pause to give in to it. But we keep accounting for it.

How did death come about?[20] In a Congo myth a woman who loses all her loved ones is left alone on the earth. She leaves home to find God and to ask why. After a long and weary journey she poses the question. The answer she receives is that God is mighty and cannot be called to account. The theme of resignation before a natural, God-willed event occurs also in the Gilgamesh epic. Roaming the world in search of eternal life, Gilgamesh eventually discovers an herb that makes humans young again, growing on the far side of the waters of death. While Gilgamesh is resting on his way back to the world of the living, a snake steals the herb. Thus snakes no longer die, but only change their skins. But the answer for humans:

> Gilgamesh, where are you roaming
> You shall not find the life you search after.
> When the gods created mankind
> They destined death for man
> But life they kept firmly in their own hands.

Resignation is not the only response. In a Patagonian myth death is the work of the supreme god, Waitaunewa. But humans did not accept it without protest. They accuse the god of murder and avenge themselves at every death by killing animals belonging to the god.

Sometimes human death is said to be the result of a divine death or of divine conflict. An Indonesian myth recounts an argument between a stone and a banana regarding how man should be created. The stone kills the banana, but the next day the banana's children appear to continue the fight. The stone falls into an abyss and admits defeat on the condition that man would be created as the banana wanted, but must also die as the banana does and the stone does not.

Harder to endure is death stemming from the cheating or carelessness of the gods. The trickster myths of North American Indians show death as the gods' cruelest joke. There are also "message that failed" myths: A supreme god intended to give man eternal life, but a subordinate inadvertently spoiled his intentions. In an East African myth, God sends a chameleon to man with the message of immortality. The chameleon delays, and a snake who has heard of this gift for man goes instead with a message of death. As punishment, both the snake and the chameleon are cursed, but the message cannot be reversed.

A Solomon Islands myth tells that once both humans and snakes could change their skins and be reborn. A woman left her baby in care of her mother while she went to work. The old woman went off to the river to change her skin while the baby slept. The baby woke up and did not recognize the grandmother in her new skin. The baby howled inconsolably. Furious, the grandmother finally returned to the river and put on her old skin. But the grandmother told the child that from then on all human beings would grow old, and only snakes would preserve the capacity to be reborn. Thus death arises from human shortcoming—or love. Another myth roots death in discord in the first family. In a Lotuko (Uganda) myth a child dies, and the mother implores the god to bring the baby back to life again. The god grants the request, but the child's father is dissatisfied and kills the child. The supreme god then pronounces, "From now on when a Lotuka dies, he remains dead."

Death can originate in wrong choices (a god held two nuts, life and death, and woman chose the wrong one), in guilt from disobedience (Adam and Eve; numerous other myths depicting death emerging from a bundle or box forbidden to be opened), or in sexual offense (primordial incest or mortality as the price of procreating children).

The descent to the underworld to rescue one who has died young, to search for immortality, to escort the dead, or to receive initiation in sacred mysteries is a common theme in which the human imagination reaches to the world of the dead to find otherwise inaccessible knowledge or ability. Ascetics and mystics do it through privileged vision, shamans through ritual descent, and heroes through action.

Sometimes there is a test of strength between love and death; the survivor follows the beloved to the land of no return. The best-known example in the

West is the Greek story of Orpheus. Orpheus sets off for the underworld to recover his wife, Eurydice, who was bitten by a snake and died still young. With his music and songs Orpheus relieves suffering and wins the favor of the gods. Eurydice is promised to him on condition he not turn back to look upon her on the road up to the land of the living. Just as he is about to step into the light, Orpheus is overcome with doubt, breaks his vow by looking back, and loses his wife, who melts back into the shadows and must remain forever with the dead.

Greek mythology is rich in the imagination of death and the underworld. Persephone, daughter of Demeter, is abducted by Hades, king of the underworld, who loves her on first sight. Demeter grieves and then refrains from all activity. Withdrawing her harvest blessing, she makes the earth sterile until Persephone returns. Zeus orders Hades to give Persephone back, but this is not possible, because no one who has consumed food in the underworld can return, and Persephone has eaten six pomegranate seeds. Persephone will live half the year underground with Hades and half with Demeter. Thus the earth is sterile during the winter, when Persephone is separated from Demeter. Those who know the metaphorical power of winter do not read this as merely a simple story to account for the earth's seasons.

Styx, son of Night, is one of several rivers that flow through the underworld. Charon, the ferryman, is a sinister old man who requires a coin from everyone who crosses the river. Cerberus, the three-headed dog, guards the entrance to the underworld, allowing the dead to enter but preventing anyone from leaving.

Zeus sends Thanatos (Death) to seize Sisyphus, but Sisyphus puts Thanatos in chains, so there are no further deaths for a while. When Thanatos finally is able to take Sisyphus to the underworld, Sisyphus secretly tells his wife to leave him unburied. Then Sisyphus asks permission from Hades to go back and punish his wife. But he has no intention of returning to Hades ever again. So the gods give him an eternal task to hold him, trying in vain to push a great rock to the top of a steep hill.

To reimagine death mythologically is to journey down to the underworld, to negotiate the subterranean caverns of the psyche, to wrestle our dream world into the daylight. At the end of such an imaginal task, death will not appear agreeably freed from its hoary archetypal roots, sanitized, and packaged in plastic. The gore still clings to it. We are irresistibly fascinated and repelled. To reenter the world of myth is to invite the discovery that we are umbilically connected to death, that we and death are actors in the same cosmic drama. Perhaps horror films offer modern versions of such mythologies, and Hollywood is the most important producer of contemporary myths.

Myths can become uprooted from their imaginal ground. No longer nourished by the collective unconscious, no longer replenished by living experiences flowing in and out of their stories, no longer enacted in cultural appropriations and constructions of death, they dwindle into premodern artifacts to be handled and scrutinized by college sophomores or museumed by meticulous scholars using scientific technique.

But whenever humans strive with wonder and fear to accomplish an appropriate end, the mythological imagination will be summoned, because everyday language is tested at the boundaries of life, where its limitations for telling all the truth are exposed. Under such conditions of communication failure, we strain for primordial meanings—and eschatological ones—that can give us truth large enough to live by.

In myth we read other worlds forward and ours backward in our quest for meanings. Death, we discover, is another journey lying ahead of us, and it may be that it carries us to the world of sacred beings. So we are uncertain and ambivalent at its boundaries, where life and death, endings and beginnings, nothingness and God intersect. We are challenged to discriminations that can bring re-creation out of chaos, to symbolic acts (rites of passage) that replicate primordial movements and demonstrate the participation of death in another, ultimately real, and dangerous world. Through myths that recount contests with chaos and darkness, we replicate these struggles and make them manifest in our own experiences. Death and life, the living and the dead, sustain each other; their exchanges ferment the mythological imagination and invite us to see in the dark more than we have seen in the light. Two worlds come together in one world amidst the reciprocities between death and life. Both birth and the grave are fertile enclosures and disclosures. The refining of death parallels and effects the refining of self, community, and cosmos.

Myth frees us from the limits we impose and lets us call out the sacred power of death and unite it with our living. Myth is an imaginal geography that lets us see our traversal through multiple worlds. The contours of the invisible world that we trace as we follow death all the way upriver turn out to be echoed outlines of the world we are living. How impoverished a landscape we see without myth. How safe and shallow the life that ignores it.

THE PSYCHOLOGICAL IMAGINATION

The psychological imagination measures the weight of death and grief on the human psyche with the critical questions and analytic tools that have matured in psychology.[21] Failure of such imagination leads to a truncated view of death and a flattened sensitivity to the emotional responses that death evokes. Death's wound to the psyche goes unnoticed and unaccounted for, and the crater death leaves in the heart of the griever is left unexplored.

But no act of imagination fully prepares us for death. If we glimpse its form as a dark imminence, take its size, lay out clothing appropriate for death or mourning, and instruct the engraver to make room for second thoughts, we still find ourselves and all our efforts remeasured by death. The severe mercy of grief work forces outward the too narrow boundaries we have set for the space of death in our lives. Alexander Pope wrote:

> *Grief tears his heart and drives him to and fro*
> *In all the raging impotence of woe.*

The passing of a loved one tears a great hole in the soul. Desperate searching is a common response:

> *By the waters of the woodland*
> *I have looked for you*
> *Weeping in the meadow I lay down*
> *I light the lamps of my heart.*
> *I call your name*
> *From the deeps of the world*
> *From the hollow place*
> *You do not come.*
> *What hath become of you?*
> *My lad. My lovely one.*[22]

Grief is the name we give to our emotional response to death of self or significant other, though sometimes we are surprised by a grief attendant on "insignificant" deaths or difficult passages. Grief stimulates the imagination (or is it the other way around?), so that lost images are pulled back into consciousness and larger stories gather.

On the death of another, we glimpse her life's course with sudden keenness. If the journey has been cut short, we carefully touch her hopes, caress her still-lively dreams, sorrow over broken promises, remain unwilling to lay all to rest.

Part of ourselves must be laid to rest, too. In the death of another I am wrenched by the death pangs of a mortal self. The part of me I locked inside her is to be buried, while I violently protest. The part of her lodged within me has also died, so death has come inside me. The structure of my soul is suddenly a jumble. Imagination races. How much of me is missing, lost, dead, left? A death knell is sounding for me.

It is not only the future of me heading toward death that plays on the imagination. At least at an unconscious level, a whole past history in which I have suffered the anxieties of separation, especially in early childhood, is replayed. We all learn to make meaning and to grow in a matrix of separation anxieties. In grieving now I express all the fears for my own existence that I have learned over the years, including when I thought my mother had abandoned me at the department store. Mourning the disappearing loved one, I begin to retrace all the times I have felt helpless, a history that death writes large. I am apprehensive that her death may be cuing acute danger to the interpersonal core of my very self.

As an infant and child, I experienced good and bad. Could I protect the good against the bad? Could I prevent the good from disappearing? Perhaps I have left those fears behind because I learned a basic trust of the good in my life. Mourning now reawakens those early concerns about losing the good objects that I had incorporated. I begin to obsess about them. I begin worrying again about my ability to defend myself against the bad. Will my deteriorating inner world ever be restored? Can the good come home to live inside again? Or must I leave my present human project and set out on the dangerous journey back to recover myself or rejoin myself to the lost good?

Grief varies with the complexity and intensity of one's relationship to the deceased. A bewildering variety of emotions present themselves to the imagination stimulated and charged by death. Depression signals our inability to protect the good we thought we had safely connected ourselves to. Defending against life, we turn our existence into mourning. We surrender the remaining vital part of ourselves to the domination of the part already dead.

Grief throws up tremendous energies. Profound ambivalence toward the dead may arise. We project onto the deceased any hostility we felt toward them and begin to imagine the malevolence they must have directed toward us. Fearing for ourselves, we defend against those we have lost. We are afraid and also guilty. If we ever wished the other person dead, we now stand condemned because our wishes apparently were omnipotent.

Or, the death of another may trigger early vulnerabilities stemming from parental admonitions we failed to heed during childhood. The superego becomes more punishing. We feel anxious for failing the moral demands thrust on us by others, and by our existence. Two projects get united. In the deceased's interrupted destiny, we fear we have lost our own destiny. Perhaps the person has left because of our ambivalence. We may also feel guilty for being unable to play the proper role at the other person's death.

Guilt burgeons, fueled by the powerful energies of grief. We defend ourselves by directing hostility outward, onto the deceased. Or we displace it onto others, or turn it inward in self-loathing. We punish ourselves with depression, or with excessive activity, or by developing bodily complaints. We justify ourselves by prolonged mourning, excessive idealization, or attention-getting behavior.

Under the mounting stress of grief we try to defend ourselves by building up an internalization to replace the lost relationship, regressing from loving the external person to loving her incorporation in us. Or we may turn our feelings toward the deceased in upon ourselves and in effect become in part that person. The emotions or even physical character of the other person may come to replace our own. We may develop strong attachments to externals: rooms, clothes, a cemetery plot.

The complexity of grief is related to the fact that the intense life energy directed toward a loved one is interrupted by death. This drive continues to seek satisfaction but is blocked. Death destroys the equilibrium between the id and the ego. Suddenly the ego must cope with excessive libidinal energy seeking discharge. The self is overwhelmed and becomes helpless. This surplus libidinal energy drives grief. The self feels driven, but with no place to go.

In Freud's imagination of grief work, the mourner, as a result of reality testing, must begin to withdraw libidinal attachment from the lost object. This is a struggle because one never willingly abandons a libido position. But in gradual acceptance of reality, every dimension of the lost object is brought up, hypercathected (great energy is poured out upon it), and detachment is finally achieved. Each object to which the libido has been bound must be liberated. Mourning is complete when the liberation of the libido from the lost object is finally fully accomplished. Object loss is transformed into ego-loss and finally the ego becomes free for new associations, free to invest emotional capital elsewhere. But part of the reborn ego's new equipment is the lost object, present and appropriable in a new way.

When this entire process ends too soon, it represents an exteriorizing that wants to channel meaning away from the painful inner self, or it may provide a direction for aggression, or a transfer of dependency to a new object in its most extreme form—fetishism, that is, a recathexis of an early ego state to a substitute for present reality. But when the process is healthy, the mourner is rebuilding links to the external world. Insofar as this is a world of good objects, the ego is replacing lost love objects and even reestablishing the lost love object as an active force. The inner world, which had been in danger of collapse, is reconstituted, as all the internalized good objects (besides the deceased) that were lost are reestablished. Thus the foundation is recovered for the courage to be. Anxiety produced by uncertain potentiality stimulates movement that leads to personal growth and the integration of new experiences, feelings, and meanings. Anxiety signals a threat to the ego, which can become a motivation to change. Mourners who have early experienced a basic trust or who live against a horizon of meaningfulness will have higher separation tolerances and greater success in completing grief work.

There are endless imaginings of the process, tasks, and stages of grieving. These, in effect, are grief "stories." Here, for example, is a coping story: The griever experiences a breakdown of reality testing under a narcissistic compulsion to keep the deceased in the world. Denial negates external realities to protect the ego from complete disintegration, and repression keeps the now unsatisfied instinctual demands of the id at bay. There follow searching behaviors, hyperactivity, calling for the deceased, and roaming, as one imagines the lost love object as only temporarily absent. Mania may set in as a denial of depression through triumphs of power and euphoria. All of these are narcissistic coping mechanisms. Aggressive coping strategies may follow. Protest reproaches the deceased for abandonment or expresses aggression by devaluing or ignoring the loss. Searching for the guilty may represent a regression to childlike notions of fixed causes or adult cravings for explanations and may move to ultimate levels by naming God as the one who administers death penalties. Identification with the aggressor means directing aggression against the self instead of against the deceased, restoring the deceased to dominance, and revenge-taking. Survivor guilt and penance may also be involved. Finally there may be objective libidinal coping, in which the conflict between the libidinal attachment to the deceased and the reality principle is worked out. Helplessness may be a means of securing attention and support or represent symbolic death and exhaustion. Recollection involves a slow dissolving of ties that moves from regression to adaptation. Incorporation may include such behaviors as regressive overeating but also finally the reconstruction of the deceased within the mourner through introjection, identification, and internalization. Finally, substitution means the lost love object is replaced by another person, new activities, caring for a new life.[23]

The grief process is also commonly imagined in stages. The most obvious to the eye are shock, intense mourning, and readjustment. A more elaborate list includes shock; the expression of profound emotion; depression and loneliness; physical symptoms of distress; pain, guilt, hostility, and resentment; the inability to return to usual activities; a gradual recovery of hope; and a successful struggle to readjust to reality.[24]

Another way to imagine grief is to identify its tasks. The mourner must find support from others; emancipation from the deceased; acceptance of reality; means to express sorrow and loss; verbalization of ambivalence, hostility, and guilt; formation of new relationships and connections; and discovery of larger meanings, hope, and direction.[25]

The term "grief work" denotes a process that is difficult, strenuous, exhausting, and unavoidable. Consider nine areas of grief work: accepting what seems like interminable pain; renewing a relationship with the deceased; talking about one's feelings; coming to terms with new feelings, including thoughts that one is losing one's mind; talking through how to deal with changed feelings; reflecting on and dealing with hostility; finding ways to think and feel about the deceased in the future; verbalizing guilt; and reflecting on new modes of living.[26]

I have been describing how the psychological imagination, quickened by the power of death and mortality, can create a grieving that is adequate to the human condition. But such a grieving is not finally an individualistic process or product. The full imagination of death compels the individual to stretch. A healthy imagination will seek the help of others and ground the individual in larger communities of meaning. If the pathologizing responses to death that the imagination inevitably churns up are not to become permanent postures in the world, with all life experiences filtered through the distortions of death, if mourning is not to settle into melancholy, imaginative grief must find a language of connection to the rest of the human community.

Shakespeare wrote:

> *Give sorrow words. The grief that does not speak*
> *Whispers the o'er-fraught heart and bids it break.*

We must today retrieve a language conversant with life on the boundaries and sedimented with mystery and pain and hope, a language replenished with symbols that are reminiscent of other voices and larger stories.

Ritualized language is the learned mechanism through which the mourner comes to reduce anxiety, overcome separation, and release the negative emotions of hostility and guilt. We think and talk our way free from the libidinal energy still cathected to the deceased. Ritual itself is a powerful symbolic language. But in the weeks and months following the funeral, language partly substitutes for the emotionally charged acts that need to be performed, understood, and accepted. In this vessel of language we clarify, alchemize, search, touch. In words we reestablish the threatened and disrupted self. Present words of comfort evoke the love and protection that accompanied the first hearing of such words whispered to us as children. Words call the names of the good objects that are resurfacing and of the bad objects that we fear and from which we are getting free. Words express the helplessness and helpfulness of regression. Words usher us into the inner world of grief and give us entry to the outer world of reality we must learn to retest. We talk our way into new connections with a new world. Through the good-byes we say aloud in empty rooms we honor and also loosen the ties with the lost object. Language was the communicative link with the other. Through it we now reinforce the internalized presence of the other, but also relate to it in a new way, freeing a resurrected ego to return to the world. Now language begins to reach out by the power of love to make new unions and overcome separation. Through the soul of language we find our way back to the center, to meaning. Grief is partly a talking cure. In words we feel our way to the new and perhaps touch the presence of God hovering in the symbolic power of language.

But our culture lacks the imagination to encourage us to speak such a language and has adapted us to live without it. We ourselves are unsure there will be caring listeners. Long denial has eroded the textured words that could be vessels of transcendence. An unimaginative culture invites silence or the use of words that anesthetize or say nothing. Society forbids the living to appear moved by the death of others. There is a conspiracy to deny words their power to search and to explore us, to carry us through our grief work to the courage to live again.

THE ANTHROPOLOGICAL IMAGINATION

Funeral rituals are created by humans. Death itself is a cultural construction. From earliest days to the present, the anthropological imagination has been stimulated by the encounter with funerary rituals. Archaeology is indebted to burial sites for early indications of symbolic activity among prehistoric peoples. The effort to imagine what was happening in rites of last passage brought forth a full range of interpretations and reflections regarding the work that humans, individually and collectively, do with death. Studies of ritual process revealed how death invites the reimagination of the social system and of the self. Theories about cultures as collective representations of society and elaborate systems of symbolic meaning followed.

Conceptualized as "cultural performances," funerals elucidate the cultural values by which people live and interpret their experiences. Viewed through the rituals of death, life and living become more transparent. How transparent? Are we entitled to assume that individualism, materialism, and commercialism are the deep cultural values illuminated by the contemporary American funeral? The ritual impoverishment of the contemporary "death system" is telling.

The imagination of death in exotic cultures produced false starts. British anthropologists Tylor and Frazer intellectualized the anthropological project as reconstructing the questions and solutions to which death gave rise. To the threat of death, "primitives" asserted the soul and afterlife, which led to ancestor worship, which led to belief in a spiritual being.

A breakthrough occurred when Durkheim shifted from questions about prehistoric origins to ones about social functioning. He tried to account for the anxieties not of individual personalities but of society. Conceptions of death are not explanations, but rather what needs to be explained. Death threatens the continuity and permanence of society and evokes rites that restore equilibrium. Funerary practices counteract the centrifugal forces of fear, dismay, and demoralization and provide a powerful reintegration of social solidarity. Death, "a sacrilege against the social order," requires this social reality to be recouped and regrafted onto the living and onto the deceased as ancestors. Society emerges triumphant over death not by losing the dead, but by assigning them a place in a total social system with room for both living and dead.

Durkheim looked at suicide, which seemed obviously a psychological phenomenon, and demonstrated that it varied with various "social facts." Hertz then demonstrated that emotions, which seem private and individual, could be taken as socially conditioned facts as well. Did death rituals organize and orchestrate private emotions? Was weeping a social construct? If so, it is not just emotional need or psychological functioning that accounts for funeral rituals. Mourning is a social and cultural task.

In societies that practice "secondary burial" (recovering the initially buried remains and ceremonially reburying them) Hertz saw that corpse, soul, and mourners are on parallel journeys, moving through a rite of passage, with the corpse a kind of natural symbol for the states of the soul of the deceased and the mourners. What is happening to the corpse stands for what is generally happening. When the journey is over, the clean white bones remaining are reburied in a second funeral site, the soul has established itself in a new society of the dead, and the mourners have reintegrated themselves into the society of the living.

Death leaves other cultural work to be ritualized as well. The legal and emotional roles of the deceased are dismantled and redistributed. Property and relationships are rearranged. Elaborate funerals minimize social conflict and threats to the stability of roles and rights. Death is not finalized until the social roles of the deceased have been redistributed among the living. Thus culture, rather than nature, speaks the last word.

Van Gennep saw that three-stage rituals move people from one culturally defined status to another (alive/dead; single/married) and are not merely archaic relics of past social forms, but a universal logic of human social life. Victor Turner brilliantly expanded our conceptualization of the second stage of such rituals, the liminal, which van Gennep had already observed to be the most developed.[27] The liminal is the "betwixt and between" stage, between normal social roles and close to some transcendent or sacred core of social and moral values, as well as dangerously disorderly and chaotic.

Building on such insights, Lévi-Strauss's structuralism viewed the human experience of death as the core of a universal language code. Death rituals use this language to mediate the opposition between life and death by asserting that death is an integral part of life. All myths and rituals, with their binary oppositions, are attempts to resolve unwelcome contradictions in life. Because such basic contradictions cannot be overcome, myths and rituals move from statements in strong form to weaker or mediated forms. Such messages are endlessly repeated or enacted, since no final resolution is achievable. Greek funeral laments, for example, are "rich in metaphors of mediation because the process of dying and the body of the dead are mediators of the opposition between life and death and between nature and culture. Dying is a transition from life to death, culture to nature."[28] Such contradictions cannot be resolved, only endlessly expressed. Ritual talk is a continual coming down first on one side of the opposition and then on the other, always seeking mediations or weaker expressions of the binary opposition.[29]

Such understandings helped move beyond a social functionalism that reduced all rituals to subtle statements about or reflections of society. (Today we need to free ourselves from reducing all rituals to psychological needs.) Influences run in all directions. Perhaps social solidarity bubbles up out of the dialectic of sorrowing and comforting, of personal emotions and obligatory displays. If there is a reassertion of social order at the time of death, *might such social order be an effect, rather than a cause of funeral rituals?* Does a society responding to the sacrilege of death create death rituals, or do such rituals create society? The question of what rituals create and what creates rituals is wonderfully complex.

Death is not just an empty stage for other, more primary social dramas. Indeed, turning social functionalism on its head *makes death the primary variable, not society.* (This is akin to those who turn psychoanalytic theory on its head and make separation anxiety a product of mortality, not the other way around.) What if death becomes the be-all and end-all? Then social structure and culture/nature are examined through the lens of death, not vice versa. Instead of "familiarizing" death by demonstrating its domestication by other issues, one could "defamiliarize" social order (things are not what they seem) by the way one studies death.[30]

Because death is the ultimate marginal situation, it threatens not merely social structure but every system of meaning for an individual or a culture. It is the most terrifying threat to the taken-for-granted realities of everyday life, the insult of the final triumph of nature over culture. We band together in groups against death, we reduce terror by legitimating death or providing recipes for

good deaths. We produce meaning systems that give an account of death sufficiently persuasive that we are not immobilized. "World-construction" and
"world-maintenance" are required.[31] Through interactions with others, we
project our subjective experiences into reality. Such world-constructions then
seem prior to our individual experiences. Our constructed worlds are subsequently internalized by individuals as structures of subjective consciousness.

But we have to maintain the worlds we have constructed if they are to keep
making sense. Conversation with others, necessary for world-maintenance,
steps up at death. Funeral rites are such conversations, oblique talk about
important cultural themes and about the special necessity of affirming meaning in the face of death. They are metasocial commentaries, reflections in time
of peril about ultimate meanings of individuals and society, reflections that
take on the character of religious conversation.

In the face of death all across human history and culture, gripping metasocial commentaries, existential conversations about world-construction and
world-maintenance, have occurred. The early Greeks held funeral games in
honor of the exceptional dead and of aristocrats, asserting group solidarity
and high culture through athletic competitions and poetry contests. Puritans
in early America felt the death of one of their group as a devastating blow to
the dwindling circle of concerned survivors.[32] Every death complicated their
covenant with a seemingly capricious God who had sent them on an "errand
into the wilderness." Each Puritan death seemed to require a theodicy and a
reexamination of their mission. Despite their antiritualism, during periods of
societal stress and instability they adopted highly elaborate funeral rituals and
abandoned their unadorned style of grave marking. In daily conversations
they kept reminding themselves through their *New England Primer:*

> *T is for: Time cuts down all*
> *Both great and small*
> *X is for: xerxes the great did die*
> *And so must you and I*
> *Y is for: Youth forward slips*
> *Death soonest nips.*

Sometimes such world-constructing commentaries take the form of rituals to
complete in death what didn't get done in life. The death weddings still practiced
in rural villages in Rumania are a startling example.[33] When a young person dies
unmarried, a death wedding placates the soul of the deceased and protects
against the dangers arising from unfulfilled lives. Otherwise the deceased may

return in search of a mate and become a menace to society. The turbulence between sex and death is quieted, the Otherness of untimely death is socialized into the life cycle, and an ideal and pure marriage is effected. A total social system remains intact: Kinship responsibilities keep the dead eternally alive and keep sexuality in marriage, tempering the anxieties of the living regarding untimely death. The rites of the wedding of the dead are a form of alms given by the living to the dead and a marvelous exercise of social imagination.[34]

Funeral rites may construct an idealized society that rights the inescapable wrongs of normal life. The Dobuan, who see in-laws as a constant danger, epitomize through their funeral rites the desire of the lineage to turn back on itself and to abrogate all relations with outsiders. In life husbands and wives alternately reside in each other's villages. At death, however, each finds a permanent haven in the mound of his or her own village, where the person is at last free from outsiders. At death the corpse is immediately claimed by its own lineage, and in-laws are not allowed to watch the rites. The spouse remains in the village of the deceased for one year of arduous mourning and then must leave and never return. So in the lineage burial ground the Dobuan construct their utopia, in which absolute boundaries reign between descent groups. In that perfect land, which only the dead know, generations succeed without the unpleasantness and danger of exchange or differentiation. The afterlife is rid of in-laws.

In Lugbara thought death comes in from the wilderness, a place of unrestrained female sexuality, uncontrolled by men and always threatening to engulf male order. Funeral rituals then serve to hang on to the souls of important men, even if they must release the spirit to a timeless wild. Such rituals keep chaos at bay and reinforce the male order that has carefully been built up in the life of the group.

Even human physiology may be an icon of the changes in meaning that death brings, demonstrating the place of life and death in the same cosmic order. In the rites of some South American indigeneous groups, the last breath of the deceased is ritualized into a final exhalation so that it becomes congruent with a larger cosmic ordering of breath. This is how it happens. When the time is right, the heaviest women of the younger generation are called to sit down hard on top of the dying person, whose groans and moans are the sounds of the evil spirits' breath leaving the body. After the nearly asphyxiated person's groaning ceases and he is almost dead, he is folded chest over knees. Then heavy and ample daughters and daughters-in-law seat themselves on top of him until a strange crackling noise of shattered ligaments indicates the spinal column has given out and the body is reduced to a bundle. So the physiology of the dying moment modulates meaning in the world of the living.[35]

What messages do we send with modern rites, what metaconversations are being staged? Blauner argued that bureaucratization is the key variable in understanding the modern funeral, just as it is the key variable in modern societies.[36] A funeral industry is the mate of a health care industry, which is the mate of the bureaucratization of all contemporary society. The devaluation of the aged is represented by the bureaucratic phasing out of individuals from society in anticipation of their death. This parallels a modern reduction in the significance of death, which results in a reduction in the significance of funeral rites.

Parsons and Lidz suggest that the style of death in modern American society is a reflection not of denial but of a mode of acceptance appropriate to our primary cultural pattern of instrumental activism.[37] Such activism maximizes rational control over the conditioned elements in our life situations. Death becomes a technical matter, and we see in our death system the metasocial commentary of a technological society. The open casket and embalming allow society to see the deceased in a manner that makes his or her former capacities recognizable. A control mechanism is emphasized; suffering and loss of capacity are deemphasized.

Death rituals that can so effectively perform varying "cultural work" have, of course, stimulated the political imagination as well: "rite makes might."[38] Mark Antony turned Julius Caesar's funeral into a political act that drove the Brutus faction from the city. Some African-American funerals effect political reversals in death.[39] If the larger society accords to a minority community minimal respect, treats them as objects, blocks their mobility, they may retrieve posthumously the esteem denied them while living. During slavery, the churches became surrogate families and afforded dignity to the dead. In contemporary Harlem, numerous community funeral parlors give final elegance to lives of deprivation.

Death is not only a problem, but also an opportunity—"an occasion for furthering social, cultural, and political ends."[40] Political, social, and religious sytems can use funeral rituals to call themselves into being or to accomplish revitalizations. A purgatory whose inmates could be moved along by prayer both led to the extension of communal ties between the living and the dead and became a marvelous instrument of power for the medieval Church.[41]

Funeral rituals can be overtly political.[42] On June 16, 1989, several hundred thousand people assembled in Heroes Square in Budapest for "the most important political event in Hungary since the revolution of 1948." Imre Nagy and five compatriots, executed after the 1956 uprising, were disinterred from their unmarked graves. "Amid great ceremony and intensely emotional display they were given a second burial, and their revolution a second birth."[43] An opposite example is the disinterring of the pre-Reformation hero John

Wycliffe and the scattering of his remains by English Catholic counter-Reformation forces. More elaborate was King Charles II's second funeral for Oliver Cromwell, whose first had all the trappings of royalty. The king had the body of Cromwell exhumed, dragged through the streets, hanged, beheaded, and the head stuck up on a pole on Westminster Hall. The skull remained there for seventeen years until it was finally blown down in a violent storm.

In Ireland, "a cult of death has emerged in the political realm, where powerful symbolic performance and emotional display is a feature of dying, wakes, and funerals. The cult of political martyrdom has a long history of its own in Ireland and has enjoyed an ambivalent relation with the Catholic Church."[44] Those in power and those wanting to seize power have seen that "the experience of death is so powerful emotionally that its cultural organization is a source of potential political power."[45] Both Church and state have extended their hegemony by promoting new and powerful cultural forms involving rituals, texts, and devotional objects. Death played a critical role in the spread of churchly power in late antiquity through the cult of saints.[46] If the Church had learned how to use death's power ritually to invoke social units and cultural values, the IRA was willing to imitate. As "English firing squads succeeded in ritualizing" the deaths of IRA militants and "framing them as religious events," the IRA, in organizing the political funeral, "has learned from the Church as well as the army, reappropriating the funeral with all its pomp and adding, by dint of the menacing presence of British soldiers, the charisma of dramatic opposition."[47]

Great funeral rituals can gracefully deconstruct as well as construct. Winston Churchill's funeral in 1965 not only was the last rites of the man himself, "but was also self-consciously recognized at the time as being the requiem for Britain as a great power."[48] One man's last passage marked the end of an era. Interestingly, the power of ritual was thenceforth increasingly used in Britain to celebrate something that had *not* passed—royal family and the monarchy.

Modern states show no lack of imagination in their use of death rituals. A Japanese emperor's funeral thus could become a celebration of the new Japan (or a last hurrah for Japanese totalitarianism). Combining Shinto rites with the ritual of a state funeral, "the Japanese government turned Emperor Hirohito's last rites into a semi-sacred celebration of the nation's emergence as an economic superpower. . . . In death, Hirohito brought the nation a respect his Imperial Army and Navy failed to win in the Pacific War."[49]

President Reagan's 1985 visit to the military cemetery in Bitburg, Germany, was a less successful exercise in imagination. A ritual visitation by the American president and the German chancellor, Helmut Kohl, was supposed to symbolize the mutual clasping of hands over the graves of the war dead. The Bitburg ritual was planned partly because Chancellor Kohl resented having been excluded from the ceremonies at the Normandy landing the year before. When French president Mitterand tried to make up for it by inviting Kohl to ceremonies at Verdun and the two solemnly embraced amidst a sea of crosses, he succeeded only in ritually absolving Germany from the wrong war. What was needed was absolution for the Second World War, and on German soil. Reagan's consent to visit Bitburg was repaying Kohl in ritual currency. But to millions of Jews and others it seemed a betrayal of Holocaust victims, for Bitburg, in effect, had been deconsecrated by the burial there of thirty-eight of Hitler's SS troops. A visit to the Bergen-Belsen concentration camp earlier in the day was hastily arranged, although Reagan had first announced he would not be visiting any concentration camp. But this juxtaposition of the Bitburg and Bergen-Belsen dead seemed to place them on equal symbolic footing and only provoked further outrage. An editor of the *Jerusalem Post* cried: "Do not drag our dead into your reconciliation with Kohl's Germany. Do not mention our victims in the same breath with those who lie at Bitburg." An obtuse *Chicago Tribune* editorial the day before lamented "a time when symbolism has replaced rational debate as the medium of political exchange." But we know no other way as powerful as ritual and symbol.[50]

Thus, *in funeral rituals we get our cultural work done, as well as our cosmic, or religious, work.* Hindu cremations in the holy city of Banares align death with a perpetual cycle of time. Cremations are sacrificial acts that reenact the original cosmogonic sacrifice and rekindle the fires of creation at the very spot where creation began.[51] In just the same way Golgotha, the place of Christ's crucifixion, is thought to be at the navel of the earth. Christ's blood drops on Adam's skull, and humankind is redeemed and reborn. Or the gods may desire human blood: The death of humans replenishes the earth. An Aztec sacred writing goes:

> And four days passed by, and the sun was in the sky.
> All upon the earth feared amid eternal shadows.
> Went the hawk to ask: the gods wish to know the reason
>   why you don't move.
> And the sun answered,
> Do you want to know why?
> I want the blood of humans
> I wish to have their sons, I desire to possess their offspring.[52]

So humans lend their deaths to the universe and receive the light of the sun in return.

At one time a bad death was one deprived of elaborate cultural trappings.

In such a case the individual could not swell with cultural and cosmic meaning; none of the overlays of society, culture, and religion was available. The Greeks thought a bad death was one away from community, lonely and unseen, the body unburied and rotting like that of a wild beast. In view of the so-called opposites of culture and nature, the death mediated through the community of culture demonstrates the connection between humans. To culture belong fire and burial in a grave. The unmediated death represents the world of animals. To nature belong the raw and nonburial.

A good death is one in which time and place are determined, social death is dissociated from mere bodily function, and a victory of order over biology is dramatized. Thus pleas to die in a social context where death rituals will be performed properly are found in laments that invoke the horror of dying in a foreign land, a place where no one is obligated to perform the necessary rites. So death rituals function to get the truth about the human condition told. And such truths get told only in community. Each of us must have others to throw a little earth over him or her.[53]

Death rituals across time and cultures stimulate our imaginations and enlarge the boundaries of death. We may rediscover ourselves by way of the discovered Other. But closer looks invite risks. Even if in rituals "doing is believing," even if rituals carry strong messages of order, continuity, and predictability, even if sacred rituals link the celebrants to their very selves and turn individual history into a single reality, still, rituals appear in dangerous circumstances and contain the possibility of failure.[54] Underlying each ritual is an ultimate danger: "the possibility that we will encounter ourselves making up our conceptions of the world, society, and our very selves."[55] Death rituals can come to be seen as products of our imagination, culture as our construction. A ritual fails when it is seen through, not properly attended, or experienced as arbitrary invention. But it is always just as possible that rituals, when they deliver the goods and provide enough order and meaning for the moment and for meditation later, will be experienced as revelations. *Human agency then is acknowledged as discovery rather than invention.* And in the personal integration achieved through ritual, the self is also discovered and the individual life is remade as a mythic event. Thus is our experience and possession of the world changed.

This is work no culture can afford to leave undone. Danforth found in his study of funeral laments in rural Greece that it is almost exclusively women who perform ongoing death rituals.[56] The more the bereaved defines herself in relation to the deceased, the more death threatens her socially constructed world. The marginal women of rural Greece whose role is to nurture and maintain social relationships in life are the ones who keep doing it in death. As they say, *ponos* (a kind of painful connection to social bonds) pulls them to the graves daily.

I think these women of rural Greece are a bit like monks. They do one important task—not the only task life demands, not the task to which everyone is called, but a task indispensable if all the truth about being human is to be voiced. They spin part of the web of meaning in which we suspend ourselves. Meanwhile, others in society lay the weight of their lives along other lines of contradiction, other opposites that need mediation if life is to go on. The women do not lack imagination; they do the work imagination envisions and to which they are called.

Who are *our* contemporary equivalents of such women? Who today is most connected to a socially constructed world that death will collapse? Clergy? Religious communities of faith? Does death create these groups in order to make meaning in the face of its challenge? Do they do ritual work because they have the most to lose, or do they have the most to lose because they do ritual work?

What is the task for persons of anthropological imagination as they look at their own culture? Are we to be left bereft and alone if ritual connection to social bonds fails? Anthropologists have measured death's claims and found them immense. All over the landscape of the heart, to every precinct of society's ideal of itself, death's boundary lines run, its districts gerrymandered through every aspect of life, its deeds claiming ownership of diverse cultural forms, so many poets and priests and commoners in its employ.

We cannot pass all this by in order to preserve our youth, whistling away in a mined landscape. It won't do to look away from ourselves limping along in hunchbacked finitude or blocking out siren calls with the white noise of omnipresent transistors. We can be saved from despair or shallowness by the cultural outpourings with which we respond to death. Whether we use our imagination wonderfully to create or humbly to receive, it is the vessel in which discoveries, revelations, and mythical constructions are mixed with the reality of death.

THE RELIGIOUS IMAGINATION

Imaginal thought pressed to the ultimate becomes religious thought. In the religious imagination humans face death facing them. Stalking the tracks of death, its traces dropped in dreams and daydreams, we stop short when it turns to question us. We learn new ways of seeing after languishing in its darkness; set free, we see better in the light as well. Intrepid and amazed explorers, we search death's boundaries. We hope finally to trace our own last breath back to the mouth of God. Dying, we imagine, must be a sacred art.

But death is no easy journey. Its wound to human consciousness is a universal experience. The religious imagination of the East has seen how illusion and attachment weigh down human death. St. Paul connected death's sting to sin. Human finitude is heavy because death hangs over every quest for self-transcendence. Cruelly arriving death seals our moral failures, freezes unstarted creations, causes dreamed selves to be stillborn, and mocks even our most joyful celebrations with reminders of unfinished business. The more penetratingly we inspect the self, the more we agonize over paths not taken, promises unkept, unfulfilled identity. It is not simply moral failure, sin as we usually think of it, but crises of meaning and finitude that feed the existential anxiety evoked by death. Never simply friend, never only velvet touch, death comes to sting. Death is powerful because sin, or false knowledge, burdens the inhabitants of the world. Death devastates because we are always unfinished, flawed, finite, misled.

A homely response to the sting of death was the creation in some folk cultures of "sin eaters," curious and pitiful figures shunned by all because of their assigned familiarity with evil. They derived their income and station by taking upon themselves the trespasses of the deceased. Summoned at death, they were passed a loaf of bread and a bowl of beer over the corpse by the survivors. After consuming these, the sin eater was paid and the bowl and platter burned.

An enlarged imagination is necessary for coming to terms with death. Death is natural and spiritual. The easy victory that comes in naturalizing death and thereby taming it also renders it opaque to the human spirit, or romanticizes humans into uncomplicated animals. Death is dialectical because humans are. We are a mystery to ourselves, a riddle that forces larger questions on us. Religious imagination is stimulated as we experience ourselves being addressed. If we have been created in a divine image, it is embarrassing how we grope for our true likeness. But within such embarrassment lies the opportunity for radical discovery— unless we surrender radical and painful amazement to penultimate meanings.

An appropriate death is a construction of religious imagination, a death in which we are granted the opportunity to finish ourselves as body and spirit, nature and culture, to give ourselves up to the completion of being and receive a new relation to the world. In death a person's history of freedom reaches its final form. One has always had, consciously or unconsciously, to do with God. Death might be the radical challenge to decide finally for God. To decide for God is to accept a radical helplessness and to allow oneself to be engulfed by the incomprehensible mystery that is God. Thus, to suffer death becomes an act of inner liberty.

Such a self-offering need not be confined to the biological moment of death, an undependable contingency. The self-transcendence of such a dying may migrate through the whole of life. Memento mori is there in every accomplishment of freedom in which one accepts the finiteness of life and nevertheless affirms before God ultimate meaning. Today such an *ars moriendi* is difficult because so much dying has become styleless, that is, unshaped by a community of faith and trust.[57]

The Christian Religious Imagination

The religious imagination may find in death unexpected encounters with God.[58] Elusive presence is discovered at the edge of the abyss. The manifestation of sin and brokenness is reimagined as the opportunity for graceful presence. Over the course of Israel's history this emerged in the Hebrew scriptures as the discovery that God's presence extends even to the underworld, that nothing can assert separation as strongly as God's love can assert connection. Christian proclamation about death and dying is tied to the central Christian narrative, the incarnation, death, and resurrection of Jesus Christ. The Christian imagination, particularly in the Roman Catholic tradition, invites the faithful to die the Church's mode of dying, that is, a sacramental dying, a paschal journey, with Christ, through death into the life of God.

When Jesus accepted death into his vocation, he transformed it into an opening up to the divine presence. The "crucified God" reveals the unexpected power of life in death. Jesus, at the crucial moment of despairing trust, hanging on the cross, took over the absurdity of human death as his own and thus opened it up to a new future, which included resurrection. Moving toward God in his dying, Jesus let his death become the point of entry into the life of God. His death and the world's dying are taken up into the history of God. Uninvited and alien, death nevertheless offers unexpected opportunity for the consummation of self in freedom and hope. Death becomes the quintessential occasion to pass into the life of God.

Death is not simply conquered from without, but opened up from within. The free offering of the self to God in the midst of death is revealed as a possibility, expressed as a dying with and in Christ. Death is turned into the completion of the human pilgrimage, the lifting of the earthly city into the city of God. The lesser mortalities that taunt human passages—failure, divorce—are similarly opened up.

Some imagine that in death the individual enters for the first time or in a new way into an open, unrestricted relation to the cosmos as a whole. Perhaps near-death experiences are hints of a next state that is beyond space and time. The risen Christ may symbolize the opening of the soul to a new relationship with the world, unmediated by a physical body and beyond space-time limitations.

In twentieth-century Protestant theology, the historical doctrinal locus of eschatology, which referred to the "last things," including death and judgment, shifted to the center stage. Early in the century eschatology focused on

Jesus as an apocalyptic visionary. Later, eschatology permeated all theology as "the crisis of ultimate concern" that overshadows all of life, the presence of the eternal in the present moment. The dialogic partners for eschatological theology were Marxism, existentialism, critical theory, and other gaping postwar questions, such as the Holocaust or the death of God. In this theology an individual's death was generally swallowed up in larger concerns about the world, the community, the survival of a viable Christian faith, and even the question of God.[59] Personal death and survival become less important than the largest questions of meaning and suffering projected onto a cosmic stage.

In *The Crucified God,* Jürgen Moltmann sought again to make the cross the center of Christian theology.[60] "The death of Jesus is the way God's full participation in human suffering and death is enacted; to make the cross central repudiates forever any definition of God as a being immune to pain. Here, the death of Jesus is not his defeat by an enemy, but his complete and final act of solidarity in the human condition of mortality and oppression. . . . It reveals more clearly the permanent character of God as a participant in the pain and alienation of creation."[61] The cross is the foundation of Christian imagination because it is there that God locates his presence for humanity. The cross is criticism because it calls into question all other images of God (and of death). The focus on divine suffering provides a new home and a new hermeneutic for death imagery. Moltmann is willing to say that "in the death of the Son, death comes upon God himself, and the Father suffers the death of his Son in his love for forsaken man."[62] Jesus's death becomes the quintessential *death in God.*

The religious imagination inevitably produces models of dying. For Socrates or the Platonic view there is "natural death." Much recent Roman Catholic theology idealizes the death of martyrs, who die triumphantly by surrendering their life to God in a great consent, through which their death is taken up into the life of God and death's power is broken. Moltmann wants to emphasize Jesus's death as "judicial murder" so as to make the point that God's involvement in human suffering takes the form of victimization at the hands of authority. Thus Moltmann places twentieth-century victims in solidarity with Jesus's death.

The Jewish Imagination

Early Hebrew scriptures see humans as returning somehow to the earth or to a shadowy world at death. These scriptures focus instead on the creative power of God and his ongoing living relationship with the whole Jewish community—the people of God. Simply to observe that early Judaism lacked a notion of immortality misses the point. "Better to say they left immortality in God's hands, never daring to assert that the human being possesses it by rights, and yet daring to hope that God would bestow a share in eternal life upon those who belong to him."[63] Eventually, some kind of resurrection comes to dominate faithful expectation, as the urgency of God's setting things right with his people and with world history grows ever greater.

In ancient Israel the individual person was never considered immortal. Humans are a living mixture of earth and the breath of God. At death, the clay returns to earth and the breath goes back to the Creator. The promise to Abraham comes to epitomize "ancestral and cultural transcendence." That is, through the power and promise of God, the Jewish people or nation become the carrier of identity, transcendent meaning, eternal life. Within such an ongoing pattern of meaning, the exodus from Egypt came to function as the transcending of death. Later, under the pressure of heartbreaking times and threats to Jewish continuity, apocalyptic thought blossomed, with its hope that dry bones might once again live.[64] Messianic hopes were connected to an age and a people, not to individuals.

The Jewish tradition continued to evolve, guided by the rabbis. During the Middle Ages important influences from Plato and Aristotle were incorporated. While the view of God as the creative presence and of the Jewish people as eternal heirs to special promise and divine covenant continues strongly into the twentieth century, a wide range of views of the afterlife, including denial and disinterest, came to coexist. While physical resurrection remains a defining feature of Jewish orthodoxy, reinforced by liturgical avowals, Jewish reform movements arising during the eighteenth and nineteenth centuries accommodated themselves to the climate of modern Europe and tended to reject rabbinic authority. Somewhat like liberal Protestantism of the same period, Reform Judaism rejected any literal belief in resurrection. Twentieth-century Jewish discourse, outside the Orthodox tradition, focuses on the absolute commitment to this world as the setting for the encounter with the divine. Eternity is the religious dimension of life, not of afterlife. The Jewish imagination of death and life after death is massively challenged by the Holocaust; what remains is a powerful and continuing search for ultimate meaning amidst absurdity and destruction.

Ritual as the praxis of ongoing meaning, as a community-rooted style of living and dying, has become more important than doctrine. At death, the dying person makes confession. Within the community the great Shema is proclaimed: "Hear, O Israel, the Lord is our God, the Lord is one" (Deuteronomy 6:4). During dying and death the body is not left unattended. Burial—ideally in a simple pine box—occurs as soon as possible after death. After the graveside service the community of close relatives pray the mourners' prayer, the Kaddish, an essential part of Jewish mourning, a ritual to be observed for a full year following death. Its essential cadence is: "The Lord gives and the Lord takes away; blessed be the name of the Lord." Then: "To the departed whom we now remember, may peace and bliss be granted in life eternal. May they find grace and mercy before the Lord of heaven and earth. May their souls rejoice in that ineffable good which God has laid up for those who fear Him, and may their memory be a blessing unto those who treasure it." For the seven days following burial, the family observes shivah, an intense period of mourning in the home. All life can be a preparation for death. The highest Jewish holy day, the Day of Atonement (Yom Kippur), calls the whole community to fast, visit the synagogue, reflect on sinfulness, and diligently pray. Out of working through the meaning of sin and death in the midst of life comes the renewal of the people of Israel.

The Hindu Imagination

The Hindu imagination of death, as evidenced in the great texts, proceeds through famous dialogs between an archetypal seeker and an immortal teacher. Reduced to its essence, the question is: What is the purpose of life, given the certainty of death? The answer comes: Freedom from the question just asked and from all separateness through realization of the *atman*, the deathless self.

In a story from the Katha Upanishad (eighth to fifth centuries B.C.) Nachiketa journeys to the court of Yama, king of death, who is away from home when Nachiketa arrives. On Yama's return, he grants Nachiketa three boons, one for each night he waited. He is to be restored to his relationship with his father, and he is to be taught how to perform the fire sacrifice to Agni, which leads to the realm of immortality. His last request is for knowledge of the soul's fate after death. Yama offers him alternative gifts: wealth, beautiful women, fast chariots, numerous sons. But Nachiketa wisely says that these things do not last and only wear out the senses. So Yama agrees to teach him the great secret of the *atman*. It is not born, does not die, hides in the heart of every living creature, and is part of *paratman*, the eternal, total soul. When the body dies, the true self, *atman*, does not die. *Atman* is realized through intense meditation. Beyond *atman* is *paratman*, unmanifest, the container of all the gods and all that exists. All that is manifest will end. One who knows the true self puts death to death. This realization and emancipation, called *moksha*, frees one from the vagaries of karma and from the wheel of rebirth, *samsara*. Freed from the illusion of separateness, Nachiketa comes to learn that:

> *Death is ever-present within the body and world;*
> Atman *is undying;*
> *To realize it one must die to fears about living and dying;*
> *The only teacher about death is Death itself;*
> *Through wholehearted and disciplined surrender one*
>   *attains immortality while yet alive.*

In the Bhagavad Gita (fifth to second centuries B.C.) the warrior prince Arjuna waits in his chariot on the eve of civil war, in anguish that he must soon be killing his own relatives or be killed by them. His charioteer is Krishna himself. Krishna teaches him that death is natural and unavoidable, but not real. Only *atman* is real, recognized and realized through the yoga of devotion and surrender.[65] To realize *atman* while still alive is to merge already with *brahman*, undifferentiated ultimate reality. To actualize *atman*, and not only to recognize it, is to practice the sacred art of dying. Ultimately the yogic paths to such actualization bring one to the paradox of actionless action. The performer dies into Krishna and becomes *atman*. Krishna expresses this:

> *Let a man close up all the body's gates,*
> *Stem his mind within his heart,*
> *Fix his breath within his head,*
> *Engrossed in Yogic concentration.*
> *Let him utter* Om, brahman *in one syllable,*
> *Keeping Me in mind;*
> *Then when his time is come to leave aside the body,*
> *He'll tread the highest Way.*
> *How easily am I won by him*
> *Who bears Me in mind unceasingly,*
> *Thinking of nothing else at all—*
> *A Yogin integrated ever.*[66]

The *bhakti yoga*, the art of dying in one of many Hindu traditions, requires surrender. To die mindfully, yogically, is to be absorbed in devotion to Krishna. At that point rituals, texts, and temples fall away. Reciting mantras or offering selfless acts of mercy, the *bhakta* welcomes death in the midst of all-absorbing love. There only remains placing water from the Ganges in the dying person's mouth as the family chants Vedic mantras, carrying the deceased to the cremation grounds in new or clean clothes, the eldest son walking round the pyre three times, and setting the body afire to free the soul. But all of life can be an anticipatory dying.[67]

> *Between the doors*
> *of birth and death,*
> *stands yet another door,*
> *wholly inexplicable.*
>
> *He who is able*
> *to be born*

at the door of death,
is devoted eternally . . .

(Therefore)
Die before dying,
die living.

The Buddhist Imagination

In response to ominous predictions before the birth of Gautama Buddha, the king, his father, sheltered him from all knowledge of unpleasant things. Then one day in his late twenties Prince Gautama experienced the Four Passing Sights—a leper, a man decrepit with age, a burning corpse, and then the fourth sight, a meditating yogi, who promised an avenue of escape. Shocked into awareness of suffering and death, Gautama resolved to follow a spiritual path dedicated to overcoming them. He took a vow of death to the world, left his wife and son, cut his hair, and traded his rich clothing for rags. He took up the life of an ascetic. He determined to conquer death within life by dying liberated, so that he would not have to be born again. At dusk on the night of his enlightenment, Death appeared before Gautama and challenged his right to sit on the seat of enlightenment beneath the bodhi tree. Contending against Death during the three watches of the night of enlightenment, Gautama gained ever-deepening insight into the nature of death. He saw how spiritual perfections accumulate through the course of rebirths. He saw the parade of suffering through life. He saw the flux of the whole universe, that all things except nirvana arise and pass away.

He came to see four noble truths: that life is permeated by suffering, that suffering is caused by desire, that there could be liberation in disattaching from desire, and that this could be accomplished by following an eightfold path toward enlightenment (right understanding, right resolve, right speech, right acts, right livelihood, right effort, right mindfulness, right concentration). Fully enlightened at age thirty-five, Gautama began teaching. At age eighty he died his final death in a grove while the trees dropped their blossoms and gods came to honor him. His Great Death was one of complete composure and equilibrium. His final instruction to his disciples was: "Compounded things decay; strive earnestly."

Buddhism turned away from Hindu religious constructions toward the ultimate liberation that was nirvana, the release and liberation that comes from spiritual insight or enlightenment. It is the extinction of lust, hatred, and delusion. Nirvana is both provisionally achieved after enlightenment while still embodied and finally achievable after the dissolution of the body. The saint after death is like an extinguished fire, and even Death cannot discern where the saint has gone.

Buddhist meditation in the context of death, like the meditation of Catholic monasticism, includes the development of mindfulness about one's death and may use corpses as objects of meditation. One finds a quiet spot and says, "Death will take place," or just "Death, death." More, one may enhance such awareness by an eightfold meditation: all stand before death as before an inexorable executioner; no means can avert it; even supreme buddhas die; the human body is shared with eighty families of worms; bodily life is dependent; one cannot rely on signs that tell when death will come; life span is limited; individual consciousness is but a moment. Meditations on corpses—swollen, discolored, festering, severed, mangled, dismembered, cut, bloody, worm-eaten, and skeletal—are meant to eradicate lustful states of mind. Alternatives are the seeking of a pure mind and ten kinds of merit to avoid fear of death and seeking a completely peaceful mind at the time of death.

Tibetan Buddhism, the Vajrayana school, teaches its practitioners in great detail how to enter into the death experience prior to dying. The Tibetan Book of the Dead, a manual on the art of dying, is its most famous vehicle. The manual was intended to help practitioners die consciously. It assumes the importance of right knowledge for enlightenment and of a certain kind of consciousness at the time of death. Ideally, a Buddhist has memorized the book and recites it to himself as he lies dying, or a priest recites it to him. The ritual function is to assist the dead in their journey through the realm of the dead, initiating them to a pure state of consciousness, but this is a journey they have been practicing throughout their lives. Focusing on the gap between death and rebirth, the bardo state, which lasts forty-nine days, the Tibetan art of dying offers opportunity for awakening or rebirth.

The manual prepares the adept for three states: the moment of death, when one is to be prepared to recognize a great, bright, colorless light and in this way attain liberation immediately; a dreamlike state, in which one encounters peaceful and then wrathful deities as manifestations of one's own mind; and a hallucinatory embodiment, to be overcome after the Lord of Death assigns a realm of rebirth based on one's karma. The culmination sought is the "ejection of consciousness," in which the dying person keeps the mind free from earthly distractions, visualizes a seated Buddha over the head, surrounded by a rainbow arch, visualizes consciousness as a ball of fire in the abdomen which then rises up the spine until it leaves the top of the head, and experiences the mixing of self-consciousness with the Buddha-mind. Throughout, right practice can achieve the final avoidance of rebirth—if one can be freed from karmic illusions and concentrate on the pure Buddha realm. If not, a new body must be found by the forty-ninth day. The to-be-born-again are encouraged to concentrate on the womb about to be entered and to enter it in a state of supreme equilibrium. The *bardo* body will be attracted to a lovemaking couple and enter the woman's body at the moment of ejaculation.

Japanese Buddhism developed its own path.[68] The concept of *mujo* (in Sanskrit, *anitya*), or impermanence, became central to apprehending death. *Mujo* relativizes death by making every moment a type of dying and change all-pervasive. Endings are distributed throughout life, and only illusion makes us see death as extraordinary. In accepting impermanence, one moves from illusion to enlightenment and to an eventual great death. The Japanese thoroughly imbibed the theme of impermanence. Their memento mori is an image of scattering blossoms or falling autumn leaves. The entire world of phenomena, not just cremation grounds or corpses, becomes a theater for meditation on death. Observing this, one develops an inner sensitivity, which is an appreciation for beauty as well as truth. Memento mori becomes aesthetic awareness, and cherry blossoms and melting snow teach an *ars moriendi*. The twelfth-century poet-monk Saigyo wrote:

> *With each night of Fall*
> *Grown colder than the one before,*
> *The cricket's cry seems*
> *More feeble—as each night it*
> *Moves farther into distance.*

Things gain in beauty to the extent they are ephemeral. The fourteenth-century writer Yoshida Kenko offered this: "If a man were never to fade away like the dews of Adashino, never to vanish like the smoke over Toribeyama, but lingered on forever in the world, how things would lose their power to move us."

The most precious thing in life is its uncertainty. This perception and an aesthetic came together, truth beyond the veils of illusion and beauty. So death is not an ugliness to be beautified, but a beauty to be discovered. Death is somehow transcended thereby. In art and literature death brings the individual into unity with a larger totality.

If, as Buddhism teaches, there is no individual and continuing ego *(atman)*, then death should be faced with equanimity. One demonstrates free, unprotesting entry into death with no illusion or anguish.

In the West the best-known strand of Buddhism is the Zen tradition, which emphasizes the direct, intuitive, spontaneous realization of the Buddha mind.[69]

In China and Japan a series of "ox-herding" pictures was created to illustrate the process of enlightenment. Each picture is framed in an asymmetrical, brushed, free-form circle (*enso* in Japanese). In the first six circles a young man looks backward, searches for, discovers footprints of, perceives, catches, and then tames and rides an ox, his Buddha nature. In the seventh the young man and the ox rest quietly; the ox is forgotten or internalized. In the eighth picture there is only the empty circle alone, the formless form. As ox and self are forgotten, the seeker enters *shunyata* or emptiness, the limits of self abandoned. This is the Great Death of Buddhism, which is also a rebirth. "In the final *enso*, he enters into the marketplace, barefooted, bare-breasted, dusty and blissful. The last picture in the series depicts the herdsman awake, and returning to the world with false desires extinguished. His spiritual death results in a movement from controllable passions to spontaneous compassion. Adapting to the needs of any situation, he is free from past personality. Having accomplished the sacred art of dying, he is changed, yet nothing is different."[70] A Zen poem expresses this consciousness:

> *While living*
> *Be a dead man,*
> *Be thoroughly dead—*
> *And behave as you like,*
> *And all's well.*[71]

One prepares for a Great Death through the methodless methods of *zazen* (seated Zen) and *koan*. In *zazen* one cultivates the cessation of ordinary consciousness until absolute stillness presents itself. Wide awake and fully dead, one awakens to nirvana. In the stillness of sitting, the world also sits: one surrenders the actions of the world and notions of self. The point is to cease sitting even while one sits, to overcome dualism by ceasing to identify the self even with the awakening itself.

The *koan* method is to challenge ordinary dualistic consciousness by meditating on an utterly illogical concept, for example: Without speaking and without not speaking—speak! The *koan* is meant to drive the dualistically calculating mind out of existence. It exhausts the proclivity toward intellectualization. This Great Death, or *shunyata* (absolute void, emptiness), becomes the Great Birth, or *satori* (sudden enlightenment). In the achievement of Great Death/Great Birth, the dualistic self is annihilated.

In the practice of Zen all life can become life after death, if one dies artfully before dying. This is the process of such an artful dying: The problem of dualistic consciousness is faced; distractions are removed; nondualistic consciousness is the focused solution; all alternative solutions are exhausted; one dies to all subject-object dichotomies; and one is reborn or renewed as the no-self self. The secret of Zen is to come to experience nirvana before one dies. Then there is no death left to die.

CONCLUSION

An "appropriate death" is an imaginative religious construction, prepared, assisted, and effected by a sacred art of dying. Entering a hermeneutic circle, we imagine death imagining us. Scouts for expanding human awareness, we seek to discover a death adequate to the human condition. We take account of its sting, we come to see the loss of our true self and our need for enlightenment, we find beauty in impermanence and the presence of death in every moment. A rich imaginal mixture is created: water from the Ganges or a sacred host on the tongue; snow on a cherry blossom; sin eaters carrying the sting from camp; angels and devils; conscience and karma struggling for the soul at the end. With the arts of dying we hope to have mastered over a lifetime, perhaps leaving us no death to die, we concentrate the imagination on a Great Death and focus death into a powerful transition to another world or another life. In the divine dialectic we hope death will proffer us, our dying finds an opening to the life of God, and God enters our personal history.

All this can happen if we do not back away: away from the uncertainty of afterlife and the fate of the soul, away from the history of the human imagination of death now undervalued and neglected in a death-denying age. For in trying to be certain or coolly secular or ironically detached, our age has placed "beyond reach much of what we know about human beings, about ourselves. We leave ourselves poorly equipped to understand human culture and less able to probe the working and meaning of the imagination, that labor that is distinctively human."[72]

But death has occasioned the breakthrough of the human imagination. "Poking through the breakpoint of death into the otherworld is an act that orients the human being in this world, brings into full power the imagination of the living, and enables human labor to take new account of material existence."[73] Death is the great test of the imagination, the great trial of our capacity to use symbols. To envision life after death, to construct mythic geographies, to reconstruct a true self—these are distinctively human labors. We are our best selves and most accomplished as a community whenever we try to look further than we can see.

Chapter 3

The Lost Art of Dying

*Of all footprints
That of the elephant is supreme;
Of all mindfulness meditations
That on death is supreme.*
—THE BUDDHA

A LOST ART

A bell at St. Andrew's Church in Dorset, England, cast in 1608, is inscribed: "I sound to bid the sick repent / In hope of life when breath is spent."[1] In a page of the *Rohan Book of Hours* (1418–1425) a naked corpse lies amidst skulls and bones. From its mouth comes a scroll: "Into thy hands, O Lord, I commend my spirit. You have redeemed me, O Lord, Thou God of Truth." Above, a devil has seized the departing soul but is being attacked by the archangel Michael. In many medieval illustrations angels and devils contend over the deathbed.[2] Scenes of fornication, murder, and robbery contrast with images of St. Peter, Mary Magdalene, the penitent thief on the cross, or the converted St. Paul testifying to the efficacy of repentance. In some books a sick man is kicking the physician and overturning the bedside table on one page, while on the opposite page patient martyrs and the suffering Christ stand by patiently exhorting the dying to keep the faith.[3]

Thomas à Kempis wrote in the fourteenth century: "Why dost thou not provide for thyself against the day of doom, when no man shall be excused nor defended by another, but every man's burden shall be enough for himself? Now thy labor is fruitful, thy weeping acceptable, thy mourning audible, thy suffering is satisfactory and purgatory. Be now busy and sorrowing for thy sins, that thou mayest stand safe in the day of judgment with blissful men." Those who wanted to heed this admonition could conduct a life review with the assistance of *ars moriendi* (art of dying) picture books, like a fifteenth-century text that summarizes the good and pious life in seven works of charity: admonishing the sinner, feeding the hungry, sheltering the homeless, clothing the naked, visiting the sick, visiting prisoners, burying the dead. The reward comes as angels convey the departing soul heavenward in a napkin. The greatest tragedy was to die unshriven or unreflected. Across the centuries Christians have prayed: "Father, you made us in your own image and your Son accepted death for our salvation. Help us to keep watch in prayer at all times. May we be free from sin when we leave this world and rejoice in peace with you for ever."

Since St. Augustine in the fifth century, death, judgment, hell, and heaven were the four last things of pious meditation. These were not narrow matters of religious indoctrination; they stimulated focused reflection on the large questions of human life, death, and afterlife. While the subjects of these antique meditations seem macabre or even repulsive to the twentieth-century mind, it formerly was held that nothing less was adequate to the complexity and mystery of the human condition.

By the time the *ars moriendi* tradition was flourishing, it was not merely piety but also prevailing common sense that demanded an art of dying. While some primitive societies had viewed death as the result of someone's evil intention, among the Christian communities of late antiquity there was a celebration of death and an emphasis on the soul's passage and resurrection.[4] Death marked the entry into the real life of a Christian. But death held some terror for Christians in the early medieval West. "In a world of disorder, among people for whom Christianity was an alien faith conveyed in a foreign tongue, the question of personal salvation had less easy answers."[5] New occasions teach new duties. Earlier rituals had marked the easy passage of the soul into the next world. Then emerging rites of penance, confession, and reconciliation with God and the community carried the dying through a set of ritual movements that prepared them for death. "The ritual process paralleled the experience of death. . . . Before they could meet death with any equanimity, they had to be ritually 'passed on' while they still lived."[6]

The ritual focus had shifted from the triumphant soul to the distressed dying person. For the frontier Christians living in fear of death, its rituals become a rehearsal for getting it right when it came. In the fourteenth century, devotional books "formed part of a calendar of torment inscribed upon time as well as space, in that each saint was commemorated on his or her day, often with specific prayers, antiphons and masses. . . . The tortures of the saints were recited aloud as part of a *performative structure of death*."[7] The entire *ars moriendi* tradition follows in this train.

The fifteenth century provided the first conditions for the appearance of natural death, an inevitable, intrinsic part of human life. By the end of that century death had come to play the leading role among the last things. It was seen as an independent force, not merely the shadow of the self, one's own mortality. Death was thought of not necessarily as a lifelong self-consciousness, but as the event of the last moment, the egalitarian executioner of all. Once death appeared as a natural force, people wished to master it through manuals of *ars moriendi*. Though attention to an art of dying long preceded them, these manuals began to appear in the fifteenth century and continued for the next two hundred years. The most widely circulated version appeared in 1491, and over a hundred incunabula editions were made before 1500 from woodblocks and from movable type. They took their place alongside books on the proper way of manipulating a table knife, conducting a conversation, weeping, blowing the nose, and playing chess.

If some attention to the art of dying prevailed throughout the medieval period, there were still differences along the way, and the culture of death has continued to evolve into the present age. Philippe Ariès is well known for his taxonomy of "deaths" from the early medieval period to the modern age.

He began with "tamed death." From the time of the *Song of Roland* in the eighth century, the recumbent deathbed figure participates in a ritual organized and presided over by himself. It is a public ceremony. At least until the eighteenth century deathbed portrayals always included children as well. That the bedchamber should become a stage for a public actor playing an appropriate and expected cultural and religious role at the hour of death is astonishing to us, but it is a scene and occasion to which we might well aspire to return. In an age grown comfortable with sex, and recently again childbirth, but not with death, it is good to be reminded that the medieval artist saw in life's beginning a far more controversial subject for representation than its end. "Whereas death was often a public event witnessed by crowds of onlookers and, even for the poor, an eminently social experience, birth was, by contrast, the secret of the midwives, forbidden to the male gaze and a breach in nature much more disturbing and dangerous for all the living."[8]

Next, in Ariès's view, came "one's own death," with overtones of terrifying judgment. From the twelfth century on, changes began to occur that gave a more personal meaning to one's familiarity with death, corresponding with greater concern for individual identity. This shift appears in portrayals of the Last Judgment, displacements of this judgment to the end of each individual's life, macabre themes and interest in physical decomposition, and a return to funeral inscriptions and personalization of tombs. The cosmic book in which the people of God were all included became an individual account book. The Franciscan Dies Irae intoned: *"Liber scriptus proferetur / In quo totum contine-tur / Unde mundus judicetur"* (A book is brought forward in which everything is written down by which the world is to be judged).

Eventually supernatural beings entered the bedchamber. The Trinity, the Virgin, and a whole celestial court were portrayed there, contending with Satan and an army of demons. God was there to observe how the dying conducted themselves during this trial. In this final temptation the dying, reviewing the contents of their "book," might see their lives characterized by despair, vain-glory, or excessive attachment. But the old style of dying was not yet lost, either. The iconography of the fifteenth-century *ars moriendi* combined the security of a collective rite for the dying with the new anxiety of personal interrogation. Thus *et moriemur* (we shall all die) gave way to *la mort de soi* (one's own death).

These *ars moriendi* traditions continued under Protestant auspices. Jeremy Taylor's tract of 1650, *Holy Dying,* describes how we learn to taste of death through the fragility and vulnerability of life, and warns against the folly of putting death out of mind. To consider life deeply, one had to consider death seriously.[9]

In the eighteenth and nineteenth century, Ariès found "thy death." A mor-bid fascination with and a romanticization of death became sublimated replacements for the erotic-macabre obsessions of previous centuries, and the relation of the dying person to the family came into focus. A cult of memory and sensibility emerged.

The brutal revolution of the twentieth century brought "forbidden death." Attention shifted from individual and family to hospital and physician. The romantic death became the forbidden death, the invisible death of the twenti-eth century. How did this modern denial of death come to outweigh the joy of last communion between the dying and survivors (the romantic ideal) or between the dying and God (the age of faith)? The hospitalization of death ban-ished the emotions. Mourning atrophied because the community had become disconnected from the death of its own members. Society no longer had to defend self-consciously against a raging nature, now domesticated by technol-ogy. A mass of atomized individuals replaced the sense of solidarity among the collective members of the group. Added to this was a shame in the face of death. Society had lost the capacity to face darkness and attempted instead simply to banish it from reflection. The choices seem to be either to ignore a scandal that could not be prevented and so force the bereaved into silence or to feign indifference and call death merely a natural event. But as a result, neither the individual nor the community had the resources to face death directly.

Meanwhile, the old savagery of death of a thousand years earlier crept back under the mask of medical technology. Death in the intensive care unit became the new *danse macabre*. "The death of the patient in the hospital, covered with tubes, is becoming a popular image, more terrifying than the *transi* or skeleton of macabre rhetoric. There seems to be a correlation between the 'evacuation' of death, the last refuge of evil, and the return of this same death, no longer tame. This should not surprise us. The belief in evil was necessary to the taming of death; the disappearance of the belief has restored death to its savage state."[10]

Hegel said that history is the record of what humans do with death. Early in this century the poet Rainer Maria Rilke wrote in his notebook: "Who cares anything today for a finely-finished death? . . . The wish to have a death of one's own is growing ever rarer. A while yet, and it will be just as rare as a life of one's own."[11] People had begun to die the death that belonged to their disease. Or they died a death assigned by the hospital. Rilke went on: "Formerly one knew (or perhaps one guessed it) that one had one's death within one, as a fruit its kernel. The children had a little death within them and the grown-ups a big one. The women had it in their womb and the men in their breast. One *had* it, and that gave one a singular dignity and a quiet pride."[12] Rilke hoped it could still be true that death is a mirror in which the whole meaning of life is reflected.

In his autobiography, *All the Strange Hours*, Loren Eiseley reflects on a visit to his physician, who was then in his eighties: "'Take care now, Ed,' I told him, gazing at a wonderful photograph taken down a long lane with a rail fence and a house in the distance. He'll be walking that road soon, I thought, to the big house of his childhood." Eiseley muses: "Personally I have no compass, no directions. For me there is no clear stretch of road, but for him the picture will be hanging there. He will be all right. He will know where to go. I suppose that is why he kept it on his wall. Most of us lose our way when the time comes."[13] Testimonies showing "how difficult it is to die in contemporary North America" abound.[14]

Might we not set out again in search of an appropriate death?[15] Such a death will be some version of a good life—or more. Death could arrive as an auspicious moment for each individual, perhaps relatively pain-free, with suffering reduced, and emotional and social impoverishments minimized. The dying might be gifted to resolve unfinished business, or even vouchsafed an opportunity for self-transcendence. While such a death may seem an impossible ideal, the search for it should be encouraged. When this goal is relegated to a vision beyond all reach, every death becomes a self-fulfilling failure. Recently we have heard admonitions to "die with style" or to "die in character" (although this would surely be a tragedy for some people). Elisabeth Kübler-Ross's challenge is to find in death a "last stage of growth."

These calls for more authentic ways of dying raise again the long dormant theme of *ars moriendi,* the art of dying. But is the art of dying a lost art, like the deep blues of the stained-glass windows in Chartres Cathedral, forever unrecoverable? Did the *ars moriendi* reach the end of a long history well before this century? Is Rilke's prayer to go unanswered and the people of this age to be denied a death of their own? Could ancient wisdom from the West become available again? Is there new light from the East?

At the end of his fifteen years of research Ariès concluded that the types of dying he uncovered evolved with respect to four major variables: the awareness of the individual, the sense of society defending itself against untamed nature, belief in an afterlife, and belief in the existence of evil.[16] He believed that acknowledging evil allows the taming of death; denial of evil restores death to a savage state. Undoubtedly, the roles of these and other variables will continue to shift. Belief in an afterlife may be seeing a resurgence in contemporary America. We seem undecided whether evil is a banality whose mystery eludes us or an obsolescence shelved by a progressive age more fascinated with human potential. The individual isolated from community and cultural resources faces death alone and so is tempted to deny its reality or determine that the ravages of a death no longer tamed by faith must be repressed. Ariès disdains humanizing efforts to acknowledge death but not its shamefulness; to consult the ancient wisdom but to turn away from its awareness of evil; to reconcile death with happiness. "Death must simply become the discreet but dignified exit of a peaceful person from a helpful society that is not torn, not even overly upset by the idea of a biological transition without significance, without pain or suffering, and ultimately without fear."[17]

It is not necessary to assume, however, that the present state of affairs, given by history, is one we must accept. It is the argument of this book that current sociocultural death practices are maladaptive because they are inadequate to the complexity of the human condition. One could argue in reply that given the decline of community and cultural resources, rampant individualism and "psychological man," the medicalization of death, and the decline of the sacred, the present death system is in fact adaptive, the best we can do. But to adapt to dehumanizing conditions is to decline the important task of changing them.

Calls for a recovered art of dying are coming not only from within Western traditions. Tibetan Buddhism is another great religious tradition that places great emphasis on a perfected art of dying, exemplified in the manual of dying called the Tibetan Book of the Dead (literally "The Great Liberation Through Hearing in the *Bardo*"). In an expanded meditation on that manual, intended for Western readers, which sold two hundred thousand copies worldwide in its first year after publication, Sogyal Rinpoche addresses his audience with no less fervor or certainty than any Christian fundamentalist:

The *bardo* teachings show us precisely what will happen if we prepare for death and what will happen if we do not. The choice could not be clearer. If we refuse to accept death now, while we are alive, we will pay dearly throughout our lives, at the moment of death, and thereafter. The effects of this refusal will ravage this life and all the lives to come. We will not be able to live our lives fully; we will remain imprisoned in the very aspect of ourselves that has to die. This ignorance will rob us of the basis of the journey to enlightenment, and trap us endlessly in the realm of illusion, the uncontrolled cyle of birth and death, that ocean of suffering that we Buddhists call *samsara.*[18]

Rinpoche places as much emphasis on the spiritual discipline and cultivated compassion necessary for those who must accompany the dying as on the role the dying themselves must play. This tradition offers companions of the dying extensive coaching in how to take on oneself the suffering of others and offer them one's own happiness, well-being, and peace of mind *(tonglen);* and how to visualize divine consciousness or presence over the dying *(phowa).* There are elaborate rituals, meditations, and prayers that the dying may have prac-ticed in their living and that they now take on as their final spiritual discipline. These surround all the processes of dying: letting go of attachment, entering clear awareness, transference of consciousness, grace of prayer at the last moment, and leaving the body. Over and over the dying may recite:

> *Now that the* bardo *of dying dawns upon me,*
> *I will abandon all grasping, yearning, and attachment,*
> *Enter undistracted into clear awareness of the teaching,*
> *And eject my consciousness into the space of unborn Rigpa;*
> *As I leave this compound body of flesh and blood*
> *I will know it to be a transitory illusion.*[19]

Finally dawns the Ground Luminosity or Clear Light:

> *The nature of everything is open, empty and naked like the sky.*
> *Luminous emptiness, without center or circumference: the*
> *pure, naked Rigpa dawns.*[20]

Perhaps Westerners who cannot heed a call from within their own tradition, whether for intellectual reasons or because of painful alienation, will harken to a call from the East. For some a summons wrapped in spirituality, yet not embedded in an institutional religion they know, will seem far more attractive.

A CALL FOR GREAT DEATHS

It may be that at this time in our cultural history we have to hope for a few individuals who in their dying can move the *ars moriendi* forward to a new plane and thereby model new possibilities for us all. We require a paradigm shift, a massive script change. Erik Erikson's studies of Luther and Gandhi demonstrate how great individuals can achieve a breakthrough that solves both their own conflicts and identity crises and the historical crises of an epoch.[21] The psychosocial identity of the individual has a psychohistorical side.[22] These individuals accomplish the unfinished or forgotten work of their ages as they also deal with their own individual problems. As such great souls struggle to solve problems of human conscience and meaning, they lift their individuality to the level of a universal and try to solve for all what they could not solve for themselves alone. Responding to intensely personal anxiety or neurosis, they produce new forms of social and cultural awareness. Erikson thought there can be mental disturbances of "epidemiological significance" that arise from and confront the times and produce innovative insights. During a period in American society characterized by widespread identity confusion, he developed his theory of stages of life that resolve through identity crises. Our current death system may encapsulate issues buried deep in the sociocultural unconscious of our time. The looming crisis occasioned by this repression may produce individuals who will die the great deaths that take us beyond our present impasse and offer model ways of dying that can be authentic responses to our times.[23]

Victor Turner believed great rituals as cultural performances interact with and locate themselves in the "social dramas" of their age. Social dramas take their rhetoric from cultural performances; cultural performances take their plots and problems from social dramas.[24] I am arguing that the lost passages surrounding death and mortality constitute one of the great social dramas of the twentieth century. From the conflicts and contests of that drama can come new scripts to respond to the great and disturbing loss of plot at the end of this millennium. Great individuals staging great deaths may become the early improvisers of such scripts.

Such individuals could help create "definitional ceremonies"[25] as contributions to collective autobiography and the creation of a societal or community story. New meanings are engendered when present problems are married to rich pasts and infused into the "doings and undergoings" of the community. Compelling social dramas and the cultural performances they induce contribute to (and stem from) public self-reflection. The resolution of the great dramas of the age occurs through ritual action. Indeed, the lasting solutions occur through the ritual process more than through the political or legal processes. No social crisis surpasses that of a society that has lost its way with death, and the great answers will come more from new and old ritualizations of last passage than from legal rulings in the field of bioethics or therapeutic bromides. Perhaps the rituals that rise to negotiate life crises portray and symbolically resolve archetypal conflicts that are larger and more significant than the teeming social life that surrounds such crises.[26] Ultimately, they are more prophylactic than therapeutic.

Hinduism has held up the art of the great or good death as achieved through pilgrimage. *Saddhus* and *saddhvi*, holy men and women, devote the last stage of their lives to asceticism, holiness, and preparation for a right death. In northern India some people, at the end of their lives, leave their villages and travel to the holy city of Kashi (Banares or Varanasi) to die. These pilgrims hope that death in Banares will attain for them the reward of *moksha*, liberation from the cycle of death and rebirth. Cremation in this holy city represents a perfect alignment between the pilgrim's ascent and the divine fire ignited by the gods at the beginning of creation.[27]

If we have not had many great deaths of our own, we have recently become accustomed at least to great funerals, watched and participated in around the world in a media age, as humans respond to tragic death, stimulate and unite national and international mourning, solidify and strengthen communities and nations, and marshall available resources from history and culture. One such, of course, was the funeral of President John F. Kennedy. It is the best example of the sociological insight that great rituals produce, maintain, and renew social solidarity. Such great rituals do not only respond to social needs; they also mediate the feelings of individual actors and unite all in a symbolic mobilization of shared life meanings.

In the White House aides rearranged the East Room, at the widow's request, as it had been a century before, when President Lincoln was assassinated. The entire nation watched on TV as the body was taken in procession to the Capitol rotunda, a black-draped caisson pulled by six gray horses carrying the casket. The procession included police, military services, and clergy. Finally came a black-draped riderless horse, the symbol of the fallen leader.

The next day the caisson was escorted back to the White House. The widow led the assembled mourners on foot to the church. Cardinal Cushing of Boston met the procession at the steps of St. Matthew's, sprinkled the casket with holy water, and led the procession into the church. At this moment Americans throughout the country joined in solidarity: Times Square fell silent, cab drivers stood outside their vehicles with bowed heads, trains stopped in the countryside, buses drew to the side of the road, and subways halted. From ships at sea memorial wreaths were thrown into the ocean, and on seven thousand military bases around the world twenty-one-gun salutes were fired.

As the mass came to a close and the recessional began, a military band played "Hail to the Chief" to this president for the last time. Three-year-old John Kennedy Jr. joined in a final salute and produced a powerful image seized by mourners around the world. Through "aisles in a theatre of solemn grief" the procession made its way to Arlington National Cemetery, where at the burial site fifty air force and navy planes flew low overhead in inverted-V formations, with the point of the final V missing. Trailing this formation came Air Force One, dipping its wings over the mourners in final salute.[28]

A much more conflicted rite of last passage followed the assassination of Indira Gandhi in India. After Gandhi had put down a Sikh rebellion at the Golden Temple and her Sikh bodyguards assassinated her in retaliation, producing killing and burning across India, it fell to the cremation rites for the fallen leader to restore order to India, bring warring religious groups back together—and legitimate Gandhi's son Rajiv as her successor. The funeral was an Indian version of Kennedy's rites two decades earlier. There was a procession through the streets of New Delhi. At the funeral pyre representatives of all India's religions presented themselves, though there were few Sikhs—no doubt for fear of their lives.

Draped in the national flag and covered with garlands, Gandhi's body was placed on the sandalwood funeral pyre. Following ancient rites, her son Rajiv took a flaming stick, circumambulated the pyre three times, and lit the fire. The president, a Sikh, ascended the steps and sprinkled handfuls of rice on the flaming corpse. The pyre stood a few hundred feet downriver from that of Mahatma Gandhi's cremation years before and, in the opposite direction, from that of Indira's father, Jawaharlal Nehru, the first prime minister of independent India. Her ashes were collected and sent to all thirty-one Indian states or territories. When all the urns had completed their pilgrimage and were returned to the capital, the ashes were scattered over the Himalayas, at the request of Gandhi. Her own son flew the plane. Shortly after, Rajiv won a major victory in parliamentary elections.[29]

In recent decades, far more common than accounts of great deaths are first-person narratives of dying and of grieving, written by the dying and by those who mourn them. It does not seem that these many, many accounts—highly visible and apparently selling well in bookstores—will produce a shared society-wide vision of death and illness. There is little sign that American society will replace a lost religiously based vision of death with a new public one. There are diverse stories, but no one is authorized to speak for all. Still, these narratives are a resource and promise for the future. Those who have endured difficult journeys point the way for others. "The narrators' passion to bear witness, to memorialize, to retell how 'someone was here' will find an echo in our own urge to become storytellers."[30]

In his existential psychology Jean-Paul Sartre tried to develop a method to interpret the central theme or project that unifies a person's life. With his concept of the singular universal, Sartre pointed to how an individual person may transcend the internalized values of an epoch. So, I hope, the lives of significant figures can both express the problems and contradictions of the age and also reshape and refocus them for others. Such a serendipitous historical process can become mythic. One life history comes to be held up as a paradigm or archetype. The solution to an individual developmental problem becomes a historically significant innovation. In the arena of one individual self, the great dramas of cosmogony, death, and rebirth unfold on a larger stage as that self takes on the fundamental project of self-creation at the boundaries of chaos and order. Thus do great individuals recover forgotten truths, or discover new ones, and knit them back into the social fabric. We are in need of great deaths through which new arts of dying will be mythologized for our generation.

Finally, however, the task becomes to die a death of our own. One can study the faltering attempts of our culture to create new scripts for dying.[31] In the present time of transition, some scripts for the last passage may have the character more of improvisational theater than of fixed liturgies. We do not know what is retrievable, what is imaginable, what we require. There are few fixed expectations and defined cultural roles. In Nietzsche's language, we painfully await the birth of new gods while still mourning the deaths of the old.

IMPEDIMENTS AND PROMISES

More useful than defining a good death for our time is discovering a process through which we can recover the art of dying. I believe its centerpiece is the reimagination of dying as a last career whose chief goal is the completion of the human story and whose preface is life review. There are both current impediments to such an achievement and omens that augur well for the attempt.

The professionalization of the American death system dictates that the dying hand themselves over to experts who script the process according to their own prejudices and interests. Wherever medicalization has not been mitigated by the hospice movement or a militant consumerism, patients still require permission to die and are expected to follow hospital rules in their dying. Exit from a neo-capitalist system is permitted when the consumer, trained at great expense, must finally be written off as a total loss.[32] The professionalization that morticians have eagerly sought may function also for them as a warrant for expropriating our deaths. The morticians' impatience with the unconventional or the idiosyncratic may also stand in the way of achieving a death of our own.

It is not yet clear whether thanatologists will foster patient autonomy, assist in the retrieval of lost traditions, or instead become a new priestly class offering a death system subsumed under "psychological man" and innocent of social, cultural, and religious resources.

An entire age can produce a death system that is more an impediment than a help in dying an appropriate death. A therapeutic culture that confines its imagination to notions of lifespan or developmental psychology, to the triumph of scientific and other kinds of professionalism, and to the bureaucratized lifestyle of modern economic systems leaves the individual alone, constricted, and helpless. It reinforces the separation between private and public selves. It defines us through our activities and declines to value contemplation even in old age, which it wants to "keep active" through the trivial pursuits of leisure industries. Positive valuations of old age and significant contributions from the wise elderly toward their own appropriate dying must include a cultural framework wider than the individual and wider than a single, isolated unit of life called retirement, distinct from education and work. We must learn to look for meanings that belong to the whole of life and transcend the individual.

The retreat to privatism "is unsuited to provide any abiding sense of meaning that transcends the individual life course. That absence of enduring meaning creates a special peril for old age when the temptations of narcissistic absorption are greater."[33] The denial of religious or cosmic meanings, which began with the Enlightenment, weakened collective senses of meaning and by the twentieth century had bequeathed an exclusively individual preoccupation with the meaning of life. But it is precisely in old age that "individuals alone cannot invent meanings to save themselves from despair."[34] Such a quest must be a collective enterprise that takes place in a wider public setting. Yet there is despair about the integrity of that larger social order and a turn away from the transcendent, partly because of secular presuppositions and partly because the contemplative consciousness to which the numinous is especially transparent has been discounted in an age of activism.

The negative residue that continues to fall on the sick and the dying impedes both our seeking wisdom from the aged and their discovering in dying anything other than a horror to be repressed. Whether marginalized by a youth-glorifying society, by economic rationalization, or by our own dark projections upon them, the aged do not readily appear to us as a fertile resource for accomplishing tasks significant to the human project. The assault of sickness on the psyche can be so great that it seems to pry us loose from our very humanness. We must recover the humanity of the sick and envision them in a larger context than that of our own repressions.[35]

A recent distraction is cryonics—deep-freezing a newly dead body, or head, to be resurrected at a later time when an appropriate cure is available.[36] Such are the digressions of a technological age.

But there are some promising signs that a recovery of the art of dying might be under way. Bioethicists have led the call to see in dying the patient's "last quest for responsibility."[37] There are discussions of planned exits and elective deaths. These follow legal precedents for informed consent and ethical commitments to truth telling, which grew from the sense that patients own the truth about their lives and have the ability to make informed choices. The hospice movement embodies many of the best of these impulses, and a wider consumer movement attends to patients' rights. Significant help, as we shall see below, can come from poets and storytellers, often volunteers, who can help aging people and others turn their memories into meaning.

Also of good promise for a recovery of a death of our own is the legacy left by existentialism. Part of the current interest in death began with Kierkegaard and Nietzsche, Doestoevski and Tolstoy, Heidegger and Sartre. The knowledge that from birth we are dying and destined toward death pervades and fecundates a whole way of philosophizing. Schopenhauer declared that death is the muse of philosophy, and Camus more recently asserted that suicide is the only genuine philosophical issue. In psychology, existential analysis pays special attention to the contribution of extreme or limit experiences such as anxiety, dread, and death. A common existential theme is the challenge to cultivate awareness of death as a means of heightening our sense of living. The knowledge of death gives life urgency and challenges us to live authentically and to complete our being. Heidegger argued that the awareness of death confers a sense of individuality, since each must die his or her own death. To shut out the consciousness of death is to refuse one's individuality and to choose to live inauthentically. In religious terms, the escape into impersonality to avoid the terror and possibility of authentic existence may be called original sin. Contemporary culture is a display case for such behavior.

This insight is not unique to Western existentialism. Chuang Tzu said: "The birth of a man is the birth of his sorrow. The longer he lives, the more stupid he becomes, because his anxiety to avoid unavoidable death becomes more and more acute. What bitterness! He lives for what is always out of reach. His thirst for survival in the future makes him incapable of living in the present."[38] Rinpoche contrasts Eastern laziness as "hanging out" with Western "active laziness"—cramming our lives with compulsive activity, so that there is no time to confront the real issues.[39] "Sometimes I think that the greatest achievement of modern culture is its brilliant selling of samsara and its barren distractions. Modern society seems to me a celebration of all the things that lead away from the truth, make truth hard to live for, and discourage people from even believing that it exists."[40]

A central existentialist theme is that the possibility of choice is the major fact and determiner of human life. Through choice we come to be who we are. Sartre urged us to shake off the incubus of false authority and to transcend convention by free acts of self-determination. But this is no easy matter, for we suffer under the crushing weight of existence (Sartre), of awareness of the fragility of Being (Jaspers), and of feeling homeless in the world (Heidegger). From this dread of being we may be awakened, however, to freedom and to a higher level of existence. Such awakening from the superficiality of normal existence could underlie an authentic art of dying.

Crucial to Jaspers's position is the idea that it is not sufficient to know about death, even our own; we must see it as a limit or ultimate situation in which we confront absolute failure. This awareness, not evaded or obscured, can lead us on to a fully authentic existence. Learning to confront death is the condition for the good life. But this is not just a mental discipline based on the power of reason over emotions, nor is it merely passive resignation.

Heidegger identified our ability to run ahead of ourselves in thought and so experience anxiety in the face of nonbeing as the root of all fear. To turn such existential anxiety into fearful living is the great temptation. It results in an avoidance of our nature as beings facing death. But facing such anxiety offers the possibility of new freedom, of a new mode of being. The later Heidegger could speak of anxiety giving place to wonder and amazement, and homelessness yielding to the reassuring closeness of Being. A humanization of death can occur when we realize our freedom in the face of dying and constitute ourselves through accepting such finitude.

Sartre focused on the absurdity of death. One can resolve to await specific death but not death as such, which always eludes our grasp. Sartre was less sure than Heidegger that death can be individualized as "my death." The essential task is to enter into the complete subjectivity of freedom that would make such ownership a possibility. Death in its essential unexpectedness would always withhold itself from our waiting, unless death were only to come at the end of old age. The fact of chance requires that we become something other than a being toward death. Death will not assure us that it will come as the harmonious conclusion of a melody. Death may fall outside our possibilities, or nullify them. But when we see this about death, we may eliminate its constraint through acts of freedom.

Religious existentialists wanted to see beyond this confrontation with nonbeing to transcendence, to an experience with the Other, with God. In absolute failure, in desperate foundering, in the renunciation of the self and of all claims, the reality of God is disclosed as the only ultimate reality. Learning to die means learning to keep the awareness of the ultimate situation of death open, to choose freely a genuine foundering, in order to attain through it the only true Being—God. As the Buddha was approaching death, he said:

> *Of all footprints*
> *That of the elephant is supreme;*
> *Of all mindfulness meditations*
> *That on death is supreme.*[41]

Death and our decisions to approach it in a certain way are thus re-visioned as privileged moments of human freedom. Christian theology especially has built on these themes. Roman Catholic theologies of death and dying have recently opened up the following perspective: A dialectic between matter and spirit, necessity and freedom, constitutes the whole of human life but reaches its highest point in death.[42] We can experience death as an external rupture from without or as an active consummation from within. The very moment in which we seem to experience complete domination can become the one in which we express ultimate freedom. The decisive choice in the face of death, however, is not limited to a given empirical moment, but can become a lifetime disposition. Such a disposition, unfettered by contingency and absolutely free in a total awareness and presence of being, is pointed toward an afterlife that follows.

Of course, it can be argued that this view seems to depend on moments altogether too rare and undocumentable; that dying in fact reduces us to the passivity of birth; that the moment of death may not be the time that life reaches its inner consummation and identity; that the moment of death may not be the one most privileged moment of human existence. Yet the limitations of these insights do not render them valueless. The point is a life lived and a character developed that is open to freedom and to God and also a dying process that is open, as best it can be, to an ultimate consummation.

This Christian insight into the possibility of opening up death through seeing it aright (that is, seeing the figure of Christ through it) is wonderfully caught by St. Augustine. His words evoke the "great deaths" I have called for earlier in this chapter and which were achieved, in the life of the Church, by the saints: "The precious death of the saints, for whom the death of Christ had already merited so much grace that they hastened to lose their own lives in order to find him, proves that the right use of death, which was originally intended as the punishment of sin, may bring forth abundant fruits and holiness."[43] For Augustine, heroes in the history of death are the saints, and in his *City of God,* he accounts for their triumph over mortality in "the right use of death."[44] A medieval illumination by Remiet depicts the martyrdom of St. Denis, the patron saint of Paris. The saint has been decapitated by a grinning executioner. The saintly bishop stands, his halo in place where his head should be. He calmly holds the mitred head, its eyes closed, a dead head, in his living hands. Thus are the saints living triumphs, in their deaths.[45]

Is it time, again, for a vigorous art of dying? There are the existentialist themes of freedom, choice, and authentic living arising from genuine encounters with dying. There are movements in the culture that offer advocacy of the individual against the professionalization and medicalization of living and dying. There are calls in philosophy and religion and elsewhere for quests that recover social contexts and larger cultural meanings beyond those of the individual in the final stage of a life cycle.

If there is a chance to recover a genuine art of dying, some will fear the kind of remythologizing that might follow. Will angels and demons struggling over the soul of the departing offer a medieval gloss on modern consciousness? Will the public again watch while the hapless person struggles between abandoning or clinging to the faith? Is the reenlargement of death only a ruse for Christian dogmatic repristination? To allay such fears, it may be good to begin with a demythologized present, with calls only for baby steps toward a death of our own, one that sounds not unlike self-actualization. Later will come movements toward a remythologized death that draws on ultimately religious resources and offers, beyond self-actualization, self-transcendence.

No doubt evil can come from such attempts. We should not let the rosiness of the human-potential movement or the enthusiasms of therapists running the last stages of growth therapies deceive us into thinking only good can come. A new flowering of humanity might occur, new pourings of meaning into culture and society. We may get a richer education when the dying become our teachers, as Kübler-Ross hoped. But it is not yet clear what will be learned.

If light canopies the dying process, darkness may lurk under the bed. It is a truism of religious insight that good and evil are inherent in every opportunity for human freedom. The capacity for good and evil to run side by side, as they do everywhere in the human condition, is here too. Confronting a death of our own invites us to ripen or to wither, to grow or to diminish. We may become a candle burning more brightly because of a strange inner intensity or one slowly depleted by lack of oxygen. An air of futility may hang over our bed, or we may stir with a sense of new accomplishment and completion. The last passage may become a lockstep, fate-decreed "becoming dead," or a processual, open-ended "being dying." Death may offer still another opportunity for emotional constriction and denial in which we stoically refuse to let feelings surface and choose to ward off sentimental self-indulgence, or a chance for a new emotional expressiveness. We may perfect denial patterns or risk a style of open awareness. Whether death will become a telos, an accomplishment and fulfillment, and not merely a finis, an end, remains to be seen. A death of our own may come as a gift indeed, but not without strenuous effort and religious engagement.

The dialectical possibility of moving in two different ways, or in both simultaneously, raises the question of a different dialectic, now unfashionable, that between body and psyche. While there is much to be said for "listening" to the body and following its wisdom, as the holistic health movement has it, there is also the issue of whether we want to let the physiological decay that slowly creeps into every aspect of bodily existence or the sudden massive trauma to bodily systems become the last truth about us.[46] Dying may be just that time when psyche and spirit more freely express themselves, emerging to tell truths untold by the body—or by a materialist culture. The contingency of pain and the assault of disease may contend with our efforts to achieve a death of our own. The body as a "natural symbol" may reach the edge of its capabilities for the generation of meaning, and we may need to look elsewhere, or beyond.

Will we reach new stages of growth stimulated by the dying process, or will we "die in character"? For some, and for their survivors, the highest good would be to die in that character they have spent their lives becoming. When others die in character, it will only be an occasion for lament to all who knew them. Meanness can harden in dying. Death can invite hiding from self or disclosings of self, but which self is to be hidden, confronted, disclosed, reinforced? For some the imagination of death will reflect the same deformed and afflicted perspective that has been the channel for imagining life. He whose living has been an unrelenting protest and defense may choose a similar dying. She whose life has been a passive suffering of unlived possibility and helplessness may be able to offer only these in her dying. One may choose from among the sicknesses of our culture the one that is a metaphor of his living. Another may die a death that enacts the characteristic lack of love in her world. Some dyings will be stylized versions of the pathologies we have spent years practicing in our living. Others will be breathtaking breakthroughs that astound everyone and lend dignity and hope to the human prospect.

In Hoffmannsthal's play *The Fool and Death,* Claudio is trying to convince Death that his time has not yet come.

Remember, before the leaf glides to the ground,
It has drained all its sap:
I am far from that point: I have not lived!
My young days have slipped away,
And I never knew that even this meant life. . . .
Half hearted, my senses numb,
In every consummation mysteriously inhibited,
Never feeling my inner self aglow,
Nor ever swept away by mighty waves;
Never upon my path met God
With whom one strives, until He grants his blessing.[47]

But Death argues that Claudio should have been able "to animate this chaos of dead things with relatedness, to make your garden out of it." In his life review Claudio begins to attain the reflectiveness that will allow growth. He asks:

Why did this happen to me? Why, Death
Must you be the one to teach me to see life?

In the end, Claudio transcends the previous character of his life and resolves his conflict with Death through a new growth in insight, achieving in his dying a deepened living:

Since my life was death, then Death be my life!
You can pour more life into one hour,
Than my whole life contained. . . .
Never, with all my living senses
Have I perceived so much, and so I call it good! . . .
For only as I die, I feel that I am.

Like good and evil lying side by side as possibilities for human achievement, impediments to and promises for an authentic art of dying lie side by side in our age. We can choose which to fix our attention on as we contemplate the recovery of a death of our own. A situation and a time fraught with possibility beckon us to get on with it, to embrace the imaginal task of reenvisioning death and dying.

Chapter 4

The Last Career

Later life is a season in search of its purposes.
—THE OXFORD BOOK OF AGING

ACCEPTING A LAST CAREER

St. Jerome once referred to someone as pregnant with his own death. This metaphor invites reflection. Of what are the dying to be delivered? The art of dying may be thought of as the art of a good delivery. "Deathing" has emerged as an analogue of birthing, with accompanying Lamaze-like techniques and the participation of a coach.[1] The substantial something to be delivered after the pregnancy of dying is the final form of the life we have lived. Death presents us with the urgency, nourished by our own anxieties about meaning, guilt, and finitude, to deliver a completed story. The gestation of dying is the time for life review and story completion. This is pregnancy as a new and also last career. The question is whether we can be socialized into such a role, whether we can be persuaded to accept new images, expectations, and norms, whether this is a pregnancy we are willing to see through.

Jerome's metaphor is suggestive. How do we think of this pregnancy? Is it the result of rape, or perhaps a movement of the Spirit of God, or a movement of our spirit back to God? It has been said by a Tibetan Buddhist that death can be simple: You breathe out, and you don't breathe in. Death is the end of our taking in and the ultimate breathing out of ourselves back into the universe, or into the lungs of God.

In the introduction to *The Oxford Book of Aging,* one of the editors calls later life "a season in search of its purposes."[2] In the modern period of Western history aging has undergone a profound transformation, under the influence of secularist, scientific, and individualist pressures, from a way station along life's spiritual journey to a problem to be solved by science and medicine. Old people have been turned into patients or pensioners. But as the millennium comes to a close the editors are hopeful about bridging the gap between existential mystery and scientific mastery, about reclaiming the moral and spiritual dimensions of later life. Age can be a *growing* old and not just an accumulation of years. Creativity can remain powerful in old age. The product may be not a painting or a poem, but an altered self-image, a change in how one lives, the deepening of a relationship, a profound response to the limits and uncertainties of existence. This passage, too, is a becoming as well as a perishing. But stereotypes of the aging blunt the imagination. What the aging need is not customary rubrics and cultural fixities, but surprise, tension, paradox, ambiguity. We say time sweeps aside all pleasure and accomplishment. What if God has made everything beautiful in its own time? Aging as a last career can take up such beckoning metaphors not as intangible abstractions but as real possibilities that we can ritualize in social and cultural life. Such a career can heed the poet Rilke's lament that "love and death are the great gifts given to us that mostly are passed on unopened" or the Hasidic saying "There are three aspects of mourning: with tears, that is the lowest; with silence, that is higher; and with a song, that is the highest." Aging reimagined as a last career becomes a new frontier awaiting bold and courageous pioneers.

The task of our last career is to negotiate successfully a final identity crisis, the one in which we are challenged to come to an acceptance of life as a whole as it draws to a close.[3] Erik Erikson divided human life into eight stages. In each stage the individual is confronted with a crisis of understanding and the opportunity to meet and accept the task or fail it. In each stage the developmental task is to resolve the crisis successfully. With the ideal completion of each stage come basic virtues or character traits, the sum total of which is the completed person. In infancy, for example, we were challenged to arrive at a basic posture of trust or mistrust. From that passage came hope. In adolescence there was identity or identity confusion. From that came fidelity. Old age presents the opportunity to arrive at integrity or despair over or against the life we have lived. Out of this last stage can come wisdom. We must have had some success in solving the seven earlier crises if we are to resolve the crisis of the final stage. For Erikson, integrity as the goal of the final stage means we have arrived at the conviction that life has had meaning and purpose, that our living has made a difference, that our humanity has been fulfilled, that our life is part of the flow between past and future.[4]

Modern psychologists write of self-actualization and self-transcendence. St. Paul is recorded as having expressed at the end of his life (2 Timothy 4:7):

"I have fought the good fight, I have finished the race, I have kept the faith." A sculpture that stands in front of the Faculty of Medicine at the University of Madrid depicts a young man on horseback ready to begin a race, reaching back to receive a scroll extended by an old man almost prostrate on the ground. The old man's face is serene. Erikson notes: "He knows that for him all human integrity stands and falls with the one style of integrity of which he partakes. The style of integrity developed by his culture or civilization then becomes the 'patrimony of the soul,' the seal of his moral paternity of himself. In such final consolidation, death loses its sting."[5]

When life's tasks are unfinished, we want to delay the course of our last career. But if we can celebrate great consummations, we are ready. In "To the Fates" the poet Hoelderlin poignantly depicts this tension:

> A single summer grant me, great powers, and
> a single autumn for fully ripened song
> that, sated with the sweetness of my
> playing, my heart may more willingly die.
>
> The soul that, living, did not attain its divine
> right cannot repose in the nether world.
> But once what I am bent on, what is
> holy, my poetry, is accomplished:
>
> Be welcome then, stillness of the shadows world!
> I shall be satisfied though my lyre will not
> accompany me down there. Once I
> lived like the gods, and more is not needed.[6]

The poet Sarojini Naidu sounds the perennial plea that death tarry until we have lived fully:

> Tarry a while, O Death, I cannot die
> With all my blossoming hopes unharvested,
> My joys ungarnered, all my songs unsung,
> And all my tears unshed.
> Tarry awhile, til I am satisfied
> Of love and grief, of earth and altering sky;
> Til all my human hungers are fulfilled,
> O Death, I cannot die![7]

While Erikson seems pessimistic about the prospects of a person who has not successfully negotiated earlier stages and thinks it likely that despair will overwhelm the short time left, there may be opportunities for grace, forgiveness, repentance, and love at the end, which can transform dying into something beyond what was attained in living. These are precisely the great themes of those Jewish and Christian traditions that neither romanticize the human condition nor assume one's own gifts are ever enough.

Death comes to inquire about our identity, and it is the task of this last career to supply the answer. We may resist. Jung wrote: "It is just as neurotic in old age not to focus upon the goal of death as it is in youth to repress fantasies which have to do with the future."[8] Jung imagined the curve of life as a parabola. Our conscious clinging to life may stay in the air while the curve of the parabola sinks downward with ever increasing speed. Refusing to follow our unalterable course, we become stiff, rigid, suspended. But all of life, not just our aging years, is part of this process of individuation. In every stage there are stories to be told, stories which require the larger language of mythology to describe their true contours. This is life as "soul-making," to use James Hillman's term.[9]

Recent Roman Catholic sacramental theologies regard the stages of life as invitations to offer consent: the consent of the growing individual who says yes to a religious tradition and grasps a larger story as the stories of adolescence are negotiated in the sacrament of confirmation; the yes to a faithful relationship and to a specific partner as the career of marriage is undertaken; the yes to grace that arrives in the midst of darkness, doubt, despair, and sin in the sacrament of reconciliation; the yes to God in the center of mortality's no. Death comes seeking our consent, though it will also take us without it. Thus death may appear as rapist, pillager, or plunderer, or as friend or sweet lover. This duality is expressed in Matthias Claudius's poem "Death and the Maiden":

> The Maiden:
>> O, go away, please go,
>> Wild monster, made of bone!
>> I am still young; Oh, no!
>> Oh, please leave me alone!
> Death:
>> Give me your hand, my fair and lovely child!
>> A friend I am and bearing no harm.
>> Be of good cheer, I am not wild,
>> You shall sleep gently in my arm.[10]

We may try to withhold consent temporarily—not to avoid a last reckoning, but to attend to unfinished business. In his film *The Seventh Seal* Ingmar Bergman shows us a knight who has returned disillusioned from the crusades and now, with plague all around, confronts a personified death. The knight proposes a chess game with Death and then requests time for some noble act—having achieved nothing with his life so far. We may seek a reprieve to pour reluctant meaning into our world or to express a rage that cries across the abyss of mortality to a farther horizon. But responses of emotional rigidity as death comes beckoning, or attempts to hide amidst the foliage of a consumer culture, are pathetic as answers to the call to take on a last career.

Even if the preparation for consent to death is a lifelong process, as the existentialists so clearly see, even if death refuses to arrive at a proper time, still, a certain time in life will invite us so persuasively and so relentlessly that it seems appropriate to call that time the beginning of a new career, a last career.

It is commonplace to note that our previous careers and the depth of our previous consents are the assets accumulated over time and now to be unpacked for this final time of reckoning. But some hope chests will be nearly barren. Others will have chests full of things they have accumulated, but not wisely. If structures of meaning and of religion have been cultivated, they may now bloom as validations at life's close. This needs to be said against those who can only imagine the last career as an unrelieved series of losses. A last career can also invite growth beyond the past, new postures and attitudes, new constructions and reconstructions, new dramas of worth and of honor. It is possible the final telling may surpass the content to be told. There is hope for those with meager hope chests.

There is a question of style in the forging of a career. How will one answer the call? Consider some past mythologies of dying that may still be available:

> The hero's death. Enveloped in images of violence, the person dies bravely, nobly. Death is an enemy to fight. At the last it's better to take your own life than be victimized by death. A flamboyant death.
>
> The man's death. This is the death of resignation. There is nothing anyone can do about death, it is inevitable, so accept it. Death is a sleep, a blessing, a return to nature, or the end of one's earthly task. A submissive death.
>
> The fool's death. I am not really dying. Death is a kind of cosmic joke. This is the senseless, aimless death.
>
> The martyr's death. To give your life is noble; sacrifice for love or for a social cause, or to protest against life's stupidity. I will permit myself to be killed. My death will be important to society. The victimized death.

The morbid death. Death is a grim reaper; his approach is terrifying, fearful, painfully unholy. Death is an executioner, man is the victim, avoidance and denial the only remedies. A bizarre dying.[11]

Beyond all these, consider two archetypal styles of dying, those that are *congealing* and those that are *eruptive*. We may go shrinking and thickening, like a hard-boiled egg, or fluid and expanding, like a broken raw egg.[12] Death may fix us or extend us.

I find more useful than any of these the idea that there are six styles of living, each with positive and negative dimensions, and implications for styles of dying:

> An accepting life style that meets death as an inevitable part of creation.
> A defiant life style that rebels against death as personal destroyer.
> A sensual life style that fears death as the denial of human meaning.
> A humorous life style that dances with death around the edges of ultimate mystery.
> A tragic life style that experiences death as always too soon.
> A questing life style that seeks to find in death the meaning of existence.[13]

Also illuminating is the thesis that there are only two basic opposing responses to death: *overcoming* and *participating*.[14] Overcoming responses conceptualize death as an external contingency with overtones of failure, defeat, or humiliation. The individual has strong needs for achievement and independence, technological resources are at hand, and cultural values require the assertion of power against external forces. Participating responses, by contrast, conceptualize death as an internal locus with overtones of honor, reunion, or fulfillment. The individual has strong sensitivities for cooperative behavior, sharing, and affiliation. Technological props are not conspicuous, there are channels for meaningful expression, and cultural values support a natural and intimate relationship with the environment.

The choices of posture and style in a last career are bewildering. Which self will make them? How will it play to the relatives? To history? We become anxious in the face of all the possibilities. As Sartre warned, before a yawning open-endedness we are tempted to retreat to false consciousness, to pretend we lack the freedom to act at all. The antidote against inaction is to focus on the task connected to this last career and to fix its connection to the completion of life as a whole. If the chance for a last career is a precious gift and opportunity—a grace—then we can fully realize it by taking up its attendant task with diligence and enthusiasm. A gift of a new career coming as a surprise may alert us to a task long forgotten. When the gift is discovered and accepted, it becomes an unexpected *kairos*—an opportune moment. To accept the gift is to obligate ourselves to reciprocity. We owe a debt (to God? to society?); the relationship must be respected and the debt repaid.

In our age of activism and lack of interest in the contemplative or spiritual life, the task of this career is frequently depicted as not losing hold of the reality principle, not getting out of touch with life. But the ultimate fulfillment of the self involves considerably more than holding on. Unfortunately, we have lacked just the framework into which such a last career could properly fit, the web of culture and religion within which the aged could move with freedom, empowerment, and enrichment.

In *Prophetic Anointing: God's Call to the Sick, the Elderly, and the Dying*, James Empereur attempts to retrieve the sacrament of anointing in order to empower a marginalized group in our society and commission them for the holy task of symbolizing in their own sickness and dying the overcoming power of Christ in the mystery of suffering and death. Anointing becomes a sacrament of vocation. It is a liturgical celebration of the ill and aged Christians living in the midst of the Church. It ritualizes their ministry to the young and healthy, and it articulates the Church's recognition of the paschal mystery concretized in sickness and old age. The Church stands in solidarity with its marginal members, discovers in faith new meaning in their condition, and unites with them in worship of the One who has conquered death. The anointing of the sick or elderly is sacramental because through it the Church defines and realizes itself and proclaims itself as a certain kind of community. To the recipients, this sacrament of anointing promises transcendence in a meaningful human future. To all believers it announces freedom from those postures and attitudes which suffocate brokenness with meaninglessness and loss of integrity.[15] All this evokes the possibility and power of ritualizing. Not only can death itself be ritualized, not only can the process of dying be reenvisioned through *ars moriendi*, but we can ritually attend to and empower this entire period of life.

To that end, we need to move beyond the therapeutic mind-set that dominates the welfare state. "At the moment when the meaning of old age vanishes, we find that enormous economic resources are expended to prolong lives which have been deprived of any purpose."[16] But we can interpret pain, illness, and death, and the meanings we give them become our culture. We mislead ourselves and surrender the work of culture when we allow ourselves to imagine that medical science will indefinitely postpone death as a human problem. "A problematic arises: How do we give meaning to something that we seek to eliminate by all means? This issue is linked up with a more general character-istic of industrial—or postindustrial—societies, namely, that entire aspects of the human condition are becoming meaningless."[17]

The last career is shorn of significance, and old age is devoted to mere sur-vival, with the help of the medical system and human service professionals. There is prolongation without a mission. "The collapse of subjective meaning so often experienced in late life is a result of modern social policy: for exam-ple, the growth of retirement and the rise of bureaucratic systems in the human services."[18] Add to this the diminishment of traditional communities of meaning and the self is left completely isolated. This is the worst possible scenario; the task of meaning itself has already, in a mindless culture, been dis-placed to old age, but an old age from which any sense of last career has been expurgated. The necessary response to this situation is to give back to old age as a last career its heavy cultural markings, socialize ourselves into high expec-tations for the accomplishments to be gained, and ensure that this period is fertilized by connecting it organically to culture, religion, and history.

Shakespeare's Sonnet 73 provides a rich and true description of the pathos of aging:

> That time of year thou mayst in me behold
> When yellow leaves, or none, or few, do hang
> Upon those boughs which shake against the cold,
> Bare ruin'd choirs where late the sweet birds sang.

Joseph Sittler sees in this a call not for new solutions, but for courage, acqui-escence, resignation, acceptance. These years "are a time of remembering, gathering up and sorting out, discriminating between the abiding and the evanescent, a time of perhaps unmarked passage from knowledge to wisdom, from simple awareness to insight, to what Jonathon Edwards called 'consent to being.'"[19]

It is time to move beyond an American cultural system that maximizes individual choices and achievement but expects only a dramaturgically pas-sive dying. (By contrast, in the medieval period people lived harsh lives over which they frequently had little control, but practiced a positive dying.) The task that preoccupies the last career and which prepares for the final story-telling is the task of life review, which, when appreciated for what it fully can be, is the first step toward a fulfilling last career. The dilemma in which old age finds itself, beset by unkind circumstance yet open to late-blooming power, is wonderfully caught by William Butler Yeats:

> *What shall I do with this absurdity—*
> *O heart, O troubled heart—this caricature,*
> *Decrepit old age that has been tied to me*
> *As to a dog's tail.*[20]

But in another poem Yeats hints how he can turn his rage into art:

> *An aged man is but a paltry thing,*
> *A tattered coat upon a stick, unless*
> *Soul clap its hands and sing, and louder sing*
> *For every tatter in its mortal dress.*[21]

LIFE REVIEW: AN UNCERTAIN BEGINNING

The belief that when death is imminent an entire life will pass before one's eyes is well known. It may be that in a decadent consumer society, it will be the life of Elizabeth Taylor or Paul Newman or Madonna that is more arresting than our own. Or perhaps, in our final days, we will as our last request desire to know how the plots of our favorite soap operas are going to turn out. If the concept of life review is to be redeemed as the first act of a last career, we will have to rescue it from the trivialities that have accrued to it. Life review is best done over time, grieving or rejoicing as scenes from the past insistently present themselves or are carefully retrieved. We recover ourselves through memory, retrace how we have come to our present stature, fill in the history that has poured into the mold of our present self.

Pondering one's own life, one contemplates leaves floating calmly down a creek and observes their fate, as they approach tiny rapids, but one is not able to predict which way the current will catch and carry them. Søren Kierkegaard said: "Life can only be understood backwards, but it must be lived forwards." Louise Bogan has written: "At first we want life to be romantic; later / to be bearable; finally, to be understandable." We look with some wonder, some dis-appointment, some gratitude at the eddies of our existence, especially as we near the mouth of the river and our journey out to sea. J. A. Valente's poem "The Dying Man" catches this mood:

> *The dying man saw*
> *mysterious gestures, forgotten faces*
> *pass before his eyes,*
> *birds of another country once his own*
> *but in a foreign sky.*

Through the open window came the earthy
colour of the storm.
He heard the rustling of the olives
far-off, in his distant childhood, wind-tossed now.

The air crackled with sharp reports.

He saw the fields, the sun,
the south, the years, the distance.

An opaque sky stretched
over a foreign land.

In a slow voice
he assembled all that was scattered,
the heat of all those hands
and shining days,
into a single sigh,
huge and powerful
as life.

Finally rain broke over the dark siege.
Memory expanded.

May a song
bear witness for him
that in his struggle he won self-completion.[22]

In a celebrated article Robert N. Butler interpreted reminiscence in the aged as a life review.[23] Since then the notion of life review has attained almost mythic status, but Butler's initial thought was to help rescue the elderly from contempt in American society. Impending death triggers an appraisal of the lifelong conflicts, some perhaps hitherto unconscious, that have marked one's life. New and more sensitive understandings may result. Serenity and wisdom may result, or deepened depression and even despair. Such reminiscence is often identified as psychologically dysfunctional and its content lost or devalued. Onlookers sometimes wonder whether it is beyond control or volitional, escapist or a meaningful agenda. Does it obscure the present or lead to a deeper grasp on life? The aged are Janus-like, facing death and also looking back. If unresolved conflicts resurge, there is the potential to integrate them as part of a lifelong unfolding of character. Importantly, the aged have the time necessary for this task and need not be distracted from it by the "defensive operation of work." There is time for a dialectic in which the past plays upon us and we play with it.

This is not necessarily a happy experience. In Henry James's short story "The Beast in the Jungle," the insights of aging descend upon the detached, intellectualizing self, who finds himself gazing into the sounded void of his life, stupefied at the blindness he had cherished. There can be panic at the closing of the door, terror at the dangerous truth that the capacity to project the self into the future has atrophied.

To capture the promising possibilities, the term "gero-transcendence"[24] has been coined to describe a shift in old age metaperspective "from a materialistic and rational vision to a more cosmic and transcendent one, normally followed by an increase in life satisfaction."[25] This is more than Erikson's ego-integrity, in which the individual looks back at the life lived from within the same paradigm. Here the individual looks forward and outward, with a new view of self and world. It is more than the "disengagement" described by gerontologists and much more than the prevailing positivist paradigms that characterize much gerontology.[26] It is the final stage in a process toward maturation and wisdom. Gero-transcendence brings a new feeling of cosmic communion with the spirit of the universe, a redefinition of time, space, life, and death, and a redefinition of the self.

Dealing with guilt may be an inevitable and long-overdue dimension of life review.[27] Postponed intentions, buried animosities, unfinished business, or moral turpitude may lie in wait. We may find ourselves having to decide all over again about our lives. It is not clear how we will resolve the life we recover through reminiscence. "Hidden themes of great vintage may emerge, changing the quality of a lifelong relationship. Revelations of the past may forge a new intimacy, render a deceit honest; they may sever peculiar bonds and free tongues; or they may sculpt terrifying hatreds out of fluid, fitful antagonisms."[28] But the possibility of growth may make life review irresistible.

William Carlos Williams, whose poetry Wallace Stevens nicely calls "rubbings of reality,"[29] writes in "The Desert Music":

> *Memory is a kind*
> *of accomplishment,*
> *a sort of renewal*
> *even*
> *an initiation, since the spaces it opens are new places*

inhabited by hordes
heretofore unrealized,
of new kinds—
since their movements
are toward new objectives
(even though formerly they were abandoned).

No defeat is made up entirely of defeat—since
the world it opens is always a place
formerly
unsuspected. A
world lost,
a world unsuspected,
beckons to new places
and no whiteness (lost) is so white as the memory
of whiteness.[30]

The reexamination of our performances, submitting the lines we have spoken to critical review (by friends, relatives, God), reminiscences about the settings of our lives, other actors, stage managers seen and unseen—all help us see our lives as performances and make us wonder what alternative performances might have been.

The great French historian Fernand Braudel studied not only the prevailing moment but also its opposite, inquiring about the harvest of contrary experiences that fought hard before they went down. The task of resurrecting the voices of the losers has lately been assumed by feminist and ethnic historians. To do history in such a way is to reopen, momentarily, the options that were closed. Thus the past is recovered as a living thing. We face the options as they were faced once upon a time. We become aware at every stage what the alternatives and the limitations were, what might have been and why it was not.

Literary deconstructionists see that "the real" or "identity" may only be a fictive unity standing in for what was unstable or incoherent. What meanings can be teased out of the text of a life? The claimed subject of the text is surrounded with other possible meanings that are marginalized or discounted so that the main claim is foregrounded. After identifying various opposing meanings, the critic may show that each term's identity has been artificially stabilized by repressing what it actually has in common with the other. Each meaning, each identity is an unstable fiction. All that exists is the multiple play of difference. In the landscape of postmodernism, "the objectivity of self-knowledge is eclipsed in favor of pluralism. In the postmodern world, meaning is to be found only in a fictive version or metaphor of the self."[31]

Which selves do we review? The postmodern move signals not the end of the private self, but the death of the *indivisible* self. The concept of a divisible self serves the interests of postmodern claims about "our relationship with a collective identity; a cyclical rather than a linear sense of time; and myth as an alternative to narrative and history."[32]

The insight that identity also includes the roads not taken or the voices repressed is powerful and significant. The notion that any real difference between appearance and reality has collapsed can be promising, although it can also reduce life to intellectual games. A life review that uncovers a living history in which the options not seized are no longer buried from view will be a much richer one and more pregnant with possibilities for final story construction. This retrieved information may better enable us to reach a final version of self in this life, a version that may include reworking and retitling some of the original material.

I think this is the way it can work. Other selves, voices repressed, undervalued, neglected, defeated, are recalled, get stage time, speak their lines, and perhaps demand a curtain call. Who else might we have been or become? What other moves, what other stages now call for attention? They come to the theater now, multiple selves, lost friends, strangers, dangerous enemies, the ones we once were or decided not to be, the ones whose lines we could never learn to speak, personae we could not convincingly bring off, might-have-beens, have-beens, not-to-be's—a crowded stage, competing for bows and applause, regrets, boos. To give these selves stage time now is to deconstruct the life we decided to go with, perhaps to destabilize it. Probably we have reified the one public presentation of self we have chosen to let ourselves become, as if there could have been no other. In many acts of bad faith, we have pretended this is the way it had to be. Now we look through, peel the layers off history, see the bewilderingly dense texture of existence. Approaching our final flow into the ocean in this delta region, our life course is fertilized by anxiety and expansiveness: long-dormant seeds sprout, surprising and terrifying us. We are frightened to find ourselves in the whirlwind of creation and re-creation. "To reconstruct a self, an old self may have to be shattered. Sometimes the world-vessel must be pulverized. To discover who we are, we may have to divest ourselves of everything, go beyond the imagined limits of ourselves. We may have to leap out of the familiar, jump off a cliff, go to the very edge of the world where all the dragons live."[33] When all the actors have reappeared, in dream time and waking time, when darkness and light have been acknowledged, when our public persona has been unmasked and the hidden selves disclosed, we are better prepared to carry our life review on to its conclusion.

We will not have been unmindful of the risks in such a venture. It is said Winston Churchill once sent a pudding back to the chef because it lacked a theme. Cosmic editors, or critical friends and relations, reviewing our life may demand a rewrite . . . or repentance.

Worse, like the protagonist of "The Old Man and the Sea," we may lash to the side of our vessel what we have managed to haul in, then row desperately homeward, trying to reach shore before other forces take away our catch. We should not like to appear pathetic to bemused onlookers onshore who will mock the remains of what we had thought to present proudly. The teeming sea has stripped us clean, and there is no fleshly form to admire. It is ourselves we have lashed to the side of the little vessel, and we have rowed mightily to get us home while something is still left.

We may not have turned out to be the grand specimens our mothers hoped for. Our Mae West bloom, filled out with ersatz culture and refined consumer goods, has deflated. Could our bones at least fill a charnel house next to some great cathedral, in huddled proximity to the bones of the saints? The pursuit of ultimate meaning and the attempt to show, for all to see, a fine specimen could leave our vessel broken to pieces.

No wonder, then, that some will seek to mythicize their pasts rather than struggle to make sense of them. Instead of laboring for insight or taking heavy responsibility, they embrace self-justification as their only task. A finally authentic self is a goal, but not a guaranteed attainment. Untranscended ego-preoccupation can simply become the narcissism of old age: the withering of any taste for the other or for larger concerns. Easy harvests produce root metaphors of self-deception. As a complacent culture breaks into applause, we proudly offer degenerated wish fulfillment and sentimentality, "ersatz spirituality in humanistic costume"[34] playing the role of last judgment. This cultural mood shows up in contemporary near-death experiences and the life review that is often a part of them. Judgment is out of the question, and mercy is unnecessary. "The encounter with deeds is from start to finish a reassuring and therapeutic exercise. There is no sense of being judged by an external being; rather, the emphasis is on self-evaluation, learning, and growth."[35]

This raises the ticklish question—for moderns—of guilt and repentance, and perhaps of the need for grace and forgiveness. It is not easy to restore the moral component of death and dying to public discussion and cultural attention. Modern understandings of death focus on technical, physical, and psychological aspects and ignore the moral component—the dimension of human responsibility in relationships. As life draws to a close only an immature person would want to ignore questions about the moral life one has led —responses one has made to relations and situations, accountability for interaction, and solidarity with the human community.[36]

Once deathbed penance was a ritual prescription. Any public penance was a preparation for death, because it brought another world to bear on this one. Deathbed penance compressed a life of penance and "brought the full ritual lexicon of Christian rites of passage to bear on the period immediately preceding physical death."[37] To engage in it was to have begun the movement beyond the borders of this world.[38]

If we do not lose faith in the tasks of this last career, if we hold open the possibilities for renewal inherent in searching life reviews, we may accomplish authentic preparations for genuine story completion. We are not ashamed to see that the home movies we thought to be in their final form need editing, repentance. We are ready to attempt retroactive insertions that can pull threads of meaning through the fabric of our existence. We see we may have to insert branches in bare spots, as my father tried to teach us children to do as we turned the Christmas tree round and round looking for its best presentation. New namings may be necessary if we are to get hold of ourselves. We cast our net again and again, undiscouraged by small catches. The specter of death, that elusive presence in this last career, has tweaked our mortalities over a lifetime and now arrives as an insistent invitation to the last dance with our names clearly engraved on it. We are determined not to give up, not to post in our obituary notice "No services," as do those who fear the mourners will arrive with discreet inquiries and find even the hired preacher at a loss for praise of the deceased.

Let others scoff or confess that there never was any meaning beyond hair appointments, shopping expeditions, and ball games. As the momentous knock grows louder we seek a last authentic consent to meaning. We hope to leave as our legacy a patina for others to touch and value, labored over as we learned to tell our story, oiled by last travails with divine dreams and designs, hand-rubbed, perhaps, by God.

Chapter 5

Finishing the Story

Our hearts are restless till they rest in Thee.
—ST. AUGUSTINE

A biography is always constructed from ruins.
—LOREN EISELEY

Called or uncalled, God will be there.
—GERMAN PROVERB

Death lies in wait
A missing brother—
Full of the missing words.
—WILLIAM CARLOS WILLIAMS

Jacob's story was a symbol perfected in death.
—BARBARA MYERHOFF

THE PROMISE OF STORYTELLING

Fifty percent of deaths of the aged occur in the three months following their birthdays, while only 10 percent occur in the three months preceding their birthdays. People hold on to observe a final milestone. The completion of story has its own inner drive and promise. But we do not know what form it will take; sometimes we do not know how to begin.

In recent decades there has been a recovery of the significance of narrative or story in theology. Earlier theologians had already turned to narrative as a way around the Enlightenment's emphasis on isolated, objective facts or truths that privileged science and rationality. The biblical traditions were thought to gain a better hearing in narrative terms. The story of God's actions was seen to interact with individual human stories. Attention turned to the "narrative quality of experience."[1] Human character is displayed through narrative, and communities are shaped by the stories they tell. The lifeless rituals one so often encounters have become disconnected from the storied lives of the participants or from the larger story of religious communities.[2]

Anthropologists have turned a critical eye on narrative[3] as they examine the relationship between ethnographer and ethnography.[4] The anthropologist was recognized also as the teller of his or her own story. The subjectivity of the author has again emerged from behind the screen of Enlightenment rationalism and objectivism. In both theology and the social sciences the objectivity of the historical record and the confidence in the truths of lucid rationality have come under heavy fire. Critical theory, especially deconstructionism, has emphasized the interaction of author and audience and prevailing cultural pressures in the retrieval of narrative.

First-person accounts by the dying and by those who have accompanied them proliferate. An example is *Final Negotiations,* in which Carolyn Ellis struggles to tell a story within a story.[5] The inner story is that of her nine-year relationship with a sociologist who turns out to be dying of emphysema. The framing story is about her struggle to integrate autobiographical and sociological writing. At the beginning and at the conclusion of her "experimental ethnography" she engages in critical dialogue with the sociological and anthropological literature on autobiography and narrative.[6]

The primary characteristic of a good story is its open-endedness. Individual readers or hearers can take it along with them, and the story continues to evolve beyond itself. It is less important to discover the "correct" interpretation of a story—even one's own—than to reflect on what you do with your interpretation. A good death completes a story and is a gift to the next generation, to the future. The bequest of a good story is the ongoing process it sets in motion—stories never remain frozen. The story itself, especially its last chapter, is the record of the process of achieving a death of one's own.

When Elisabeth Kübler-Ross's theory that we die in stages (denial, anger, bargaining, depression, acceptance) began to dominate thinking about death and dying, one of the more interesting objections to it was that stories have moral primacy over stages.[7] Putting the dying into stages risks controlling them with second-order generalizations. To invite them to put themselves into stories is to honor their individuality and not assume we know more than they do. Stories are primary texts; each person is best viewed as a narrator or storyteller. Stages are likely to take people's individual, narrative-rich dying away from them and replace it with theory. When the dying are encouraged to become storytellers, they maintain their status in the community. The dying function as "artists" to the very end, crafting their own stories.

There are obvious reasons for writing first-person narratives about dying and grieving.[8] People do it to inform others about a disease process or the reality of caretaking, to encourage others and share with them the message that difficult situations can be endured with hope and courage, to advocate changes in the health care system, or to plead for public funding or concern. But most compelling is the motivation of "writing as bearing witness." It is reported that the murderous Khmer Rouge in Cambodia singled out for death anyone who wore glasses—because they could presumably read and write, and so bear witness. A compelling version of the witness theme is "to make sure I'm alive when I die."[9]

There are compelling calls to storytelling. Gaston Bachelard's words are often quoted: "What is the source of our first suffering? It lies in the fact that we hesitated to speak. It was born in the moment when we accumulated silent things within us." Isak Dinesen wrote, "All suffering is bearable if it is seen as part of a story." Black Elk said, "A man who has a vision is not able to use the power of it until after he has performed the vision on earth for the people to see." This is the so-called performative character of narrative. Composing and playing out one's dying offers not only closure, but disclosure. Looming death is the pressing invitation to finish the story. Writing is a disclosive and empowering act. Try this exercise: Imagine you are at the end of your life. Without hesitating, without thinking, record the story you have lived in five sentences. Stories heal because we can become whole as we trace them. Think of life as a dream from which you are about to awake. The "dream police" are arriving in twenty minutes. Everything in life not written down will evaporate upon their arrival. Whatever you forget to record that is most precious, that formed you, that sustains you, will disappear.[10] Might an artful dying grant us the gift to look back over our life and know the entire story we have been living?

Many projects with the elderly encourage them, through life review, story writing, and guided imagery, to work on completions to their life stories.[11] The movement toward story completion does not always take a form we might have expected. Fragmentary, half-submerged figures move through one disguise after another. Life review does not compose itself into a coherent narrative or orderly progression of memories, but is more like quiltwork. We progress toward story completion whenever we find recurring configurations of images that suggest important questions or partial answers. A final resolution may never be reached. "Peace may be won, but it is usually something like a truce between renewed outbreaks of conflict."[12] We are searching for "a redemptive metaphor of self that is both an emblem of the meaning of our lives and a plausible legacy."[13]

The move from reminiscence toward storytelling is difficult in our society, which sees this power of old age as vestigial, out of touch with the kinds of information that can be stored in the memory banks of a technological society. Currently there is a struggle between those who think the reawakened interest in oral histories and roots augurs well for the storytelling of a last career and those who regard this with amused disdain, as a self-indulgence and a useless preoccupation. We need great storytellers who turn their last chapters into examples for us all.

The surrounding culture can reward or discredit storytelling ventures. It may also shape, perhaps insidiously, the kinds of stories we put together. Consider four kinds of autobiographies in our age.[14] Following the dominant paradigm, the *psychological* autobiography is the one most readily facilitated by human-services professionals and easily assimilated into some variety of psychotherapy. Mental health and adaptation are the main themes. The *spiritual* autobiography, by contrast, seeks salvation or deliverance and plays on the stage of a universal spiritual drama. Myth and history coincide. "Like parallel lines that meet at the horizon, individual lives lose their separateness at the 'still point' of eternity. . . . Time and memory are taken up in eternity and the act of reminiscence becomes an act of prayer or meditation."[15] The *literary* autobiography manifests artistic creativity. It is the search for an appropriate metaphor for the self, but its deconstructive forms move beyond previous notions of normative self-disclosure to a sense of multiple selves, of making up our stories as we go along. The final metaphor of the self may be a chosen fiction. The *philosophical* autobiography moves well beyond psychological reductionism to address such questions as "the status of time and memory, our knowledge of other minds, the intersubjectivity of language, and the nature of the self."[16] Life review turns back on itself to reflect on its own purposes and assumptions.

The most promising life review and story completion is one that leads to the recovery of a public world. It is not in our private worlds that we will discover the secret of reminiscence, but in the structure of the stories themselves, in the disciplines of poetry, history, and autobiography. What really is the tale we are seeking to tell? "In the words of *Black Elk Speaks*, it is the story of all life that is sacred, the story of the human journey from birth until death. It is a journey through the public world, the waking world restored by the act of remembrance."[17] Quoting Dylan Thomas's "Fern Hill"—"Time held me green and dying, though I sang in my chains like the sea"—Harry Moody remarks: "The singing of the song and the telling of the tale *must* become public in order to shine through the natural ruin of time. The common world outlasts any single generation, but it survives only if it becomes illuminated in a 'public realm.'"[18] To fail in the recovery of a public world is to fail to participate in something larger than a single life story. Our own society is most likely to coach the elderly to make reminiscence a "sentimental journey" into nostalgia. We should call for the necessary dream work of an age, one that promises a legacy. The public story (and stories in public) is indispensable to the recovery of a death of our own, for it helps break the grip of the prevailing psychological paradigm that sees only the individual, remaining innocent of society and culture. Public stories point in the direction of community ritualizing.

How does one begin such storytelling? By placing an X in the center of a page, a workshop leader answers.[19] In workshops on storytelling and life review, she requests participants to overcome their terror of the blank page by spending several minutes filling in the boundaries of a map of their childhood, letting details around the X assemble as memory recovers them. She invites all to see their stories as parts of one big story that tells of the life journey of the hero, introducing them to Joseph Campbell's *The Hero with a Thousand Faces*. Storytellers unlock closed doors, open old trunks, and acknowledge the truth that we always know more than we can tell. They come together in memory-raising feats. A poet arranges reminiscences into poetry. This "transforms what feels in prose like an easy-to-lose scrap of life into a framed, full-bodied, resonant, and somehow complete poetic moment. I want them to see the poetry in their lives."[20]

The ill can be reimagined as "wounded storytellers."[21] They move away from passivity and victimization, turning illness into story and fate into experience. A common bond of suffering unites them in shared vulnerability, from which they emerge as brave actors. Tiresias, blinded by the gods, is such a wounded storyteller. It is he who reveals to Oedipus the truth about his parentage. The patriarch Jacob wrestles with the angel, and his hip is thrown out of joint as the price of his story. Through storytelling the wounded are transformed from those who are cared for into those who care for others. They become potent healers. The wounded recover their voice through the difficult act of storytelling. The whole body speaks. Eventually everyone becomes a wounded storyteller. "It is our promise and responsibility, our calamity and dignity."

To tell a good enough story, we must go deep enough: this is storytelling as archaeology. We should experience the pull of the future: this is storytelling as eschatology. We should seek a story aesthetically ripe and set in the midst of stories larger than our own: this is storytelling as poetry and myth-making.

STORYTELLING AS ARCHAEOLOGY

Loren Eiseley subtitles his autobiography *All the Strange Hours: The Excavations of a Life*. He writes: "A biography is always constructed from ruins but, as any archaeologist will tell you, there is never the means to unearth all the rooms, or follow the buried roads, or dig into every cistern for treasure. You try to see what the ruin meant to whoever inhabited it and, if you are lucky, you see a little way backward into time. The search may carry one high up into mountains where someone fled in extremity or deep into arroyos where bones protrude from the walls or into caves, from which one hopes to come out again."[22] The journey back is delicious but also perilous. Eiseley goes on: "Each man goes home before he dies. Each man, as I, physically or mentally, it does not matter which, goes shivering up the dark stairs, carrying a taper that sets gigantic shadows reeling in his brain. He pushes through the cobwebs of unopened doors. Or, rich and happy in his memories, he runs swiftly up the steps of a mansion that has no terrors and bursts into the lighted room of peace to find the fire dead upon the grate and the rocking chair still swaying slightly."[23]

The search for a way home, the attempt to uncover a root metaphor of the self, may drive our younger years as well. When I was in graduate school, I often spent Sunday afternoons far from my East Bay apartment looking at real estate for which I had no money. Impatient realtors would say: "Tell us what you're looking for and we'll tell you whether it can be found in this area and at what price." Always I would describe acreage with small hills, productive rolling fields, long and winding paths and fences, live streams and shade, and always a forest backdrop. I never found what I could afford or even what I was looking for exactly. A few years later I went back to eastern Iowa for my parents' fiftieth wedding anniversary. I drove out into the country one day and saw immediately what I had been describing to the California realtors. It was the landscape of my childhood. I had carried it around in my consciousness as a way home, as an orientation point for my navigations through graduate school, as an ideal destination for my journeys into a new world.

The completion of story requires an archaeology of the imagination. Can we deepen events into experiences and turn the experiences into imaginal possibilities? Can we glimpse through dream, image, or fantasy the larger metaphors in all our lives? Can soul making ensue? "The dimension of soul is depth (not breadth or height) and the dimension of our soul travel is downward."[24]

Amidst the excavations, we are certain to discover unfinished tasks. When we pause to listen carefully, we hear echoes just now reaching us. Eiseley calls this time "the human autumn before the snow. It is the individual's last attempt to order the meaning of his life before a spring breaks in the rusted heart and the dreams, the memories and the elusive chemical domain that contains them fly apart in irreparable ruin. Oncoming age is to me a vast wild autumn country strewn with broken seedpods, hurrying cloudrack, abandoned farm machinery, and circling crows. A place where things were begun on too grand a scale to complete."[25] The limit that is death pushes against us as we labor between cosmos and chaos.

We glimpse that we are a story being told, that our dreams are dreaming us. The soul is not a projection, but the projector. The soul's house is always under construction and filled with occupants, not all of whom are acknowledged or recognized. There is enough room for mass immigrations, the resurrection of the repressed. A pantheism of personified images reenters the commerce of our daily lives, "released from the mental reservations that restrain such primitiveness and from the conceptual prisons of small-letter descriptions."[26]

Under the time pressure of finitude and mortality, we work away at excavations for a story. While laboring over these excavations we come face-to-face with all the forgotten symptoms our soul has thrown up over the years. In these symptoms lies the opportunity for insight and, if we are fortunate, growth. The approach of death itself may throw up new symptomatology. It is worth recalling that the great insights of depth psychology have all derived from souls in extremis. If we grant ourselves *Seelsorge,* the old pastoral "cure of souls," we give ourselves permission to handle these unearthed shards with gentleness and without disgust.

Part of the record unearthed by our imaginal archaeology will be the course of what James Hillman calls "pathologizing." We create illness or abnormality or suffering out of our experiences and proceed to imagine life through this deformed and afflicted perspective.[27] Through such pathologizing the soul speaks. "We owe our symptoms an immense debt. The soul can exist without its therapists but not without its symptoms."[28] Jung said that analysis is dreaming the myth onward. Imaginal archaeology at the end of life is the attempt to urge our story toward its end, or its continuation.

I emphasize pathologizing and the archaeology of ruins lest the warm glow of humanistic psychology, so dominant in the modern death awareness movement, transfuse the last chapters of our lives with denial, on one hand, and artificial growth, on the other—a growth that may arrive prematurely or superficially under the coaxing of rosy-minded therapists and other well-wishers. Health, hope, courage, love, and wholeness are not the whole story of our lives. Not everything about human nature yields tenderness, creativity, joy, and play. Human stories also have darker sides. Life and death are never without shadows, and these should not be dismissed as "regression values." Flights of easy transcendence never escape the shallows.[29]

The soul sees by means of its afflictions. Pathologizing is a vital way of seeing. In our wounds are mouths shouting our myths and eyes to see what cannot otherwise be seen. Pathologizing need not present itself as a hospital patient to be taken seriously.[30]

Allowing the soul to speak through us in our dying and death is not the highly personalized, idiosyncratic, solipsistic exercise our culture is likely to imagine.

Soul projects itself through human life, enters everything human, but not every-thing about us is our own individual soul.[31] We do not own the great archetypes and myths that speak through us, and they cannot be measured on personal scales. I do not believe that Rilke's call for a death of our own is best fulfilled as an individualistic enterprise. In great human choices and decisions we play out mythic stances. World and history are also the soul's landscape. Religious com-munities and culture nurture and sustain that landscape. Our age will tempt us to limit our excavations and thus the insights we gain, to the outlines of isolated, if heroic, selves. But we are more than "the little self-important man at the great sea's edge, turning to himself to ask how he feels today . . . counting his personality inventory."[32] Intellect and imagination weigh as much as gut experiences or emo-tional problems. The soul's redemption requires more than coping mechanisms.

The human heart on its way with soul making cannot walk just those paths marked "trust your feelings." A dying in which depth of soul speaks will be more than discovering one's feelings. Larger questions beg to be asked. Cosmic soul must be larger than the body. If soul is confined to the natural body and bound only to individual lives, we leave insufficient place for life's other side, death, and for the great connections between the living and the dead, between present and past and future. A culture without soul cannot give death its due because it has left no place to do so and recognizes no place to do so. This happens as we watch our culture converting death into illness or stage theory so that it can be man-aged under the paradigms of scientific medicine or psychotherapy.

The archaeology of the imagination does not limit itself to light conversa-tions with peers, but searches for a language of soul, a language that can voice the archetypes that precede and constrict us, a language through which God could speak. Plato said one should exert one's competence in language "not for the sake of speaking to and dealing with fellowmen, but for speaking what is pleasing to the gods." Imagine a death of our own that comes after the exca-vation of our life down to the level of soul. By such a death we might become a lyre on which God plays, or feel our lips burned into eloquence by the divine presence. The prophet Isaiah was overcome at his comissioning in the Temple when he saw a vision of God and then one of the seraphim flew to him and touched his unclean lips with a coal from the altar.[33]

An age that attends to such stories, such last passages, will find itself invited to archaeological expeditions of its own. Great deaths may be lived, solving and resolving the issues of an age. The soul of an age will find its voice. Humans fresh from their depths will become the voice of soul and speak wisdom to their times. The way back is the search for a voice from the beginning that will speak at our end. The goal of an archaeology of the imagination is to see through the past.

STORYTELLING AS ESCHATOLOGY

The archaeology of the imagination enables a reenvisioning of the meaning of our lives and of unfinished business. But back is not the only way to look. Another posture of recovery, another hermeneutic of retrieval, is the one that stretches forward, straining toward an infinite horizon. This move toward the future, toward final things, is the way of eschatology. For some this will be a complement to archaeological expeditions. Others may find eschatology the root metaphor of human existence, even as James Hillman finds the journey back or down to be preeminent.[34]

Jewish and Christian theologies are rich in eschatological thought and have left a great deposit of it in the Western traditions.[35] In the Jewish Passover liturgy, for centuries believers prayed, "We await Elijah's arrival, we ask God to inspire us by the example of all the martyrs for truth and faith, the witnesses to God in darkness and suffering." A place set before an empty chair for Elijah was a powerful eschatological symbol. The present ritual moment can be a springboard to eternity. In some Jewish thought the messianic moment of redemption will come when the whole of Israel keeps a single Sabbath; then, when the messiah comes, the eschatological Sabbath begins.[36] Christian hymns sing of a future in Christ.

> *Will the circle be unbroken,*
> *By and by, Lord, by and by?*
> *There's a better home a-waiting,*
> *In the sky, Lord, in the sky.*

Tombs, even in the modern world, are stones that cry out through their epitaphs, like this one from a cemetery on Long Island:

> *This body sleeps in dust*
> *Immortal joys await the host*
> *In perfect beauty may it rise*
> *When Gabriel's trumpet shakes the skies.*

Basic to the Jewish and Christian ideas of salvation is life, but it would have been a disappointing theological enterprise that could not find its way beyond human mortality. To be sure, abundant life here and now on this earth, so-called realized eschatology, has been fundamental in these traditions and undergoes periodic recoveries of significance. But so is a life projected despite death, a life that overcomes death and turns it from a terminus into a way station.

The unconquerable power of love empowers projection beyond death. From Plato to Ionesco, from the Song of Songs through the troubadours, "runs that presage of love conquering all, stronger even than death."[37] In Psalms 16, 49, and 73, in St. Paul's evocation of "being-with-Christ," and in St. John's "abiding in love," love is pictured as stronger than death. If earthly love promises eternity, God's love grants it. In Christian theology such a love works itself out in history. "The death of the individual challenges the love of God and tests the identity of both humans (are we an absolute value?) and God (Is God love?). The response to the challenge corroborates the immortality glimpsed in any life born from and for love."[38]

But if life and love are to go on forever, humans themselves must be elevated if we are not to face a tedious eternity. Jewish theology warns that our greatest concern should be not to continue our existence, but to exalt it. "The cry for a life beyond the grave is presumptuous, if there is no cry for eternal life prior to our descending to the grave. Eternity is not perpetual future but perpetual presence. God has planted in us the seed of eternal life. The world to come is not only a hereafter but also a *herenow*."[39] Christian theology, especially Roman Catholic and Orthodox, sees heaven as the goal of the process of divinization implanted in time by grace. The "beatific vision," the promised seeing of God, engenders likeness to God. Such a vision exerts pressure out of the future onto society and onto the world and onto our as yet unconsummated humanity—a human solidarity with all humankind and beyond the boundaries of space and time, and a full vision of God.

Ludwig Feuerbach, followed by Marx and Freud, dismissed Christian eschatology as mere projection, wishful thinking, and mystification. He thought heaven represented the human desire to become like God, to transcend contingency by sublimating it. The projective element in every vision of an afterlife must be acknowledged, even if Feuerbach's reductive assumptions are rejected. Leaving aside for now the confessions of Christian theology, it is time to ask whether projection is a significant and healthy force in human story construction during and before one's last career. Many psychologists, with often unreflective commitments to empirical and even positivist science, look on the fuzzy projections of "life after life" by Kübler-Ross and her followers as the same dangerous mystification that, according to Feuerbach, characterized nineteenth-century religious thought. Is it certain that projection is inappropriate to the human condition?

To avoid special pleading on behalf of theology, I turn to the German philosopher Ernst Bloch's nontheological discussion of the human propensity to project.[40] No less suspicious of the masquerades of human thought than Freud, Bloch still argued that Freud, attending so fully to the unconscious, failed to consider the important role of the preconscious or the not yet conscious. Feuerbach, Bloch thought, was so intent on nailing down time in his materialistic universe and so distrustful of human imagination, that he paid no attention to "the infinity of the unfinished." Against Freud's and Feuerbach's excessive constraints, Bloch posed an eschatology whose principal themes are possibility, process, daydream, *novum*, utopia, and hope.

Reality is matter, as Freud and Feuerbach saw, but matter is possibility. Life is in process, still undetermined. The final essence of things is not yet unveiled. "The world is full of disposition to something, of tendency toward something, of latency with something, and this something toward which the world is tending is the outcome of intention."[41] What we now predicate of something is not yet its final form.

Consider the implications of Bloch's thought. A philosophy of the not-yet invites a psychology to match. Humans, too, are in process. In the depths of our humanity is a pressure impelling us forward. We keep aspiring to more than we can reach. This tension produces in us an affect of expectation, which eventually becomes a posture of hope.[42]

This expectation and hope fills our preconscious, and that preconscious is the workshop in which the new is forged or imagined. Here in the human preconscious is a "twilight to the future," a "psychic portrayal of the not-yet-become." If night dreams look back, the preconscious comes out in daydreams that hope, that "give way to the waking imagination, whose natural tendency is anticipation."[43] When daydreams are allowed space, they give way to utopia, where possibilities are fulfilled. Bloch imagined that wish-images might actually reach their objective, thereby justifying their validity. We move from a world of contradictions to a homeland where we are transformed by hope.

Any attempt to achieve a death of our own faces the question whether present culture is conducive to such a quest. Is the ground fertile? Are the symbols at hand rich enough? This discussion of recovering the validity of projection faces the same question. If the worldview one begins with is confined to naked empirical facts, then possibility and process and projection are likely to be repressed. If our system is closed, projection and hope and a new future are idle mystifications. If our ontology is open, we can look at the present as a state of fermentation and of genesis of the future.

"Process theology" moves in similar directions. Wanting to free itself from a static (classical) theism and from a God who cannot be moved by the world or human suffering, it conceived a limited God who is subject to becoming, to process—a God unfolding in the course of the world. God and the world are seen as correlates, each necessary to the other. Process theology draws on the process philosophy of Alfred Whitehead and Charles Hartshorne and makes event, becoming, and relatedness, rather than being, ultimate categories. A popular Jewish version is expounded in the phenomenal best-seller *When Bad Things Happen to Good People,* proposed as a theodicy in the face of human suffering. It, in turn, draws on efforts in Jewish theology that reenvision theism in response to the mass death of the Holocaust.

Carol Zaleski in *The Life of the World to Come* straightforwardly asks whether we are rationally and morally entitled to believe in life after death, and she emphatically answers yes.[44] William James defended the right to believe before all the evidence is in. Earlier ages that came to terms with death better than our own does also set greater store by an afterlife, giving "the lie to the modern conceit that belief in life after death is an evasion of the reality of death."[45] Indeed, the methodical contemplation of one's own mortality—and of a reality that eclipses the present—has always been an important spiritual discipline.

In a series of meditations, Zaleski chooses Holy Saturday as a metaphor for Christian life that lives amidst the coincidence of opposites—the death of Christ and of all on Good Friday, and the hope of resurrection on Easter. Holy Saturday becomes a little cosmos, and the liturgical offices (in the Catholic tradition) of lauds, vespers, and compline trace in their natural rhythms the mystery of death and resurrection through a single day. The Church awakes, watching with Christ, and sleeps, resting with Christ. Thus is consecrated also the sleeping and waking of nature.

Zaleski ponders near-death experiences: separation from the body, sometimes accompanied by a spectator perspective; journey motifs; encounters with beings of light; life review; immersion in light and love; return to life; transforming aftereffects.[46] She decides to call these real experiences mediated by the religious imagination. Perhaps they give us a glimpse into the workings of the eschatological imagination, the primary vehicle of religious hope. Near-death experiences are first sightings, visionary anticipations, filtered through images engraved on the psyche and embedded in the culture, all rehearsals for the final drama.[47] Perhaps near-death experiences mediate through open-ended symbols what is not sayable in conceptual language. If God, the unknowable, wishes to be known, what other recourse is there? If God descended into the human condition in Christ, Zaleski asks, might God not also descend into our cultural forms? It would be iconoclastic to deny the possibility of such a courteous descent. We can test our experiences in such cultural forms. Do they transfigure us or lend themselves only to self-serving ends? Do they merely confirm the satisfaction of continued personal existence or also summon to possible judgment and review? The narrow ego-self, too confident in eschatological imagination, should not expect to survive the translation to eternal life intact. The Spanish philosopher-poet Miguel de Unamuno thought we owed it to our humanity not to stifle the desire for immortality: "We must needs believe in that other life in order that we may live this life, and endure it, and give it meaning and finality. And we must needs believe in that other life, perhaps, in order that we may deserve it, in order that we may obtain it, for it may be that he neither deserves it nor will obtain it who does not passionately desire it above reason and, if need be, against reason."[48]

The eschatological imagination has played with the symbols both of resurrection of the body and of immortality of the soul.[49] The symbols are sometimes made polar opposites. Some New Testament scholars insist that only resurrection of the body is a biblical idea. For Zaleski, immortality of the soul retains its validity in Christian theology if it "is not an abstract quality, not something a soul possesses by rights, but an eschatologial transformation that happens to a whole person—an alchemical change reaching down to one's very basest matter and transforming it into gold, into light."[50] Perhaps there is too much to lose in an outright rejection of all immortality language. We risk "estranging believers from the literary sources and imaginative resources of their own tradition."[51] More important than which metaphor predominates is the alchemy that results from God's sacrificial descent into our mortal condition. St. Augustine calls this the wonderful exchange by which we make it possible for God to die and God makes it possible for us to live. But the logic of the exchange also requires that we die to ourselves and no longer self-sufficiently belong to ourselves.

If the right to believe in a life after death can be defended, can the right to imagine what it might be like also be defended? Most modern Christian theologians decline the invitation. But Zaleski believes that "if we do not permit ourselves to form images of personal and collective existence after death, then we have no way of testing who we are or of sounding our deepest ideals."[52] To be sure, the history of heaven is the history of humanly constructed ideals. There are heavens of contemplative adoration, of friends and family reunited, of lovers, of favorite causes, of tweeds and hunting dogs, every one a projection against the dome of the sky. But don't we find our bearings through such projections of the good life and of good society? *We do not better ourselves by starving the imagination.* In any case, the function of such images is to provide orientation, not information. We must, as Paul Tillich reminds, keep the afterlife from degenerating from a life-giving symbol into a narcissistic projection. Whether we must choose between the dream of heaven and authentic engagement with the eternal now, as Tillich seems to have thought, is a question some might answer in the negative.

Is it time to take a stand against the iconoclasm toward heaven so prevalent among both religious and secular contemporary thinkers? The relentless efforts to demythologize may stem more from the embarrassment of intellectuals with popular piety than from the needs of authentic theologizing.[53] Such theologians should strive for a "second naivete."[54] There is genuine folly in suppressing imagistic ways of thinking about death. Why not let such images emerge from our own experience and reflection, or even as playful experiments? The censorship of certain symbols as obsolete is a misguided enterprise leading to symbolic impoverishment. "We should bear in mind that the archaism of symbols is part of their appeal, that some symbols may go into retirement only to return in full vigor at a future time, and that religious traditions are better served by a plurality of symbols than by forced consistency."[55]

Zaleski scorns efforts to cook images of postmortem existence down to a single conception. Why? "It would render unintelligible many of the things people do for the dead. Again, this would mean the breaking of vital links between the society of the living and the dead."[56]

Commonplace arguments against heaven based on eschatological boredom may only betray a lack of imagination. The imagination of afterlife is not a distraction but an orientation. "Christian eschatology is the story of divine love calling creation back from death," a story rich in images, all of them needed until, with Dante, we can say, "Here power fails the high fantasy," and let love lead the rest of the way.[57] A life lived against a horizon of hope can be a richly human life, moving toward self-transformation. The pull of hope and heaven on our stories should be not denied but welcomed; the pressure from the future should be given its due.

But we should be careful in the exercise of the eschatological imagination. Jurgen Moltmann, who has devoted more attention to this topic than any other modern theologian, warns that a simplistic obsession with last things can spoil one's taste for penultimate ones. Then "the dreamed of, or hoped for, end of history robs us of our freedom among history's many possibilities, and our tolerance for all the things in history that are unfinished and provisional. We can no longer put up with earthly, limited and vulnerable life, and in our eschatological finality we destroy life's fragile beauty."[58] Eschatology is not the "final solution."

STORYTELLING AS POETRY AND MYTH MAKING

We are unfinished creations. Storytelling is an imaginal act. As we bring our lives to completion we want to adorn them with aesthetic richness and situate them in larger journeys and aspirations. This effort is not limited to the lone individual creatively engaging the self. Culture provides rich voices that speak through individuals, and individuals pour meaning back into the community.

The connection between reminiscence and creativity should not be lost. This is a task for a whole generation, a whole culture. Reminiscence touches the dream, which touches eternity, provoking meditation on time and history. "The artistic imagination is rooted in the soil of dreams, but its branches reach toward heaven. . . . Between the subterranean depths of psychic life and the enveloping transparency of the sky, the air of a common world surrounds all our actions. This bond between dream and public world is also the link between art and history."[59] Goethe brought together the poles of art and objectivity in the title of his autobiography, *Dichtung und Wahrheit* (Poetry and Truth). Any literal separation between poetry and truth leads to other false separations, finally condemning our wish for meaning to a privatized self-satisfaction, winnowed from public and cosmic aspirations.

As it is possible to create an environment that fosters poetry, it is possible to stimulate approaches to story construction that pay off in the creation of larger meanings. We must learn to ask and answer questions elliptically rather than literally. For example, "How are you?" and "What is it like?" can be answered analogically, allusively, by images, by similitudes, by models, by metaphors, by evocations. Familiar categories are enlarged into allegories. "How old are you?" can become "What is it like for you?" or "What does it mean for you?" The task is to ply familiar language in evocative ways. Through such questions meaning as given, discovered, or imposed will play with meaning as created and imagined. This can be a communal task. While a group can only witness (and marvel at) an act of self-discovery, they can join in creation. This call for joint discovering, it must be acknowledged, comes at a time when "the great cultural systems of participatory meaning have largely lost their compelling power" and "such recollecting and drawing together are left to individuals."[60] Against the fact that old age has been lengthened but drained of substance, that a cultural sense of the whole of life has been lost, that we are without paradigms for a last career, we labor away to create and rediscover meaning.

Story construction is the task of mythopoesis, the work of poetry, the work of turning our lives into larger myths that can bear the weight of significant meaning. "The poet labors in the workshop of the mind, gluing together odd ceramic splinters of the self. The poet works alone, but never by himself. He works without a plan, but guidance is at hand."[61] Elderly people can search for archetypal images that will contain and carry their stories. Jung understood that archetypes, whether in experience or words, summon voices stronger than our own. We find "refuge from every peril and outlive the longest night. Whoever speaks in primordial images speaks with a thousand voices; he enthralls and overpowers, while at the same time he lifts the idea he is seeking to express out of the occasional and the transitory into the realm of the ever-enduring."[62]

Can our personal destiny be transfigured into the destiny of humankind?

In "Minerva's Doll" Janet Bloom offers a lovely interpretation of a writing workshop she conducted at a senior citizens center. A woman named Minerva was able to attend to her own personal story through writing about the life course of a favorite doll she had had for many years. Minerva wrote the following poem, which became the catalyst for reflections in the group and from Bloom as well:

> Of all the objects I own, in my house, and I love,
> is an old Spanish doll that adorns my bed.
> This doll was brought to me from Spain more than
>   thirty years ago.
> This doll body is made of rags;
> but the head is made of clay;
> and the arms are like plastic.
> She was very beautiful. I said "was"
> because now the head is coming apart.[63]

No one in the group initially treated the story as symbolic of Minerva herself, who was then facing a cataract operation and whose face was deeply wrinkled. Nor did Minerva consciously connect her condition with the crumbling face of her doll. Bloom asked Minerva if she wanted to expand her story. Minerva wondered how she could. Bloom replied that she thought it was very beautiful the way it was, but she also thought Minerva knew more about the doll and could tell more if she wanted to. How could Bloom the poet have fielded the inside of Minerva's story while others were fielding the outside of it? How much should she have revealed of what she saw in the doll story? Should she have invited comments from Minerva on a relation between her operation and her doll? She decided to "jiggle something loose" but not in any obvious way.

In subsequent sessions Bloom invited the other members of the group to write descriptions of the face of Minerva's doll. The following were offered:

> The doll appears as if once
> she was a very precious and beautiful lady.
> Today after the years she has gone through
> the marks are left on her face.

> Minerva's doll is a flapper;
> it is a very old doll of many years.
> But having so many years she looks good.

Her face is a little scratched
but she can paint it with paint
called varnish and it will be perfect.
I feel very happy to see
a doll of so many years.

The face of this doll to my understanding
was painted. And with the years it's happening
as it happens to us human beings,
that the face changes.[64]

Near the end of the course Minerva was scheduled to go into the hospital for her operation and brought her doll for Bloom to see. She said she wanted Bloom to see it before Minerva went into the hospital. "The way she said it, I felt as if she were giving me her soul, as if she had said, 'I'm going, you keep me.'"[65] A legacy was pressed into the poet's hand. Minerva had thrown her lifeline to Bloom onshore, to let her know. Suddenly they had a life-and-death bond, a reverse umbilical cord attached at the end rather than at the beginning of life.

At the close of her account Bloom decides that more got said through indirectness than would have through directness. She is pleased she did not try to pin down the symbolic equation between Minerva and her doll, to label and box and point at things, as if they held no mystery. By not confining the doll symbol to Minerva's concerns about blindness and death, Bloom opened the symbol up like a window in an airless room. Instead of nailing down meaning like corpses into coffins, she let meaning get out alive.[66]

Maybe, Bloom thinks, the terror of death is a terror of having nothing to say about it. But in symbols we find there is plenty to say. To offer a literal interpretation of Minerva's doll story would have been death to ongoing conversation. Circumnavigating the void, however, meant finding new ways of approaching it. "Because we were only dimly cognizant of what the doll was meaning, it acquired full meaning, true meaning; it swam in the sea of our thought."[67] The poet did not pin a subject down until it squirmed. She didn't jab the life out of it. Bloom remained a poet, and in doing so, she gave Minerva her death, and her completed story.

A much more deliberate and self-constructed death was that with which the Japanese writer Yukio Mishima planned to bring a symbolic ending to his life. He sought to fashion his death as the highest form of art. His samurai suicide would culminate his obsession for control and his view of life as theater. He cherished a romantic impulse toward death and through his bodybuilding tried to make his body a suitable vehicle. Although he thought death at age twenty was the most aesthetically desirable, his own body was not yet fit at that age. He hoped, then, to die at age forty-five, in his view the outside age before his body would become irredeemably corrupt. Mishima was fascinated with the possibility of creating a work of art and then immediately dying, deaf to either praise or blame. In his fiction he had written of a privileged moment one may be given, for which one's whole life has been a preparation, a moment that invites a perfect gesture that crystallizes and embodies truth. Against the contradictions and compromises of his earthly life, Mishima posed his perfect death. In fact, Mishima's ritual suicide, or *seppuku,* exhibited none of the perfection in which life is raised to fine art. Instead of a rite with the elegance of a Japanese tea ceremony, he produced not an aesthetic triumph worthy of a *samurai* but a clumsy disaster.

In "The Death of Ivan Ilych" Leo Tolstoy shows a dying that is on its way to being tragic but becomes instead the very act that makes us fully human. Ivan has been caught up in the web of secrecy and delusion with which society hides both life and death. He comes to grieve for the meaninglessness of all that has been important to him and, in the face of bewildered and rejecting onlookers, including his family, weeps bitterly. But through the death-affirming peasant Gerasim, Ivan comes to see his own death for the radical event it can be. Death is not the intruder who attacks from without; through it Ivan is offered the possibility of a final creative act. He comes to his true self by letting go. It is not the image of a rosy Christian afterlife that Ivan has recourse to, but rather Jesus's paradoxical saying that in losing the self one finds it. At that point all the fear and pain and even death itself, which has been oppressing him, drops away. The unchanging truth of what it means to be human alone remains.

Anthropologist Barbara Myerhoff has recounted a successfully staged last chapter of life, which, following T. S. Eliot, she calls "a symbol perfected in death." This is the story of Jacob Kovitz, who died in the middle of the public celebration of his ninety-fifth birthday amidst two hundred family and friends gathered to honor him at a Jewish senior citizens community center in Los Angeles. The human passion for continuity, and its social, cultural, personal, and spiritual variants, came into focus on the day Jacob died. "His ritual death was an assertion that his community would continue, that his way of life would be preserved, that he was a coherent, integrated person through his personal history, and that something of him would remain alive after his corporeal departure."[68] In the elaborate plans for this event, death was transformed from antagonist to partner. In making his death a mythic and symbolic drama, Jacob transcended it. Amidst uncertainty, anxiety, impotence, and disorder, ritual provided pattern and predictability and asserted continuity.

This is how it happened. A Yiddish culture of East European Jews, survivors of shtetls now extinguished by the Holocaust, emigrants originally to the industrial cities of the eastern United States, reasserted itself in a neighborhood of Los Angeles. It was a community of about three hundred people, mostly between the ages of eighty-five and ninety-five, who were living in harsh circumstances but had "outlived their enemies." They had created a career out of their aging. A kind of patriarch in the group, Jacob celebrated his birthdays with parties that were great fêtes. Characteristic of these parties were a Hebrew blessing, welcomes and introductions, a festive meal, speeches, entertainment, a speech by Jacob, family donations to the center, solicitation of donations from others, a birthday cake, and song.

Amidst this customary occasion of honor and continuity, Jacob, who seemed to have sensed or even timed the hour of his death, had to receive oxygen several times during the speeches after the meal. He referred several times to his struggle with the angel of death and with great difficulty read his own speech, including mention of the provision of funds for five further birthday parties, up to his one hundredth, whether he was present or not. He sat down again, rested his chin on his chest, and died shortly after, backstage, in the arms of his sons.

Jacob's party was a successful ritual, his storied dying an act of poetry and myth making. It communicated an attitude, a posture. Jacob gave his last breath to the group. The rabbi's Kaddish prayer enlarged and generalized the significance of Jacob's death. His death reminded all that sometimes people die meaningfully, properly, purposefully—not always helplessly, accidentally. Death does not always have to find the wrong people at the wrong time. This time death made sense and invoked some higher order.[69] This was Jacob's final gift. Clothed in the Kaddish prayer, "the life of the mortal man, Jacob, was made into a mythic event, enlarging and illuminating the affairs of all those present."[70]

Individual acts of mythopoesis, the recording of "great deaths" by writers, and loving chronicles of deaths by family members all constitute outpourings of meaning into culture, bread cast upon the water that can return to provide fertile contexts for individuals dying deaths of their own.

Years ago at the great annual flower show in Bonn, Germany, I spent time in a one-acre section devoted to cemetery landscaping and planting and sculpture (scarcely imaginable at an American garden show), sponsored by the Association of Cemetery Gardeners. This group was trying to reawaken the interest of the German citizenry in cemetery art and landscaping in view of increasing demands for economic rationalization. Their pitch caught my attention. Their burden was to reimplant in public consciousness the notion of the cemetery as a space for culture and tradition. In such a reenvisioned cemetery, gardeners wanted to offer themselves as partners to the citizenry. They hoped they could persuade the readers of their literature that this could be an intentional, community-based task.

In a pamphlet distributed by an association of stonemasons and sculptors, the reader was encouraged to think of monuments in stone as means of reaching beyond the past into a lived culture. In stone we see our cultural development from earliest times into the present. Stone is a developed expression of our cultural history. To be a cemetery gardener is to be an environmentalist; to be a cemetery sculptor is to be an instrument of cultural development, a protector and renewer of what is precious for rest and reflection. In this they asked for the support of the public. The care of graves is not merely a service to the dead, but an assignment for the community. The thought that death should provoke and evoke a cultural outpouring that could enrich the community and the human spirit has been with me ever since.

In our own dying and in our remembering of the dead we can offer poetic constructions that pour new meaning into the world. In our words and ritual actions we add to the bulk and substance of soul in the world. We construct sinews of credibility that connect our constructions of meaning to the whole human project. We spin webs of culture around the logos, the meaning, that we say lies at the heart of our quest.

Hillman remarks that Jung's psychology is a cultural advance over the Freudian style of talking cure (free associations while reclining on a couch) because in Jungian analysis we sit face-to-face, knee to knee, and struggle to find words, interwoven with thought, image, and feeling, that carry soul, that make soul.[71] Our dyings and deaths and memorializations become a culturally available *Bildungsroman*, signals of character development that can move others.

Such evocations always invite and assume the presence of a larger community. The recovery of a death of our own is a gift to the community. Such a death will become, in one way or another, a public death. From the storm and turmoil of dying, a cleansing of consciousness may result, the possibility of the new emerge, and gifts to the future be offered. As Boris Pasternak writes in "The Passing Storm":

> *The air is heavy with the passing storm.*
> *The earth lies calm and free and glad again.*
> *Through all its pores the flowering lilac bush*
> *Drinks deep the pure cool freshness of the plain.*
>
> *The world's reborn, transfigured by the storm.*
> *The gutters shed a flood of rain. Now fair*
> *And vast the blue beyond the shrouded sky,*
> *And bright the ranges of celestial air.*

But more exalted far the poet of power,
Who washes clean away the dust and grime,
When by his art emerge transformed the harsh
Realities and truths of naked time.

For then our lifetime sorrows with the storm
Retreat. Free from the past of tutelage,
Our century proclaims the hour has come
To clear a passage for the future age.

No swift upheaveal swelling of itself
Can make the way for our new age to be;
Our hope—the message of a spirit kindled
By truth revealed and magnanimity.[72]

STORYTELLING AS RELIGIOUS QUEST

Above Jung's door in Zurich was engraved in stone the proverb "Called or uncalled, God will be there." The Latin root of *religion* means "to bind together, to connect." When the contradictions of our living and dying, and of the culture in which we find ourselves embedded, threaten to tear our story apart or render it untellable, when biology rends us from spirit, when finitude contests with freedom, memory with hope, we may hear a summons to go beyond self, a call finally to take note of the signs still scattered through the culture that point toward God. In that direction may lie the possibility of resolving our contradictions and binding ourselves together into one story of retrieval and ultimate becoming. The spiritual autobiography focuses on the soul more than on the self. It aims at the ultimate meaning of the author's life and is written for God as the chief reader, as St. Augustine first saw so clearly in his *Confessions*. In deconcealment comes the final revelation of self as soul-before-God.

In the last chapter of our lives we find ourselves pressing against the limits of death and of language. Ideologies of life-span development and therapeutic assists for our last career are offered by value-free social sciences. They promise that the final question, the religious one, need not be raised. But it is to larger fields than those envisioned by therapeutic models and tended by "psychological man" that we must look. The same culture that offers us few resources has loaded an almost unbearable agenda onto old age. Not only has meaning throughout the life cycle been displaced onto old age exclusively, but death/finitude/judgment have been displaced from the no-longer-acknowledged afterlife into the present life. The eclipse of faith has left us not with a lighter agenda, but only with lighter resources. So new priesthoods offer their best—ersatz spirituality and not entirely truncated transcendence—in an effort to transpose the hope of salvation into the acceptable categories of life attainable in a symbolically impoverished old age.

Something more is needed. At the time of his dying, the great scholastic synthesizer St. Thomas Aquinas saw that the end of life invites moving beyond the great task of bringing one's own life to perfection and offers instead an opportunity for doxology. The unquiet fourteenth-century saint Peter of Luxembourg stayed at his desk throughout the night jotting lists of his sins on scraps of paper and collecting them so they could be near him always. Peter kept finding more and more to confess, eventually forsaking sleep entirely. His spiritual advisors appointed two priests to hear his sins at intervals during the day, so that he could desist from further writing. Peter banged on their door during the night until they finally locked him out. "Peter of Luxembourg's compulsion to document his blotted soul aims at the dissolution of normal self-centered consciousness, not at self-expression. He seeks to empty his body of the world for the glory of the divine. Utterance becomes literally destructive of the ego."[73] The actions and the voices of saints and mystics "do not give voice to a self as we have come to define it, but to a soul aspiring to nonbeing. In confession, one speaks oneself out of conventional existence and into another world."[74]

Today, self-absorbed psyche has replaced spirit, and autobiographies are driven not by boundless desire for salvation, but by the need to declare a self to the world. In another time autobiography as confession meant the accusation of oneself as the past and the praise of God as one's future, a backward glance that unmasks the future as God's future for the soul. In St. Augustine's *Confessions* he loses himself in the larger story of the human spirit striving for grace. One autobiography is self-mythologizing, the other is, in effect, God-mythologizing, or praise of God.

It is not the goal of an accurate story that should hold us fast, but that of finding a story large enough. Concern over content gives way to concern over sufficient expansion. The new works we look for must somehow open us to a larger domain. In his poem *Paterson,* William Carlos Williams writes:

> *Death lies in wait*
> *a kindly brother—*
> *full of the missing words.*[75]

We come to see ourselves working on this story in order to find a larger story. We encounter archetypes trying to tell us, rather than we them. We seek the blessing not precisely of self-discovery, but of discovering ourselves in a prototypical narrative. In searching for a death of our own, we are taken beyond the self. From preoccupation with self-justification we are summoned to self-transcendence.

There are religious ways to speak about this, though the language of romanticism has also been offered. *Sehnsucht,* or the romantic longing to see more, what is beyond attaining, may be a religious impulse. St. Augustine wrote, "Our hearts are restless till they rest in Thee." In C. S. Lewis's *The Voyage of the Dawn Treader,* Lucy must go into the Magician's house and find a spell. As she searches the Magician's book she finds one particular spell, for the refreshment of the spirit, more like a story than a spell. She forgets she is reading at all and comes to live in the story as if it were real. When she finishes, she wants to begin the story again, but discovers that the pages will not turn backward. She finds she cannot remember the plot of the story; it all begins to fade. Ever after, what Lucy means by a good story is one that reminds her of the forgotten story in the Magician's book.

For Lewis, the very nature of human existence, conveyed in the Christian stories of creation, fall, incarnation, redemption, and resurrection, is best understood within narrative form.[76] Restating the Augustinian theme of the restless heart, Lewis says we are always trying to capture something, to cure the aching wound that the mere unfolding of time and mutability inflict upon us. Is there hope for finite creatures to find true refreshment of spirit? Thinking abstractly about something, which then distances us from experiencing it, is not the way. Lewis thought the answer lay in story. The storyteller is trying to catch a theme by means of plot. For us who are both finite and free, temporal plots are after timeless themes; the temporal story wants to net the eternal. Our lives are the same sort of net; we move through successive experiences seeking to catch something that is not temporal at all. Our hearts are restless for the eternal.

The human can touch the eternal but not fully rest in it. Yet every moment of human experience is "tensed": that is, it lies within the tension of memory of the past and anticipation of the future. Memory and anticipation are signals of transcendence, pointing us beyond ourselves. The story keeps moving on. "The creature who is made to rest in God is in this life best understood as a pilgrim whose world is depicted in terms of the Christian story."[77] Thus stories may be the most adequate way to convey the feel of human existence. Finishing the story becomes the quintessential human agenda.

Humans flee from the temporality of their existence, seeking refuge in false infinities of their own making. We are tempted to talk about the universal but give up the quest to experience it. Then we are tempted to immerse ourselves in experience and not hear the call toward that which transcends it. Lewis's pilgrim of "feeling intellect" avoids both temptations and so does not miss that larger importance in our nature.[78] We should construct stories "which expand the imagination and give one a world within which to live for a time."[79] In telling and finishing such stories, we do not content ourselves with particular experiences that point nowhere. We become open to the way in which experiences call us away from themselves. We find a larger story.

Lewis resolved the question of story and the meaning of human life through recourse to the Christian story of incarnation. "The Christian story affirms that in one human being that other and more real world has entered our history, that we need not transcend our finitude in order to find that more real world. The universal is particularized, located in time and space. The author has written himself into the play."[80] The further we get with our story, the more reminiscent it becomes of another, forgotten story. The taste for the Other grows stronger, and comes to outweigh our stories. Our life becomes a plane intersected by God.

In another elaboration of a theology of story, John Dominic Crossan lays out this scenario. In storytelling we create the world; in myth we establish the world; in action we investigate the world; in parable, the binary opposite of myth, we subvert the world. The final work on our story may take us into the parabolic task in which the smaller stories of our lives are subverted in favor of a larger story.

As we enter the world of a parable we find ourselves inspecting the seams and edges of the story in which we have been living, the myth we have constructed about the meaning of our lives. In parable we suddenly become self-conscious and critical about that version. The parabolic situation shows the limitations of our story, shatters our easy assumptions about it. Parable becomes the "dark night of story."

I suggest that our last career, including life review and story completion, can become an entry into parable that reopens for fresh examination and subversion the life story we have chosen. We have proposed; now parable disposes. The parable functions to reverse our assumptions, to force us to consider an alternative story.

Biblical parables always pose this question: What if God does not play by the rules built into our taken-for-granted story? In Crossan's analysis, the deep structure of any parable, by the art of its surface and texture, gets into the hearer's consciousness and is felt in full force only when it is too late to shrug it off. The deep structure of our last career as parable even more absolutely cannot be shrugged off. Above all, the function of the parable is to give God room or, to say it in nonreligious language, to make room for acting on the basis of a reversal of preconceptions. When our last career presents itself to us as a parabolic event, the deep structure of our accepted world is shattered and the relativity of our story is made manifest. With the removal of our defenses, we become vulnerable to God, to transcendence, to other versions of story, to divine story. Crossan suggests such a transformation occurs in the Christian story because Jesus died as parabler and rose as Parable. "Jesus announced the kingdom of God in parables, but the primitive church announced Jesus as the Christ, the Parable of God."[81]

Arriving in force and challenging both our biological and spiritual being, death invites us to decide whether we will respond in a supreme act of freedom that brings our whole history to a definitive end, summed up in the self-disposal of faith, hope, and love toward God—or in an act of despairing rebellion against the absurdity of life. How will our story end? Will we yield everything up to God, or will everything be taken by force? Will our dying be clothed in the metaphor of self-transcendence or in that of the ultimate protest of complete autonomy? The latter may create variations in story line: despair, sometimes coupled with hedonism; attempts to reduce death and the human project to triteness and banality; hunkering down with "natural" deaths. The final freedom in the stories to be written during our last career is the freedom to determine ourselves in a definitive and final way vis-à-vis God. The dying person in the Christian tradition is invited to immerse—as she or he did in baptism—a human story in a divine story, the Christian's dying in the paschal mystery of Christ's death and resurrection.

Death and our participation in it can be experienced as fate or act, the end of us or the fulfillment of us, what we suffer or what we will. It can be both an irruption from without, a destruction causing our greatest passivity, but also an active consummation from within, brought about by the self offering itself up to God. In Jesus's death this dialectic is expressed in his two addresses to God: "Why have you forsaken me?" and "Into your hands I commend my spirit." Christ did not suffer death but enacted it, thus rendering death a theonomous possibility for us, that is, an event that can be transparent rather than opaque to the purposes of God and the ultimate meaning of our human story. We cannot escape this ambiguity, these dual possibilities, and so we are caught in the necessity of hope and faith—or the temptation of despair. Our last story will act out the possible meanings of death: emptiness and futility, or ultimate fullness; the culmination of sin and finitude and guilt, or surrender to the mystery of God; radical dispossession, or final inheritance. Both have always been parts of the truth of our lives.

It remains to be seen whether in the last analysis we shall enter that deeper, all-embracing openness to the universe and to God. That is the new creation symbolized in the Christian hope of resurrection, the final appropriation of the redemption enacted through Christ's transformation of death. Thus, in T. S. Eliot's phrase, we become symbols perfected in death.

Chapter 6

Along the Ritual Way

To lose ritual is to lose the way.
—TOM DRIVER

*Human beings are by nature actors who cannot
become something until first they have pretended to be it.*
—W. H. AUDEN

INTRODUCTION

Petrarch wrote: "A good death does honor to a whole life." The argument of
this book is that good deaths honor the human condition—and also God.
These concluding chapters are about the ritual way of participating in such a
death. So far, I have argued that a resurgent death awareness in the final third
of the twentieth century, sparked by the threat of mass death in nuclear war
and then by AIDS, or coaxed along by the death education and patients' rights
movements, has not gone nearly far enough in addressing the mystery of death
and the adequacy of our responses to it. I have tried to take the reader beyond
the imaginal constraints of a death-denying culture and to pilgrimage across
space and time to wonder anew at the contours of death and dying. I have
invited a recovery of the lost art of dying. I have sought to reimagine aging as a
last career filled with fruitful images, expectations, roles, and norms. Such a last
career moves through life review toward the completion of life story. I have displayed the narrative construction of the self, accomplished in community and
with imaginative breadth and depth. It is now time to complete the argument
of this book and the recovery of a death of our own by turning, in these last
three chapters, to the performative construction of the self-in-community.

My persistent assumption is that the less interesting things about death are those assumed to be important by the institutions in which we mostly die: its biological definition, management, and problems. It is a curiosity of our times and a legacy of modern science that we should have come to think that biology has displaced all other questions and now presents the most salient issues and answers.[1] But I am claiming that death is above all a *cultural* construction, not a biological fact.[2] That college students regularly find this an astonishing claim is good evidence that medicine, science, and unexamined empiricism have become their common sense, leaving the insights and conclusions of anthropology or religious studies or arts and letters far behind. But to die ungrieved on a foreign shore, or unnoticed at home with the request "No services," is to die culturally naked. More recently, but in an equally wrong-headed fashion, consumerism has postulated that the most pressing question is how to get death done cheaply and without being gouged by the various professionals who have taken it over. Death will not be limited to economic rationalization.

Making meaning, producing culture, and naming God trump our physical nature. Giving preeminence to science and biologizing our very beings are themselves acts of cultural construction. Realizing this sets us free to carry on with the imagination and invention of death. We do not have to accept that at this time in human history we have come to a blind alley, that we are helpless victims of a modernity that has bequeathed us empty, unritualized deaths discontinuous with human history and unworthy of the human condition. We *can* get somewhere from here. At first improvising and moving haltingly forward, we can create or discover deaths adequate to the meanings we need. In rituals as great cultural performances, we can re-produce ourselves and offer the results of our ritualizations as a new cultural outpouring.

Through ritualization we can solidify, articulate, and display the recovery of a lost passage and bequeath it to culture and society. The ritual way is a way of retrieving dying and death, as well as living and life. In ritual constructions the world as real and the world as hoped for, ethos and mythos, can momentarily be fused.[3] To use structuralist language, the ritual way invites and practices mediating rather than disavowing the oppositions of life and death. The evasions and sublimations of mortality invite ritual resolutions that carry us beyond the present cultural impasse. As we seek to overlay our biological givens with new cultural constructions, we should look to ritual for the space and time for rehearsal, for the opportunity for trial and error in our world-construction and world-maintenance. Cognizant of the decay of mediating institutions in a contemporary America where neocapitalism has become the apotheosis of individualism, we may pause to recall a time when a densely rit-ualized culture produced a rich social life. How different our era is, for exam-ple, from the fourteenth century, when rituals, feasts, and festivals aplenty filled the eye with splendor and public spaces with a dynamic interplay of per-sons, communities, and experiences.[4] With many warrants for new construc-tions of death and with the promise of culture performing itself anew through ritual, we gain the courage to proceed.

A BRIEF NOTE ON THE AMERICAN FUNERAL

Sixty thousand years ago, as we know from excavations at Shanidar, Iraq, Neanderthals buried their dead with ceremony and included in their graves food, tools, and ornaments.[5] Some kind of burial rites may have existed since Lower Paleolithic times (500,000–250,000 B.C.). Today funerals range from the simplest comforting of a grieving widow within a small support community to rich liturgical celebrations in the life of religious communities.[6] "Funerals are the occasion for avoiding people or holding parties, for fighting or having sex-ual orgies, for weeping or laughing, in a thousand different combinations. The diversity of cultural reaction is a measure of the universal impact of death."[7]

The contemporary American funeral, overall the most elaborate in the industrialized West, offers a peculiar configuration of rapid removal of the corpse, embalming, institutionalized viewing, and disposal, most frequently by burial. While funerals once sent the deceased on their course, the preoccu-pation today is with the mourners. The unexamined truism is that "funerals are for the living."

We call funerals rites of passage, and they culturally mark status changes. They carry the mourners through stages of separation, then liminal transition, and finally reincorporation. Such transition rites have come to be seen as a uni-versal logic of human social life and by no means simply a relic of an earlier superstitious era. "The first movement opens up the way into death and the final one closes it up again. Only in the rite's central space does the door stand open, and the two worlds mingle in timeless confusion and fruitful chaos."[8]

In American funerals we see, sometimes only dimly, the traces of these stages, both for the dying and for the survivors. Stage one begins with the gradual separation from the living through anticipatory grieving and con-cludes with the medical declaration of physical death. Stage two begins with the rapid removal of the body and concludes with the funeral service, though today the latter typically does not preoccupy itself with the "journey" of the deceased. Stage three occurs when the new status of the deceased is declared:

"with God" or, committed to the ground or ashes, in the timeless world of the dead. For the living mourners, stage two is of unknown and unexamined length and is almost totally without social or cultural support. While this open-ended period of liminality typically can provide powerful, if also terrifying, threshold experiences, American culture suggests that suppressing grief and getting right back to work is "the best medicine." Typically, individuals are left to make their own way into the stage of reincorporating themselves into the life and community of society. There are no prescribed societal closures around the new status of the bereaved, nor any means of dealing with the "pollution" of the bereaved. So some individuals get stuck in melancholic grief, and others foolishly rush their reintegration.

An important exception to this carelessness in American culture is the ritually prescribed mourning period—an entire year following death—that many devout Jews still follow. From her daily journal, *Mornings and Mourning*, Esther Broner tells the inspiring, hilarious, poignant, depressing story of her attempt to honor her deceased father by saying the Kaddish, an eleven-month-long ritual of daily mourning usually performed by the eldest son.[9] As a somewhat eccentric and unorthodox woman performing a traditionally male task, she is faced daily with suspicion and hostility, and sometimes caring and friendship. Searching for connection and community, she persists against infuriating and heartbreaking odds. In *Mourning and Mitzvah*, Anne Brener provides sixty guided exercises for walking the Jewish mourner's path through grief to healing.[10]

It is easy enough to catalog the purposes of the funeral. Consider these six: provide a rite of passage for the soul of the deceased; offer a ritual way of disposing of the body; declare the dead person's status in society; help the survivors acknowledge their loss; help the survivors grieve; reaffirm the ability of the social system to exist after the loss of one of its members.[11] Funerals have social, psychological, and religious agendas.

The *religious* agenda sees a funeral as a service of worship that glorifies God by offering a kind of theodicy that fits God, humans, and death into a larger system of meaning. Christian funerals are witnesses to the hope of resurrection, while admonishing the living to "number our days and apply our hearts unto wisdom."[12] Secular societies have not been able to render the religious dimensions of the funeral irrelevant. In the modern West there is a remarkable persistence of religion, in spite of the predictions (or hopes) of sociologists. Death itself remains sacred even for moderns because we are ultimately helpless before it and unable to tame it. No more than early peoples do we understand the state of being dead. When medical technology finally fails in its campaign against death, we are at a loss as to how to proceed on the far side of this world. At the least, we may revert to "ceremonies of acceptance" provided by the funeral director.[13]

It is said today that the *social* function of funerals is no longer necessary. An early tradition in anthropology saw funerals as powerful antidotes to the centrifugal forces of fear, dismay, and demoralization, with the potential to provide powerful means of reintegrating a group's weakened solidarity and reestablishing shaken morale. Funeral rituals were thought to promote and maintain social forms, as the community acted in assembly to re-create its collective self-representation and strengthen the ties that held it together. Modern societies are no longer threatened by the death of their members (with such obvious exceptions as the death of a president or other great leader). A bureaucratic system makes people appear interchangeable and readily replaceable. Ceremonial recognition, no longer performing indispensable functions, wanes in the face of bureaucratic efficiency and rationality. Demographic shifts in American society have come to mean that the majority of those who die are no longer central to the stream of life. Their deaths have little consequence for the social order. Some scholars predicted that the American funeral would not only diminish, but eventually wither away.[14] Yet funerals are the chief ceremonies among the elderly and provide for them a key social setting and the possibility of reinforcing their membership in the community.[15] Is devaluing funerals yet another way of devaluing the elderly?

The decline of the social significance of funeral rituals leaves the *psychological* dimension preeminent. That most literature on death and dying follows the dominant psychological paradigm and the ready assumption that funerals are fundamentally about assuaging individual grief is evidence of this. Does the contemporary funeral answer the need expressed in Alexander Pope's couplet "Grief tears his heart and drives him to and fro, / In all the raging impotence of woe"?

Grief is the whole syndrome of responses to one's own dying or to the death of another. Whether it is rooted in infantile separation anxiety or whether anxiety about mortality is fundamental, we need not decide here. Depression, guilt, and hostility are often connected to it. The central feature of grief is the dying of part of one's self. Bereavement includes the amputation of part of the emotional structure of life. The task of the funeral is to initiate the mourners on the long journey of grief work. One view of an appropriate funeral sees it as providing an "experience in which a person can face the reality of what has happened, let memory become a part of the process of grieving, and, in the experience, express honest feelings, accept the community support that is freely proffered, and attempt to place the death in a context of meaning accept-able to the individual experiencing the trauma of separation."[16]

The American funeral has recently been criticized for its commercialism and materialism, but nearly every age has worried about and even legislated against excessive funeral expenses. There is also the question of whether a materialistic society will produce a materialistic funeral: We get the funerals we deserve and want. Funerals mirror cultural preoccupations and regnant values. More point-ed has been the pillorying of funeral directors as opportunists who take advan-tage of people in need. This was the great crusade Jessica Mitford began in her *The American Way of Death.* The Federal Trade Commission, in response, pro-duced its 1984 "Funeral Rule," requiring that funeral directors provide detailed information, itemized pricing, and legal requirements, so that consumers can make informed decisions. In fact, survey after survey reports a very high degree of satisfaction with funeral directors. In a number of surveys clergy seemed resentful at their displacement by funeral directors as ritual-stagers and grief counselors.[17] More cynically, it is also suggested that the public deals with guilt over relations with the deceased by paying lavish atonement money to the funeral director. The clergy believe such atonement should be worked out with God, but if psychology is the dominant paradigm, the funeral director will seem much closer. The most worrisome criticism of the funeral from the viewpoint of this book, and one that perhaps would arise only in an age of secular and eco-nomic rationalization, is that the religious, emotional, and economic obliga-tions of the funeral are simply burdensome and inappropriate.

The American funeral has not stopped evolving from earliest Puritan times to the present.[18] The undertaker changed from cabinetmaker or liveryman (furnisher of goods) to embalmer, businessman, professional, and grief coun-selor (provider of services). There is a corresponding evolution from body-shaped plain coffin to beautiful, form-denying casket; from shroud to attractive clothes; from private home to funeral parlor; from family-provided services to the purchase of services from professionals. If the earliest Puritan colonists suppressed ceremonies and emotion, already by the late seventeenth century there were elaborations: washing and laying out the corpse, fine gloves for all attending, church bells, feasting. When religious rites were pro-scribed (in the Puritan protest against the elaborate liturgical forms of Angli-canism and Roman Catholicism), social rites ran ahead. Eventually both became elaborate. Eighteenth-century laws were not able to prevent extrava-gance, although funerals regained simplicity on the frontier. During and after the Civil War embalming developed into a common custom, and by the end of the nineteenth century undertaking had become a common business.

Why is the American funeral what it is today? Philippe Ariès is confused by the American funeral, which does not seem to fit his theory that the proscribing of attentiveness to death fits hand in glove with modernity. He finds us to be a death-denying culture, just as Europe is, but the American funeral is much more elaborate than he would have expected, full of commercial exploitation and the perversions of a cult of happiness.[19] More, the American funeral looks like a denial of the absolute finality of death and a sign of repugnance toward physical destruction, but without the accompaniment of ritual and solemnity. The taboo on death is broken. The embalmed body is displayed in a neutral setting, and its purpose is to play down death and give the appearance of life. Americans turn the deceased into the living in order to pay tribute one last time. They honor the dead while refusing the status of death. Are these the meanings that readers of this book have taken away from funerals they have attended?

Other students of the American funeral do not draw such radical conclusions. Two paradoxes in the American rituals of death trouble Metcalf and Huntington in their survey of death practices across time and cultures.[20] The first is that throughout American culture they find a remarkable ritual uniformity, but one grounded in an indeterminate ideology. They wonder whether this can be explained by economics (it's all a product of capitalism and materialist values, from the funeral parlor to embalming) or psychology (it's due to fear of death and guilt). The second paradox they call "puppet death." In an activist culture where the individualized actor is celebrated above all, the individual is inexplicably reduced to a dramaturgically passive role in dying. All significant action is consigned to professionals, from physicians to morticians.

Or is the American funeral consistent with the "instrumental activism" typical of the American cultural orientation and the American response to death one of realistic and calm social acceptance and control?[21] What if American funeral practices are congruent with prevailing cultural assumptions but, at the same time, plainly inadequate to the human condition? "The symbol system of the society fails to correspond to the exigencies of the human reality."[22] Is it true that we live amidst a cultural system "that systematically relegates the dying to indignity, humiliation, and oblivion because it cannot stand to be reminded of its own poverty of resources before death"?[23]

What conclusions will anthropologists in the future draw from these facts, particularly regarding embalming? How much of contemporary funeral ritual represents artifacts left over from another time and how much is genuinely disclosive of significant, pervasive cultural needs and goals of the present? In 1990 Paul Irion surveyed the most recent evolution of the American funeral and made the following summary and evaluation of the new funeral orders that were developing. In terms of the goals of this book, are these contemporary trends promising?[24]

1. The new funeral orders manifest an integrated, more comprehensive understanding of the function of ritual.
2. The emerging new orders see the funeral as community function, not as private exercise.
3. The new funeral services show awareness of the importance of facing the reality of death.
4. The funeral is set within the context of the mourning process.
5. They are responsive to the dynamics of pluralism.
6. Corollary to the encouragement of broad participation, the new funeral orders recognize that there are ministries other than that of the clergy.

DEFINING AND APPRECIATING RITUAL

Ritual provides a way to recover and display ourselves as fully human. In rituals we make ourselves fully real, and we interact with the real that is everywhere around us. Neither marginal nor optional, ritual is one of the constitutive means through which we articulate who we are and what we want to become. Over the course of a culturally rich life and drawing on multiple traditions, we may develop "a virtual repertoire of ritual capacities together with both individual and collective resourcefulness in mobilizing them."[25]

To open the imagination to ritual, I begin with Roland Delattre's definition: "Those carefully rehearsed symbolic motions and gestures through which we regularly go, in which we articulate the felt shape and rhythm of our own humanity and of reality as we experience it, and by means of which we negotiate the terms or conditions for our presence among and our participation in the plurality of realities through which our humanity makes its passage."[26] Thus, ritual involves (1) going through motions and gestures; (2) articulating human reality; (3) negotiating relationships; and (4) passage.

Thoreau saw in carefully rehearsed motions a spiritually formative power. To resist the distracting commotion of life, he proposed to dwell in the world according to the rhythms of an alternative reality, and ritually to renew the resources for such a life by frequent journeys upon the inward sea. Susanne Langer called this capacity of rituals "a disciplined rehearsal of 'right attitudes.'"[27] Without rituals, we lack "mental anchorage."[28] With them, we bring together how things are and how things are done. Effective rituals provide a directed process of spiritual formation.

Ritual also brings to expression aspects of humanity and of experienced reality that remain otherwise unarticulated. In an age tempted to believe that only the inner life of the individual is real, ritual expounds a life and realities that go beyond the self's feelings. Because it opens us to self-transcendence, *ritual should be understood less for what it achieves than for its capacity to make significant achievement possible.* We come to such achievements in the context of a community of other ritual actors who together discover that meaningful action is possible. In creative ritualizations we work ourselves out. Ritual inarticulateness and incompetence are thus a real detriment to and deprivation of human development, while "ritual resourcefulness is among the principal conditions for whatever success we may enjoy" in constructing coherent culture.[29]

Ritual further provides a formative way among the competing claims of experience and circumstances of life. Through ritual we work out our relations between sacred and secular, individual and society, family and polity, thought and feeling, public and private, physical bodies and social bodies, structure and process, ethos and worldview.[30] A ritual storehouse of such achievements becomes a ritual powerhouse.

Finally, ritual negotiates "*the human passage through the world, which from another perspective is also the world's passage through our humanity.*"[31] The liminality of ritual passage is the marginal, negotiable, subjunctive, structurally impoverished, symbolically enriched threshold of experience it proffers. On that threshold, as the cultural richness of the world passes through us, we are offered the opportunity for creative articulations of our humanity and of the (sacred) reality that surrounds us.

Ritual is less a monument at the end of a road than a road to a monument. "Ritual is, first and foremost, a mode of paying attention. It is a process of marking interest."[32] It is not so much a response to the sacred as a means by which we make something or someone sacred. The space marked off by ritual becomes a focusing lens: We begin directing attention through it in new and more intense ways.[33] Thus it is through ritual that we pay attention to death and give death its due, acknowledge its mystery, mark its difference, render it sacred, link the world of the living with the world of the dead. We provide a place where we can take death with ultimate seriousness. Through ritual we rediscover, create, install, re-place such a place. In that safe place, we set about to dis-place the ordinary variables of life that overpower us and perform the way things ultimately are.[34]

Three gifts of ritual, in Tom Driver's rendering, are order, community, and transformation. Ritual does not merely remind individuals of an underlying *order* in the cosmos; it establishes such an order and makes it palpable.[35] How so? Through the creation of "shared worlds" and ritual's rendering of "part for the whole," participants glimpse, touch, and taste an imagined universe. Conversely, this imagined universe depends upon ritual for its instantiation. "Ritual performs the world, bringing it from chaos and the limbo of potentiality into actualized (actionful) form."[36]

Rituals establish a social world and restore it when it has weakened—above all through death. This reordering capacity of ritual is profound. In the daily life of religious communities, liturgical orders "unite, or reunite, the psychic, social, natural, and cosmic orders which language and the exigencies of life pull apart."[37] Even the idea of a Word that orders the universe arises from the order-establishing power of ritual performance. Creation was a liturgy through which God brought the world into being. As ritual establishes transcendent order, it expresses and discloses the sacred. Sometimes it relativizes or even mocks temporal order, intimating "an order that transcends time, an ultimate or absolute order of which the temporal order is merely a contingent part. . . . Liturgy's challenges to the temporal are in the service of the ultimate, for they keep the conventions of time and place in their places by demonstrating that they are not ultimately sacred."[38] This is true above all at deathbeds and funerals, where rituals enact and proclaim truths that contradict obvious reality and point beyond it. Events, including death, come to be seen *sub specie aeternitatis*.

Ritual's second gift is *community*. When we come together in ritual, we are effectively united. "A ritual is a party at which emotions are welcome. If the emotions are too strong, threatening to swamp the party, the ritual scenario can be used to guide and moderate them; and if the emotions are too weak, draining the event of its energy, the ritual can invoke them."[39] Ritual separates us from everyday roles and statuses and carries us across a threshold into the "what if" or "as if," where structure is weak but symbol strong. Here we encounter what Victor Turner named *communitas*, the soul or essence of ritual, a state of "antistructure," a potentiality for a deep I-Thou connectedness, a spirit of unity and mutual belonging. When ritual is most powerful it unites the world of the living with the world of the dead, bringing together two communities into one. Such a ritually empowered community is the only one that can give us the death, and the life, we need.

Transformation is ritual's third gift. We should seek to restore magic to religion as its inner ritual power. "When people divorce religion from magic they end up with metaphysics on the one hand, empirical science on the other, and religion gone."[40] Two truths are best discovered through ritual: that the sacred has a personal character and should be addressed performatively; and that without such performance communal life is drained of power.[41] We perform rituals as if everything is alive and personal. The "social magic" of rituals, their character as "transformative performance," comes from their power to envision a reordering of the world, to expose societal and cultural contradictions, to effect reversals, to imagine, "to give to aery nothing a local habitation and a name."[42]

Through ritual attentiveness we create the space we need to articulate and constitute our humanity. Ritualizing, we engage in the larger work of culture. When the ritualization of death and dying is neglected or ignored, we leave unfinished business, indispensable work undone, opportunity unfulfilled. In ritual, participants "attain their faith as they portray it."[43] Within ritual actions, "the world as lived and the world as imagined, fused under the agency of a single set of symbolic forms, turn out to be the same world."[44] It is no small capability to hold together the worlds of the living and of the dead, the worlds of faith and biological givenness, the worlds that we are and that we seek to be. This drama plays against a backdrop of chaos. The "undiscovered country" of death sends humans on religious quests and floods us with metaphysical anxiety. In such crises, more than passive endurance is called for. Ritual turns sufferers and endurers into participants and actors. We cross thresholds into alternative orders of existence. The results are long-lasting: The dispositions that such rituals induce may have their most important impact "outside the boundaries of the ritual itself, as they reflect back to color the individual's conception of the established world of bare fact."[45] Under the disclosive power of ritual and the satisfaction of expressive ritual action, humans move back and forth between ritual and everyday life, between reflecting and reforming their world.

If ritual is the means through which we constitute our humanity, we may also come to see, with many ritual scholars, that ritualizing is both our *evolutionary possibility* and our *evolutionary task*, deeply embedded in animal nature and handed forward to us as ritualizing animals. Clifford Geertz[46] argued that some form of human culture appeared before physical evolution stopped, and that nature and culture must have proceeded together. Culture became a part of human development before the evolution of the brain was complete. Thus, human nature does not precede culture; *humanization occurs along cultural pathways*. What it would mean to be *Homo sapiens* continued to unfold through culture. Ritualization, a dimension of animal and human, nature and culture, is a vital means through which human evolution continues and humanization achieves new completions. In this ongoing process, ritual does not only store and repeat the known, but extends the frontier.

Consider, then, ritualization as an evolutionary mandate. What vistas does this open up? I have argued that finishing one's life story should be taken up as the defining task of a last career. We should commission the elderly to take up such a last career, to finish their own stories and to bequeath them as gifts to the culture that follows. What if old age could be unfolded as a new evolutionary stage in which cultural rather than genetic development is waiting to occur? What if the richness of culture is as important as the human genome?

If the human life span has had a one-hundred-year biological potential for a very long time, if the actual life span has lengthened dramatically only during the last two centuries, if in precivilization the last third of the genetically programmed human life span was only a potential and not a reality, then one might entertain a remarkable conclusion: "The human genome was formed largely during the millions of years of prehuman and human evolution when old age was virtually nonexistent. Under these conditions, strengths or weaknesses after age sixty-five could play no role in natural selection." Thus: "Old age, in comparison to youth, may be a period of the human life cycle which is relatively less guided by our genes and relatively more susceptible to manipulation. Biologic evolution has permitted our species to reach age one hundred, but it is cultural evolution—creation of a favorable environment—that will convert this potential to a reality."[47] If death is a cultural construction, if ritualization is an evolutionary mandate for the work of culture, if the last third of the possible human life cycle is particularly poised for cultural work, then *the elderly, privileged with time for a new career, might commit themselves to the recovery of a lost passage through a new ritual outpouring into culture.* It is past time that we offer the aging a ritual "prophetic anointing" for just such a task.[48]

Ritualizing is evolutionary, inevitable, culture-producing, humanization-completing, imaginal, creative. It is central to a human rhythm of change and conservation: pathway and shelter, verb and noun.[49] In ritual we do it all: we are creator and interpreter, speaker and audience, actor and spectator, maker and consumer; there is no longer a distinction between composer and performer. "There is usually a 'conductor,' a master of ceremonies, a chief priest, a central protagonist, whose actions provide the temporal markers for everyone else. But there is no separate audience of listeners. The performers and the listeners are the same people. *We engage in rituals in order to transmit collective messages to ourselves.*"[50] We become human by learning the ritual repertoire of the human community.

RITUAL PROBLEMS AND PROMISES

All this might lead one to expect that individuals, minorities, dominant cultures, religious communities, and governments all would be engaged in a headlong rush to capitalize on the power of ritual. This is scarcely the case. Rituals have fallen on hard times, and the encounter with death has steadily become deritualized in modern times. Why? Everything from secularism to ecclesiastical fussiness is blamed.

Secularism and modernity are commonly thought to provide inhospitable ground for ritual. Max Weber described a secularizing "disenchantment of the world" characterized by the ascendancy of modes of thought based on empirical observation, technical mastery, and scientific knowledge—none of them fertile ground for ritual.[51] In America such a world combined with "middle-class values," a bureaucratic ethos, an anticeremonial and classless society, and frontier plainness and simplicity to produce a worldview hostile to ritual and its meanings and agendas. The bureaucratic ethos holds that activities must have some extrinsic end or they have no value. "Expressive" values give way to "instrumental" values. Ritual gestures do not engender quantifiable results. They do not yield to cost-benefit analyses. For rationalism and positivism, rituals are sentimental or merely imaginal. Rituals seem at best playful and at worst subversive; we prefer to stay closer to the social shore.[52]

Ritual life may suffer where individual autonomy is emphasized and pressure to conform to community norms is weak. The triumph of individualism throughout Western cultures provides the antithesis of the climate conducive to ritual work. Modern individuals assume ritual must be about self-expression; they cannot imagine "participation in expressive action whose meaning ultimately steps beyond immediate social life and connects with the timeless truths of the gods."[53] Once public life itself was a kind of ritual. Then individual personality intruded and belief in the public domain declined. Everything came to depend on intentions. "The self of motivations intervenes in an intimate society to block people from feeling free to play with the presentation of feelings as objective, formed signs. Expression is made contingent upon authentic feeling, but one is always plunged into the narcissistic problem of never being able to crystalize what is authentic in one's feelings."[54] Many decline to participate in funerals because they are suspicious of their own or other participants' feelings. Funeral rituals that invite public mourning become awkward, if not impossible, for people who believe grief is only private and personal.

The devaluation of ritual was rooted in the emergent social sciences of the nineteenth century, and in much of Protestantism before that.[55] Magic, science, and religion were seen as mutually exclusive; true religion occurred rationally between the individual and God, the world was left to science, and magic was a vestigial embarrassment.[56] Protestantism had arisen, in part, as a massive protest against the eclipse of the Word by medieval ritual. "The Puritan preference for word to the exclusion of rite was based on an anthropology that granted priority to the individual over the community, to mind over body, and to the conscious over the unconscious."[57] Freud saw religious ritual as a public counterpart of private obsessive practices.

Religious communities and traditions must bear some of the blame for the decline of ritual. Liturgical commissions produce static, dogmatic, text-based liturgies, using time but not space, theology but not the arts, privileging words but granting no quarter to the "epistemological primacy of body." Rituals can fail gesturally, posturally, and actionally, just as they can fail theologically or ethically.[58] It is time to acknowledge that even liturgical affirmations in words are more performances than statements. Effective liturgy and ritual are always "more than words can tell."

Protestant rationalism and Roman Catholic sacerdotalism have done harm to ritual, one displacing it with doctrinal discourse and the other manipulating it for clerical hegemony. Liberation theology, however, sees in ritual the potential to produce social change, to form a community and lead it to its commitment in history.[59] But too often the sacraments become the *gift* of the ordained to the laity. Rituals lose their legitimacy if their sponsoring institutions have lost theirs. Protestantism stripped the funeral ritual of all eschatological purpose. Protestant doctrine meant that each generation could be indifferent to the spiritual fate of its predecessor. Individuals kept their own accounts; no one could receive atonement through the prayers of descendants. Societal relationships were atomistic. Life no longer looked to death for its perspective.[60] No longer tied to the world of the dead, death ritual steadily lost utility for the mourners.

Apart from historical and doctrinal changes in the life of the churches, certain attitudes about ritual itself throw up impediments to effective and authentic ritual life. It is well known how frequently and wonderfully liturgical niceties and liturgical etiquette are mocked, inside and outside of church life. This is typified by the story, probably apocryphal, that the Russian Orthodox hierarchy was debating the length of vestments while the revolution was brewing. "Rubricism" refers to a religious mind-set in which liturgy and ritual come to be about performing received traditions correctly, divorcing ritual from the vital and changing lives of real people and communities. Ritual becomes less a celebratory feast than an obsession about recipes.

But ritual will have its ways. Its promise may be reasserted in unexpected quarters. As W. H. Auden said: "Human beings are by nature actors, who cannot become something until first they have pretended to be it. They are therefore to be divided, not into the hypocritical and the sincere, but into the sane, who know they are acting, and the mad who do not."[61] One expression of our alienation from ritual life is that we forget that rituals are human cultural constructions, the result of our own human activity over time and space. If the culture of secular modernity or of historic religions does not produce fertile ground for ritual fulfillment and evolution, then alternative (sub)cultures and institutions will be found or created. In the late twentieth century ritual is resurfacing.

Any urban bookstore today is likely to carry Michael Harner's *The Way of the Shaman,* an argument for new realms of spirit when the Age of Faith is over.[62] The author claims to be "bringing into personal life the paradigmatic consequences of two centuries of the scientific method." Shamanism is a methodology, not a religion, and its methods work surprisingly quickly, he blithely assures his readers, achieving in a few hours what might take years of silent meditation, prayer, and chanting. Thus it is ideally suited to the lives of busy people. To work, it does not require faith or changed assumptions regarding ordinary reality.

There are more credible approaches. Parashamanism is a term for the religiosity of countercultural movements. Its distinctive characteristic is its "penchant for inventing, borrowing, and performing ritual in search of healing, which is understood holistically or ecologically to be a state of integrated selfhood."[63] Such invented rites have their liabilities, chief among them "spiritual consumerism" (workshop-to-workshop collection of rituals that are never fully digested), cultural imperialism (indiscriminate appropriation of the sacred resources of other cultures), and spiritual experimentalism (tasting but not testing). At its best, shamanism is an invitation back to a dimension of ritual mostly lost through the triumph of static religious institutions and priestly power.[64] The shaman invokes; the priest represents. Revitalization of religious ritual may require overcoming the dominance of the priestly type by moving again toward the shamanic.

Neopaganism and new religions of the goddess have conspicuously attempted to create, rediscover, and improvise new rituals—to escape the repression they experience in patriarchal rituals or to recover a ritual life long suppressed by major Western religions. In the anthology *Magical Religion and Modern Witchcraft,* a folklorist aptly titles her chapter "Ritual Is My Chosen Art Form: The Creation of Ritual as Folk Art Among Contemporary Pagans."[65] Authenticity is sought in an ancient past whose ethos was close to the earth. Folklore offers a romantic recovery of such a past. Typically, New Age rituals are collaborative productions; there is a low degree of separation between leader and congregation. Neopagans are conscious of foregrounding ritual within a dominant culture that is inimical to it, above all because they seek personal and planetary healing and transformation. Equally important for those seeking historical links, rituals appear to be the sole and most promising remnant of pre-Christian religions. Folk rituals survive forgotten or suppressed doctrine. Restaging such rituals of the past induces feelings of timelessness and liminality—and a reconnection with nature.

For neopagans art and ritual are inseparable; ritual is likened to performance art. Some Wiccans refer to their religion as "the Craft," a metaphor for ritual and artistic creativity. The encouragement of ritual improvisation, of course, produces variety—rituals that are transformative and powerfully participatory, rituals that are pedantic, rituals that go on forever, rituals that don't work. No matter how participatory and collaborative, many such rituals nevertheless depend on creative facilitators. Some typically look to living folk traditions, some to the experiences and scholarship of academic culture (Frazer's *Golden Bough* and Campbell's work on myth and symbol), to popular psychology (from inner child to Jungian archetypes), to mass media and popular culture (*Star Trek* or the ethnographies of the Discovery Channel), and to their own intuitions and imaginations. All come together in the process of *bricolage,* combining disparate elements into an artistic whole. Rituals are created for and evolve by means of the many neopagan festivals and the networking so common to the movement. Ritual training workshops are common.

Will ritual artists become the new unacknowledged legislators of the world? Will the ritual vacuum be filled with empty art or with imaginings adequate to human need? What are the chances we will overcome the ritual deprivation of recent centuries? Does the capacity of ritualization to evolve carry its own promise?

RITUAL EVOLUTION

Rituals change. Rituals effect change. That is the driving presupposition of this book. We must see that rituals are human products and that we can therefore give ourselves permission to improvise new rituals that will respond to death in ways that are more adequate to the human condition as we experience it.[66]

First, we ought to recover a sense of ourselves as ritual actors.[67] A study of Yoruba ritual tries to move toward an African orientation that "assumes the instrumentality of performers in invoking or even breaking rules, producing structures, and mobilizing resources and support."[68] Never merely rigid, conservative, and structurally static, ritual also allows for transformative performances by human agents.[69] Empowered ritual actors and new rituals can pour new meaning into culture and accomplish the work of culture that is now neglected or ignored. Culture and society themselves become subject to change. Changing rituals bring about social and cultural change.

The essays collected in *The Invention of Tradition* startlingly illustrate this.[70] There are illuminating studies of the invention of the highland tradition of Scotland and of Welsh traditions as vital elements of nationalistic or ethnic consciousness. Other essays demonstrate how new rituals are invented to demonstrate power and authority in colonial India and Africa. Most surprising is the demonstration that the royal rituals of the British monarchy that so charm and impress late-twentieth-century television audiences were only invented in the late nineteenth century. In his introduction to this collection, Eric Hobsbawm calls "invented traditions" those that were "actually invented, constructed, and formally instituted and those emerging in a less easily traceable manner within a brief and dateable period . . . and establishing themselves with great rapidity."[71] (Americans were startled to learn in the summer of 1996 that most of the Olympic ceremonies they believed to be historic legacies had existed for only several decades, and that not a few originated in the 1936 Olympic Games in Nazi Germany.) The rituals of these invented traditions seek to establish continuity with a suitable historic past and to inculcate certain values and norms of behavior. In fact, these rituals did not originate in the mists of time, but are responses to new situations that take the form of reference to old situations. The comparatively recent historical innovation, the nation-state, has had to invent traditions that are "exercises in social engineering . . . often deliberate and always innovative."[72]

The final chapter of *The Invention of Tradition* surveys the forty years before World War I as a particularly fertile time for the invention of traditions. This was a period of profound and rapid social transformations that demanded new ways to express social cohesion and structure social relations. For an emergent modern France, for example, the invention of traditions came to include secular equivalents of the Church, public ceremonies (the celebration of Bastille Day can be dated to 1880, ninety-one years after its actual occurrence), and prolific public monuments. Germany, England, and America had also invented mythological figures: Deutsche Michel, John Bull, and Uncle Sam. The Fourth of July and Thanksgiving Day were marshaled to turn immigrants into Americans, and from the 1880s onward the American flag was worshiped in every American school. The rituals of nationalism, especially for emergent middle classes, became a new secular religion, a substitute for the social cohesion achieved typically through a national church, a royal family, or other such cohesive tradition. Transnational labor movements discovered May Day in 1890, though not in the United States. While traditions can be invented and thus manipulated, the most successful inventions are those that meet a felt need. Such traditions escape the control of their inventors.

Theory followed. Victor Turner associated himself with a shift in theoretical emphasis in anthropology "from structure to process, from competence to performance, from the logics of cultural and social systems to the dialectics of socio-cultural processes."[73] This postmodern turn emphasizes the processualization of space in contrast to the spatialization of process. Movement and process became more important to the anthropological observer than system and stasis. Kelly and Kaplan argue that the 1990s are producing a theory of ritual as part of history making in all societies.[74] Rituals can be acts of power in the fashioning of structures, in the building of definitions. The special power of ritual acts lies in the *lack* of independence asserted by the ritual participant. It is the limits on individual agency in ritual presentations that make the larger claims for ritual possible. We are constantly entering and exiting ritual roles in which our action is authorized outside of ourselves, and that is how we remake some forms of authority and disempower others. Practice has usurped structure as the reigning image of the real in anthropology. The new question is the place of ritual and structure in practice. Rituals in ongoing practice are a principal site of new history being made. A history of rituals, then, is a history of the reproduction, contestation, transformation, and deconstruction of authority. Social process is performative.[75]

In this book I have moved from *description to diagnosis to prescription.* I have been arguing that the ritualization of death in America is inadequate, that we face death with resources woefully small for death's magnitude, that the present inadequacy of the American death system is a social drama requiring redress. That drama offers a contemporary plot for a much-needed evolution of death rituals in our society. As ritual evolution occurs it may become the means through which we recover a death of our own.

Death, then, presents us with opportunities, if also problems.[76] Death, if we do not look away, invites us to construct and discover the rituals we need. How do we proceed? Rituals have life spans; they surge and subside.[77] We might call for a new category of public servant, "civic magician," who would become expert at designing public celebrations.[78] We must let rituals gestate, not rush too fast to construct them.[79] Nor, as I hinted above, should the search for openings to transcendence in death be restricted to "official religious traditions." We must also "include variant experiences of sacred power and patterns of religious behavior that may beset a culture in convulsive change and turmoil."[80] There are experiments in classrooms.[81] Turner was often concerned by the great distance between the academic study of ritual and religious participation in it, especially if academic meant "detached" and religious meant "naive." Drama and play are third, mediating possibilities that do not force such dualistic choices.

It would be a painful irony if churches (and other religious institutions), with their long histories rich in symbol and ritual and theological interpretation, were unwilling or unable to participate, if not take the lead, in ritual improvisation and evolution. Their historical traditions and communities should preserve them from vapid creations and culture-bound technicization of the sacred but could also excuse or prevent them from undertaking new imaginings. Are religious communities up to it? Christian sacramental performance should be liberating and open to God's comings. "Far from standing quiet in the dead seriousness of a funeral, or even the high seriousness of a museum, and far from confining itself to the safety of good taste, a sacrament of the grace of Christ tends toward improvisation and irony."[82] We should hope for ritual effervescence in "the freedom of the performance situation." Churches should break open their ritual forms and be broken open by them, precisely because their rituals celebrate the breaking of bondage. "Christian sacraments celebrate something that is humanly absurd, something literally unbelievable and beyond all worldly expectation. The sacraments are about deliverance from oppression, including the grip of death. The outlandishness of this in the face of our natural mortality and in the presence of pervasive human misery is what puts the sacraments in an ironic relation to their own tradition. Full of tradition, the sacraments are not fully at home inside tradition."[83] We must not value their form more than their spirit.

A "liturgical movement" has been under way within Christian churches for many decades now. Liturgical renewal began blossoming in the Roman Catholic tradition in the 1960s, evoked by the Second Vatican Council, and soon migrated through Protestantism as well. Most of the church bodies have in the last three decades produced new liturgies. Indeed, a flood of liturgical innovation washed over church life, some of it blessed and some unblessed by ecclesiastical authorities. While these innovators have been attentive to recovering earlier textual traditions, they almost completely ignore all other dimensions of ritual. The more adventuresome liturgies—and many embarrassing failures—arose from individual communities and clergy working at the margins.

Human Rites: Worship Resources for an Age of Change collects these new "liturgies from the ground up."[84] The editors solicited from eighty correspondents rituals for occasions or circumstances not catered to in the churches' prayer books. They reflect public worship settings and small, idiosyncratic community needs. Especially do they reflect a breaking down of barriers between liturgy providers and liturgy users. The Anglican editors assume that liturgy will be open to change because one of its chief functions is to help people with changes, as through rites of passage. They hope to inspire and not only to provide ready-made "alternative liturgies." They refer to *human* rites because they emphasize the capability of liturgy to be humanized, and they want to give people permission to mark changes in ways fully concrete and suitable to themselves.

The several death-and-dying rituals in this collection are more about doing through words than doing through ritual actions, but they do coax along concrete actions of human caring: expressing love through conversations, touching, sharing favorite things; remembering through naming and making; sharing through doing and being; participating in practical things such as writing a will or planning how and where to die. There are evocations of crying and ways to say good-bye. There are many special prayers, especially for infants who have died, for the stillborn, and for mothers who have suffered miscarriage. While these human rites are gentle and human and evocative, they also show how completely tied most of our ritual imagination still is to words.

There are also promising signs among the professional liturgists working in the churches. They are trying to restore the integrity of the discipline of liturgics and to move toward authentic ritualization that transcends both ritual as fussy etiquette and ritual as mindless repetition. Tripp tries to recover the connection between liturgy and pastoral practice.[85] First, he reminds us that theology and scripture and perhaps even ethics emerge out of worship. Therefore reflection about and education for ritual and worship must proceed in critical dialog with biblical studies, church history, ethics, and constructive theology— and they with ritual studies.[86] Second, he wants unambiguously to reconnect ritual to the laity, because worship and ritual life express and realize the calling of the laity and connect the holy to the material. Lay alienation from ritual should become a vital sign of tension in religious communities and perhaps, then, a new locus of revelation. (It occurs to me that rituals should be seen as the canary in the coal mine. When they begin gasping, radical action is necessary.) Third, he insists on essential connections between liturgy/ritual and the role of the ministry. All ministry is essentially liturgical, and it derives its mission and role from ritual need. Fourth, a religious community realizes itself and expresses its "marks" through worship/liturgy/ritual. If troubling, it may also be beneficial that in ritual actions churches express their unity and their disunity. Proliferation and diversity of rites are inevitable and should occasion the fostering and guiding of creativity. Ritual evolution should be conscious but not contrived, and always a call to faith and authentic living (and dying). Finally, he wants to reconnect religious ritual communities with the world community, by emphasizing that any and every community is also a ritual community. Thus religious communities must acknowledge and confront all other communities. Conversing with and challenging the pretensions of secular communities and their assertions, the religious ritual community becomes an invitation for healing and wholeness.[87] Religious ritual is fed by vigorous culture dialog and itself enriches, challenges, and corrects culture.[88] If all this is true, then ritual learning must be central to every religious community.

Aidan Kavanagh, a Benedictine monk teaching liturgy at Yale, provides a clever, wry critique and commentary on contemporary liturgical renewal. While occasionally a bit fussy himself, he offers advice that could contribute to healthy ritual evolution. He begins with ten affirmations:

1. Tradition and a certain good order are qualities of Christian liturgical usage.
2. The liturgy is hierarchically structured.
3. The liturgy is an act of the Church.
4. The liturgy requires focal points in space and time which are constant and stable, and which have about them a certain sober splendor.
5. The fundamental criterion against which all liturgical things, words, gestures, and persons are measured is the liturgical assembly.
6. The liturgy happens in space and time.
7. The liturgy is neither a text nor an audio-visual aid.
8. The liturgy forms but does not educate.
9. Because the liturgy is a species of the genus ritual, it is rhythmic and repetitive.
10. The liturgy assumes the closest correlation between visual, sonic, and kinetic media of expression.[89]

There follows much pithy advice. Avoid disorder and last-minute improvisation. Let liturgical ministers preside within the assembly, not over it. Do not clericalize the liturgy. Ritual activity is a cool medium that seduces people into common activity; electronic media are hot and isolate people into passivity. Rituals do not educate, but free people to learn things that cannot be taught. Ritual reverence is a virtue, not a neurosis; God can take care of himself. Ritual is essentially antistructural and exists to undercut and overthrow the very structures it uses. Archaism is a form of antistructure: It is not the obsolete but the equivalent of the unconscious, and ritual exists to conjure it. When ritual completely loses its archaism, it becomes so adapted to contemporary culture that it looks like the PTA or a political caucus. Liturgy is to the divine logos, as style is to meaning. Ritual style is not to be abjured; it "intensifies meaning and injects it into the larger experience of the race, freeing imagination and overwhelming the emotions and senses along the way."[90] Ritual style lets the worshipers escape into the open. Style raises meaning to revelation. "What one witnesses in the liturgy is the world being done as the world's Creator and Redeemer will the world to be done. The liturgy does the world and does it at its very center, for it is here that the world's malaise and its cure well up together, inextricably entwined."[91] If God issues logos, not rules for ritual (rubrics), then the task of the assembly is to find the ways to bespeak logos, and not merely tinker with ceremonies.[92]

Kavanagh speaks sharply against both ritual rigidity and ritual looseness. The former is a regression into fantasy born of an obsessive fear of risk and ambiguity, but authentic ritual is shot through with the ambiguity of metaphor and symbol. The latter offers a breeziness of uninhibited expression rooted in the "spontaneous me," but joy, meaning, reality all lie deeper. "Liturgy sympathizes with its culture's plight, but it never seeks to give cheap or superficial fixes for its culture's wants. The liturgy's duty is to enflesh and serve *logos*."[93] True ritualizing is not the gifted poet who gives it up to write doggerel for television commercials. It transcends the trendy, or it dies at its hands.

Even the best contemporary efforts still lack a full ritual imagination. Could it be that mainstream Christianity and its liturgical governors need to recover lost gifts, gifts more at home in some marginalized communities, just as classical music has need of the improvisatory power of jazz? Consider Yoruba ritual, remnants of whose tradition persist among African-Americans: "Periodically repeated, unscripted performance—including most ritual, music, and dance in Africa—is improvisational. Most performers—maskers, dancers, diviners, singers, and drummers alike—have been trained from childhood in particular techniques enabling them to play spontaneously with learned, in-body formulas."[94] Needless to say, we are a very, very long way from such a practice or even such a readiness in Christian liturgical celebrations.

The longing for ritual liberation has recently produced feminist criticisms of existing rituals and feminist pioneering of new rituals.[95] There are good reasons. The obvious is the historic use of ritualizations constructed and performed by men to keep women marginalized. Another is that dealing with death is something of a gendered experience. Men die first, and women take care of them.

Surely a first step, taken decisively but not without powerful resistance, is the use of inclusive language in rituals that depend on received texts. In many Christian churches, this first meant that the texts of hymns and of the liturgy were revised to eliminate exclusively masculinist forms. Jewish feminists have made similar moves, ranging from liturgies performed by women alone to attempts to alter the common traditions. Eventually a need for inclusive language in the biblical texts was recognized. First there were inclusive-language lectionaries, which amended the texts typically read in worship. Much more recently there has appeared an inclusive-language Bible. But more than linguistic revolutions are needed if ritual is to be inclusive and not exclusive, if it is to empower and not to marginalize.

An article entitled "The Missing Element of Women's Experience" begins with Adrienne Rich's admonition to women that they study their lives, take themselves more seriously, refuse to accept common incantations, and give themselves to silence or a "severer listening."[96] For centuries or even millennia women have been circumscribed with ritual texts that were androcentric and sometimes misogynist. Men have preserved and transmitted ritual traditions. Male experience was the primary reflection of divine-human relationships. To these rituals, women may need to offer a severer listening, or even silence— that is, absence. Besides the linguistic elements that need revision, styles of embodiment, the authority of ritual leaders and ritual texts, and styles and metaphors of connection are areas of ritual requiring feminist critique. It is just such ritual imagination that has been lacking in the work of professional liturgists. Most churchly liturgies continue to pay little or no attention to the epistemological primacy of the body.

Feminists are at work revising the male-biased bases of culture. One way is the creation of rituals to promote and sanction a turning away from the old to the new. "As in traditional societies, feminist ritual provides an emotional, descriptive, intensified and sanctifying version of emergent ideological systems. Feminist ritual offers an imagistic revitalization for women and a participation in the concrete, bodily expressive creation of new images of the feminine which helps alleviate the stress of liminality."[97] Women are using ritual means to gain and transfer power precisely because men have used rituals as "their most profound display of cultural authority and their most direct access to it."[98] Men have used rituals to warrant their creation and definition of culture and to exclude women and keep them in their place. They have created sacred space and denied women access to it. Making their own claims, women have seized ritual as a source of power, vision, and solidarity. "In the context of ritual women are creating a space in which to feel better, to feel more, to feel the past as well as the future."[99] For these women, ritual provides a formalized consecration of female bonding and offers them a visceral language for the restoration of symbols that are vital. The ritual turn to the body is particularly important. The "out-of-place," alienated, polluting body of woman, in the midst of the embodied community, raises to critical consciousness the need for feminist liturgies that pioneer the introduction of woman's body into hitherto androcentric ritual.

Evolving rituals shaped by women for women show certain distinctive characteristics.[100] Women can become the subjects of the liturgy, the ones who shape and lead. Such rituals are in constant tension between tradition and freedom. They show a strong predilection for symbols—water, oil, bread, flowers, candles, fabrics, earth, wine. They overcome the long invisibility and exclusion of women's history, their concerns, their significance, their persons; they correct the silencing of women. God and religious traditions are reread and God is reimaged from the position of women. New (repressed) sins are confessed. The earth as creation is recovered, and separations are overcome.[101]

It is time now to turn to the quarries that harbor the materials for the construction of new rituals. As we examine them, we gain ideas on how movement or space or music or community can be planned responses to human need and ritual possibility. If rituals as cultural constructions can change, so can we. There is no reason not to plot ourselves (whether as mourners or as those seeking "a death of our own") along the various continua that emerge. Self-consciously and in community (and aided by religious traditions and recoveries) we can create and design the rituals we need, rituals that have promise of taking us where we want to go. If four modes of responding to death are overcoming, participating, fearing, and sorrowing, the dominant American one is ignoring or neglecting.[102] Some ritual opportunities present themselves only once. The "teachable moment" is there, and then it is gone. While efforts at retrieval can be attempted later, they will never be as effective as seizing the moment of dying, and also the time of the funeral and the days just preceding and following death.

Chapter 7

Ritual Quarrying: Bodies in Motion

By their performances shall ye know them.
—VICTOR TURNER

*Ritual negotiates the human passage through the world,
and the world's passage through our humanity.*
—ROLAND DELATTRE

INTRODUCTION

Rituals may recall us to other times and other places, or even to some totally other time *(in illo tempore),* but they take place in real time and space, with physical bodies and within flesh-and-blood communities, using human words and actions and symbols, drawing often on the ingredients of material culture, appealing to all the senses from smell to sound, and setting material bodies in motion through a vocabulary of gesture, movement, and dance.

An intriguing question is whether some ages have mined more promising ritual quarries than others. Are we to assume that a ritually impoverished culture such as ours will yield only meager resources for the construction of rituals? Must we rummage through other times, spaces, and imaginations for the construction of our rituals, as playwrights or novelists sometimes do? Are other symbols and cultures retrievable by us? Was there some perfect century in which to die, as there perhaps was to be an actor, a musician, a scientist, or a theologian? Ritual cannot be reduced to its ingredients and can fail in spite of them. The richness of ritual, however—its power to offer its gifts and transform people, space, and time—depends, in part, on the ingredients assembled to assist in ritual work. Robert Browning wrote:

> *I would hate that death bandaged my eyes, and forebore,*
> *And bade me creep past.*
> *No! let me taste the whole of it.*

Good and great deaths call on rich cultural resources for their staging. Great lives, moreover, will have thrown up wonderful accumulations for such a staging. Drawing from all the available resources, *we compose a death and decompose a life.* We move back and forth between grief and hope, sounding all their notes. But we arrive finally with ritual as hopeful action.

Cultures become most fully conscious of themselves in their ritual and theatrical performances.[1] "A performance is a dialectic of 'flow,' that is, spontaneous movement in which action and awareness are one, and 'reflexivity,' in which the central meanings, values and goals of a culture are seen 'in action'; as they shape and explain behavior."[2] In rituals as cultural performances, we find invaluable means for reading a culture and its meanings. It is time to take up the task of creating and renewing the performances through which we explain ourselves to ourselves.

The last decades of the twentieth century have seen a rediscovery of the body as a focus of cultural reflection and critical theory, above all in the work of Foucault.[3] "Embodiment" has become a preoccupation in theology and ethics, in feminist studies, and also in ritual studies. Thomas Berry and Matthew Fox have developed "creation spiritualities" that attempt to recover the value of the earth's physicality.[4] Sallie McFague images the universe as God's body in order to reenvision God's positive relation to the physical world —and vice versa.[5] In *Metaphorical Theology* McFague argues that metaphors are crucial to our understanding of God; in *Models of God* she experimented with new metaphors to retrieve God's immanence.[6] For Christians, Incarnation has always been at hand as a paradigm of God's concretizing grace, power, and love in the world. Christ's bodily resurrection carried that forward. Anticipating our discussion of the body of the deceased, we can reflect on theological treatments of Jesus's body: the Protestant empty cross, the suffering Christ of so much Roman Catholic iconography, and the more recent artistic treatments of the *Christus Victor*—the risen Christ, crowned and wearing eucharistic vestments, radiating, as it were, from the cross.

In the first three instances of ritual quarrying below, I treat physicality in three concentric extensions: the body, the community, and ritual space or site.

Ritual space can be seen as body enlarged, community as the body whole. I close this chapter by setting all three in motion—ritual as movement and passage.

THE BODY IN RITUAL AND RITUAL EMBODIMENT

Consider the significance of the human body for anthropology. It is an architecture and then a ruin, overlaid with culture. "Without burial, without a cult of bones, we would know nothing of the existence of Peking or Neanderthal man."[7] The culture of bones discloses the existence of Neanderthal man.

Robert Hertz argued that one could best interpret what was going on in funeral rites in Borneo by paying attention to the role of the body—the corpse. In that culture secondary burial is practiced: at the end of an intermediary period, the corpse, by then "dry," is exhumed, ritually processed, and moved to another location. There is thus a green funeral and a dry; the body's fate is first putrescence and formlessness and then, as dry bones, hard and imperishable. The fate of the body models the fate of the soul. As the corpse is formless, so the soul is homeless. Ceremonies are necessary to deal with the threatening soul, an object of dread, just as the fresh corpse is repulsive and polluted. A great feast concludes the period of the two burials "by honoring the now dry bones of the deceased, confirming the soul's arrival in the land of ancestors, and marking the reestablishment of normal relations among the survivors."[8] In fact, there are three dramatis personae here: the corpse, the soul, and the mourners. The evolution of the mourners from grief back to affirmation of life, their own rite of passage, is echoed in the course that the corpse follows. The corpse, the soul of the deceased, and the mourners are all set on a ritual passage at death, but the marking of this passage occurs through and upon the corpse.[9]

Christian rituals in early medieval Europe depicted the role of the mourners as those who "worry the dead on to their destination."[10] From the seventh century on, the living occupied themselves in the process of purifying the dead so that the dead could move toward their ultimate destination. Rituals grew to commemorate the dead through posthumous expiations, including eventually the development of the idea of purgatory. Such rituals reflected the growing conviction that the immediate destination of the dead was not the bosom of Abraham, but some intermediate state. Masses that once had symbolized or triggered the final incorporation into heaven, the end of the soul's passage, now effected the release of the dead from purgation.

In many cultures, including ostensibly Christian ones, a preoccupation with ghosts reflects a concern about restless dead who have not reached their proper destination.[11] If the dead are not successfully transformed into an ancestor, or a saint, they wander about and disturb us in the form of ghosts. One function of funeral ritual is to ensure that the dead reach their proper destiny. Ghosts are the foggy screen upon which we project our unfinished business with the dead.

No culture worried more about unfinished business with the dead than the Greeks. The souls of the dead could not enter the Elysian Fields until their bodies were buried. The Trojan War was held up so that Hector could be given a proper funeral; he had begged not for his life, but that his body not be thrown unceremoniously to the dogs. A third of the *Iliad* is concerned with reclaiming the bodies of Hector and Patroclus in order to bury them according to custom.

The body, then, is to be watched, observed, noted, prayed over, worried about; in it and on it and around it we project the meanings of our culture and religion. The body is marshaled, shanghaied, enlisted, manipulated, romanticized, politicized, naturalized, and theologized in order to speak larger meanings. In funeral rituals the body of the deceased and the bodies of the mourners come together, and they both have meaning. Bodies are never simple physical objects, just as death is not a simple biological phenomenon. Both are culturally inscribed, even culturally constructed, as are the embodied rituals themselves. A notable cultural construction of the body is the conversion of the king's body into a metaphor for the body politic. "The death of a king sets off a tremor of ritual activity that climaxes in a display of national pomp unrivaled even by the coronation of a successor."[12] That so many have a stake in royal death rites makes them a political drama. The corpse serves the ends of the living.

In England and France the king has two bodies, a body natural and a body politic. His body natural is mortal, subject to all nature and infirmity. The body politic cannot be seen or handled but is managed for the public good. Because the body politic is devoid of infancy or old age, defects or infirmities, what the king does in it cannot be invalidated or frustrated by any disability in his natural body. "His Body politic, which is annexed to his Body natural, takes away the imbecility of his Body natural, and draws the Body natural which is the lesser, and all the Effects thereof to itself, which is the greater."[13] This becomes a kind of Christology of kingship, mimicking as it does the Christian theological language describing the two natures of Christ. At death this intellectual-political position becomes trickier. The body politic does not die but is conveyed over from the old body natural, now dead, to a new body natural. Hence "The king is dead; long live the king." Even in revolution the metaphor holds. Parliament, in the name of the body politic, summoned armies to fight and execute Charles I, the body natural.

Royal funerals have come to embody this ideology. Beginning in 1189 with the funeral of Henry II, the royal corpse is publicly displayed during the funeral procession. The display of the dead body natural warrants the ascendence of the new king. It may well be that ritual action preceded ideological rationale, which evolved later. (The ancient slogan *Lex orandi, lex credendi*—"The practice of prayer precedes the development of doctrine"—suggests how ritual action often precedes and evolves ahead of doctrine, a good reminder that we can run ahead in ritual and catch up later in ideology.) When the funeral for the deposed Edward II had to be delayed for months until his son Edward III could be present to make a show of filial piety, an effigy was created to allow for a grand funeral. Thereafter the use of an effigy permitted the staging of increasingly grand funeral tributes. Further manipulations of the king's body occurred when corpse, heart, and entrails were casketed separately and buried in different locations. William the Conqueror's body was interred at St. Etienne, his heart at Rouen, and his entrails in the Church of Chalus. Carving up monarchs' bodies and burying them in different places may be a way of "imitating the holy martyrs, whose relics were scattered throughout Christendom."[14]

We come to see the body as a "natural symbol" through which the social world can be ordered.[15] The body so interpreted sustains a particular view of society and even the cosmos. Meanings flow back and forth between the body and the cosmos or the body and society. Foucault even insisted that the body can be understood only through socially given forms of knowledge. The body does not yield its meaning by itself, but as a product of forms of power and knowledge that impinge on it. Political technology has encompassed the modern body and rendered it docile, disciplined, and productive.

The body, then, invites us to "read" it as a symbol system, just as the biological body is read by the clinician or the pathologist. There emerges a semiotics of the body that "concentrates on the metaphorical relations which occur between the body and some aspect of social life."[16] The body becomes signified and signifier, a cognitive map through which we read the external world. The modern undertaker inscribes an image of peaceful and restful death on the body that is a mirror of human expression—or of quasi-official American ideology.[17] The body can be recognized and construed in many ways, acted upon through diverse practices. It becomes what the discourses surrounding it say it is. "Thus, the body can be viewed and treated either as a productive force or a hedonistic agent of consumer culture. It can be a source of pathology or a source of sexual excitement. It can act as a framework of orderly classification, or a point on which to express rebellion against the prevailing order."[18] In death, the social, medical, religious, and legal practices that structure and define the body come together. There the physical body articulates social practices, and social practices structure the human form. The body is both the foundation on which the modern state inscribes itself and also the point on which "private individuals can articulate their emotions, thoughts, practices and beliefs about death."[19] Over the body we weep, pray, eulogize, and socialize. Through the body we make contact with death, depict death, and lean toward the hereafter.[20]

It is not just undertakers, then, who direct a complex social drama in which the body is the most important prop. To say with Hertz that the corpse is a social being that needs attending to is to tell only half the truth. The other half is that we socially attend to the corpse in order to make social, cultural, and religious statements to and for ourselves. In the drama surrounding the body, there are many interested players. In seventeenth- and eighteenth-century funeral notices, the mourner was invited "to accompany the corpse" rather than merely to attend the funeral.[21] The corpse takes center stage and rivets to itself religious questions and cosmic concerns.[22] After the Anatomy Act of 1821, some players were outlawed: grave robbers and anatomists. The body is "the hub of the organizational system which surrounds death and the dead."[23] The players in the drama around the body may change, but the activity continues. In the Middle Ages "death ritual was not so much a question of dealing with a corpse as of reaffirming the secular and spiritual order by means of a corpse," as we see in the prescribed medieval treatments of kings, criminals, saints, heretics, and stillborn infants.[24] An interesting example of a transformation of the body thought to be brought about through ritual is seen in the popular idea that someone who survived after receiving the sacrament of extreme unction was to refrain from sexual intercourse, going barefoot, or eating meat.[25] It should not be a surprise that there is a gendered division of labor among the players, for example in nineteenth-century France, with male clergy in charge of official services and women attending the body. Such women "burial experts" described placing the dead in shrouds "as if they were babies."[26]

The living body of a monk was treated metaphorically as a corpse.[27] The blessing pronounced over a monk who had just taken his vows was *mundo huic mortuus,* "dead to this world." For three days and nights the would-be monk wore his hood up and spoke to no one. On the third day the abbot lowered the hood and the new monk was thus resurrected into a new existence. Sometimes a mass for the dead was said over an anchorite.

The disposal of the corpse follows many different cultural practices. The body may be eaten. Sometimes the products of the body's decomposition are mixed with the kinsmen's food; sometimes a liquor is made from its ashes. A late-twentieth-century form of anthropophagy is the harvesting and transplanting of healthy organs.[28] There is also immolation, exposure to wild animals or birds of prey, and burial under piles of stone, in caves and houses, under water, in trees, on platforms, or in urns and niches. Mummies were really only vessels intended to trap the astral body. "The Egyptian tombs, so obviously houses of the dead, were merely a receiver, a medium, intended to receive psychic radiation from the beyond. The mummy was simply a symbolic object summoning the psychic reality it represented."[29]

In India, cremation "aligns death with a perpetual cyclic renewal of time; for every cremation in Banares may be seen as an act of self-sacrifice which reenacts the original cosmogonic sacrifice and rekindles the fires of creation at the very spot where creation began."[30] Japanese Buddhist cremation may reflect "little respect for dead bodies or the desire to preserve them but rather . . . the hidden idea of dead bodies as filthy and fearful."[31] The pressing need is to liberate the life principle, the soul. This done, the ashes can be treated with reverence. While Romans and Greeks periodically practiced cremation, the Jewish tradition rejected it in favor of earth burial, and cremation was proscribed throughout European Christendom. The Enlightenment proposed it again, partly as an attack on the Christian doctrine of resurrection. During the French Revolution there was an attempt to make cremation obligatory. It gained popularity among free thinkers, then liberal Protestants, and by 1964 was even allowed for Roman Catholics, so long as it was not intended to deny Catholic teaching. Arguments for cremation range from the ideological (purification by fire and liberation of the soul) to the utilitarian (cost, space, sanitation) to the sentimental (natural, tasteful). At least from 1949 on, the Chinese Communist Party committed itself to change Chinese ways of death fundamentally, above all insisting on cremation rather than earth burial.[32] The first American crematory began operation in 1876. By 1920 only 1 percent of American funerals used it, having lost out to the embalming movement.[33] Now, however, cremation is widely practiced.

While kinds of rites for the body vary greatly, the relevant question is: What do we wish to be saying through them? Must we assume that in modern rites the body is "dramaturgically passive"? In the literature of the first memorial societies, which arose to bypass the funeral industry, funeral services are appraised in exclusively economic terms. The funeral director is seen as untrustworthy, the body is to be avoided, rituals are unnecessary, and grief is unrecognized. Social, psychological, and ritual dimensions are scarcely significant. The fundamental need is to dispose of the body swiftly, simply, and economically.[34]

Is the lavish attention paid to the body by the embalmer and makeup artist at the funeral home a better practice? Joseph Matthews describes his actions after seeing his father laid out in a mortuary. "There is a kind of glory in the face of an old man. Not so with the stranger lying there. They had my Papa looking like he was fifty-two. Cotton stuffed in his cheeks had erased the best wrinkles. Make-up powder and rouge plastered his face way up into his hair and around his neck and ears. His lips were painted. . . . I called for alcohol and linens. A very reluctant mortician brought them to me. And I began the restoration. As the powder, the rouge, the lipstick, disappeared, the stranger grew older. He never recovered the look of his ninety-two years but in the end the man in the coffin became my Papa."[35]

The Irish wake offered quite another kind of attentiveness to the body—sitting it up as a participant in the community's hilarity. In the rites for Richard Nixon, the body, as is the custom for military or national figures, was never left unattended. The body must be "present" to play its part and to be played with. If the *dying* played a more active role than our medicalized model of dying presently allows or expects, the *dead* might also be less passive. If the dying could once again hold forth from their beds, convening social occasions and the beginning of adequate ritualization, practicing their *ars moriendi*, then perhaps the dead body could also again be permitted its prominent role in the funeral ritual itself.

Once there existed the convention that the deceased continued, well after death and interment, to play an active social role. He or she beckoned and addressed passersby through an epitaph on the tomb. In the world of antiquity highways were lined with tombs from which the dead still spoke to the living. The intention of early Christian epitaphs was unambiguous: "Wayfarer, hail, whether you be friend or stranger. And why go by on the run? Stop and listen, being yourself burdened with care about death."[36] A well-worn epitaph, first used in medieval times, went: "What you are I was / What I am you will be." In early nineteenth-century America, this inscription was ubiquitous:

> *Thou traveller that passest by*
> *As thou art now, so once was I*
> *As I am now, thou soon will be,*
> *Prepare for death and follow me.*[37]

The body of the deceased can even speak through its orientation in the grave. In primitive times humans were often buried in the fetal position, with arms and knees bound to chest—to facilitate rebirth or to keep the deceased from walking about and disturbing the living. Early Christians were buried with their feet to the east, whence they thought Christ's Second Coming would appear. Muslims are buried lying on the right side, head north, feet south, and face turned toward Mecca. Buddhists are buried on their backs with head at the north, Buddha's position as he entered nirvana. In the Roman Catholic and Anglican traditions, during a funeral mass the body of a priest lies head toward the altar; of a lay person, feet toward the altar.

Sometimes society plays with the body one more time, to get it right. So in 1793, during the excesses of the French Revolution, Cardinal Richelieu's body was removed from his family plot and decapitated. Abelard and Heloise were twice disinterred: In 1630 an abbess had had their skeletons exhumed and buried separately, thinking it indecent to have them lying together in deadly embrace in a common grave at the Convent of the Paraclete; in 1817 sentimentalists exhumed them again and buried them together.[38] Mirabeau and Marat were buried in the Pantheon; then, when revolutionary sentiments shifted, they were expelled. "The equality of the dead achieved by the destruction of tombs was to lead to a posthumous massacre of kings, queens, princes, and princesses when they were dragged from their burial places in the royal abbey of St. Denis."[39] On August 6, 1793, French workmen smashed all the royal tombs and the bodies were thrown into a common grave north of the church. After the restoration of the monarchy the abbey of St. Denis once again became a royal necropolis, and the remains of Louis XVI and Marie Antoinette were transferred there, too.[40] In 1936 Republican rebels in Spain exhumed a great many bodies of clergy and nuns and displayed them in churches and in the streets as an attack on the political conservatism of the Catholic Church.[41] Reversals have happened to Stalin and, more recently, to Lenin. Chairman Mao may be waiting his turn.[42]

In our evolving rituals of last passage, what should be the role of the body of the deceased? Looking at many American funerals, especially the trend toward "memorial services" (a delicate term for bodiless rituals), one might conclude we have nothing to say about or through the body.[43] I argue, however, that for many reasons we need the body to be present: to ground and concretize the ritual; to overcome the dramaturgical passivity to which we subject the dying and the dead in an otherwise activist society; to allow the deceased in some way to remain or become again an actor, a real presence; to symbolize that this is a ritual of passage; to signal and enact movement; to stand witness against our propensity for death denial; to acknowledge the material and earthly embodiment of the life and legacy of the deceased; to register that we are all physical beings; to initiate appropriate grief work; to connect to the mourners' own mortal bodies; to point in the direction of hope; and, in general, to maintain focus on the larger action and meaning of the ritual. *Good ritual keeps its eye on the body.*

I am arguing that the body of the deceased is normally an indispensable prop in a last-passage drama. But what exactly do we do with the body—or what does the body as a presence require of us? We surround the body and embrace it as a community. We place it strategically. We reverence and honor and acknowledge it. We move it in, out, and perhaps even around. We look at it and walk past it. We speak to and over it. In the Lutheran liturgy for the burial of the dead, for example, the minister, standing at the coffin for the "commendation," says: "Into your hands, O merciful Savior, we commend your servant, _____. Acknowledge, we humbly beseech you, a sheep of your own fold, a lamb of your own flock, a sinner of your own redeeming. Receive him/her into the arms of your mercy, into the blessed rest of everlasting peace, and into the glorious company of the saints in light."[44] (It was a tremendous disappointment to me when the Lutheran minister at my father's funeral declined to speak these words. He didn't want to be giving God instructions about the afterlife, he chirped. I was left like a child denied the exact words of a familiar and beloved story.) Eventually we carry the body, commend it, lower it, and shovel earth over it. In effigy (in effect) we recall it through pictures, videos, artwork, and sound. Around and with it we move back and forth between grief and hope.

The contemporary problem is that the human body has dwindled to fit the reigning metaphors of its culture.[45] We have come to resemble the impoverished meanings with which our society is content.[46] People, including the ill, need to be "brought into bodily contact with a 'nest' of the sacra (objects, gestures, postures, and spaces) of their culture."[47] It is a long time since ritual focus turned to the body and its transition from the deathbed to the grave. Once "the treatment of the body mirrored the state of the soul. The body that is washed and reclothed, carried in procession, and incorporated in the earth is a symbol of the soul that is purified, transformed, and incorporated in the other world."[48] Are we quiet about the body because we have nothing to say about the soul? Who is left of Hertz's three dramatis personae—body and soul of deceased and body of mourners? If our culture has dis-membered us, it is now time in our ritual evolution to member and re-member.

If the corpse has lost its way in modern ritual, so have the *bodies of the living*—the mourners and their accompaniers in ritual. If the dead body once was so significant to cultural meanings and manipulation, the bodies of the living, the ritual celebrants and performers, are equally crucial. The body, not the mind, is the locus of transformation in ritual. The body is the vehicle for ritual movement and gesture. Christian ritual studies still overwhelm the body with attention to speech and texts.[49] "We wrongly think of liturgies as arising only from tradition and history, not from the body as well."[50]

Ritual is a performance carried out, not disembodied words recited. It makes most sense when we see the community as prior to the individual. In ritual the mind comes into contact with the embodied world. *Nihil in intellectu nisi prius fuerit in sensu* (Nothing is in the intellect unless it has first been in the senses). "In liturgy, the world is encountered *in sensu,* and reveals itself as sacrament through an almost experimental acting out of the ritual, through an exploratory assumption of the prescribed words and gestures, whose meaning is revealed in the doing."[51]

In the case of Christianity, ritual was set free to be public ceremonial, to be an embodied carrying out, when the Church was recognized and legally authorized in the fourth century. Christian ritual became a public performance. This was especially true in the East, where the divine liturgy as a kind of staging of heaven became most fully embodied at the great Church of Holy Wisdom in Constantinople. Publicly embodied ritual eventually developed "ceremonial high spots." In the East it was the Great Entrance, the procession in which the elements for the Eucharist are brought forward. In the West, by the thirteenth century, it was the elevation of the Host after the words of the consecration, marked by bells, lights, incense, genuflections, and, of course, the gestural language of elevation—all the ceremonial resources of the medieval church.[52]

A study of African Christian liturgy begins with the observation that in worship the assembly displays itself before God.[53] In gesture the body displays itself in time and space. Such gestures vary widely across cultures. In the dominating Christian culture brought to Africa, with Greco-Roman dualism sedimented into it, body motions were regulated by moderation, and the body itself was held suspect as a fallen instrument of sin. So dance was excluded from the liturgy. "God-like immobility or the absence of emotion was preferred to the 'undisciplined' flexing of the body. Immobility symbolized perfection. God is the unmoved mover."[54] But the African body is the center of the total manifestation of the person in gestures. "Its corporate or individual deployment reveals the person. Consequently, the dance features prominently in diverse experiences of the human community in its contact with the universe. . . . The rhythm of the dance puts one in tune with the original rhythm of the universe as interpreted by ancestral memory."[55] Individual bodies and community are "in motion" toward each other, toward completion. They go the distance.

The body of the deceased is significant because so much human experience has happened through it. Our own physicality connects to its physicality. The bodies of the mourners, of those participating in ritual, are the locus of experiencing the human condition, of doing theology, of negotiating and "reading" our way in the world. A feminist theologian claims the wisdom of her grandmother's expression "a body knows."[56] As a theologian, she thinks not just about her body or through her body, but in her body, as she writes amid her experience of near-death, breast cancer, manic depression, and being lesbian. She claims her most formative insights have come from her body as knower, rather than from her rationally trained theological mind.

Epistemologically, the body is primary.[57] No good rituals are disembodied. The body generates the metaphors for imagining the world. "The body is a specially marked-off preserve, a repository of ultimate value. The human body does not merely front for or point to the sacred; it is sacred, a locus of revelation and hierophany. Not only does skin 'think,' skin 'reveals.'" Ritual knowledge is gained by and through the body. Ritual knowledge has an "incarnate" character.[58]

It is easy to portray a disembodied ritual, because one witnesses so many of them. The audience—one cannot call them participants—sits immovably and passively, listening to words. In embodied rituals there are live bodies moving and being moved, shaping and being shaped by ritual action. They, and the body of the deceased, become the locus of ritual action and enactment.

Sometimes ritual calls attention to the locus where liberation is waiting to occur. The liberation promised in some feminist rituals may begin precisely at the point where the body of woman is experienced and recognized (or shunned) as an alien body in the midst of the embodied community. The belief that the female body can pollute ritual and sanctuary has a long and well-known history, and may still be seen in the exclusion of women from the Roman Catholic and Orthodox priesthood. A recovery of the body and of embodiment, then, may also bode well for evolving ritual's escape from the bondage of androcentrism, because it raises to critical reflection the issue of the alienated body of woman in the midst of the embodied community.

THE COMMUNITY IN RITUAL
AND COMMUNAL RITUAL

An Irish priest announces: "Every member of this parish faces death." He hears titters from someone near the back of the church. He repeats: "Every member of this parish is mortal." The snickers turn to guffaws. Thunderously he proclaims: "No one in this parish will escape death." Laughing uproariously, the dissident shouts back: "I'm not a member of this parish." How large or how small is the community summoned by death? For how many, besides the deceased, is death a command performance? How necessary to death rituals is the community? Once the last of Christianity's Seven Works of Corporal Mercy was the burial of the dead. In the late medieval period this mercy was often administered through what sociologists today call a "mediating institution": the guild. One type of guild was a secular organization of the laity, a kind of early funeral society, for the purpose of providing proper burials—and for the provision of chantry priests to say masses for the soul of the deceased. More typical of our time are the "eighteen empowering rituals for confronting death" offered by a recent book.[59] Each is only a "personal ritual," and none involves a community at all. Nor are they really rituals, but journal-writing or guided-imagery exercises, done apart from community, space, and body.

It is unfortunately a truism that we lack today a reasoned and cultivated appreciation for community. To be sure, we see that society guards us against aggression and violent death and protects private property. But our dominant cultural legacy is unlimited acquisition of material goods by competitive individuals. In death, the society that guaranteed private property deserts us, leaving us bereft of a community of solidarity and support. This does not represent a perennially human incapacity to deal with death, but a neocapitalist culture's inability to deny limits and to unite with others to face human need. This lack of a moral base is a self-inflicted wound and not a necessary result of living in the modern world. A community-based acceptance of death could create a new kind of culture, one that reaffirms the past, respects limits and the priority of needs over wants, and agrees on a conception of equity. The mark of a narcissistic culture is the isolation and aloneness of people in total competition with everyone else. Even if neocapitalism has given us liberty and prosperity, it has been at the price of fellowship with others and the ability to cope with death as a community. "The biggest toll in the invitation to getting and spending is that it forbids us to glance at that limited side of our nature manifested by death, the side that would question the significance of a bigger pile. . . . Because we are presented with a portrait of human behavior that emphasizes how everyone is trying to get ahead of everyone else, we can rely on no one else for comfort and support."[60]

If competition and greed are the cause of the denial of death, not its effect, might the acknowledgment of mortality invite the reassertion of the social dimension of life? A promising sequence is to acknowledge mortality, which leads to recognizing limits, which allows us to see through the smoke screen of unlimited and compulsive acquisition. Or, to say it differently, to recognize mortality leads to an understanding of the fragility of human existence, which leads to an appreciation of the importance of community. "Rather than threatening to deprive life of all meaning, death deepens an appreciation of life and the capacity of every person to give life to others."[61]

Perhaps, then, we might be willing, when the invitation arrives, not simply to come to a funeral, but to *accompany* the dead. It was once so. By the end of the eighth century, death rituals had come to emphasize communal participation. "The community stepped forth to aid the dying at the deathbed. It invoked the presence of that other community to which the soul would pass, compelling the souls already departed to attend to the fate of the dying person; accompanying the soul on its journey to the other world; keeping up a constant stream of supplication and sacrifice until the soul safely reached its heavenly home."[62] The fully cared-for and attended body, in burial, joined the community of bodies awaiting resurrection. Meanwhile, the soul's incorporation into the other world was no less carefully attended to by institutions created to see to its successful passage. "The performance of these rituals bound together the people who took part in them just as it bound together the communities of the living and the dead in a seamless whole."[63]

Is such an ethos permanently lost to history? The new Roman Catholic order for funerals *expects* active participation of the faithful for the first time since the early Middle Ages.[64] The Church now calls attention to the community as much as grief therapists urge social support. Recent writings on "deathing," as analogous to "birthing," stress the indispensability of a Lamaze-like coach to the dying—and by extension, to the mourner. I take the more radical, but historical, position that such coaches are also needed to speed the *deceased* on his or her journey. But we must accommodate the gathering of the community. The new funeral manuals wisely question whether funeral rites are usually scheduled at times most conducive to community participation. Nevertheless, we continue to schedule rituals not for the convenience of the community of mourners, but for the convenience of ancillary personnel such as cemetery staff. (We would not consider holding a wedding on a weekday morning when no one could come.)

Funeral rituals in rural Greece nicely demonstrate the value of community, particularly in the role of female mourners. In the women's mourning ritual, *klama*, replete with categories of performance and feeling, one woman is the soloist in pain and the others become the chorus, though each mourner may briefly engage in solo improvisation. The responses of the chorus validate the pain of the soloist with their own pain. This antiphonal response is crucial to the mourning ritual. "Lament singers cannot attain the proper emotional intensity and reality outside of the antiphonic structure and thus outside of the ceremony itself. Women may recite the narrative of a lament but are unable to sing it 'with proper pain.' . . . Any *klama* in which there are not enough skilled participants to form a chorus/soloist structure is considered 'incomplete' and 'improper.' The absence of others to 'help' a singer is considered absence of kin support and a sign of 'bad death.'"[65] The absence of chorus produces a "naked" death. One thinks of the commonplace that in African-American Christian preaching, the preacher does half the work and the congregation the other half. Nor can any teacher be effective without a willing community of learners.

A recovered emphasis on community can invite reflection on the community between the living and the dead, the community between life and death, and the community of the living that gathers to support mourners.[66] "The elaboration of beliefs in a purgatory whose inmates could be moved along by prayer" meant the strengthening of communal ties between the worlds of the living and of the dead.[67] The Protestant Reformation seriously weakened this connection, as has the recent decline in the significance of purgatory in the Catholic tradition. In nineteenth-century Brittany the domains of the living and the dead were fully interpenetrated, as folklore makes clear: "No sooner is the coffin nailed shut than you encounter the dead person again, one minute later, leaning on his garden fence. If death is a voyage, the return trip in any case follows quickly upon the departure. . . . Hence, the dead come to life again, in the final analysis, in the same places where they have always lived. . . . As long as it is day, the earth belongs to the living; come night, it belongs to the dead."[68] Warner's study of a small New England town in the 1940s found a still-powerful symbolic connection between the worlds of the living and the dead, above all evidenced in Memorial Day services.[69] Lifton argued that there is a "broken connection" between life and death.[70] We have lost the symbolic ability to form connections between the two, and the culture suffers greatly because of it.[71] Therefore death reasserts its connection to us in hidden, disguised, sublimated ways—distortions and pathologies in society.

Many Christian eucharistic liturgies have the congregation sing of being united during worship "with angels and archangels and all the company of heaven" (even if they do not constantly believe or experience it). On November 1, Christian churches with strong liturgical traditions celebrate All Saints' Day as a way of reaffirming such connections and keeping alive the memory of the departed. A reflection piece in a Lutheran publication exhorts the laity and clergy to see that the saints (the departed) are part of the church, that we worship with them—they face-to-face with the risen Christ, we under the veil of bread and wine. "Here at the altar we find our communion with the dead; for the altar is our closest meeting place between us and our Lord. That place must be the place of closest meeting with our dead who are in his keeping." It is at the altar, rather than the cemetery, that Christians should feel closest to their dead. The nearer we come to Christ in the sacrament of the altar, the author entreats, the nearer we come to the sacred dead, because all are one in the Body of Christ.[72]

There is also a powerful moral reason for holding the communities of the dead in the consciousness of the living. This necessity has been reccognized by Jewish and Christian theologians struggling to come to terms with the Holocaust.[73] The living community suffers under the unreconciled hurts of the past, under the sufferings of the dead that cannot be made good. The dead keep up a silent protest against the indifference of the living. This consciousness gave birth to the "political theology" of postwar Germany. "We perceived the long shadows of Auschwitz, and heard the cries of those who had been silenced. We became aware that we have to live and act in community with the victims of the Holocaust and in their presence."[74] This was necessary if the murderers were not to have the final triumph over their victims. The dead have rights, and they must be redressed in the community of the living. To live in hope means to live as a community that preserves its solidarity with those who have died from injustice and to seek their resurrection.

Christian liberation theologies in Latin America have accented the "dangerous memory" the community has, or should have, of the dead who have gone to their graves unjustly. A vital moral community should not be able to get such dead out of its mind. In the so-called base communities, when the roll of the disappeared and the martyrs is called, the entire congregation calls out, "*Presente*." All these are present in the community, which is the Body of Christ. "We have no need to do anything for the redemption of poor souls in purgatory, for Christ has done it all, and they are already safe and hidden in his love. But we must not forget them or suppress the remembrance of them. This may be the deeper sense of the church's tradition of intercession for the dead. . . . The community of the living and the dead is the praxis of the resurrection hope."[75] We need to keep community with the dead because of our responsibility to bring them justice. We turn them from objects of lamentation and mourning into a new community on the way to transformation.

To accomplish these and other great ritual tasks, we must put the community back in the midst of ritual, and we can create rituals that are ineluctably communal in character. "Dramas have audiences, rituals have congregations. An audience watches a drama, a congregation participates in a ritual."[76] That analogy, though facile, raises the issue of the relation between ritual-leader or actor and congregation or audience. The community within which rituals of last passage occur may be seen as a religious congregation or, at least, an audience. *Audience* need not be taken as a weak term that connotes only a spectator role. It has become common in performance studies to attend to the vital significance of audience as context. Sometimes the audience is fully participatory; sometimes there is a sharp separation of stage from audience, as in the proscenium theater—or perhaps the church.[77] Churches and other religious institutions face the same challenges and opportunities as do experimenters in theater. "The dream of Rousseau, and later of Adolphe Appia, Antonin Artaud, and others, of a theatre in which no distinction is made between actor and spectator, has inspired an important segment of twentieth-century experimentation and has led to frequent abandonment of the long-established stage/audience spatial confrontation."[78] If the congregation or audience is fully engaged, the ritual leader or actor need not apologize for his or her role. "Theatre occurs in a mystic place created by the confrontation of two worlds —the uncanny, dangerous, and fascinating space of the archetypical *illus tempus* inhabited by our representative shaman/actor and the duller and safer world of everyday reality from which we observe him. It is not these separate spaces for player and observer which make theatre, but their simultaneous presence and confrontation."[79] Churches should aspire to no less. In the thick of such a setting an actualized community transforms actors and audience.

Since rituals can focus human energy in the direction of collaborative action, humans need, for the sake of moral development, to assume responsibility for their rituals.[80] If "we perform our becoming and become our performing," then rituals require coming out, going public.[81] Ritual requires us to accept responsibility for being a community. If religious communities believe what they act out in their rituals and if they confess things that require ritual acting out, they will experience the ritual demand that they come together, that they embody themselves in order to do ritual. Ritual needs to become community performance if it is to carry power. We need to become communities worthy of the rituals we celebrate.

Death brings the community out of concealment, puts it to the test. What kind of humanity does it exhibit? If it is to pass the test, the community must reveal itself as a network of human caring.[82] The Christian community, as it is reminded by liberation theology, is one in solidarity with suffering. The Jewish community has emphasized its solidarity in remembrance and expectation. In the funeral, the community displays itself in shared suffering and in confession of God's power over sin, suffering, and death. Even if participants in the funeral have a limited relationship to the deceased or a lukewarm communal faith, "remembered losses and griefs are wounds which again bleed and join the flow of shared suffering. . . . This community sense and connectedness is more a universal community of human sufferers who gather in the church catholic with dividing fences and barriers of particularism momentarily down, and who are brought together by death and the risen Word."[83]

The religious communities that gather in the face of death can be seen as "plausibility structures." Worlds socially constructed must be maintained by specific social processes. "The interruption of these social processes threatens the (objective and subjective) reality of the worlds in question. Thus each world requires a social base for its continuing existence as a world that is real to actual human beings. This base may be called its plausibility structure."[84] Religion especially is called to legitimate marginal situations such as death in terms of an all-encompassing sacred world. The reality of this sacred world "depends upon the presence of social structures within which this reality is taken for granted and within which successive generations of individuals are socialized in such a way that this world will be real *to them*. When this plausibility structure loses its intactness or continuity, the Christian world begins to totter and its reality ceases to impose itself as self-evident truth."[85] If the firmer the plausibility structure, the firmer the "world" that is based on it, then one sees how crucial is the community that gathers around death and mourning. Religious institutions have to become communities worthy of the truth their rituals enact.

But what of death rituals that must thrive apart from *religious* plausibility structures? The rationalist, anticlerical slogan "Without God, without creed" typically and unfortunately led to "Without community and comfort."[86] Marxist societies fared no better. Russia and Eastern Europe struggled with little success to create alternative death rituals. The enthusiasts of the French Revolution suffered similar failures.

Alternative religious movements, New Age mentalities, and death awareness psychologies have been seeking secular or nonmainstream spiritual alternatives to religiously based ritualizations of dying and death. Narrative and biographical approaches are evolving as aids to the journey of aging. No doubt some will offer ersatz redemptions—leisurely life reviews devoid of fear and trembling, exempt from moral self-examination or judgment. But such efforts surely represent a "resurgent aspiration for human community and even a nostalgia for a measure of spiritual integration."[87] Christopher Lasch reminded us: "In its new meaning, the term identity registers the waning of the old sense of a life as a life-history or narrative—a way of understanding identity that depended on the belief in a durable public world, reassuring in its solidity, which outlasts individual life and passes some sort of judgment on it."[88]

It is doubtful that isolated individuals can single-handedly create self-transcending structures. If mainstream religious "plausibility structures" are weakened, even rejected by many, who will create the necessary durable public worlds, who will be the communities of meaning and support that summon and are summoned by death rituals? Here the decline of mediating structures, lamented by sociologists over the last several decades, is especially salient. If, besides churches, the neighborhood, the union hall, the guild, the school have lost their ability to mediate larger social and cultural meanings, where will the dying or the mourners who need a community find it? Some death awareness activists hope for the emergence of a critical mass consisting of all those who have had a near-death experience.[89] Will these millions become a leavening in society and culture that can produce and then socialize others into communal responses to death? Or can family, friends, coworkers, mourning-support groups, or representatives of various interests somehow find each other and construct the communities necessary to accomplish proper death rituals?

The indispensable role of community in last-passage rituals is evident. Coming together, the community offers itself as a plausibility structure within which our affirmations in the face of death become and remain believable. Judaism's developed sense of being the people of God provides the vehicle that carries Jewish theology and meaning. Christian theology posits the Church as the Body of Christ, the extension of the incarnation. Crucial to the idea of "Church" is that it embraces both the dead and the living in one community, the church militant and church triumphant. Jewish thought envisages the "bosom of Abraham." Religious traditions, above all, must offer themselves as a counterculture to a society that has lost community and the art of building it. A working community lends support and witness as mourners move between grief and hope. Such a community declares and experiences solidarity in mortality and in the imaginal task of transcending death. It accompanies the dying, surrounds the mourners with care and concern, and participates in sending the body of the deceased on its passage. It represents a living tradition of responses to death and stands together as the counterpart to the community of the dead. Such a community makes ritual possible.

Effective rituals are communally embodied. They require communities to do their work. The Jewish Kaddish, for example, is an eleven-month-long ritual of daily mourning that *requires* a minyan—at least ten (men). The dramatic action and movement of ritual, its enrichment by the arts, especially music, the positioning and utilizing of a site, the speaking and hearing of words—all enact themselves through participants gathered together. Martin Luther was willing to call the "mutual consolation of others" almost a sacrament itself. In community ritual this sacrament realizes itself.

Material culture—for example, the visual arts—can play an essential role in ritual. Communal food and drink may also be seen as a kind of material culture. Eating and drinking together, whether festively or mournfully, are powerful, meaning-laden activities in all the world's religions.[90] The Jewish seder is one example. The Christian Eucharist is another. The early Church linked funeral meals to that quintessential meal, the Lord's Supper, which already in the second century was being called the medicine of immortality.[91] After his resurrection Jesus is recorded as eating and drinking with his disciples, in order to reestablish real physical communion with them. In recent Roman Catholic thought there is an emphasis on how the very elements of the first creation, bread and wine, become in the Eucharist pledges and first fruits of the new heaven and new earth. The Eucharist is seen as the most significant of many "meal stories" in the New Testament that foreshadow the arrival of the kingdom of God.[92] Eating and drinking following a funeral is a community-solidifying activity. For those who are mindful, it may also reach toward a heavenly banquet to come, one where sorrow has been put to rest, death conquered, and perfect unity with God and the community attained—as the Church, for example, never ceases to remind itself in its eucharistic liturgies.

SPACE AND SITE

Space or site is the third concentric circle for ritual action—expanding out from body to community to ritually constructed space.[93] Here ritual action locates itself. The site becomes "shelter and setting for the liturgical assembly. Liturgical worship happens in space, and space is shaped into place by the meaning people discover within it."[94] It is not difficult to imagine the universe or heaven as the ultimate extension of this space. In the Confucian tradition, ritual site is the locus from which ritual effects harmony throughout the cosmos. In the Orthodox Christian tradition, it was thought that the divine liturgy is a staging of heaven. Christian liturgies in the West imagine a larger concentric circle of "all the company of heaven" joining in the local eucharistic celebration. This calls to mind Geertz's conception of ethos and worldview, the world as lived and the world as imagined, being joined at the site of ritual as cultural performance.

The early Christians loved to build their churches over the tombs of martyrs. Such a mausoleum-church became a place where the living and dead would live in close contact. The martyr's sarcophagus became the first altar, and the shape of future altars. Under the papal altar in St. Peter's in Rome lies the tomb of the apostle Peter. The papal mass is celebrated over a tomb. When there were not enough martyrs to underlie all the churches, their bodies were broken up and bits of the bones distributed throughout Christendom as relics.

The Church, surrounded by its cemetery, symbolized the Christian social unit. Eventually the rising bourgeois class introduced its dead inside the church.[95]

Pope Gregory the Great thought some benefit might derive to the dead from prayers offered by worshipers reminded of them by passing through their graves in the churchyard. (Perhaps some benefit accrued to the living as well.) Later medieval church architecture was shaped in part by the popular demand for individual requiem masses, which led to a proliferation of altars around the perimeter of the church building. This is an elementary example of the role place can play in connecting living and dead. Social and cultural geography, the landscape of the psyche, and the geography of transcendence come together in the geography of ritual. *Space is crucial to ritual.*[96] Ritual action and ritual embodiment require space. Ritual constitutes space as sacred by its occurring there, in one view, or occurs there because the space has been recognized as sacred, in another view. In ritual we discover, recognize, or constitute "power spots." The place of ritual becomes the *axis mundi,* the center line of the world around which meaning and life evolve, the place where the tent pole is driven that centers the cosmos.

One way of marking ritual space is through the use of incense. In many religions of the world, including Catholic Christianity, incense stimulates the sense of the worshipers, conjures the sacred, and alerts the community to sacred action. Its fragrance can also mark a personal space as temporarily sacred, as it does for some meditators.

Another "marker" of sacred space or sacred person is the use of vestments, special clothing for ritual officiants. In the nonliturgical churches and, of course, in many invented rituals occurring in "natural" spaces, ritual leaders eschew such special clothing, perhaps to make a statement. "If the celebrant . . . today decides to wear 'ordinary clothes,' they immediately cease, psychologically, to be ordinary clothes, and become another form of symbolical ecclesiastical garb, their very ordinariness making an extra-ordinary theological or sociological point."[97] Perhaps those who find themselves leading invented rituals of last passage in unusual places should consider availing themselves of special clothing—to mark their role and assist in the successful marking of ritual space and action. All ceremonial clothing represents a complex pattern of communication, whether planned or not. Criteria for choosing or developing such clothing should include the aesthetic, the symbolic, perhaps the historical, and the functional.

To imagine the significance of space or site, consider the city and its contours as theater, as Marvin Carlson does in *Places of Performance.* In the medieval town, a space we have long since abandoned, the cathedral was the symbolic center. Nowhere else was so rich a trove of symbolic referents concentrated. Victor Hugo saw that Notre Dame in Paris was the central repository of signs for its culture: "Legend, allegory, doctrine, the whole sum of medieval knowledge of the world, divine and human, was here represented in painting, sculpture, stained glass, and space. At the same time this fabric of symbols, rich as it was, also served as a setting, a container for the even more central symbolic systems of the performed rituals of the church, by which the citizens of the city were led to a direct participation in the divine mysteries."[98] Liturgical drama grew up between religious ritual and the aesthetic space that enclosed the ritual. Eventually that drama moved beyond the confines of the cathedral and gave rise to the first Easter plays, which may have been staged in front of the cathedral's west portal, with its powerful images of death, resurrection, and last judgment. The cathedral itself lay always on an east-west axis: "To the east lay Jerusalem and the presumed site of the lost Eden, and the celebrant entering the cathedral moved in this direction to reach the high altar."[99] This passage evoked cosmic journeys, echoed by the liturgical dramas that may have been enacted outside. The mystery plays were also performed in the marketplace, the stage upon which Everyman played his role. Stressing the similarity between the physical world of their biblical subjects and that of their audience, the plays "were extremely well served by a space redolent of those vernacular and contemporary concerns, just as the more abstract and ritualistic liturgical drama was well served by the surrounding iconography of the cathedral."[100]

In such a world we can still see how culturally and theologically crucial is the space that ritual requires. Today, most ecclesiastical spaces tame ritual through the presence of pews (almost unknown before the fifteenth century) and the restriction of movement: "Since spontaneous movement is the analogue of liminality and freedom, this principle has been violated by most church architecture, which has reflected a hierarchical structure and an ethic of obedience in the church."[101] The funeral home is hardly an improvement. Indeed, it is so much the worse, for there, far more than in the church, business rationalizations drive the kind, use, and availability of space. An even worse example is the English crematorium, a grotesque instance of a dead end in the evolution of ritual and its sites in a postreligious age:

> Few funerals now take place in church. Too often one is asked to meet at the crematorium, and what then ensues is dismal: an unaccompanied funeral car glides noiselessly under the *porte-cochère*, the coffin is transferred to a stainless steel "hors-d'oeuvre" trolley and wheeled into

the chapel, which looks more like a waiting-room in a university college hospital than a dignified setting for the disposal of the dead. Ten minutes later, to the accompaniment of slurred canned music, the curtains jerk their way noisily round the catafalque as the coffin sinks slowly through the floor, like a Wurlitzer organ at the Roxy Cinema, to the furnace below. We have only ourselves to blame for putting up with such banalities. Outside, as the mourners exchange greetings and inspect the wreaths, a plume of black acrid smoke rises from the ill-disguised chimney, bearing its load of burnt plastic and Terylene up, up and away to make its contribution to the "greenhouse" effect. Cremation may be "clean" but it's certainly not "green."[102]

The evolution of ritual needs, especially among the postreligious, has led, in funerals and in weddings, to explorations and experimentations with alternative space—backyards, parks, nature, theaters, and other sites that are in some way iconic to the people involved. To be sure, these alternative spaces often have an ersatz, sometimes kitschy, and occasionally grotesque quality to them. They represent early, insistently sentimental, and not deeply thought-out efforts to break out of traditional constraints. But they may be moves in the right direction. Where space is driven by ritual needs for movement, embodiment, enactment, it is most likely to be successful and authentic. Then the ritual itself discovers, creates, or constitutes its space. It may be well to remember the insight of the early Church—revived among evangelical Christians in the twentieth century—that the gathered worshipers themselves, enlivened by the Holy Spirit, are living stones in God's temple. There is no requisite, sacred architecture. The "house churches" that have sprung up in many ages may also be a model for community gatherings around human last passages. Still, there are problems, including a characteristic absence of powerful symbols, with the multipurpose-room approach. Can ritual intentionality reconstitute such a room as sacred space? "It goes counter to Christian instinct, therefore, that the place in which the Church assembles should be devoid of all evidence of Christ's presence, or that this presence should be regarded as temporary, capricious, or discreet so as not to restrict him or inconvenience the assembly. He restricted himself by becoming incarnate, and the assembly's only inconvenience is his real absence."[103]

The cemetery is one distinctive space that needs to be recovered for death rituals. Redolent with symbolism, history, memory, material culture, the cemetery as ritual site stands ignored or avoided by a death-denying culture. The great majority of death rituals do not include a cemetery site for most of the participants. When they do, some of the powerfully symbolic action (read:

dirty business) of the cemetery is safely done before the mourners arrive or after they leave.

Private homes can be very useful spaces because their everydayness requires interesting mental juxtapositions when they suddenly become the site of sacred ritual. They also signal or invite improvisation. The home becomes the site of the medieval morality play in which the commerce between the sacred and the secular awaits reimagination.

Whatever the limitations of the church and its architecture, it is vastly preferable to a funeral home because it is replete with symbolism and is the site for ongoing stagings of the sacred. Down its corridors, from font to altar, have come the newly baptized, couples to be married, the sick to be healed, and, now, precious bodies to be sent on their way to God. The church is dense with allusions to such rites of passage—sacred story and sacred time, sacramental substance, innumerable powerful memories. For those meaningfully connected to a religious tradition, ecclesiastical sites or buildings should be a sine qua non for some part of death rituals.

For some, however, the church will be a place of great negative valence. For them, everyday sites need to be enlisted. But because the corpse needs to be present for a death ritual to be fully effective and given American law's obsession with the threat of pollution posed by the corpse—there will probably be significant constraints on the kinds of space selected. It is important to recognize the very significant room for creativity and improvisation in extensions of ritual action *after* the burial of the body. Where cremation has occurred and ashes become the vehicle of ritual action, natural sites are especially inviting.

I want to observe also that space need not be static. We have seen Victor Turner's emphasis on the processualization of space, in contrast to the spatialization of process.[104] The furniture of our mind may need changing as much as the pews in the church do.

Finally, I offer a word about time, often radically contrasted with space as an alternative construction of reality, but not here.[105] Jewish and Christian traditions have shaped time as a medium of divine initiative and given it an eschatological thrust.[106] Time, already sanctified by the divine presence within it, "is a holy creature with which the liturgy puts one in meaningful touch. Once in touch with it as marking the implacable unfolding of divine purpose, one is able to perceive its true nature to be not an endless succession of bare moments but a purposeful thrust home towards its holy Source."[107] Just as the Christian liturgy, for example, is only whole when celebrated over the entirety of its annual cycle, the "liturgical year," a rite of last passage is fully adequate to the human condition when it takes up into itself not only spatial presence, but sleeping and waking, grieving and hoping, death and life, and when it lifts the participants above the present moment into eschatological thrust toward ultimate Life. An effective ritual of last passage does not merely await a distant end-time; it celebrates its unfolding presence and surrounds the ritual participants within it.[108] Moltmann tries to move beyond the polarities of linear and cyclical time by speaking of an eschatological imagination, rooted in the Christian liturgical year, which achieves the "rhythmicization" of time, an expectation in which time vibrates and dances.[109]

MOVEMENT AND PASSAGE

Recent trends in anthropology and ritual studies assert the primacy of ritual over symbol and myth, reversing earlier assumptions. "Although rituals forge a link between bodily activity and symbol-making, and although ritualization is the earliest form of language, we do not well understand ritual unless we realize that within its frame of reference, action is primary and symbolism subordinate."[110] Whatever the priority, rituals are never only about words, as many liturgical studies seem to imply. *Rituals are gestural, postural, actional, performative.* Partly they are this because they involve bodies and communities and sites, which have a three-dimensional presence in the world. Rituals move, and they transpire in movements. They evoke and display some larger divine movement. Death rituals, above all, signal, assist, portray, and effect *passage*— of the deceased, of mourners, of communities and social systems.[111] The essential message of the ritual itself is a message about exits and entrances. It is precisely the lack of movement and passage that makes many rituals, including funeral rituals, so lifeless and unempowering. Rituals can fail gesturally. The loss of the primacy of the body gives us rituals that are both disembodied and unmoving. It is worth remembering that movements connected to death rituals have ranged from relatively modest processionals, recessionals, and circumambulations to gouging of eyes, the tearing of garments, the knocking out of teeth, sexual orgies, and the frenzied *danse macabre.*[112]

When the kinetic arts of ceremony decline, other ritual elements, such as oratory and music, begin to change as well, usually for the worse. Liturgical speech functions less to direct the assembly toward its purposes, and more to address individuals in their places. Liturgical music becomes music to listen to, rather than music to move by.[113]

It is a well-known feature of American classrooms that seating dictates the conduct of the class, and it is an equally well-known truth of American churches that pew arrangement defines liturgical action by nailing the congregation in place. Real liturgical movement requires taking to the aisles.

Within a site made sacred through ritual, the community must be coaxed to express its movement between grief and hope.

Rituals move, in part, because they may invoke—or once evoked—larger movement. The Jewish Passover ritual invokes the historic experience of the Jewish exodus, but the divinely planned flight from Egypt, the movement from captivity toward freedom, *was itself a ritualized movement,* as close study of the sacred texts demonstrates. The stylized ritual movement of Passover stems from the raw ritual movement the exodus once was. Protest and resistance and flight can be seen as ur-ritual. Such ur-rituals can restore action to political and social movements. Aided by theological reflection and interpretation, primordial movement can become stylized in regularized rituals. So the ritual movement of the Jewish exodus became a political and social movement that forever after, throughout the Jewish diaspora, evoked the memory and the possibility of new passage. The Jewish archetypal community—the people of Israel—is performatively constructed over time through Passover ritual. Every Passover is eschatalogically aimed at a movement back to Jerusalem.

The form and structure of ritual should be iconic: There should be continuity and suggestion between form and meaning. If the form is intrinsic to the message carried, then the ritual can put both form and meaning into social circulation. How odd it would be, then, for a ritual commemorating and invoking a formative ur-ritual-movement to go on and on without ever itself any longer moving. Van Gennep saw ritual as the enactment within a structured sociocultural space of the disturbing movements and changes of life. But one could also say that ritual may set lives in necessary and appropriate motion.

In the Christian tradition, the death and resurrection of Christ is referred to as the "paschal [passage] mystery."[114] There is a dynamic unity between Jesus's life, death, resurrection, and outpouring of the Spirit on one hand, and the community of believers, on the other. The Gospels proclaim the ritual movement of Jesus toward Jerusalem, toward the cross, toward death, toward the taking of death up into a new life in God. *Jesus is performatively constructed as the Christ (Messiah) through his ritual movement into and beyond death.* For the devotee seeking to follow Christ, a small imitation of Jesus's movement occurs in Catholic "stations of the cross," as the parishioners move, within the church, from one artistically depicted, symbolically rich station to the next, meditating along the way on Christ's death and passion and shaping themselves in the images of the paschal mystery. The ultimate passage is from crucifixion to death to resurrection, a movement commemorated in the mass or Eucharist, but also in the sacrament of baptism. Recent Protestant liturgical reforms focus more on baptismal movement (down into the water, dying, up out of the water, rising) as the central metaphor for funeral liturgies, while Roman Catholic reforms choose the eucharistic or paschal metaphor. One reason given for rooting modern funeral rituals in the life and death of Jesus is that "paschal faith cannot tolerate the denial of death or cosmetic life purchased at the price of a funeral."[115] Contemporary disciples, no less than Jesus before them, face death honestly and are challenged to see in it a movement up into the life of God.

How far Protestantism will come on this road remains to be seen. "A performatively grounded hermeneutic exposes the ritual avoidance that is still deep in the heart of post-Protestant theology."[116] Ritual enactment seems to the Protestant temperament too much like "doing good works" instead of relying on grace. Protestants are also very cautious about formalism, including even such stylized ritual gestures as making the sign of the cross or genuflecting before the altar.

This brings us to the body's own passage—movement through death and toward God—as the central metaphor that should inform and shape death ritual. In the Middle Ages the corpse continued its role as public actor, a role initiated in deathbed rituals, by being brought by the community on a passage that led from home through the town to the church and ultimately to the churchyard. The viaticum, the Eucharist given to the dying as a profoundly necessary late rite, was "something for the journey," something wonderfully iconic: The Eucharist—the "medicine of immortality"—given to the dying was to invite and effect solidarity with the very paschal journey of Christ himself through death and into the life of God.

Today such ritual action is fragmented and discontinuous and therefore hardly noticeable as a passage. In contemporary death rituals, the body is often forgotten, having been prematurely disposed of; the passage of the deceased is completely ignored; and even the mourners—the ostensible and only target of most modern death rituals—do not experience ritual movement in the direction of their grief work or toward hope. Nor do they participate in "worrying" the dead on their way. Yet a ritual commendation in the contemporary Catholic office "Pastoral Care of the Sick" still catches this movement: "Go forth, Christian soul, from this world in the name of God the almighty Father, who created you; in the name of Jesus Christ, Son of the living God, who suffered for you; in the name of the Holy Spirit, who was poured out upon you, go forth, faithful Christian." A prayer in that same pastoral office invokes the Christian's immersion in Christ's own paschal journey:

> *Your son, our Lord Jesus Christ,*
> *by dying for us, conquered death*
> *and by rising again, restored life.*

May we then go forward eagerly to meet him,
and after our life on earth
be reunited with our brothers and sisters
where every tear will be wiped away.

Were the Middle Ages more conducive to such ritual movements? Lewis Mumford thought moving pageants or processions, above all religious processions that wound about the streets and monuments before entering the church for the great ceremony itself, were the key to the medieval city. "These great processions united, as did the ceremonies of the church, spectators, communicants, and participants. Even the tortuous windings of the medieval streets contributed to this effect, by affording those in the procession glimpses of other participants so that they became spectators as well, as they can never be in a formal parade on a straight street."[117] This is a remarkable example of reflexivity in ritual. Ritual participants catch themselves turning into what they are doing. Such great processions and dramatic pageants claimed the entire city and the involvement of every citizen as they moved through it, erasing all boundaries between performance and public space. It is a time and a space now lost to us.

We need "travel agents" who can remind us about ritual passages in death and help us book them. These travel agents would serve like Sherpa guides who direct our journeying toward Mt. Everest and prepare us for it, final escorts. The imaging of death as the start of a dangerous journey is a commonplace among cultures across the world. To place again an *obolus* in the mouth of the dead, as the ancient Greeks did in order to ensure a successful crossing of the river Styx in Charon's boat, might deconceal the imminent passages we face and move us beyond the repression of the rituals necessary to them. In West Africa, death is not a barrier separating two worlds but a transition that allows one to pass from the village of the living into the village of the ancestors; the African "takes care to transform physical death into a ritual death."[118] Both the dead and the living face journeys through a liminal state and toward a final or resumed state.

Christian sacramental ritual attempts to endow the great events in individual and collective life with a particular meaning and content, one derived from the life of Christ. No doubt this also draws on the Hebrew scriptures, where there are constant exhortations to the people of Israel to move nomadically along with God, just as they archetypally did out of Egypt and in the wilderness journeys. Just as Christ moved through a messianic passage, so the community is called to move. The individual—better, the community—travels with or in Christ through danger and temptation, from tribulation to hope. Recent Roman Catholic liturgical reforms have tried to recover the paschal character that emphatically defined the early Roman liturgies of the dead that had emerged by the eighth century. The following description evokes that early liturgy, replete as it is with verbs of movement:

> When the Christian is about to depart *(exitus)*, he is given communion, which is a token of resurrection. The story of the Passion is read to him until the moment when his soul is about to leave *(egredere)* his body, when the response *Subvenite* is pronounced: "Come, saints of God; advance, angels of the Lord . . ." and then Psalm 113 is recited, "In *exitu* Israel" with the antiphon "May the choir of angels receive you *(suscipere)*." After death, the body is placed on a litter and carried in procession to the church. There no eucharist is celebrated but instead an office consisting of psalms is said, with a very expressive antiphon: "May the angels lead *(ducere)* you into God's paradise, may the martyrs receive *(suscipere)* you on your arrival *(adventus)*, and may they introduce *(perducere)* you into the holy city of Jerusalem." A second procession takes the body from the church to the cemetery while Psalm 117 is recited, with the antiphon, "Open the gates for me, and once I am within *(ingressus)* I shall praise the Lord."[119]

This ritual speaks of the beginning of the soul's movement and is clearly a paschal transition ritual. Psalms 113 and 117 had been part of the structure of the Jewish paschal meal. "The Christian death celebration is the accomplishment of a paschal 'exodus': the dead person undergoes his exodus from Egypt, his liberation from exile, his entry into the Promised Land, where he is received by angels and saints who come to meet him."[120] The liturgical action conducts the dead from earthly home to celestial Jerusalem, stopping at the church, which is halfway between earth and heaven.

> Throughout this journey the Christian is not alone: at the start the earthly community accompanies him as far as it can, and on arrival he is welcomed by the inhabitants of heaven: that is, by those who have travelled before him (saints, martyrs and patriarchs), by the envoys of the master of the house (the angels), and finally by the master of the house in person. The dying Christian therefore passes from one community to another, and his "transition" is related to Christ's Passion, either directly (the reading of the Passion), or more often indirectly by referring to the exodus and liberation of Israel. The death of each human being is trans-signified by its relation to the Passover of Christ, and is inserted into the great migration of all the people of God on the way towards the kingdom of heaven.[121]

Even when, in the evolution of liturgy, the peaceful *transitus* of the eighth century was replaced by a dramatic vision of judgment, and the perilousness of the journey became more prominent, passage was still the dominant metaphor.

The current recovery in Roman Catholicism of those more ancient traditions preserves the sense of movement and passage. As the dying person prepares to leave life, the pastoral liturgy tries to cancel the threat of solitude. Through gestures of human community such as the laying on of hands and anointing with oil, God's accompanying presence is evoked. The Body of Christ is given as viaticum, food for the journey, something for the road. A climate of prayer and support surrounds the dying on the journey out of life. "The living are trying to help the dying person to remain in control of himself in the face of death. They recommend him to God who made him and recite at his bedside, or help him to say, the most ordinary prayers, the prayers of his youth. This latter concern corresponds to the need to return to the origins, to the safety of early infancy, which so often appears on the approach of death."[122] Avoiding mention of purgatory, hell, or Satan, the revised ritual concentrates on the journey of soul and body from one world to the other. The *transitus* continues into eternity and the life of God. In effective, movement-filled rituals, the body is speeded on its way—not just talked about in absentia. Still today, in the Subvenite of the Catholic funeral rite, the Church prays:

> *Saints of God, come to their aid!*
> *Hasten to meet them, angels of the Lord!*
> *Receive their souls and present them to God the Most High.*
> *May Christ, who called you, take you to himself;*
> *may angels lead you to the bosom of Abraham.*
> *Receive their souls and present them to God the most High.*
> *Eternal rest grant unto them, O Lord,*
> *and let perpetual light shine upon them.*

This Christian ritual enactment is not proclaiming an abstract theological truth. Anthropologists and sociologists have recognized the acute status transition death represents, both for the deceased and the living, and the necessity of ritually recognizing it. Some scholars are fond of calling undertakers and other death-related professionals "transition technicians." Sending the dead to another community or world allows humans symbolically to represent the persistence of human society and to mitigate its transience. Social existence continues, even if physical existence does not. Death rituals must also symbolize and initiate the grief work that will culminate in the mourners' reincorporation to ongoing life and carry them some distance toward hope as well. But for the believer, even more is true: Rituals of movement and transition recognize and proclaim another world, not merely the continuity of this one, a world that transcends and transforms this world.

One can describe such ritual goals, which effect status transitions, psychologically. The dead are treated respectfully and ritually in ways that evidence communal expectation regarding them. They are formally released from the world of the living, and anxiety regarding them is reduced. Their new status—being dead now—is socially and publicly recognized, as is the significance of their lives. They enter the community of the dead, which is ritually recognized as connected to the community of the living. Religious institutions may be the only ones left to perform these vital social functions. They can become the servants of a society that no longer takes any interest in the deceased.[123]

Death rituals as status transitions are equally important to the mourners, who go away from the funeral with a secure, ritually defined position that has its path marked out. The ritual offers them both limit and release for their emotions, and the eventual redistribution of them. It begins the reduction of anxiety about their arriving eventually at a new place. Ahead of time, to be sure, it grants them a new status, toward which they then progress in ritualized anticipation. The ritual publicly announces and recognizes the mourners' transition journey and informs society they should be approached in new ways. Ultimately, it is foretold, they will be reintegrated into society, social organization will be stabilized, and communal values will be reaffirmed.[124]

To stay with psychological paradigms, death rituals initiate the long process in which libidinal energy is slowly withdrawn from the deceased and redirected toward life. A psychologically reductionist view of death ritual might argue that all "sending the dead on their way" ever was is this withdrawal and redistribution of energy and emotion. Even if so, though this is hardly the position argued for here, the ritual would provide a powerful and indispensable psychological service to survivors. The freezing of libidinal attachments and the emotional stunting connected to an inability to grieve are increasingly remarked upon as individual and even national problems.[125] Without an effective ritual of passage, grief arrives stillborn and hope is deferred.

All this suggests that what we do in ritual—first—is what we come to do later mythically, theologically, actually. *We do it right, ritually, so that we will get it right later.* Death rituals enact and initiate larger mythic passages. When last-passage rituals are unsuccessful or nonexistent, then vital life passages become lost passages. The connection between life and death, between the living and the dead, and ultimately between the living and the living atrophies. It was once said that heaven and earth are joined at the graves of the saints.[126] The living and the dead become one common society via safe passage granted from one to the other. This calls for a recovery of gesture, posture, action, performance, and movement in those rituals that, above all, must connote and accomplish passage.

In the traditions gathered in the Tibetan Book of the Dead the living play an essential role, both in accompanying the dying and then in sending the newly dead on their way through the *bardo* of becoming. "The qualities of the mental body during the bardo of becoming that make it so vulnerable—its clarity, mobility, sensitivity, and clairvoyance—*also make it particularly receptive to help from the living.* The fact that it has no physical form or basis makes it very easy to guide. The manual compares the mental body to a horse, which can be readily controlled by a bridle, or to a huge tree trunk, which may be almost immovable on land, yet once floated in water can be effortlessly directed wherever you wish."[127] Such efforts, carefully described and coached, are thought to be most effective and needed throughout the forty-nine days of the bardo of becoming, above all in the first three weeks, when the dead are still strongly linked with this life. Continuous readings of this manual are typical, both to move the dying along in their final days or hours and, once death has occurred, to move the soul along to its next state.

If we look, we will find many opportunities for ritual movement and gesture around the body of the deceased. As more and more people seek a dying of their own at home, caregivers and others can offer certain ministrations to the newly dead. Even acute-care hospitals, under the influence of the hospice movement, are now likely to allow the family time alone with someone who has just died. The surreptitious collection of the body by someone from the funeral home need not be the ritually void, death-denying event it now routinely is. The movement of body to the ritual site or, after the funeral, to the cemetery could in some cases recover the meaningful movement through the city or past places of work that once were done. Within the ritual itself, there should surely be a procession in and out of the ritual space, down corridors rich with meaning, and there should be accompanying gestures as well: laying a pall over the casket, signing it with the cross, positioning the casket in a particular place, touching the head of the casket, circumnavigating it, censing it, surrounding it, setting candles around it. At the cemetery, the community can recover its participation by shouldering the coffin, touching it, laying souvenirs upon it, lowering it into the grave, shoveling earth upon it. Some ritual gestures will likely be performed by the leader in the name of all gathered—or of God.

Mourners, too, should be moving. There are accompanying, touching, commending, hugging, bearing, sending, and commemorating movements and gestures. Material culture has its role. In place of an offering of money, in place of the "offering of gifts" that precedes the Eucharist, the congregation at a funeral could bring forward remembrances of the deceased, souvenirs of the relationships between the departed and the mourners.[128] Between the mourners themselves there are embracing, handshaking, and passing-of-the-peace gestures. Kneeling and rising are classic worship postures, as are lifting up hands, bowing heads, swaying, dancing, hand clapping. Choir and officiant processionals and recessionals and liturgical dance are other ritual movements made by a few, enacting meanings for the many. The movement of life, the movement of the soul, the movement of the congregation of mourners all come together in the familiar old spiritual:

> *I looked over Jordan, and what did I see,*
> *Coming for to carry me home?*
> *A band of angels coming after me,*
> *Coming for to carry me home.*
>
> *Swing low, sweet chariot,*
> *Coming for to carry me home,*
> *Swing low, sheet chariot,*
> *Coming for to carry me home.*
>
> *If you get there before I do,*
> *Coming for to carry me home,*
> *Tell all my friends I'm coming too,*
> *Coming for to carry me home.*
>
> *I'm sometimes up, I'm sometimes down,*
> *Coming for to carry me home,*
> *But still my soul feels heavenly bound,*
> *Coming for to carry me home.*

Chapter 8

Ritual Quarrying:
The Arts and Letters of Hope

*Through art, we are able to break bread with the dead,
and without communion with the dead
a fully human life is impossible.*
—W. H. AUDEN

MUSIC

Music is a language in which meaning has been encoded that is not communicable in any other way. It takes its name from the Greek muses, who preside over all the arts. Music has always been connected to ceremony, narrative, religion, ecstasy, dance, ritual, theater. Confucius thought music could portray six emotions—sorrow, satisfaction, joy, anger, piety, and love—in ways that brought individuals and communities into harmony with the universe, thus restoring order. Pythagoras joined music and mathematics and thought music reflected celestial movement and order, produced as it was by the turning of the spheres. Later Greeks developed elaborate theories of music's power and connected it to ethics because of its identifiable effects and functioning.

It has been said that the Christian liturgy was born singing—the Hebrew Psalms may suggest the same for the Jewish liturgy before it. No other symbol evokes the communal dimension of liturgy as well as singing, inviting collective participation and enacting in its performance unity in diversity. For monastics music added a sweetness and savor to the text, and for Martin Luther, who made music a central dimension of Protestant worship, "*die Noten machen den Text lebendig*"—music brings the text to life. Though all kinds of music evolved in the Christian tradition to glorify ritual action and inspire the community, singing achieved a privileged position because of its intimate connection to sacred texts. (The early Church and the later Orthodox Church excluded instrumental music.) Eventually there developed what would be a long alliance between culture and religion, which may have benefited music more than it did liturgy. With the Enlightenment this began to come to an end, and in the nineteenth century there came a rupture between sacred and profane music. Modern music continued to develop outside the Church, and ecclesiastical music too easily related itself to an idealized golden age of piety.[1] Yet hymn singing as an essentially congregational activity—revived and dramatically extended by the sixteenth-century Protestant Reformation—continued, at least to some extent, to open itself to vital interactions with culture and society.

Kant and Hegel deprecated wordless music. Schopenhauer connected music to dynamism, process, and will. For Nietzsche it was the Dionysian art, essential to symbol making. Its artistic function is to order and intensify elements in the natural world. The nineteenth century saw a debate between the referentialists and the nonreferentialists, the latter arguing for a formalist, absolutist view of music, in which music simply means itself. In the twentieth century Susanne Langer argued that art is the symbolic analogue for, and the indispensable presentation of, emotive life, and that artistic form and content are an indissoluble whole. Contextualists connected music to psychology, society, culture. Some now argue that listening to music for its own sake, apart from ritual or story, is a recent phenomenon. Humanistic psychology is likely to emphasize music's contribution to self-actualization. Aesthetic existentialism looks to music for inner freedom. Spiritual disciplines seek in music stimulus to moral obligation and, ultimately, to self-transcendence. It is worth noting that many find music criticism meaningless or redundant, a recognition rather than a bestowal of meaning, and nothing more than the rationalization of intuitive musical understanding.

Death and its ritualizations have called the arts to service, and the arts have offered emotional intensifications of death.[2] W. H. Auden is often quoted: "Through art, we are able to break bread with the dead, and without communion with the dead a fully human life is impossible." Music is an inescapable dimension of death ritualization. *Music may even have arisen as an elongation of the emotional cry of grief at a funeral.* From that source it evolved into the high-art form we know. To be sure, all the arts offer themselves as enrichments in the ritualization of death, and death's evocation of them has produced some of the greatest art. But no art is more indispensable than music.

Great deaths abound in music, above all, in opera. Consider the liner notes to the compact disc *Opera to Die For:* "Death, with its attendant agonies, delusions, vendettas, skullduggery, jealousy, rage, heroism and despair, has inspired composers to some of their most extended and complex essays in melody and expressive eloquence, holding opera audiences in thrall for three hundred years."[3] The *liebestod* fantasy, in which death becomes the opportunity for reunion with a dead lover, is the well-known conclusion of Gounod's opera *Romeo et Juliette.* First Romeo, thinking Juliet is dead, drinks poison. Wrapping her still-drugged body in his arms, he sings: "Be consoled, poor soul, the dream was too beautiful! Love, heavenly fire, survives even the tomb! It rolls back the stone and, with blessed angels, like a flood of light, is lost in infinity." Awakening to Romeo's dying and with none of his poison left to share, Juliet stabs herself and sings, in Romeo's arms, "Come! This moment is sweet! Oh, infinite, utmost joy to die with you! Come! A kiss! I love you!" They close the opera singing, "Lord! Lord, forgive us!" The *liebestod* reaches its apogee in Wagner's *Tristan und Isolde.* Tristan, mortally wounded in battle, dies despairing that Isolde will come to him. Appearing at last and finding him dead, she too dies of grief. Each welcomed death as a means of reunion, eternalizing their love. But death is no less stirring at the end of Bach's *St. John's Passion.* As Jesus hangs dying, the chorus sings the great Lutheran chorale, "Lord, let at last thine angels come / To Abram's bosom bear me home / That I may die unfearing."

Music is singularly apt for announcing the beginning or ending of ritual because of its capacity to demarcate sacred space and time, the threshold we cross on the way into and out of ritual. It creates a world out of sound, "a ritual space with acoustic, not visible, boundaries."[4] Thus music serves as one of the most familiar markers of ritual and ritual settings. In typical (Christian) worship sites one finds organ and piano, abundant hymnody, sung liturgies, often soloists and choirs.[5] Joyous brass choirs, tender (sometimes homely) guitars, stately drum rolls, triumphant processionals, and confident recessionals have played their roles in funerary ritual. Those outside the traditions that are rich in sacred funeral music can avail themselves of other appropriate music or of original compositions written by self or friends for the occasion. While canned music is now part of the stale packing of funeral parlors, all recorded music need not on that account be rejected.

The power of music to represent death's meanings may begin as part of an art of dying. Therese Schroeder-Sheker has developed "prescriptive music" as a palliative treatment to tend the complex physical and spiritual needs of the dying. In her Chalice of Repose Project in Missoula, Montana, she and her music thanatology interns have attended deathbed vigils in hospitals, hospices, geriatric homes, and private home settings. Listen to her story: She was a novice attendant to the dying in a geriatric facility. She talked with a priest about her doubts about working with the elderly, in view of her young age. He advised, "Protect them." Subsequently she was attending an elderly man who was dying of emphysema who was often vicious, brittle, and selfish.

> One evening when I entered his room, it was clear he was nearing death. No more mechanical ventilations, tracheotomies, or surgical procedures were available to resolve his disintegrated lungs. He could take no more in, could swallow no more, and, in his complete weariness, there was little he could return to the world. The room was filled with his fear and agony. Without much thought, I closed the door quietly and climbed into his hospital bed and propped myself up behind him in midwifery position. With my head and heart lined up behind his, and my legs folded near his waist, it was possible to bolster his diminished body and even suspend his weight slightly. Before I had time to think, I had been singing quietly to him, and rocking very gently. I made my way through the entire *Mass of the Angels*, the *Adoro te devote* of Thomas Aquinas, the *Ubi Caritas*, the *Salva Regina*, the *Mass of the Blessed Virgin Mary*. . . . All I know is that he began to rest in my arms and breathe much more regularly, and we, as a team, breathed together. The chants seemed to bring him balance, dissolving fears and compensating for those issues still full of sting. How could they do anything less? These chants are the language of love. The repertoire had become the chalice that held him up into true repose. Long after his heart ceased to beat, I was allowed to hold him.[6]

She builds on the Cluniac tradition, beginning around 900, of a Western monastic medicine that sought the care of the body and the cure of the soul. She finds in this tradition a fully developed series of infirmary practices that predate modern palliative medicine by eight hundred years. The infirmary at Cluny left detailed accounts of the *musical,* and other, ways in which the dying were tended, so as to address the physical, emotional, mental, and spiritual pain that might impede or prevent anyone from experiencing a blessed death. Building on the Cluniac customary manuscripts, Schroeder-Sheker and her associates practice an "infirmary music" that is dynamic and prescriptive, individual to each patient, unique in timing, content, and context. Voice and harp are used in this live music prescribed for the bedside.

Music therapy is the systematic application of music to engage and support life processes and produce deep relaxation in the patient. The use of music in this way presupposes a reserve of patient energy, and the therapeutic application engages interaction, participation, or response by music-making activities or in deeply responsive and controlled listening environments.[7]

Music thanatology, rooted in monastic medicine, is a music therapy solely concerned with the dying. The dying person, whose energies may be depleted, *only receives.* "The entire surface of the skin can become an extension of the ear, thus enabling the patient to absorb infirmary music, creating the possibility for even deeper emotional, mental and spiritual reception. In these vulnerable moments, the dying person becomes a chalice and is anointed with very specific music, sound or tonal substance. The sole focus is to help the person move toward completion and to unbind from anything that prevents, impedes, or clouds a tranquil passage."[8] This musical practice alternates between contraction (silence) and expansion (sound). It employs the phenomenon of entrainment, in which one source of rhythmic vibrations causes another source to vibrate in lockstep. The Western infirmary music she employs is all a development of Gregorian chant, turned to a "musical-sacramental midwifery." Tonal substance is woven over, around, and above the physical body, from head to foot—a sound anointing.

Much better known, of course, is music intended for the funeral itself—to speed the deceased on to the next life and comfort and empower the mourners. Standing above all is the genre of the requiem mass, the mass for the dead. Its text typically follows the textual structure of a normal mass, but it omits the great song of praise and the creed and adds the Dies Irae. The requiem's famous Introit is *Requiem aeternam dona eis, Domine:* "Eternal rest grant them, O Lord." There are many liturgical examples of such masses, which originate in Gregorian chant. The oldest by a known composer is by Ockeghem in 1470. By the end of the twentieth century sixteen hundred requiem masses had been composed.[9] The famous Dies Irae (Day of wrath) was added in the fourteenth century.[10] Eventually the requiem mass evolved well beyond the standard liturgy—from Mozart, to Verdi and Berlioz, to Faure's and Durufle's return to liturgical tradition, to Andrew Lloyd Weber. Brahms's *German Requiem* does not follow the structure of a Latin requiem at all, but draws its texts from Luther's German Bible. Paul Hindemith's setting of Whitman's poem "When Lilacs Last in the Dooryard Bloomed" has the character but not the form of a requiem. Benjamin Britten's *War Requiem*[11] presents the Latin mass proper, but interspersed with Wilfred Owen's antiwar poetry in English. Much other sacred music, including some of Bach's motets, also was composed to serve rites of last passage.

Given the history and power of music in the ritualization of death, how is music to serve in the recovery of a death of our own? It is well, first of all, to note that music serves ritual well. Together, they offer the possibility of rehearsing "right attitudes" (Langer) in the face of death, of working our true selves out as we come under the assault of mortality, of finding a way for ourselves and even of extending a way that takes us to new places. If ritual provides both a human passage through the world and also the world's passage through our humanity, then the many deposits the world has left in our humanity can now profitably be retrieved. The most powerful, often, is the music we first learned as children.

Music in rites of last passage ought first to give voice to inexpressible sorrow and grief, precisely because music is "beyond words." Music's ability to coax an outpouring of grief is particularly crucial in the midst of a culture that mostly represses grief. The diverse tonalities of the human condition that death evokes, the feelings, emotions, moods, are given their due in the music that ought to accompany death rituals. This surely includes the well-known ability of music to summon the familiar—music the deceased used to love, old hymns the mourners now retrieve to give them strength or comfort.

We think of music as something creative. At death we can become creative with music. Some, who have the capacity or the confidence, will try to create their own music. All can perform the creative act of selecting music (perhaps recording it) for ritual use. Music provides an armamentarium from which we can creatively choose to "treat" the occasion of mortality and grief—but also to effect robust joy, confidence, hope. Mourners can take the time to ask what they need. How might various musics assist us?

Ultimately, music will help us create what ought to be or could be, in place of what threatens to overwhelm us. As music assists our human improvisations we catch sight of larger orders, we fuse the way things generally are with our view of what they ideally should be. Great music offers us self-transcendence and beckons us to overreach ourselves—also and especially in response to death.

This raises the issue of the aesthetics of music appropriate to rites of last passage. To begin with, a critical aesthetic scarcely seems the issue of first importance at the time of death and commemoration. Music that "works" in evoking memories or summoning forgotten comforts, whatever its aesthetic shortcomings, should not readily be rejected. Nevertheless, if music is to serve *communal* ritual, aesthetic questions ought not to be dismissed. It is not inappropriate to seek art forms that are larger than the merely personal, that go beyond the sentimental and the idiosyncratic. So music that offers familiar comfort ought eventually to give way to music that offers a breakthrough for the human imagination. The southern folk hymn envisions it:

> *And when from death I'm free,*
> *I'll sing on, I'll sing on.*
> *And when from death I'm free,*

I'll sing and joyful be,
And through eternity,
I'll sing on, I'll sing on,
And through eternity,
I'll sing on.

THE VISUAL ARTS

Heinrich Boll wrote: "The artist carries death within him like a good priest his breviary."[12] Wordsworth thought the poet had a "disposition to be affected more than other men by absent things as if they were present," that the poetic imagination operates most powerfully within the spaces of absence or dislocation.[13] The psychoanalytic imagination sees in art the reparation of loss, the attempt to memorialize or resurrect lost love objects.[14] The origins of architecture, sculpture, and dance are essentially funerary.[15] It is worth pausing to ponder: What is there to *see* in rituals of last passage? How disclosing is visual culture? Introducing his book on medieval death illuminations, Michael Camille notes Johan Huizinga's assertion that our perception of former times is growing increasingly visual.[16] Moderns owe their conception of Egypt, Greece, or the Middle Ages much more to sight than to reading. What do we see, and what will future generations see, in the visual culture surrounding our deaths? Of course, there's more to seeing than meets the eye. What we come to see in death and its icons could be understanding, clarity, and even spiritual transformation. The 1990s saw a turn to "visual culture." Image history, poised to take precedence over art history, is softening calcified disciplinary boundaries. The classical terms *art* and *history* evolve to the contemporary terms *visual* and *cultural*. As our eyes become more accustomed to a visually saturated environment, they may open to see much more that surrounds death. There will be more to see than medieval art or royal ceremonies and sculptures.

We do not need to assume that a rich visual culture surrounding death belongs only to the past—even if we choose also to reserve aesthetic judgment (or religious critique) of the material culture that today surrounds death and dying. Kitsch, of course, is never far from death. A funeral parlor in Osaka, Japan, invented a "laser funeral" in 1991—a sales gimmick and technological razzmatazz.[17] After passing a snack bar and the display area for funeral gifts (sold on the premises,) you go upstairs to a bowling alley of a room, forty feet wide. At the conclusion of a traditional Buddhist ceremony, there is a send-off not unlike a near-death experience. You can see what it's like to go to heaven because it looks like that's what the casket is doing. The casket, laid out on a flat little trolley is briefly opened and flowers are placed inside. Then the deceased begins his or her last ride as the car is pushed along with mourners gathered on each side. At the end of the track dry-ice vapor pours out of ducts in the floor and ceiling and laser lights cut a greenish arc through the fog. A bright light beams on the casket. While the music swells and the family is engulfed in the vapor curtain, the casket hurtles straight on down a ramp, through the laser "arch," and then drops into a hearse in the garage below. The family pronounces the experience definitely worth the money because the deceased deserved a final, great ceremony.

The aesthetic can be transparent, or opaque, to death and mortality.[18] The ritualization of death—not to mention the articulation of the sacred—has always drawn on the arts. The arts and artists may have an especially ready connection to ritual because ritual affinities lie closer to the arts than to words and concepts. Historically, the aesthetic and the sacred came together in a powerful synergy with death. Once it was taken for granted that the arts were a particularly apt vessel for the sacred, that art and religious thought served each other. "By combining the mystery of prayer with the miracle of graphic depiction man came to terms with his environment. . . . Valorized by the information that belief conveyed, and stirred by the emotion that art communicated, man embellished himself and his world. . . . As history unfolded nothing escaped either theology or the passion of art."[19] In modern life the arts and religion (if not the sacred) seem mostly estranged. This is a great loss for both.

In *The Sea and the Mirror* W. H. Auden describes the effect on us of great art: "All we are not stares back at what we are." He asks: "What else exactly *is* the artistic gift . . . if not to make you unforgettably conscious of the ungarnished offended gap between what you so unquestionably are and what you are commanded without any question to become?"[20] Think of the power of art to affect religious consciousness—for example, the image of Christ on the cross. "This was not just an object of contemplation but an actual event and a body which viewers were encouraged not just to observe but to *become*."[21] In fourteenth-century Paris the crucifixion was placed and processed at the public intersections of space and power where the boundaries of sacred and profane were negotiated. A cruciform shape inscribes itself on the imagination of all and, in gestures and artifacts, on the bodies of many.[22] Could art again negotiate the passage between our quotidian lives and the great moments, between sacred and profane, between public and private?

Death eludes or transcends our efforts to define, contain, guide, and interpret (much less control) it. Humans have culturally constructed death and surrounded it with a ritualized and aesthetic process, so that it does not stand naked and terrorizing as a single biological moment in time. The arts are summoned to tell truth about death. It is also true that some periods, such as our own, may mobilize culture, including the arts, to deny death. But mostly the artist is a seer and does not participate in cultural cover-ups. Artists who see and feel and know more about death than others may depict deeper truths about death than we wish to know or ask. Artistic visionaries disclose more authentic insights about a period than its manufactured and intentional culture displays. Because the arts can carry repressed and also verbally inexpressible meanings, they can be indispensable ritual accompaniments, mined from forgotten quarries. Hans Holbein and Albrecht Dürer produced great graphic art with death as its theme; in the twentieth century Kaethe Kollwitz's woodcuts are moving examples of the same. In the fourteenth century manuscript illuminators such as Remiet "worked in a world in which death was no less difficult to negotiate than in our own, but during a time when it was far more available to representation. Because God was not dead, every image, no matter how lifeless it looked, pointed towards the possibility of an eternal life elsewhere. What made life worth living was that Christ himself had also lived it, taking part in this fleshly pilgrimage and walking the same road between birth and death."[23] Today we face old and new questions, but now the arts are more likely to tell us of absence than of presence.

Nor is every effort today counted a success or greeted with appreciation. Bill Jones's 1995 attempt to choreograph and produce a work of dance in response to AIDS was met both with acclaim for its bravery and creativity, and with denunciation as "victim art" by the dance critic of *The New Yorker,* who refused to review it or even to witness it.[24]

Great funerary monuments, which death has summoned from the arts, are familiar bequests from past ages. Egyptian kings marshaled vast armies of laborers over long periods of time to construct the pyramids. Shah Jahan put up the Taj Mahal in memory of his most beloved wife, Mumtaz. All over Europe are exquisite marble sculptures representing deceased nobility recumbent on their tombs. Cemeteries and other sites display sublime mausoleums. The death and resurrection of Christ and the *parinirvana* (death and final release) of Buddha are celebrated in painting and sculpture throughout the West and East. Popular death sites such as Forest Lawn Cemetery, near Los Angeles, and spectacular Mormon sites, like those in Salt Lake City, Utah, have collected copies of such works and sponsored new works, occasionally with aesthetic success.

Perhaps none of these seems to us so exotic and impressive as the pyramids. More than colossal tombs, they were fortress cities of the dead. "The city of the dead involved the permanent presence of large numbers of the living whose sole function was to serve the dead—or to defend them. . . . The hundred thousand slaves who worked for twenty years on the building of the pyramids at Giza must have constituted in themselves an enormous satellite town of the future city of the dead."[25] Later generations pilfered the tombs for wealth, or used them for quarries for new building efforts, or stood in wonder or critical reflection. The French explorer Volney wrote in 1787: "The labyrinth, these temples, these pyramids in their massive structure, reveal not so much the genius of a rich, art-loving people than the servitude of a nation tortured by the whims of its masters."[26] We may allow ourselves to wonder whether all surviving culture of every age is a mortuary monument of sorts—whether deliberately elicited by and created as a response to death or left as a legacy of human cultural outpouring in the face of finitude.

Great war memorials are another kind of funerary art, and they have existed in all ages. Especially noteworthy is their proliferation in this century, beginning after World War I. Between 1920 and 1925 municipal councils of every city in France had such memorials erected at the rate of sixteen a day. Thirty-six thousand monuments became the only secular edifice to compete with the Church, both the object of a cult, each as living and as frequented as the other. "Ancestor worship, which had disappeared from the Christian West, revived around these memorials."[27] Conceived at first as monuments to victory, they became monuments to suffering. "The War Memorial is, of course, a secularization of the Calvary, and one finds in it those martyr's palms taken over by Christian iconography."[28]

Thus do artists and their patrons provide a "visual culture" that surrounds and sustains and enriches any death system.[29] It is interesting to trace the evolution in style and practice and taste in such a culture. For example, early Christian art preferred the symbols of fish, anchor, dove, lamp, lighthouse, ship, and palm. After the conversion of Constantine in 313 the use of crosses began to spread. Yet the cross as the symbol of death did not appear in cemeteries until the thirteenth century. Only since the seventeenth and eighteenth centuries have crosses been used to mark individual graves in cemeteries.[30]

Any material culture is readily available (and manipulable) for ritual use, and also subject to commercialization and market degradation. One wry observer wonders when we will begin installing TV sets in coffin lids, wired to a power supply and small satellite dish on top.[31] (But what programs would be worth eternal watching?) Many eras show the evidence of material culture in their grave assemblages. Mourning costumes historically marked social class, and widows became perfect shop windows for impressive displays of social expertise.[32] The religious, political, and social ideas embedded in such iconography serve to make ideological or cultural statements.

Art can follow ideas about death as well as help shape them. When purgatory became a dominant belief in the late Middle Ages, prayers for the dead and places appointed for such prayers (chantries) became a major impetus to the commissioning of art by the wealthy. In the fifteenth century, when death was not glorious but horrible, tomb art followed suit, and the *memento mori* theme was developed in apposite ways. The deceased, not glorified in marbled classicism, is shown on his funeral monument as a mummy or a decaying corpse or a skeleton. Perhaps the best-known example is the tomb of Cardinal Lagrange, who died in 1402, now in the Musée Calvet in Avignon, whose befitting inscription reads: "Wretch, what reason hast thou to be proud? Ashes thou art, and soon thou wilt be like me, a fetid corpse, feeding ground for worms."[33] After the Reformation in England, when such ideas went into decline, tomb art turned from the undiscovered country of death backward to the glories of the lives of the nobility.

Revolutionary France sought secular icons for its death system in order to further its program of de-Christianization. A secular state wanted monuments that in no way suggested religious practice, and sculptors were commissioned to develop a new mortuary iconography that owed nothing to Christianity. Thus, in place of the former crucifix or statue of the Virgin, "pagan" forms of mortuary art began to reappear: menhirs, obelisks, pyramids, draped urns, broken columns, and, in place of the cross, the Gallic cock.[34] Burial places, too, had to undergo the same reimagining. State officials took the lead in reinventing a funerary ceremonial that did not borrow from the religious ceremonial of the *ancien régime*.[35] Whereas once men and women were born and died within the bosom of the church, they now died under the authority of the state.[36] The funeral pall was replaced by a blue, white, and red drape. Does the current U.S. practice, even in the Christian community, of emphasizing the American flag as a casket covering unwittingly stem from this French de-Christianization program?[37]

It is one thing to de-Christianize or desacralize the visual culture of death. It is quite another to imagine a new one. Contemporary Americans who are decidedly post-Christian or post-Jewish or postreligious, if they are not completely to ignore or be indifferent to the possibilities of culturally enriched funeral rituals, including their visual dimensions, must imagine new ones. In some cases funeral establishments have attempted to create an ersatz visual culture—either one suitable for all faiths or one that changes with the pulling of a curtain—but these have mostly been so banal as to be an embarrassment to everyone forced to use them.

Americans have recently become interested in the colorful popular culture of the Mexican Days of the Dead, November 1 and 2.[38] While it seems unlikely that such a culture could readily be imitated, it may stimulate the imagination or provoke reflection. Sugar skulls, coffin candies, skeleton puppets, bread of the dead, and board games and picnics in cemeteries are all unlikely in death-denying America. For all this, Mexican families prepare during October and may stay up all night on October 31. Spirits of dead children arrive at 4 A.M. on November 1 and leave by 8 A.M.; adult spirits arrive at 3 P.M. that day and leave by 8 A.M. on November 2. Graves are decorated with flowers, candles, and incense; children's graves get toys and plaster figures. Special altars are set up in homes. Food is exchanged, especially the bread of the dead, baked as an oval with a knob on which a painted face or angel appears. Larger loaves may have hearts and crosses made of egg whites and colored sugar. This celebration of All Saints' Day on November 1 dates back to the ninth century. All Souls' Day, November 2, emerged in the fourteenth century amidst increasing preoccupation with purgatory. On that day there were often exhibitions of relics or even skulls of the local dead, and processions from the church to the cemetery.

Coffin quilts are part of the visual culture that Appalachia produced.[39] A coffin-shaped patch with the name of a family member was initially sewn on the border of a quilt while the person was alive and well. When that person died, the cloth coffin was removed and resewn in the cemetery section at the center of the quilt. A far more monumental quilt has been produced by the Names Project as a memorial to AIDS victims. From October 11 to 13, 1996, forty thousand three-foot-by-six-foot panels of this quilt were displayed at the Mall in Washington, D.C. The quilt was two hundred yards wide and eight tenths of a mile long. Seventy thousand names of the dead are stitched into the quilt; all their names were read by two thousand volunteers standing at five microphones.[40] Nearby, visitors are deeply moved by the Vietnam Veterans Memorial with its stark call to meditation or regret.

Once visual culture prepared people for death during their own lifetimes, showing them ahead of time how they were to act their roles in the prescribed rituals. Didactic art coached the populace in how to die the good death and depicted the dangers of a bad death. Such art served the purpose of religion, but also of the state, admonishing the citizen to make a proper will. In twentieth-century art, death is more likely to be portrayed anonymously—Everyman, not a hero, dies; the dead, rather than the dying, is portrayed; there is little plot or drama and no interest in allegory or admonition.[41]

In post-Reformation England, visual culture was used to depict two bodies, the natural body and the nurtured or socialized body. The natural body was simply the corporeal remains, a source of danger to public health or dignity. But the disposal of the natural body was followed by efforts to preserve the social body as an element in the collective memory. John Souch's *Sir Thomas Aston at the Deathbed of His Wife* presented both bodies, separately, in a single picture. Funeral monuments, too, were meant to establish a permanent image of the social body.[42] Rituals as well as artifacts balanced the two states, the two bodies, and attempted to do justice to each.[43]

Chinese ceramic sculpture, going back seven thousand years, is being rediscovered as among the most remarkable evidences of the visual culture evoked by death. Funerary sculptures produced as burial objects, especially from the fifth century B.C. on, came to substitute for human sacrifices—an eloquent achievement for art. "The complete substitution of funerary figures for human and animal sacrifices was an innovative measure that liberated the productive capacity of the society and raised the level of the culture. The transformation of society prompted the evolution of funerary rituals and provided the social conditions necessary for the continuing development of the art of ceramic tomb figures."[44] The most spectacular array of such figures was only discovered in 1974: seven thousand ceramic sculptures of soldiers and horses painted in bright colors, a vast funerary army guarding the mausoleum of the First Emperor of Qin (221–207 B.C.).

Today, when the visual culture connected to death is far less elaborate, we are seeing only very timid efforts to retrieve the use of the arts—as in placing a picture on the coffin during the service. In fact, the visual depictions of death that surround the living are far more likely in the late twentieth century to be violent or naturalistic than didactic or heroic or moralistic, much less transcendent.

Nevertheless, a persistent—if not high-minded—function of visual art connected to death is to distinguish among social bodies. Even if all natural bodies come to the same common denominator, society and culture make significant and lasting distinctions, and material culture portrays those distinctions—from the price of the casket to the spectacle of the monument to the quality and presentation of music.[45] In post-Reformation England "top families organized heraldic funerals entirely on the basis of rank to deny the challenge to the continuity of the social body."[46] In the nineteenth century England saw spectacular funerals and visual culture surrounding the deaths of Admiral Nelson and General Wellington. In the twentieth century the funerals of Churchill and Kennedy were great occasions for visual display. The elaborate paraphernalia surrounding funerals historically included elaborate palls with religious or secular iconography, printed materials, commemorative gloves, scarves, spoons, rings, special mourning clothing, candles and torches, tickets. Today this is almost all gone, except for flowers, mass cards, and guest registries. In the past, the ritualized monumental body, which lasted long after the funeral, helped prevent the social body from decaying as quickly as the natural body. Placed at the burial site, the monumental body "was designed to stand forever as a replacement for the social body."[47] Elaborate monuments demonstrate that "death's assaults on social differentiation had to be resisted by ritual."[48] There was a rich outpouring of cemetery art and monuments, all reflecting social station. One tombstone reads:

> *Here I lie by the chancel door,*
> *They put me here because I was poor;*
> *The further in the more you pay,*
> *But here lie I as snug as they.*[49]

A tremendous range of brass monuments was produced in the sixteenth and seventeenth centuries and again in the nineteenth, a cultural outpouring that we still reap through our rubbings. Today, economic rationalization in the cemetery has produced flat and inconspicuous tombstones that can easily be mowed over, and a postreligious art world has mostly lost connection to the sacred, and certainly to religious institutions. We are offering to those who follow us a material culture of death with very little to rub off. No epitaph of visual culture today beckons: "Stay, Passenger / And know who lies beneath this stone."

Could we change this? It is beyond the scope of this book to argue for a reunion between art and religion or the sacred. Churches and synagogues and temples, and other religious institutions, have long been remiss in their responsibility to evoke fine art in their architecture, ecclesiastical furnishings, sculpture and graphic art, and vestments, paraments, and banners. Such institutions have their own roles to play; their seminaries, theologians, intellectual leaders, and institutional bureaucracies must take the lead.

Meanwhile, purveyors of flowers, plants, wreaths, caskets, and grave clothes will respond to public demands. Commercial vendors may take the lead, as they have in imagining new kinds of cemeteries. The recent evolution of cemeteries began in Paris, London, and Boston in the nineteenth century, and it has continued into the present. Forest Lawn, in Glendale, California, is by far the most famous modern cemetery, and it has branched out to other Los Angeles suburbs as well. Forest Lawn offers everything in one place: undertaking, cemetery, mausoleum, cremation, flower shop, seven different churches associated with beloved figures of the past, a museum, abundant representations of art and sculpture, and spectacular grounds that encourage a celebration of life.[50]

About an hour from Taipei, Taiwan, is Precious Gold Mountain, with its Happy Peace Garden. The entrepreneur who owned the original cemetery on this site decided to turn the hillside into a place where the living could learn about death. It has become a "death theme park." There are gigantic statues of turtles and elephants copulating, bringing together death and regeneration. There is a hundred-foot-tall bone tower for the deposit of remains after exhumation. There is a statue of the Death Buddha, the Hill of a Thousand Buddhas, the Hall of the Eighteen Giant Wax Arhats (famed Buddhists who achieved nirvana). There is the Trip of a Lifetime, a ride through a tunnel with representations from birth to death.

Individuals, whether religious or not, may look to the visual arts as they work out last passages that honor the human condition. They will invent ways to connect personal artwork, quilts, slides, photos, videos, stationery to the dying and to the commemoration of the dying. The heuristic questions must be: What are our needs? What about the deceased do we want to remember and celebrate? How can we initiate our grief work? What homage is to be paid to God or the sacred? And then: How can the arts help us in this? Under such an impetus people will both ransack the treasures of art for fitting accompaniments to last passages and begin to create and discover new art of their own.

DANCE AND THEATER

World drama and dance have their origins in religious rites. Western tragedy and comedy originated in Dionysian festivals in Greece. The Hebrew Psalms were performed as well as sung.[51] The Augustinian tradition severed dance from its religious connections, but today we have discovered an account, in the Gospel of Thomas, of Jesus dancing at the Last Supper. Dance has a long history in religious rituals, one overdue for rediscovery on our way to recovering ritual movement and the language of gesture. Processionals and recessionals can be a kind of dance, and they should be conceived as such. Mourners, and the body itself when it is present, should be danced on their ways. The dance of death, mentioned in an earlier chapter, was a bizarre and somewhat frenzied representation of death as the great leveler and the irresistible beckoner. The medieval images of the dancing dead "replayed a traditional association between the body's liberated movement in dance and its degradation in death."[52] Or did death, in fact, set the beleaguered, dying body free to dance once again? The artistically braver (or more cultured) mourners may indeed call for liturgical dance at rituals of last passage. The invocation of dance as a powerful and moving art form is long overdue. The god Shiva was called the Lord of the Dance. A Christian song sees Christ similarly.[53] Was Christ's resurrection a dance of life? Consider Tagore's poem:

> Let the links of my shackles snap at every step of thy dance,
>   O Lord of Dancing,

And let my heart wake in the freedom of the eternal voice.
Let it feel the touch of that foot that ever sets singing the lotus-seat
  of the muse,
And with its perfume maddens the air through ages.
Rebellious atoms are subdued into forms at thy dance time,
The suns and planets—anklets of light—twirl round
  thy moving feet,
And, age after age, things struggle to wake from dark slumber,
Through pain of life into consciousness,
And the ocean of thy bliss breaks out into tumults of suffering
  and joy.[54]

There is an intimate and historical connection between theater and ritual. I call here on the art of theater in order to invite the "staging" of rites of last passage, to evoke drama, scripting, costumes, sets, improvisation. Effective rituals, especially in this age, call for imagination and risk taking. Reminding ourselves that theater calls us away from the everyday world, we can be coaxed to evoke alternative worlds. Above all, theater connotes performance. In an age of repressed ritual and the rejection of "roles," we must be persuaded to become performers again. An entire ritual, then, could be seen as a work of art, and we should summon the courage to make it such. "Ritualization is a way, an experimental way, of going from the inchoate to the expressive, from the sheerly pragmatic to the communicative. Hence, in humans it is a close relative of art, especially the performing arts. In fact, we had best think of it as their progenitor, and as the source also of speech, of religion, of culture, and of ethics."[55]

If we consider the great themes that jostle each other at the moment of death, it becomes clear that a ritual that somehow misses this drama is obtuse indeed. Ritual, like theater, plays villians in order to create heroes, gives space to defeats to achieve victories. Ritual, like theater, plays out what happens and can happen. At death there is a confrontation between God and humanity, chaos and order, self and society, mourners and deceased. Absence asserts itself, presence recedes, God absconds, humans hide. Pilgrimages are begun, or aborted. Strange that we so regularly turn high drama into ritual boredom.

Victor Turner and Richard Schechner, in their seminal collaborations, long worked on the connections between theater and ritual. Turner was convinced that the aesthetic character of theater was inherent in life itself, whose plots he saw as social drama. But Turner looked for more. Life is typically lived in the indicative—straightforward declarative statements. But in our subjunctive, "as if" moods, we turn things upside down and experiment with ideas and narratives that never were. When social dramas carried to the breaking point look for their solutions, indicative and subjunctive tangle and the players experience themselves in new ways as the drama acts back upon them.[56] The life and traditions of religious institutions, of course, should be the nurturing womb for such ritual gestations. When churches themselves are ritually constrained or unimaginative or when people are unwilling or unable to look to religious institutions for the evolution of last passages adequate to our present dilemma, then perhaps theater could be a promising alternative. Under the pressure of such an agenda, theater itself might recover its ancient connection to ritual. Wherever one looks, including to models of "archaic" societies, one might hope for a rise in the level of social effervesence that could unlock energy sources in individual participants. Even daring ritual evolutions and improvisations need not be merely new inventions, as if there were no storehouse of historical and cultural memories. Focusing on ritual or theatrical transformation, Turner thought culture could provide the engaged self "with a store of preserved social experiences which can be 'heated up' to supply the current hunger for meaning with reliable nutrients."[57]

Those who look carefully can find a dialectical relationship between theater and the social drama of life. The stage drama is metacommentary on the major dramas of its social context (wars, revolutions, scandals, institutional changes). The stage drama's message and rhetoric feed back into the evolving larger drama of society and culture. Life becomes a mirror held up to art, and the living perform their lives—equipped and encouraged by stage drama.

The insight that social process plays itself out as a kind of performance opens up the relationship between ritual and theater.[58] Both ritual and theater can provide threshold experiences that are antistructural, creative, even carnivalesque. All performance may have ritual action as its original core, and all performative behaviors, from art to ritual to play, may share certain dynamics. *The working of art is as interesting as a work of art.* Just as ethologists find connections between animal and human ritualization, we ought to look for connections among social, religious, and aesthetic rituals. It would be exciting and fruitful if ritual and theater studies came together again. Words, action, gesture, movement, script, improvisation, plot, drama, staging, role diffusion, subjunctive reimagining, ritual reordering—all suggest how far we have to go, and can go, in developing dramatic ritualizations for our last passage.

Given the dramatic power of ritual, it may not be surprising to hear the argument that Greek drama and the Olympic games originated in funeral rituals.[59] Just as the final note of certain sequences in Gregorian chant could be elongated into elaborate musical improvisations that eventually produced polyphony, so the ritualization of death could bring about powerful mediations and enactments of the meaning of life and death. Returning, perhaps, to such a root of drama, Eugéne Ionesco cast his play *Exit the King* as a stylized death ritual. Berenger I, a once great king, is dying, as are his power and throne. The play, full of absurd, pathetic humor but also possessing a stately, liturgical quality, is itself a ceremonial movement toward death.

In *An Easy Death*, Simone de Beauvoir painfully captures such drama, and the role of the mourner in it, when she sees that, at the funeral of her mother, she is attending a dress rehearsal. This comment complexifies the answer to a tired question: For whom is the funeral intended, the living or the dead? It is a dead theatrical experience when only part of the audience is captured. Powerful rituals include everyone and send all on their way. For the dying, art-of-dying rituals serve as practice for the last transit. For the dead, rituals are the means through which the community sends them on their way. For the living, the mourners, rituals remind them they are always in rehearsal for their own deaths. To that end, the more severe practice of the Christian Church has always been to minimize the difference, during funeral rituals, between the dead and the living, to include all in the drama. No one is a disinterested bystander. The bell tolls for everyone. The living are invited to see their own image in the image of the deceased, as tombstone epitaphs once commonly suggested. If life review invites the narrative construction of the self, ritual invites the performative construction of the self.

Although I have repeatedly argued that ritual suffers when it is overwhelmed with texts, it is obvious that words are indispensable. To the power and place of words we now turn.

WORDS

One of the oldest expectations of any burial, no matter how simple, is that someone would "say a few words."[60] In Arthur Miller's *Death of a Salesman*, Willy Loman's wife says to her sons: "He's not to be allowed to fall into his grave like an old dog! Attention; *attention must finally be paid!*" We love to contemplate "famous last words" spoken by the dying themselves: Goethe's "More light!"; Luther's "We are beggars"; Sarah Bernhardt's "When do I go on?"; Karl Marx's "Get out! Last words are for fools who haven't said enough!" Some of the most famous last words in the West are those of the Catholic requiem mass: "Eternal rest grant unto them, O Lord, and let perpetual light shine upon them" (*Requiem aeternam dona eis Domine: et lux perpetua luceat eis*).

It is well to choose carefully the spoken words that finish a death. A ritually impoverished age may also be short on words to speak in the face of death. We lack a religious vocabulary, now that death is merely natural—or unmentionable. We must recover a way of speaking adequate to death. Heidegger's "Language is the house of being" is often quoted. It makes especially poignant his lament that we have forgotten that we have forgotten the question about Being. But through that forgotten question we come to understand human experience ourselves. Our existence is the account we give of ourselves.

Not just any words will do. We are tempted to use words as sedatives, as if to dull the brain's mediation of anxiety.[61] Words that cover up rather than release feelings are not useful. Words can mask and defend against reality and create safe distances between people when it is precisely such distance that should be overcome. Consider the short prayer, abruptly begun at a pastoral visit, that seals off dialog, excludes all further questions, leaves God intact, and enables the minister to save face and make a quick getaway. Condolence conversations often function in the same way. But grief is work, and it must be begun. Death is immense, and we must summon words adequate to its wonder.

Still, language *can* reduce and mediate our most fundamental anxieties. Language takes shape as a security measure.[62] For the young child it was a necessary means of communicating basic survival and physical comfort needs. It came to be a means of winning and maintaining parental approval and, when the child was alone, of holding parents emotionally near. Learning to talk happens within the same interpersonal matrix within which anxiety as fear of separation is also learned. Thus oral communication becomes an early learned mechanism for anxiety reduction. Language is a means of overcoming separation. Ultimately, words as "performative utterances" become an important way in which we fully express our humanity in the face of death and reach beyond ourselves to work out and express transcendent meanings. We hope for great lines to speak when they are needed.[63] In the end, words should not fail.

Ultimate words will not fail if they are tinctured with divine words, as they are in religious ritual. In the Hebrew Bible God gets the first great lines of performative utterance in Genesis, "Let there be." The first words of the Gospel of John are "In the beginning was the Word (the logos)." The "Word of God" represents creative power, divine self-disclosure, human apprehension of revelation, and some change effected by such communication. For Jewish and Christian traditions the Word of God represents divine initiative, whether through revelation to the prophets or in the midst of the worshiping community. For Christians, Christ is identified as the ultimate Word of God—as proclaimer and proclaimed. Augustine called preaching an audible sacrament. Luther too would emphasize the proclaimed word, not merely the written. Words come from the incarnate Word. "The liturgy in this perspective is nothing other than the ceremonial of *logos*, the ritual of the Word of life's meaning, the enacted style of the world's meaning."[64] Thus in ritual the assembly succumbs to logos revealed, to the freedom of logos unfolding. Following such a logos leads "not to the brink of clarity but to the edge of chaos," to the dark and hidden things of God.[65]

Not all ritual words evoke God. Thucydides knew the power of words. In Pericles's funeral oration he evokes the "unfading praise and the most glorious of burial places" of Athenians who fell in war. "I do not mean the place where they rest, but the renown they have left behind, which will be remembered forever.... For the whole earth is a burial-place for famous men, and, to proclaim what they were, it is not enough to have an inscription engraved on a stone in their own country. In foreign lands an unwritten memorial of the choice they made dwells in all and everyone."[66]

But all words spoken in the face of death are searching for a path through meaninglessness. In *The Cancer Ward,* Alexander Solzhenitsyn gives words to a dying hospital patient, words Solzhenitsyn wanted to offer his fellow sufferers: "Sometimes I feel quite distinctly that what is inside me is not all of me. There's something else, sublime, quite indestructible, some tiny fragment of the universal spirit. Don't you feel that?" Such words echoed the poet Pushkin's words: "Not all of me shall die."[67]

Is the sacred created through language? We render something sacred through ritual as a mode of ultimate attention. Words evoke the ineffable; what is said points to what cannot be expressed. Consider the "ordering" power of liturgical words: "They mend ever again worlds forever breaking apart under the blows of usage and the slashing distinctions of language."[68]

It may be that, in the West, most formal words about death (epitaphs, obituaries, Christian sermons, liturgies, elegies and other poetry) stream out of the tradition of classical oratory, though the thundering and soothing oracles of the Hebrew scriptures can scarcely be forgotten. Greek oration developed out of formal laudation of those fallen in battle, of which Pericles's speech is the earliest example. Such oratory ranged from praise of one long dead, to general or individual epitaphs, to brief intense laments, to speeches of consolation. The heart of such oratory was a laudation combined with lament, and covering such topics as family, birth, natural endowment, upbringing, education, life, occupation, moral qualities, achievements, fortune, comparison with others. Commonplaces in both Greek and Latin consolation literature included: fortune rides all; all are mortal; live virtuously, not long; time cures all; death gives freedom from the ravages of disease and age; the examples of others give one courage; many believe in a happy life beyond the grave; reason must temper grief; the display of emotions is unmanly.[69]

Early Christian funeral orations grew out of this tradition but were saturated with basic Christian doctrines and worldview: a personal God who is creator of the world, all-powerful, just and merciful; the Trinity; the incarnation, crucifixion, and resurrection of Christ, the victor over death; the sacrament of the Eucharist as spiritual help; the role of the Church; true life in the future, resurrection of the body, communion of saints, the Last Judgment, heaven/hell. The resurrection of Christ and the ultimate resurrection of all bodies occupied a central place, though these beliefs met with great ridicule in the ancient world. This Christian rhetoric poured new life and meaning into classical forms and filled them with biblical arguments.

Christian epitaphs, a kind of distilled word, also grew out of the classical tradition, but took a very different direction, with a confidence and cheerfulness founded on Christian faith. Two typical examples are "Now a sweet world and the great design of God are yours" and "Go now therefore garlanded into God's presence."[70] If we knew nothing beyond what we could learn from their epitaphs, it would still be plain that belief in the afterlife was fundamental to the Christians, and not to the people of classical antiquity.[71]

Words about death that may find their way into rites of last passage can and will come from many genres:[72] texts from sacred scriptures;[73] orations or sermons; liturgical texts;[74] prayers; consolations; elegies; art-of-dying manuals; mantras; myths; diaries or journals; storytelling and narratives; ethical wills.[75] The elegy in particular is a rich source of words that confront absence and achieve presence.

Peter Sacks's study opens up the role of words in the ritual drama of death.[76] Originating in the classics, the elegiac form blossomed in English in the eighteenth-century work of the poets of the "graveyard school."[77] The elegy, Sacks sees, is a woven text, a fabric created in the place of a void.[78] "The movement from loss to consolation . . . requires a deflection of desire, with the creation of a trope both for the lost object and for the original character of the desire itself."[79] So it happened in classical mythology. When Daphne turns into a laurel tree to escape Apollo's advances, her "turning" matches Apollo's turning from her to a metaphor for her: "Since thou canst not be my bride, thou shalt at least be my tree. My hair, my lyre, my quiver shall always be entwined with thee, O laurel. With thee shall Roman generals wreathe their heads."[80] When Syrinx and her sisters turn into marsh reeds to escape Pan, he turns his longing to the reeds themselves, which give forth a lovely sound at the soft air stirring them: "This union, at least, shall I have with thee." The syrinx, or panpipe, takes its name from her.[81]

The laurel and flute become elegiac tokens, symbols for what is lost.[82] The resolution of loss requires a "detachment of affection from a prior object fol-

lowed by a reattachment of the affection elsewhere. At the core of each proce-
dure is the renunciatory experience of loss and the acceptance, not just of a
substitute, but of the very means and practice of substitution."[83] This is the
Freudian view of mourning as the gradual withdrawal of libidinal energy
from the lost object and the redirection of it to new objects.[84] Initially, words,
especially ritual words, mediate loss and carry the weight of the lost object.

The child's great cultural achievement of instinctual renunciation of the
absent mother becomes in later life the cultural achievement of mourning. In
the elegy the mourner learns to represent absence and *to make the absent present
through language.* Weaving a consolation is not unlike weaving burial clothes or
a shroud: elegiac words become the action of mourning, a process of work.

I have complained that liturgical studies and liturgy itself are typically so
focused on text that the performative character of ritual is lost. What if ritual
shapes the words and leaves its shape upon them? Sacks notes that ritual has
greatly influenced the form of the elegy, leaving it with a residual ceremonial
structure.[85] Thus ritual precedes the words of elegy; the text follows. To
remind us that words seek embodiment, Goody nicely notes that a funeral can
be seen as an obituary acted out, but perhaps he should have said that ritual
needs give rise to obituaries.[86] Unpacking words that can be said and have
been said, the funeral becomes a kind of verbal and ritual inquest.

Poets understand that a word is elegy to what it signifies. Any word signifies something absent. "Representation longs for the recovery of presence. . . .
Loss of the original fuels the fires of artifice. . . . Dispossession makes possible
the creation of images, and negatively, as embodied in absence, death, and
loss, animates the quest of writing."[87] Of Yeats's poetry it has been said: "Every
day, in every act of writing, a poet rehearses death, dying to the biographical
self and assuming a 'mask' or 'phantasmagoria.' . . . For Yeats, death is both the
human absence that generates the anticipatory or retrospective mourning of
poetry and the absence within poetry itself."[88]

Journal writing is a much more popular form of writing that has achieved
new currency in recent decades because of its accessible capacity to engender
and perform just these truths. In her journal Anaïs Nin found "not only a companion . . . but a source of contact with myself . . . a place where I could tell the
truth and where nobody would look."[89] Journal workshops and methods
abound.[90] I see them as part of the reigning psychological paradigm of our age.
The turn inward, for psychological and also spiritual deepening, can be
applauded, even if it leaves much social, cultural, and religious business
unfinished. It is one important dimension of the recovery of a death of our
own. Of course, journal writing of itself will not produce ritual, which, in the

usage encouraged here, is a public occasion. Nor is journal keeping a substitute for public rituals, though it can be very important as a private ritual. But individual journals, of the dying or of those who cared for them, can be rich sources of words, powerful and significant in their own right, that can be imported for public ritual use. They typically produce moments of great power in rituals, and those gathered often experience them as welcome and familiar memories, as well as an effective permission-giving for memory and grief.

Obituary-writing exercises can also stimulate words and thoughts. A typical example, never seen in a newspaper but often used in workshops, is: "_____ died yesterday of _____. She had reached the age of _____. She always wanted but never got to _____. She will especially be mourned by _____. She is most remembered for _____." Such an exercise often produces painful reflection, but may be a necessary prelude to the completion of story and the creation of a death of one's own. Another death awareness exercise is writing epitaphs. These sometimes produce the occasional humor we long for in the midst of death, as does this one found in the Elgin Cathedral:

> *Here lie I, Martin Elginbrodde:*
> *Have mercy on my soul, Lord God,*
> *As I would do, were I Lord God*
> *and you were Martin Elginbrodde.*

Storytelling, above all a communal and oral enterprise, is a wonderful birthing of words for ritual use. Tapes and videos that tell stories, taken from or given by the dying, can be powerful ingredients in rituals of last passage. Deena Metzger wonderfully titles her book *Writing for Your Life* and offers workshop exercises and anecdotes that open up the kind of writing that may well come to serve ritual occasions.[91] Journal writing liberates personal story to go public. Everyone has the right to tell the truth about his or her own life. Metzger sees the source of our first suffering to lie "in the fact that we hesitated to speak. It was born in the moment when we accumulated silent things within us."[92] If it takes a looming death ritual finally to evoke our long-silent stories, so much the more significant, then, is the draw of last passage. If life is a dream we are in danger of losing when we awake (die), then preparing for death challenges us to discover or create a usable history. "Stories heal because we become whole through them. In the process of writing, of discovering our story, we restore those parts of ourselves that have been scattered, hidden, suppressed, denied, distorted, forbidden—we re-member, we bring together the parts."[93] The resulting narratives can help us stage powerful and empowering rituals. Sometimes, as caretakers, coaches, accompaniers, or mourners, we assist another in the story he or she cannot finish.

In the search for the right words we may turn to literature, the great storehouse of words, especially if we cannot find our own. Franz Kafka wrote that "a book should serve as an axe for the frozen sea within us."[94] In her anthology *In the Midst of Winter: Selections from the Literature of Mourning*, Mary Jane Moffat writes: "Literature is one of the few resources we have in modern times for living the deep life and not being simply spectators of our own experience. Love, loss and death, of course, have always been its great themes, and a lifetime of reading has given me some knowledge of their complexities. But we can draw from books only that which we already know. The poet's intuitive gift for finding hidden likenesses in things in the objective world that correspond to our psychic life stirs and awakens in a special way the emotions of those who feel wordless in the face of loss."[95]

Finally, when thinking of the power of words, it is well to be reminded that silence is also powerful. Silences can punctuate words, as rests do the notes in music. Both words and silences take us somewhere. Ultimately, an art-enriched and word-ful and action-ful ritual is about a worldview, a hope, an affirmation.

HOPE ACROSS BOUNDARIES

I write a part of this final portion of the book during a two-month stay in India. The smoke of the cremation fires from the ghats along the Ganges stings my nostrils, intense Hindu piety presses in on me; 115-degree heat is relentless; occasional mild delirium from bad food or water settles on me. I have come to imagine the terror of dying unmourned and unclothed by my own culture, far from home. I glimpse what it might mean to view life wholly as an ordeal, to cultivate a severe ascetic practice as the only means of negotiating life passage. I have experimented with anticipatory grieving. I have tried to practice a posture of hope, a stance I previously took for granted or did not think about. Living betwixt and between, I have also gained a new appreciation for mortality—for its demands on us and for the opportunities it offers. Over it all, every night, from still another tradition I hear the muezzin's call, sounding a note I am learning to expect and treasure, even while longing for the comfort of my own community.

In the Christian tradition, the evening monastic office of compline invites eternal wakefulness and eternal rest. Just as the last passage moves between grief and hope, the posture of the office of compline moves between eternal wakefulness and peaceful sleep. Sleep alone suggests extinction; too much waking bespeaks insomnia or tedium. "What we really want is both the refreshment of sleep and the rapture of waking. This is the antiphony of Christian hope, and it is beautifully expressed by the hymns and antiphons for Compline, the lullaby with which the Church sings itself to sleep."[96] Grieving and hoping, death and life, morning light and evening darkness, sleeping and waking are the rhythms of the liturgy, and they could become a natural rhythm in our lives. Such natural symbols can become eschatological signs, markers toward the life unfolding ahead. Through ritual we gift ourselves with them. The prayer of compline intones: "May the Lord Almighty grant us a quiet night and a perfect end." Christians move from the psalter to the cross in the compline commendation "Into thy hands, O Lord, I commend my spirit."

I have opened this final section with allusions to hope ranging from India to Western monasticism. But I especially want to evoke hope across nearer boundaries: hopeful rituals that draw together Westerners across the boundaries of religious and nonreligious traditions and across the boundaries of this life and the life to come. I seek a civil religion of human hopefulness, but not a hope untinged by grief. The ritual requirements death makes upon us evoke *both hope and community. It is hope-filled communities not lacking the courage or the resources to face death that will grant us a death of our own.*

Though dying requires the mediation of grief and hope, and though grief work cannot be escaped, I believe we ultimately can be delivered to hope.[97] Just as theology, in St. Anselm's phrase, is "faith seeking understanding," and Anselm said, "I believe in order that I may understand," eschatology may be called "hope seeking understanding."[98] I aspire now to say why we might end in hopefulness.

I know that the entire community of those seeking hope is mostly far different from the one tuned to monasticism, and larger than the one that resonates with Christian symbols.[99] Is it possible we can cross boundaries and come together in hope? Might we, across varying traditions, find common ground at the far boundary, the outer limit on which death rituals come to be? There is no better ground on which to find each other than ritual. The liminal stage of ritual, betwixt and between, is inherently sacred and therefore a perfect womb for such gestation. Life passages, powerfully moving in all societies, are carried out within the authenticating framework of the sacred. The human life course is seen (by Lloyd Warner) in a kind of leaf shape, with the social personality contracted at both ends, where the sacred is dominant, and bulging in the middle, where the secular asserts itself. At the two ends, birth and death, societal definitions relax and the sacred asserts itself. There we live by hope, and community rituals are its vehicle.

If ritual seeks to draw together the world lived and the world hoped for, one can envision it standing midway between everyday life (and death) and the

Ultimate, connecting each to the other within itself. We all stand together on that frontier, where traffic flows between quotidian life and the realm of ulti-mate meaning. The dispositions toward the sacred induced or enacted in rit-ual linger to color the world of bare fact. From ritual community, we return to our everyday roles and realities with the taste of the Other still in our mouth. If rituals' gifts have been rich, we cannot forget them. Our tastes are refined.

Inside ritual we can discover hope as the hidden face of divine reality; so we shape our ritual as a *model of* the hope it mirrors. We also use ritual to lay out hope as a template for a path through this world and into the next; so ritual becomes a *model for* hope, through which we give new shape to the world that lies outside the boundaries of ritual.[100] Back and forth between the everyday and the realm evoked by ritual, we trade in hope.

All the living and the dead find themselves together in the space that ritual defines, creates, or recognizes. The living, especially those who mourn or anticipate mourning, can find each other in the company of hope. Could the vision quest toward a death of our own call together varying communities of faith and no faith? If ritual invites sinners together, why not doubters, too? Rituals will occasion traffic between religion and the secular world, whenever and wherever there are honest and authentic efforts to respond to death.[101] If death and life can come together, why couldn't we, in the diversities of our affirmations (and doubts), join together in hope?

In the introduction to this book I said I hoped to speak to all reflective read-ers and mostly to avoid appeals that implied the epistemological privilege of religious faith. I proposed that my own Christian tradition must demonstrate far more effectively than it recently has its adequacy to the human condition—this amidst the massive collapse of many Christian systems of meaning in a secular age. I wanted to show, throughout the book, what resources adequate to a recovery of a death of our own might be and what hope they might offer. But I also wanted to invite conversations with other religious traditions and with those reflective persons outside religious or spiritual traditions, so that all might come to aid each other in the struggle to find a death of our own. Together we might work at uncovering adequate resources to ritualize human passage. It is *the ritualizing human community* coming together to face death, binding living and dead, offering renewed connection for all the living, that *is the most hopeful resource we have in recovering a death of our own.*

Could ritual again deliver these goods, even in a secular age? Could doubt-ing readers of this book be lured into hopeful community? Ritual has been called the furnace within which the image of God is forged out of the power of language and emotion.[102] Less grandly and with appropriate secular caution, Antonin Artaud called for a theater that could "create a metaphysics of speech, gesture, and expression, in order to rescue it from its servitude to psychology." He saw that the contemporary world of theater found the great religious questions alien, or even alienating. Could he somehow provide for that world a metaphysical temptation, so that it would engage unfamiliar territory? What to do? It couldn't be obvious. "It is not a question of bringing metaphysical ideas directly on to the stage, but of creating what you might call temptations, indraughts of air around these ideas."[103] What if rituals of passage that were not overtly religious could still venture to draw indraughts of air around a metaphysics of hope? Couldn't they foster the inclinations that could bring us together around neglected business? Artaud noted further: "In our present stage of degeneration it is through the skin that metaphysics must be made to re-enter our minds."[104] Through ritual osmosis we might be able to absorb the ingredients necessary for a community of hope.

If minimalist staging can hint of hope, how much more must overt religious ritual recognize, create, and attend to the postures and gestures of hope. But the religious communities seem hobbled. If we live in times of important failures of nerve in the religious tradition, it is also even more necessary to acknowledge the very serious shortcomings of secular culture and society.[105] *Secularism has been unable to produce fulfilling systems of meaning, but it has also weakened the ability of religion to do so.* It has produced "a crisis in religious culture and civilization, with a gradual erosion of the social systems that 'protected' a stabilizing and all-embracing religiosity; they have caused the 'death' of a particular image of God, man and the world."[106] But a disenchanted world eventually became disenchanting. Science, the reigning paradigm, has not discovered convincing answers to the great quests for meaning. Modern psychology is caught in the impossible dualism of mind and brain. Mired in Darwinian fundamentalism, sociobiology searches the swamp for altruistic genes—though an evolutionary process pulled by an as-yet undreamed of eschatological future might offer far more promise. The biblical sense of the tragic is a more adequate statement of the human condition than Erikson's psychological stages.[107] An old age gifted with a "gero-transcendence" homing in on the sacred is more promising than most gerontological theory, but it waits to take shape.[108]

Given the cul-de-sac of secularist meanings and the mostly failed ritual experiments of Marxist governments, it does seem appropriate to look to religious communities, among others, to enrich and ground rituals of hope. Indeed, since we constitute ourselves by ritual, it is also possible the churches might use the funeral to reconstitute themselves and their worldview, clarifying their "own identity contrary to the world around" them.[109] To my mind, this would by no means be a bad thing, though the churches must avoid the temptation to say more than they know. The teachable moment will produce not a return to Christian triumphalism, but an acknowledgment that the Church does after all minister to a secular society, even as that society also seeks its own answers by its own lights. The Church, which developed many of its rituals while at the center of culture, might learn to speak even more effectively at the margins.

For religious and nonreligious people, death can be part of the process of consciousness expansion. "Human beings have an insatiable urge to domesticate mystery by making it reasonable. . . . The Christian response to death, however, is not so much an explanation as it is a confession. The Christian symbol of 'the resurrection from the dead' explains nothing, or at least it should not be interpreted as an explanation. But while it explains nothing, it confesses a great deal."[110] The Church fails to make its potential contribution to town meetings in the face of death if it modestly declines to profess its own faith out of its own traditions.

What are the prospects for bringing together all who search for an authentic last passage within and without religious institutions? What genuine and respectful connections can be created between everyday ways of seeking and theological constructions of meaning? How astute will religious communities be when they respond to the persistent and problematic questions that come in off the street or from a nonreligious culture? Could religious communities learn more effectively to sacramentalize or ritualize the answers to such seeking? Could they become adept at "popularizing the liturgical (sacramental) and liturgicizing (sacramentalizing) the popular"?[111] The churches and synagogues and temples ought to recognize that people are demonstrating a need for rites, that they would like to express whatever religious belief and hope they have, and that they may require for their sense of identity and belonging some kind of socioreligious system. When someone asks for a religious ritual, this is not a casual gesture but the fulfillment of a need to express the sacred dimension of existence. The challenge is to carry this seeking further along: not to denounce the "magic" among spiritual seekers, but to lead it from human meaning, feeling, and subjectivity to a deepened theology of hope. Providing a ritual structure and overlay is the best response to these human needs and aspirations because it realizes the symbolic dimension of the human condition and responds to the need to sacralize the decisive moments of the life cycle.[112] Hope is the ultimate ingredient in the ritual quarry; it may just be the one that finally unites us. But religious institutions need conversion if they are to become communities that can believably stage such hopeful rituals.

Hopeful rituals will require retrievals. A metaphorically impoverished age, both religious and secular, will need to draw resources from outside—from other times and places, and from the contemporary counterculture that authentic religious communities must always be. The Christian theological tradition in particular has been "set in the context of an expectation of the consummation of the world and of human history."[113] We shape such a hope and are also shaped by it. The Irish poet Seamus Heaney looks for a time when "hope and history rhyme."[114]

No doubt contemporary culture imposes limitations on hope.[115] Hope, like death and like ritual, is a cultural construction—if also a recognition of and response to divine intimations. A significant deterrent to developing a posture of hope is the *metaphorical deprivation of contemporary culture*. People die for lack of metaphor. Many deaths, much dying are failures of imagination. Alfred North Whitehead thought that "a civilization which cannot burst through its current abstractions is doomed to sterility after a limited period of progress." He said that "the death of religion comes with the repression of the high hope of adventure."[116] The dearth of metaphor in modern and postmodern consiousness impedes the reconstruction of eschatology and hope. The author of a book extolling an eschatology of hope writes: "Unless we have some sense of inhabiting a universe that carries symbolic meaning and is ultimately sacramental it will be extremely difficult to retrieve the eschatological interpretation of experience."[117]

The eschatological imagination withers under the dominance of objectifying, literalizing worldviews. The images of eschatology are poetic, imaginative projections out of the promise of our present in the light of our past experience. The formulations of eschatological hope "appeal to our participation in a personal, living and creative way in the always new and vital expression of the hope of the ancient community that is also truly our own hope."[118] But when we literalize such evocative or anticipatory images, when we impose them as doctrines, we estrange ourselves from them. Our most important hope and vision is then relegated to some realm from which we are disconnected or alienated. "It is then a matter of accepting someone's word for it that things are this way beyond death and history, exactly this way. Sooner or later the question arises as to who said it and how it could be known with certainty then if it cannot be verified now."[119] Cut off from our own imaginal ground, disconnected from the rich imagery of our traditions, alienated from our own experience and longings, we lose the ability to project ourselves into a future beyond. Rubem Alves wrote: "Hope is the presentiment that the imagination is more real, and reality less real, than we had thought. It is the suspicion that reality is far more complex than realism would have us believe, that the frontiers of the possible are not determined by the limits of the present, and that miraculously and surprisingly, life is readying the creative event that will open the way to freedom and resurrection."[120]

At that frontier God waits—impatiently, as we see in a Hasidic tale told by Elie Wiesel. An unhappy boy complains to his grandfather that his friend cheated in a game of hide-and-seek, because he gave up and stopped looking. The grandfather says: "God too is unhappy; he is hiding and man is not looking for him. Do you understand? God is hiding and man is not even searching for him."[121]

My parents were ever among the searchers, the expectant, the hopeful. When they died, they left a story within the larger story to tell. No one should die without such a story. Their story evoked work to carry on, a task to be completed. This book is that task. I wish I could enter the world's sickbed, hold the dying, sing to them of hope, calm them, deliver them to a joyous death of their own. Everything for this last act has been prepared. The quarry, so rich, has been mined. All the ingredients are at hand. I call to all readers of this book to accept this task, to make this final act their own.

You can achieve a death of your own through ritual. Ritual is a way of paying attention, of focusing, of rendering the sacred. For some of us this ritual will give body to an entire life of faith and hope. For others the investment in the ritual may be a kind of Pascal's wager. I suggest it will pay off richly. Ritual brings us together in hope, and a hopeful community empowers and quickens ritual. We enter the world of ritual to achieve a death of our own. Within ritual, we discover ourselves reunited not only with each other, not only with the world of the dead, but with hope and with God. Overcoming all the impediments of the present age, we may also overcome the impediments to God. Finally, our story is taken through ritual up into a larger story. Ritual delivers us to Life.

Epilogue

Is there something more to be said? I regret the strange silence of Christian theology, preaching, and spiritual writing regarding eschatological hope and the afterlife. I mourn the disappearance of metaphorical power from the culture and theology's complicity in a flattened language of hope. With theologians silent and the clergy discreet, I am not surprised that exotic spiritualisms and New Age searches are everywhere in evidence. The crowds, hungry for the necesary elements missing from their diets, turn to new pastures in search of them. The churches seem content to hide the old metaphorical power, out of deference to the presumed affinities of the modern age. But the bulging bookstore shelves suggest the churches have seriously misread the needs of the modern age.

In this book also, not all that needs to be said has been said. This is no flight to special privilege for Christian faith postponed until the epilogue. I would like to say what can be said with no special appeals to authority. Contemporary Christian theology is willing to be judged by its "adequacy to the human condition." I find such a theology (in my case with its Lutheran spin) a more adequate support for the hope that is within me than any alternative systems of meaning, though I mean no disrespect to them. I want to move in this epilogue from the subjunctive of a book that evokes ritual to the indicative of positioning myself in the world where rituals happen—in my case, in the theological world where Christian rituals are performed. I propose to give reasons for the hope that is in me.

I find myself in that smaller group within the whole human community that is called, in the Hebrew scriptures and the New Testament, to anticipate the kingdom of God. As such, it is a counterculture, or a remnant, though it hopes, by "standing still in the light" or by assertive cultural exchanges, to enter the world's imagination. Sympathetic readers outside this community may be relieved I held off to the end, even if they are now willing, having walked with me this far, to indulge this final step.

From Roman Catholic theology I have gained the resources fully to ritualize the human journey and also the final warrant, even in this present day, to send the dead on their way to God, not imagining that only mourners can be touched by ritual. I have learned to provide a sacramental overlay to the final passage, one that both confers the hovering presence of God and empowers the faithful yes of the believing participant. From the Orthodox tradition I have imbibed a steady incarnationalism that mantles the entire earth with a divine yes: God became human that we might become divine.

Protestant theology practices the connections between finitude and guilt and doubt and death, while medical and psychological models continue to neglect the moral dimension of dying and death, much less the ontological.[1] Nagging at the posture of hope too easily conferred by the untroubled and easy consciences of New Age psychologies and spiritualisms is the suspicion that "we have to die because we are guilty"—not that we die because it is part of nature. Fear of judgment trumps fear of extinction. A denial of death's finality that is born of despair may be truer to the human condition than a too easy acceptance of death. Terrible guilt or oppressive finitude could point to the dimension of the Ultimate. Guilt has eternal roots and demands a solution in relation to the eternal. Death itself cannot relieve it. "*In despair, not death, we come to the end of our possibilities.*"[2] We need something more than death, even an easy death, to release us from despair. More than bodily existence is threatened by despair. To believe that one has lost the eternal and oneself is Kierkegaard's "sickness unto death." In such despair, even death is not available as a last hope. One cannot escape the demand to become in freedom the person that one does not want to be. Kierkegaard understood there are worse things to fear than death.[3] Thus, merely naturalizing death is not adequate to the complexity of the human condition.

For Christianity there is only one "argument" against death—the forgiveness of sin, or, in Paul Tillich's preference, "acceptance." Estranged from our essential being, incapable of realizing it, bound to contradict it, we may, if we are fully awake, find in death the "wages of sin." To this the Gospel proclaims a state of being accepted in spite of being unacceptable. Reinhold Niebuhr also saw this, and argued that the condition of finiteness and freedom, sin and creativity, is a problem for which there is no lasting solution by any human power. This is the "Protestant principle," which discovers the ultimate seriousness of the "boundary-situation" and proclaims the ambiguity and only penultimate usefulness of all human remedies and securities. But Christianity proclaims salvation, not renunciation, an eternal yes rather than a judgmental no. The yes that confers the posture of hope is the yes "not based on anything that we have done . . . but . . . on something that Eternity itself has done, something that we can hear and see, in the reality of a mortal man who by his own death has conquered him who has the power of death."[4] Such a yes is "the coming of the

Eternal to us, becoming temporal in order to restore our eternity." Is only such an answer adequate to the human condition? The posture of hope it proffers, a hope born of facing rather than escaping the ultimate question, is what Tillich calls "the courage to be."[5] This sense of ultimate concern, which Tillich saw as the essence of religion, can transfuse culture. Culture, in turn, gives full and eloquent shape to this religious impulse. Tillich thought religion the substance of culture, and culture the form of religion. If theology spoke again with a compelling voice, would a new culture of dying form around it?

Another Protestant theologian, the ethicist Paul Ramsey, concretized the life lived in such hopefulness and corrected Tillich's "love as reunion with Eternity" to love as "covenant obedience" in community. In such a faithful community humans accompany one another—also in the face of death as the ultimate indignity.[6] It is precisely such a community that can become worthy of its proclaimed story and of the ritual life that embodies it. In its midst, within its "plausibility structure," a posture of hope is enacted.

In this last word I would like to call on the entire Christian tradition—and Judaism's messianic hope, on its own terms—once again to unite around the powerful, and annually renewed, metaphor of Advent.[7] Advent means the arrival of the future as something new and unexpected, coming as gift and promise of God. Advent is rooted in hope, not optimism. In the Christian liturgical calendar this is a time weighted with joyful remembrance (making present again the incarnation of Christ in the imaginal life of the community) and eschatological expectation (hopeful waiting upon the coming of God). Advent expectation and hope could become the root metaphor for ritualizations of death that turn endings into beginnings.

Advent, the Latin equivalent for the Greek *parousia,* the ultimate coming of Christ, is replete with powerful endings and beginnings. The "comings" of Advent are typically seen as including the Incarnation at Christmas, the recurrent coming, by the power of the Spirit, in the lives of the community, and the coming at the end of time. Thomas Merton wrote: "The Advent mystery is the beginning of the end of all in us that is not yet Christ."[8] In our end is our beginning. The signs of God's reign point toward the birth of something new. Advent, the beginning of the church year, is replete with tales of end times. Advent's themes are watching, waiting, imagining, dreaming. Its imagination is the desert watered and blooming.

Some of this Christians share with the Jewish community of faith. Think of the Passover hope, "Next year in Jerusalem." Just as ritual displays and enacts a world that transcends the everyday, Advent rehearses the community in the countercultural posture of hope.

In the Jewish and Christian traditions this hope is never merely about the future, time extended, the coming of what will be. It is about the coming of God, which always holds within itself a *novum*, the possibility of the new.[9] The God of the Hebrew scriptures said to Moses, "I will be who I will be." The God of the Old and New Testaments promises to create a new heaven and a new earth. The eschatological imagination clings to such promises through the posture of hope.

Jürgen Moltmann has culminated his magisterial systematic theology with *The Coming of God*, just as he began it with *The Theology of Hope*. He moves beyond the woodenness of much traditional eschatology with its "final solution" in order to transform the eschatological imagination into the lively expectation of a universal Easter and the arrival of a new beginning in the midst of the end. The ultimate creation stands out in front of us, and the appropriate eschatological posture is hope, the remembered hope of the raising of the crucified Christ, fresh beginnings from a deadly end. For Moltmann, the cross is the form of the coming kingdom, and eschatological hope has a cruciform shape. The oppressed are specifically included.

On a recent July 4, I was part of the audience for an evening concert at Westminster Abbey in London. That historic church has housed the rituals of monarchy and mortals. It still, in the words of T. S. Eliot's memorial there, proffers "the communication of the dead . . . tongued with fire beyond the language of the living." That night the choir sang the words of seventeenth-century poet Richard Crashaw's "Easter Day," that other Advent. In the otherness of a distant English still pregnant with metaphor, in the not-here of an exotic holy place, the music carried me across boundaries to a future time. I experienced a thrill of hope that is *totaliter aliter*—unlike anything we know.

> *Rise, Heire of fresh Eternity,*
> *From thy Virgin Tombe;*
> *Rise, mighty man of wonders! and thy world with thee.*
> *Thy Tombe, the universall East,*
> *Natures new wombe,*
> *Thy Tombe, faire Immortalities perfumed Nest.*

> *Of all the Gloryes make Noone gay*
> *This is the Morne.*
> *This rocke buds forth the fountaine of the streames of Day.*
> *In joyes white Annals live this houre,*
> *When life was borne,*

No cloud scoule on his radiant lids no tempest lowre.
Life, by this light's Nativity
    All creatures have.
Death onely by this Dayes just Doome is forc't to Dye
    Nor is Death forc't; for may hee ly
    Thron'd in thy Grave.
Death will on this condition be content to Dy.

Notes

PREFACE: MASTERING MY MOTHER'S TAPES, HURRYING IN MY FATHER'S STEPS

1. In *The Joy Luck Club* (1989), Amy Tan enacts the importance of passing on family narratives to succeeding generations. In Tan's *The Kitchen God's Wife* (1991), the narrator's mother must tell her daughter the story of her life in order for the daughter truly to know her mother's and her own identity.

2. Rainer Maria Rilke, *Prose and Poetry* (1984), p. 6.

3. Maurice Blanchot, quoted in Michael Camille, *Master of Death* (1996), p. 236.

INTRODUCTION: AN INVITATION TO EXPERIMENTAL THEATER

1. Philippe Ariès, *The Hour of Our Death* (1977), p. 614.

2. Writing a book is an act of hope, or delusion. In connection with this work, I recall a favorite ghost story in the Latin Quarter of Paris: A day after his death a student appeared to his teacher, wearing a cope made entirely of parchment and covered with tiny writing. "These words, that weigh more than if I carried on my head the tower of that church [St. Germain des Prés], are the sophisms and curiosities on which I spent my days." The master teacher is scalded by a drop of sweat from the ghost's hand. He departs the schools of logic, reciting: "I leave croaking to frogs, the morning to ravens, and empty things to the vain. / I am awakened from logic which does not fear death." Michael Camille, *A Master of Death* (1996), p. 217, tells this story in his discussion of belief in the afterlife in fourteenth century Paris. Might the scholar's bookish labors actually count against him in the afterlife?

3. Jacques Le Goff, *The Birth of Purgatory* (1968), pp. 1–2.

4. In "The Impact of the Concept of Culture on the Concept of Man" (1973) in his *The Interpretation of Cultures*, the anthropologist Clifford Geertz developed the concept of "cultural performance" to open up for analysis ritual actions that disclose the symbolic fusion of ethos and worldview, our characteristic actions and our beliefs. Geertz argued that such ritual drama occurs against a backdrop of chaos, tumults of events which threaten our interpretive capacities. In *The Anthropology of Performance* (1987), Victor Turner argued that such cultural performances interact with and locate themselves in conflictive social dramas. Social dramas get their rhetoric from cultural performances; cultural performances get

their plots and problems from social dramas. The social drama I am outlining in this book is one in which we have lost our way with death. From that drama can come new ritual plots through which we rediscover a death of our own.

5. Lasch is quoted in Eugene Thomas and Susan Eisenhandler, *Aging and the Religious Dimension* (1994), p. xiii.

6. In *First Person Mortal* (1995), p. 185, Lucy Bregman waits until the very end of her coauthored study of first-person narratives of dying and grieving to say: "Here, for the first and last time, I will speak as a Christian, having avoided a theological reading of our narratives in the interest of laying out the themes their authors themselves found important." Then she laments the almost total lack of Christian themes in the current autobiographical literature on dying and grieving, even that written by Christians.

7. His stance is quoted and discussed in Bonnie Miller-McLemore, *Death, Sin and the Moral Life* (1988), p. 157.

8. Thomas Kselman, *Death and the Afterlife in Modern France* (1993), p. 91, alludes to this.

9. Kselman, p. 108.

10. In *A Community of Character* (1981), Stanley Hauerwas has nicely argued that the church must be a certain kind of community if it is rightly to tell the stories of God. Of course, the larger argument in his collection of essays runs counter to the argument I am making here. Hauerwas reasserts "the social significance of the church as a distinct society with an integrity peculiar to itself" (p. 1) and argues that the church's most important task is not to reach out for secular dialog (as I am doing here) but to become "a community capable of hearing the story of God we find in the scripture and living in a manner that is faithful to that story" (p. 1). Christian ethics and theology can only be carried out, Hauerwas thinks, "relative to a particular community's convictions" (p. 2). Diagnosing the liberalism bequeathed by the Enlightenment as a liberation from particular historical narrative and as a claim that freedom and rationality are independent of a historical story, Hauerwas counters with the methodological claim "that every community and polity involves and requires a narrative" (p. 4). If Christians do not serve the world on their own terms, "the world would have no means to know itself as the world" (p. 10), a clearly Barthian perspective. To be useful and viable, the churches must become communities that can sustain the stories they tell—because they have been uniquely shaped by these stories. Hauerwas carries on a running argument with those who assert that Christians do not come to public policy with special knowledge and insights (p. 39). The "world" or the community called for will be created by the community that tells a unique story, and "the church is the organized form of Jesus' story" (p. 50). To follow Hauerwas's line of argument, with which I am not unsympathetic, would be to create, deliberately, countercultural Christian rituals.

11. Though not at all addressing the problem of death, Michael Harrington's *The Politics at God's Funeral* (1983) summoned believers and atheists (he was an

ex-Catholic) to address "the spiritual crisis of western civilization."

12. While mainstream religious traditions have key roles to play in the recovery of a death of our own, they may be willing to welcome all people of goodwill who are willing to address the loss of our own death in the twentieth century. It is also a commonplace in the sociology of religion to hypothesize that alternative religious traditions often spring up to meet the spiritual needs to which mainstream religions have not been attending.

13. Eric Cross, "Death in War: Britten and the *War Requiem*," in Jon Davies, ed., *Ritual and Remembrance* (1994), p. 141, remarks that in his great *War Requiem*, commissioned to celebrate the consecration of Coventry Cathedral and first performed in 1962, Benjamin Britten "was seeking to find a 'new' language and symbols appropriate to a modern secular age, a language in keeping with the historical and cultural context of a society which had largely rejected traditional religious doctrine. Thus the *War Requiem* is a non-liturgical work in which the interplay of language and symbols works on different levels, the relationship between the traditional Requiem Mass (sung in the 'dead' language of Latin) and the contemporary soldiers of Owen's poems (sung in English) reflecting the communion between the living and the dead." There come together in a powerful juxtaposition the ancient texts of Christian liturgy and the stark realism of Wilfred Owen's antiwar poetry, in which a modern Abraham declines the divine offer of a ram to substitute for his son (the Genesis 22 story in which Abraham is called by God to sacrifice his only son, Isaac). Owen's poem, in Britten's libretto, goes (p. 147): "But the old man would not do so, but slew his son,— / And half the seed of Europe, one by one." Britten wanted to produce in this great war memorial a universal, public language, not a nationalistic one, hoping to have the parts sung by a British tenor, a German baritone, and a Russian soprano.

CHAPTER 1: THE DYING AND REVIVING OF DEATH

1. In *The Prophetic Imagination* (1978), pp. 49–51, Walter Brueggemann evokes a "prophetic imagination" that cuts through numbness and penetrates self-deception. He calls for adequate symbols, which render denial of terrible experience unnecessary and which bring fear and terror to public expression. To offer society a language of grief that unmasks and dismantles the self-congratulation of existing systems is the prophet's great contribution. While Brueggemann is writing about the stance of the prophet against systems of injustice, his call for a language of grief in the midst of systems of denial is appropriate also in this context.

2. *The Poetical Works of Gerard Manley Hopkins* (1990), pp. 166–67.

3. All this could not be farther from the mentalities of the Middle Ages. Michael Camille, in *Master of Death* (1996), pp. 181–82, writes: "Remembrance of the dead played a fundamental role in medieval social and individual consciousness in rituals that were experienced at the funeral of an individual and whose repetition permeated the whole culture. . . . Catholicism at the end of the Middle Ages was 'a

cult of the living in the service of the dead,' and its two major celebrations, the Requiem Mass and the recitation of the Office of the Dead, were the major means of social cohesion among those still living." Of "tombs, idols, and relics" Camille, p. 192, continues: "One of the reasons why images became so important in late medieval culture was not because they were seen as representations of life but because they worked as powerful reminders of death."

4. Camille, p. 195.

5. Camille, p. 245.

6. Lynn Caine, quoted in Virginia Sloyan, ed., *Death* (1990), p. 101.

7. William May, "The Sacred Power of Death in Contemporary Experience," *Social Research* (1972), p. 469.

8. This is the argument of Robert Kastenbaum and Ruth Aisenberg, *The Psychology of Death* (1976), p. 160.

9. Jocelyn Evans, *Living with a Man Who Is Dying* (1971), p. 83.

10. Clare Gittings, *Death, Burial, and the Individual in Early Modern England* (1984), p. 9.

11. John McManners, *Death and the Enlightenment* (1981).

12. James Farrell, *Inventing the American Way of Death* (1980).

13. Bonnie Miller-McLemore, *Death, Sin and the Moral Life* (1988), p. 139.

14. Samuel Southard, *Death and Dying* (1991), p. xxxviii.

15. In *The Hour of Our Death* (1982), Philippe Ariès is famous for proposing a devolutionary model in which death reverts from tame to savage as cultural defenses disintegrate. His structuralism played off nature (violent and dangerous) against culture (safe), with sex and death as weak points in the cultural defense against nature, mostly carried on through religion, law, and kinship. He postulated that the proscribing of death awareness follows modernity. This summary is from Ellen Badone, *The Appointed Hour* (1989), p. 12.

16. This is the argument of Edward Rothstein in his review of Elemire Zolla's *Archetypes*, published in the *New York Times Book Review* (May 16, 1982), p. 12. Zolla asserts that we are myth-starved.

17. Eugene Thomas and Susan Eisenhandler, *Aging and the Religious Dimension* (1994), p. 11.

18. The great nineteenth-century German Protestant theologian Friedrich Schleiermacher, a participant in the Berlin circle of the new Romanticism, lamented the secularism of that circle in his book *On Religion* (1958). He saw cultural flowering alongside stunted religious development. His way back to religion was not metaphysics or even morality, but a "feeling of absolute dependence." This mode of perception or intuition is the essence of religious consciousness. Religion should flourish in every place where a living contact with the world fashions itself as feeling. How could the Romantics neglect what should have been central to their own project?

19. W. Lloyd Warner, *The Living and the Dead* (1975), p. 308.

20. Lucy Bregman and Sara Thiermann, *First Person Mortal* (1995), devote

chapter 5 of their study of first-person narratives of dying and grieving to issues of individualism and autonomy, whether celebrated or protested.

21. This is the argument Richard Sennett makes in *The Fall of Public Man* (1977).

22. See Mary Douglas, *Natural Symbols* (1973). Since the work of Foucault and others, the symbolization and significance of the body as the place where culture inscribes itself has become a fascinating new topic. A whole spate of books in the last ten years has focused on the body. To date, however, this new attention to the body and its cultural uses has not seriously impacted the pervasive individualism characteristic of popular culture. Nor has there been any significant reconsideration of the place of the (dead) body in public ritual, though I will argue precisely for that in chapter 7.

23. Here I am following the argument of Robert Bellah and his associates in their book *Habits of the Heart* (1985), in their follow-up book, *The Good Society* (1992), and in their introduction to the new edition of *Habits of the Heart* (1996).

24. Bellah et al., *Habits of the Heart* (1996), p. viii.

25. Bellah, et al. (1996), pp. ix–x. Alfred Killilea, "Some Political Origins of the Denial of Death," *Omega* (1977), provides a Marxist reading of individualism and traces the dying of death to the utilitarian political ideology of John Locke. Moving beyond Hobbes's argument that humans band together in political systems to protect themselves from violent death, Locke asserted that they come together in order to protect private property. Killilea sees that underlying the pursuit of unlimited acquisition is human isolation, which is alleviated only by outproducing and out-accumulating others. A nature lacking any primordial integrity takes on usefulness when labor is added to it, within a milieu of the moral primacy and self-sufficiency of the individual. This achievement and sufficiency of individual effort is the mythology inherited by American public life; it contributes to the dying of death.

26. Louis Dumont, "Religion, Politics, and Society in the Individualistic Universe," *Proceedings of the Royal Anthropological Institute for 1970* (1971), p. 33. In *Death, Burial and the Individual in Early Modern England* (1984) Clare Gittings builds on the work of Ariès and attempts to make much clearer and more explicit individualism as a fundamental cause of change in death systems. She especially notes the significance of the Reformation and its relation to individualism. But Ralph Houlbrooke, in *Death, Ritual and Bereavement* (1989), p. 7, while greatly admiring Gittings's work, has called into question her focus on individualism as a key variable: "The core of Clare Gittings's work, an immensely valuable analysis of expenditure on funerals between the Reformation and the Interregnum, has been set in a much larger explanatory framework which does not really fit it. The basic problem with all theses which place a heavy burden of explanation on the 'rise of individualism' is that the sorts of evidence which enable us to detect its presence, such as 'the character drama or novel, the portrait and the biography or autobiography' can usually be equally or more plausibly attributed to other causes. And their non-existence or disappearance do not in themselves demonstrate its absence or weakness."

27. Killilea (1977), p. 212.

28. Killilea (1977), p. 212.

29. In *The Denial of Death* (1973) Ernst Becker argued the opposite. Heroic, individualistic achievement is necessitated by the impossibility of coming to terms with mortality. But Becker failed to see that community and participation in human solidarity might be alternatives equally as compelling as narcissistic achievement. Indeed, it may be just the social dimensions of life that are central to affirming the value of mortal existence. Killilea (1977), p. 194, remarks that individualism marginalizes those human experiences which most challenge the assumption that death obliterates meaning.

30. Lindsay Prior, *The Social Organization of Death* (1989), p. 133, notes Hertz's well-known claim that grief is distributed and redistributed according to social principles and Durkheim's argument that grief and mourning are socially patterned, and comments: "Whilst both of these claims were preserved and developed within social anthropology during the twentieth century, they were absolutely and entirely ignored by those who studied the manifestations of grief in western cultures—a study which, incidentally, fell under the control of a normalising psychology." Later, p. 135, he contrasts the view of grief in the nineteenth century and that influenced by "normalising psychology" in the twentieth: "Grief, if anything, was a condition of the human spirit or soul rather than of the body and in that sense it could neither be normalised nor medicalised. The work of the psycho-analysts, however, was only the first in a series of processes which sought to medicalise grief. The second stage was represented in the work of Lindemann. Lindemann's work was the first to place the study of grief on an empirical footing and the first to establish a 'symptomatology of grief.'" He reviews a subsequent literature that ever more thoroughly medicalized grief and even treated it like a somatic disease. Grief became "something in the body which could be measured and assessed," p. 136.

He concludes, p. 137: "Broadly speaking, it is clear that psychology and anthropology adopted incommensurable standpoints on the study of grief, so that whilst the first concentrated on the subjective experience of grief in different populations, the second concentrated on the outward expression of grief and utilised that outward expression as an indicator of inner sentiment. In western culture, it was psychology which therefore dominated the study of grief and bereavement during the 20th century and, overall, the problem of grief, like death before it, became medicalised and individualised and subsequently fell under the control of medical personnel. Thus, the priest was ousted from the aftermath of death in favor of the doctor and grief was treated (in all senses of that word) as a private and segmented emotion. It was this segmentation and individualisation of grief which prompted Gorer to carry out his study of the phenomenon, and it was on the basis of that study that he theorised about the denial of death in western culture."

31. Nathan Scott, *The Poetry of Civic Virtue* (1976), pp. 71, 85.

32. Most communitarian literature neglects religion. So do other social and political theorists who are trying to move public discourse and social reality

beyond the individualism and rights-based norms of the Enlightenment. But some sociologists of religion, especially Robert Wuthnow in his many works and, of course, Robert Bellah and his associates, address this issue.

33. In *The Broken Covenant* (1975), Robert Bellah reopened a conversation between America's present and its traditions going back to the seventeenth century. Noting the utopian millennial expectations of the founders, Bellah lamented the substitution of a technical-rational model of politics for a religious-moral one. He noted the replacement of virtue and conscience by the notion of "interest." Even that term had been torn from its larger context of tradition and meaning, so that it was now understood only as the self-interest of the isolated individual. Bellah's book, then, became an argument that the current liberal utilitarian model of society once competed with a fundamentally religious and moral conception of America, but has now replaced and effaced the latter.

34. Medicine, of course, is not the only instance of the professionalization of death. The rise of the undertaking profession is widely commented on. Today we also have grief counselors, thanatologists, etc. Should the clergy also be charged with the professionalization of death? Perhaps not in general, but institutions such as chantries (Julian Litten, *The English Way of Death* [1991] p. 6) certainly contributed to a very narrow specialization and focusing of the sacred. Both Lindsay Prior's book and Ivan Illich's *Medical Nemesis* (1976) offer extensive bibliographies on the medicalization and professionalization of death. In *The Theology of Medicine* (1977) Thomas Szasz subjects medicine to a withering critique and argues that patients victimize themselves by attributing magical powers to their physicians. In *The Physician's Covenant* (1983) William F. May considers five images of the healer: parent, fighter, technician, teacher, and covenantor. One should not assume that everywhere in the modern world the medicalization of death has occurred in the same way. In *Cuttin' the Body Loose* (1995), William Joseph Gavin discusses, in a chapter on Japan, the very different directions and concerns that occurred as the Japanese tried to develop definitions of brain death and their relation to transplant possibilities. Gavin also discusses medical science as, partly, a cultural construction, while it mostly poses as hard biological fact.

Bregman and Thiermann (1995) devote chapter 4 of their study of first-person narratives of dying and grieving to searching analyses of and protests against medicine.

35. This is the subtitle of Robert Veatch's book *Death, Dying, and the Biological Revolution* (1976).

36. There is already an abundant literature on euthanasia and physician-assisted suicide in the field of bioethics, as well as in law. Recent examples are Tom L. Beauchamp, ed., *Intending Death* (1996) and Margaret Pabst Battin, *Least Worst Death* (1994). The series What Are They Saying on recent Roman Catholic thought, put out by Paulist Press, offers the excellent but already dated *What Are They Saying About Euthanasia?* by Richard M. Gula (1986). By 1996 Oregon had

passed a physician-assisted suicide initiative, and the U.S. Ninth and Second Circuit Courts of appeal had ruled against legal proscriptions against assisted suicide. The U.S. Supreme Court ruled that there was no "right" to assisted suicide, but that a state could legalize it.

37. For the details of this analysis I am indebted to Lindsay Prior, pp. 5, 27, 39, 113.

38. This is Susan Sontag's thesis in *Illness as Metaphor* (1977).

39. Ivan Illich, pp. 97–98.

40. Paul Starr was already documenting this in 1982 in *The Social Transformation of American Medicine.*

41. Carl Jung, "The Soul and Death," in Herman Feifel, ed., *The Meaning of Death* (1959), p. 4.

42. Maxine Kumin, *Our Ground Time Here Will Be Brief* (1982).

43. Philip Levine, *One for the Rose* (1981), p. 64.

44. Galway Kinnell, *Selected Poems* (1982), p. 61.

45. Michael Simpson, *Dying, Death and Grief* (1979).

46. Samuel Southard, *Death and Dying* (1991). Therese Rando discusses the complexity of the literature in her foreword.

47. Southard, p. xxiii.

48. Prior, p. 4, discusses Michel Vovelle's 1976 article.

49. Prior, p. 4.

50. Jessica Mitford, *The American Way of Death* (1963), p. 54.

51. D. Leviton, "Death Education," in Herman Feifel, ed., *New Meanings of Death* (1977), pp. 258–259.

52. Michael Simpson, "The Future of Death: Exploration or Exploitation," *Thanatology Today* (1980).

53. Barbara Backer, Natalie Hannon, and Noreen Russell, *Death and Dying* (1982).

54. Sloyan, p. 38.

55. Sloyan, p. 80.

56. Miller-McLemore, p. 1.

57. Miller-McLemore, p. 1.

58. Neither American nor British consumerist literature has much to contribute. Of the British Consumers' Association booklet *What to Do When Someone Dies,* Prior, p. 199, remarks: "The book's contents accurately reflect the concerns of the culture in which it is produced. It contains no mention of the ritualistic procedures through which the corpse should journey, nor does it mention any ritualistic tasks which the living should perform for the dead. Instead, it contains details of the bureaucratic and other organisational procedures through which the living must journey in order to dispose of the dead. . . . It requires 131 pages to fulfill the tasks which are set forth in the brief Foreword and within those pages one can find an outline of the system which embraces death in the modern world. It is a system replete with formal rules for establishing death, registering death, disposing of the dead, acquiring documents, utilising documents and establishing legal rights to property, pensions and the like. In short, it is a booklet which guides the

reader through the labyrinth of practices and procedures by means of which the dead are bureaucratically ordered and defined."

The same can be said of the American consumerist literature. Everything is about the price of the coffin and ways to avoid embalming and the use of "memorial societies" as a way to cheaper funerals, and nothing is about death's wound to the human condition or the potential of ritual or the necessity of religion.

59. Farrell, p. 221.

60. Camille, p. 134.

61. Eugène Ionesco, *Exit the King* (1963), p. 68.

62. Robert Jay Lifton, *The Broken Connection* (1979), p. 27.

63. Lifton, p. 29.

64. James Hillman, *Re-Visioning Psychology* (1975), p. 64.

65. Hillman, p. 67.

66. Hillman, p. 66, writes: "Highs and peaks say nothing about the worth of persons undergoing them, for they can occur also in psychopaths and criminals, having nothing to do either with creativity or maturity, Maslow's goals. Any textbook of abnormal psychology bears witness to the fact that pathologizing itself can produce peaks: kleptomanic stealing, pyromanic barn-burning, sadism, grave desecrations—all can provide ecstatic joys. So can bombing and bayoneting and so can watching them on television. Whenever the importance of experience is determined only by intensity, by absoluteness, by ecstatic Godlikeness or Godnearness and is self-validating, there is risk of possession by an archetypal person and a manic inflation. Transcendence by means of a 'high,' an idea so widespread through the different forms of humanistic practice (body-highs, weekend-highs, LSD-highs), easily turns into a manic way of denying depression. Rather than a new means for meeting a psychopathology, it is itself a psychopathological state in disguise."

67. Robert Kastenbaum, "Do We Die in Stages?" in Sandra Wilcox and Marilyn Sutton, eds., *Understanding Death and Dying* (1981), p. 111.

68. Farrell, p. 223.

69. In the fourth chapter, "The Death and Dying Movement: A Subspecialty in Psychology," of her book *Death, Sin and the Moral Life* (1988), Miller-McLemore reviews the moral views of Kübler-Ross, Lifton, and Erikson. She contrasts "the culture of joy," which sees death as opportunity for personal growth, with the "culture of care," which calls for wisdom, mutuality, and continuity.

70. Miller-McLemore, p. 85.

71. Southard, p. xxxiv, credits Bowlby and Parkes with nuanced and sensitive efforts to ground death anxiety in much earlier separation anxiety. "These studies show how loss or the threat of loss will insert deathlike anxiety into crucial stages of the life-span and deflect a child's ability to integrate trust into a developing style of life. These studies urge those who have been bereaved at an early age to give up the darkness that comes with continued internalization of a lost person and find new life and light in faithful relationships."

72. Miller-McLemore, p. 6.

73. Philip Rieff, *The Triumph of the Therapuetic* (1966).

74. Paul Ramsey, "The Indignity of Death with Dignity," in Peter Steinfels and Robert Veatch, eds., *Death Inside Out* (1974).

75. Johannes Fabian, "How Others Die—Reflections on the Anthropology of Death," *Social Research* (Autumn 1972), p. 547.

76. Fabian, p. 549.

77. Fabian, p. 552.

78. Fabian, p. 554.

79. In the appendix to *Habits of the Heart* (1985) Robert Bellah and his associates call for a return of social science as public philosophy. They recall that during the nineteenth century "the social world changed from being a community, a cosmos of callings, into an industrial-corporate society organized around competing professional careers," p. 298. Intellectual disciplines participated in this transformation and ended up, as Fabian argues, distanced from the human community and from their own humanity. Bellah decries "the assumption that the social sciences are not cultural traditions but rather occupy a privileged position of pure observation. The assumption is also that discussions of human action in the humanities are 'impressionistic' and 'anecdotal' and do not really become knowledge until 'tested' by the methods of science, from which alone comes valid knowledge," p. 301. But the recovery of social science as public philosophy will come about only when the boundary between the humanities and the social sciences is reopened.

80. Harry Moody's foreword to Thomas and Eisenhandler (1994), p. x.

81. May (1972), p. 477.

82. Abraham Heschel, *Who Is Man?* (1965), p. 89.

83. Heschel, p. 100.

84. So argues Paul Tillich in *The Courage to Be* (1952).

85. T. S. Eliot, *Collected Poems 1909–1962* (1963), p. 201.

86. Eliot, p. 201.

CHAPTER 2: IMAGINING DEATH

1. Michael Camille, *Master of Death* (1996), p. 196.

2. Such musings come hard these days except to the willful, so effectively have we segregated the living from the dead. Joseph Roach, *Cities of the Dead* (1996), pp. 48, 50, writes that in Europe the dead were once omnipresent because their spirits still occupied spaces of the living and because churchyards overflowed with their material presence. But the Enlightenment hoped to reform this scandalous propinquity, and so the dead were compelled to withdraw into sanitized memory —or forgetfulness.

There are other interesting "causes" for the decoupling of the world of the living and of the dead. Jon Davies, in "One Hundred Billion Dead: A General Theology of Death," in Davies, ed., *Ritual and Remembrance* (1994), p. 28, laments the decline of the doctrine of purgatory after the Reformation and calls it a "sociable doctrine," which "retains, indeed strengthens and enhances, friendly relationships between the living and the dead."

Interestingly, archaeologists who study burial sites talk of communities' "strategies for maintaining direct relations with the ancestors," as John Chapman notes in "The Living, the Dead, and the Ancestors: Time, Life Cycles and the Mortuary Domain in Later European Prehistory," in Jon Davies, ed., *Ritual and Remembrance* (1994), p. 57, a concept few would even imagine today.

3. Loren Eiseley, *All the Strange Hours* (1975), p. 80.

4. Shakespeare, *Richard II*, III, ii, 102–3.

5. This is Walter Benjamin's view in *The Origin of German Tragic Drama*, as discussed by Ronald Schleifer in the afterword to Sarah Goodwin and Elisabeth Bronfen, eds., *Death and Representation* (1993).

6. James Curl, *A Celebration of Death* (1980), pp. xxiii–xxiv.

7. Paul Barber, *Vampires, Burial and Death* (1988) discusses the significance of vampires in a cultural outlook on death.

8. Susan Sontag, *Illness as Metaphor* (1977).

9. Camille, p. 135, notes: "The pilgrim's fevered upward gaze also reminds us of the loss of man's natural innate heat that Aristotle believed came with orgasm and death. Women, by contrast, were described as lacking warmth and were thus not only insatiably addicted to the act of coitus, which through friction and penetration transferred life-giving warmth from male to female, but were thus at the same time associated with the coldness of heat-devouring death."

10. Goodwin and Bronfen, p. 13. Their anthology *Death and Representation* devotes four articles to "death and gender": "Painting the Dead: Portraiture and Necrophilia in Victorian Art and Poetry," by Carol Christ; "Romanticism and the Ghost of Prostitution: Freud, *Maria*, and 'Alice Fell,'" by Sarah Webster Goodwin; "Writing as Voodoo: Sorcery, Hysteria, and Art," by Regina Barreca; and "Women in the Forbidden Zone: War, Women, and Death," by Margaret R. Higonnet. A longer work is Elisabeth Bronfen, *Over Her Dead Body* (1992), which traces the configuration of death, femininity, and the aesthetic.

11. Goodwin and Bronfen, p. 14.

12. In *Society and Religion in Elizabethan England*, Richard Greaves (1981), p. 695, describes how Elizabethan Protestants tried both to curtail Catholic ceremonies and to retain the traditional pomp as an underpinning of the social order; they had to avoid so alienating the common folk that Protestantism was repudiated. An added difficulty was that funerals for persons of wealth included acts of charity in the form of grants of food, clothing, and money. Reducing the scale of funerals would mean decreasing relief for the poor at a time when the need for it was growing, but the aristocracy welcomed a decrease in such expenditures. Meanwhile, the newly wealthy in London began to exceed their social status in the lavishness of their funerals.

13. Emily Dickinson, "The Chariot," *Collected Poems of Emily Dickinson* (1982), p. 199.

14. In this section I am greatly indebted to Kees Bolle's article on myth in the Macmillan *Encyclopedia of Religion* (1987).

15. In this section I am making the larger case for the mythological imagination and its contribution to a deepening of our understanding of death. In *Rituals for Living and Dying* (1990) David Feinstein and Peg Mayo help the reader cultivate an empowering (personal) mythology for confronting death. They want to bring to consciousness personal mythology, as deep beliefs, guiding images, and unspoken rules held about living and dying. They carry the reader along the five stages through which, they believe, one's death mythology naturally evolves.

16. Hans Georg Gadamer, quoted in Gary Bedford, "Notes on Mythological Psychology: Reimagining the Historical Psyche," *Journal of the American Academy of Religion* (June 1981), p. 234.

17. Bedford, p. 239.

18. Paul Ricoeur, *Freud and Philosophy* (1970), p. 189.

19. Lawrence Sullivan, *Icanchu's Drum* (1988), p. 22.

20. Th. P. Van Baaren, in his article "Death" in the Macmillan *Encyclopedia of Religion* (1987), pp. 251ff., categorizes myths of origin.

21. Bonnie Miller-McLemore (1988) titles the second chapter of her book *Death, Sin, and the Moral Life* "Illustrations in Psychology: The Shift from Empirical to Quasi-religious Views." In it she offers a very critical analysis of the pretensions of modern psychology. In *Death in the Midst of Life* (1992), Lucy Bregman is hopeful that depth psychology is the stream of psychology most likely to "leave room" for death in its richness and for the role of religion.

22. Kim Chernin, "By the Waters of the Woodland," quoted in Robert Cantor, *And a Time to Live* (1980), pp. 52–53.

23. Yorick Spiegel, *The Grief Process* (1977), pp. 174ff.

24. Granger Westberg, *Good Grief* (1962), pp. 7–12.

25. C. Earl Gibbs, *Caring for the Grieving* (1976), pp. 116–18.

26. Edgar Jackson, *Understanding Grief* (1957), p. 157.

27. Victor Turner, *The Ritual Process* (1969).

28. Loring Danforth, *The Death Rituals of Rural Greece* (1982), p. 115.

29. Danforth, p. 152, summarizes the structuralist argument of his book. The women who perform the death rituals of rural Greece are trying to resolve the contradictions between life and death that are inherent in human mortality. As opposition between life and death is mediated, death might be overcome. Human existence is marred by a contradiction that cannot be ignored, and death continues to tear apart the socially constructed world of these women.

30. To see death more clear than anything else and to arrange other truths around it can become a powerful feminist move. Nadia Seremetakis, *The Last Word* (1991), p. 15, writes: "I am not just posing an arbitrary methodological inversion here. The defamiliarization of social order through the optic offered by death

is precisely the central task and cognitive orientation assumed by Maniat women in their performance of death rites. To examine death in Inner Mani is to look at Maniat society through female eyes."

31. Peter Berger and Thomas Luckman, *The Social Construction of Reality* (1966).

32. David Stannard, *The Puritan Way of Death* (1977), p. 133.

33. Gail Kligman, *The Wedding of the Dead* (1988), provides an illuminating study of these.

34. Kligman, p. 247, notes that "not all that is buried is dead. Death is the consummate vampire who thrives on the bodies and blood of humans. Death refuses to disappear, to relinquish its own life. Death will not be controlled—ultimately." Thus, even if urban cemeteries are silent and death weddings occur only in the countryside, the central paradox of death in the midst of unfulfilled sexual desire and marriage outlives the decline of the custom of the death wedding. "Because desire seeks expression, resolution is symbolically sought through other media" (Kligman, p. 247). So Dracula films and other new cultural texts make it possible to play with fire within the limits of control. The framework expands within which the search for meaning in the face of untimely death remains comprehensible.

35. Sullivan (1988), p. 183, offers this account.

36. Robert Blauner, "Death and Social Structure," in Charles Jackson, ed., *Passing* (1977).

37. Talcott Parsons and Victor Lidz, "Death in American Society," in Edwin Shneidman, ed., *Essays in Self-Destruction* (1967).

38. David Kertzer, *Ritual, Politics and Power* (1988), p. 102. Kertzer's book is an excellent study of the power of ritual and its political uses. It combines theoretical analysis with many telling narratives.

39. Richard Kalish and David Reynolds, *Death and Ethnicity* (1976), pp. 110–12.

40. Lawrence Taylor, "Introduction: The Uses of Death in Europe," *Anthropological Quarterly* (1989b), p. 149. The intimate connection among death, war, and religion has frequently been noted and lamented. In a clever chapter title, "The Martial Uses of the Mass: War Remembrance as an Elementary Form of Religious Life," Jon Davies (1994) discusses the sacralization of war so common in European religion, noting that an alien visitor to Winchester Cathedral could well conclude that England's religion is centered on war remembrance. Davies argues that the sacrificial character of war death is compared to the sacrificial death of Christ, so that the former is haloed with the latter.

41. Taylor (1989b), p. 150.

42. Church and state in France constantly deployed rituals to gain advantage over each other. After Bastille Day was invented as a national celebration in 1880, the Catholic Church attempted to create a new, more unifying national festival in honor of Joan of Arc. Joan's "symbolic ambiguity" might bring together the partisans of the old order and the champions of the revolution. The Vatican decision in 1894 to beatify Joan of Arc lent force to these hopes. But the celebrations degenerated into bitter and even violent battles of symbols.

43. Taylor (1989b), p. 153.

44. Lawrence Taylor, "Cultural Constructions of Death in Ireland," *Anthropological Quarterly* (1989a), p. 175.

45. Taylor (1989a), p. 176.

46. Peter Brown, *The Cult of the Saints* (1981).

47. Taylor (1989a), p. 184.

48. Eric Hobsbawm and Terence Ranger, *The Invention of Tradition* (1983), p. 157.

49. Frank Baldwin, "Chrysanthemum and Sword," *Christianity and Crisis* (March 20, 1989), pp. 82–84, provides this account. Shinto symbols, still associated by many with Japanese militarism, were carefully orchestrated into the funeral, against the protests of Buddhists, Christians, and some constitutional scholars. State Shinto had been stripped of official support by the American-imposed constitution following the war. Conservatives had attempted for years to nationalize Yasukuni, the shrine in Tokyo that houses the spirits of Japan's war dead. The year 1985 saw the first postwar prime minister to worship officially at Yasukuni, while the Chinese responded with outrage because Class A war criminals, responsible for millions of Chinese deaths, are honored there. Thus do rival parties strive to use funeral rituals to do the political work of world-construction.

50. Kertzer (1988) discusses this and other incidents in his chapter "The Ritual Construction of Political Reality."

51. Jonathan Parry, *Death in Banares* (1994), provides an extensive analysis of this.

52. David Stannard, ed., *Death in America* (1975), p. 100.

53. Danforth, p. 125.

54. Barbara Myerhoff, "A Death in Due Time: A Construction of Self and Culture in Ritual Drama," in John MacAloon, ed., *Rite, Drama, Festival, Spectacle* (1984), p. 151.

55. Sally Moore and Barbara Myerhoff, *Secular Ritual* (1977), p. 22.

56. Danforth, p. 138.

57. Miller-McLemore, p. 19, concludes that this at least makes it interesting to "play the game" of encounter with death in some other centuries, such as the fourth, sixteenth, or nineteenth, in order fully to encounter the strengths of the tradition.

58. Lucy Bregman, *Death in the Midst of Life* (1992), pp. 113–14, laments that twentieth-century Christian theology has been inattentive to the deaths of individuals. The "death" that preoccupies is that of Western European cultural forms. By contrast, the pastoral care literature focuses on personal, small-scale, individual dying but shows little connection with the theological literature.

Miller-McLemore, p. 17, notes that prior to the Enlightenment, the Christian approach to death supplanted all others and enjoyed a virtual monopoly, which produced a relative closure on the problem of death's meaning. "Much of our current moral confusion about death results from the collapse of this monolithic worldview in the seventeenth and eighteenth centuries."

59. God is less concerned with private losses than with history and transformation. Immortality is not a Platonic reward for enduring human death. Resurrec-

tion and new creation are the preoccupations. In *Spirit in Ashes* (1985) Edith Wyschogrod sees post-Holocaust theologies as calling into question individualized, privatized selfhood, the vulnerability of the individual self to history having been demonstrated by mass death.

60. Jürgen Moltmann, *The Crucified God* (1974).

61. This is Bregman's (1992), summary, p. 132.

62. Moltmann (1974), p. 192.

63. Carol Zaleski, *The Life of the World to Come* (1996), p. 14.

64. The difference between Hebrew resurrection and Greek immortality has very often been commented on, above all by Oscar Cullmann, in his *Immortality of the Soul or Resurrection of the Dead* (1958), where he highlights the great difference between the deaths of Socrates and of Jesus. David Chidester, *Patterns of Transcendence* (1990), p. 190, summarizes the distinctions. In immortality's view, the person is an eternal, deathless soul temporarily residing in a mortal physical body. In resurrection's view, the person ceases to exist at death, as the spirit returns to God and the body to dust. Only the intervention by God produces a miraculous restoration of the mixture of spirit and body that defined a human being.

65. There is a tendency in American translations to translate *atman* as "the true self." While this phrase echoes American individualism and New Age paradigms, *atman* is not "true self" in our sense at all.

66. Bhagavad Gita 8:12–14.

67. Kenneth Kramer, *The Sacred Art of Dying* (1988), p. 35, provides a useful summary; p. 40 quotes a Hindu poem.

68. I am here following W. R. LaFleur, "Japan," in Frederick Holck, ed., *Death and Eastern Thought* (1974), pp. 226–56.

69. This is the summary of Kramer, pp. 58–68.

70. Kramer, p. 61.

71. Kramer, p. 62.

72. Lawrence Sullivan, *Death, Afterlife, and the Soul* (1989), p. xi.

73. Sullivan (1989), pp. xi-xii.

CHAPTER 3: THE LOST ART OF DYING

1. In ritual studies or those with religious emphases, one could expect to find a renewed focus on dying, on the art of dying, on dying as a spiritual discipline. But also in bioethics there have been renewed calls to pay attention to dying, and not just to biological death. William Gavin, *Cuttin' the Body Loose* (1995), p. 123, notes with respect to many thorny issues in bioethics: "The problematic . . . is not death but rather dying, and just as one would not identify a melody with the last note in a score, so too one should not focus on the last moment of dying, that is, death, at the expense of the entire process of dying. This form of denial results in a depersonalization of the dying process through displacement and self-deception." Oth-

ers have called for a view of death as process rather than event and warned against a "misplaced concreteness" when death and life substitute for dying and living.

2. Michael Camille, in *Master of Death* (1996), has provided an engaging account of a fourteenth-century Parisian manuscript illuminator that is scholarly, imaginative, theoretically sophisticated, poignant, and, at the beginning of each chapter, even novelistic. Camille sets the life and work of Pierre Remiet in the midst of a culture far more open to death than our own. On pp. 156–68 he discusses "dying well," the deathbed scene.

3. Just as there is the turbulence of earthquakes, darkness, and the rending of the temple surrounding Jesus's death, in Matthew's Gospel there is great turbulence surrounding Jesus's birth—above all in King Herod's slaying of the "holy innocents" in Bethlehem, in his attempt to put the Christ child to death. In the sixth part of Bach's *Christmas Oratorio,* the cantata for the Feast of the Epiphany, Herod becomes a historical metaphor for all the powers of evil and hell the Christian ever confronts, and there is a contentious scene worthy of a medieval deathbed, with angels fighting demons. The chorus opens the cantata singing: "Lord, if proud enemies rage / Let us then in steadfast faith / Look to Thy might and help. / We will put our trust in Thee alone / So may we withstand unharmed / The talons of the fiend."

4. Frederick Paxton, *Christianizing Death* (1990), p. 202.

5. Paxton, p. 202.

6. Paxton, p. 203.

7. Camille, p. 120, emphasis added.

8. Camille, p. 88. In his chapter "The Birth of Death" Camille spends considerable time comparing death and sexuality as dimensions of the body, with due attention, of course, to deconstructionists' discussions of the body.

9. "The sum of all is this: that thou art a man, than whom there is not in the world any greater instance of heights and declensions, of lights and shadows, of misery and folly, of laughter and tears, of groans and death. . . . All the succession of time, all the changes in nature, all the varieties of light and darkness, the thousands of accidents in the world and every contingency to every man, and to every creature, doth preach our funeral sermon, and calls us to look and see how the old Sexton Time throws up the earth, and digs a grave, where we must lay our sins or our sorrows, and sow our bodies, till they rise again in a fair or in an intolerable eternity. . . . Every day's necessity calls for a reparation of that portion which death fed on all night when we lay in his lap, and slept in his outer chambers. The very spirits of a man prey upon the daily portion of bread and flesh, and every meal is a rescue from one death, and lays up for another: and while we think a thought we die; and the clock strikes, and reckons on our portion of eternity; we form our words with the breath of our nostrils, we have the less to live upon for every word we speak. . . . Nature hath given us one harvest every year, but death hasth two: and the spring and the autumn send throngs of men and women to charnel-houses; and all the summer long men are recovering from their evils of the spring, till the dogdays come,

and then the Syrian star makes the summer deadly; and the fruits of autumn are laid up for all the year's provision, and the man that gathers them eats and surfeits, and dies and needs them not, and himself is laid up for eternity; and he that escapes till winter, only stays for another opportunity, which the distempers of that quarter minister to him with great variety. Thus death reigns in all the portions of our time. . . . You can go not whither but you tread upon a dead man's bones." (From "Consideration of the Vanity and Shortness of Man's Life," a selection from Jeremy Taylor's *Holy Dying,* excerpted in *Omega* [vol. 4, no. 1, 1973], pp. 8–9.)

10. Philippe Ariès, *The Hour of Our Death* (1982), p. 614.

11. Rainer Maria Rilke, *Prose and Poetry* (1984), p. 6.

12. Rilke, p. 7.

13. Loren Eiseley, *All the Strange Hours* (1975), p. 180.

14. Lucy Bregman, *Death in the Midst of Life* (1992), p. 18.

15. The phrase "appropriate death" was popularized by Avery Weisman. See his article "Appropriate and Appropriated Death," in Edwin Schneidman, ed., *Death* (1984).

16. Ariès, pp. 602–14.

17. Ariès, p. 614.

18. Sogyal Rinpoche, *The Tibetan Book of Living and Dying* (1993), p. 14.

19. Rinpoche, pp. 223–43.

20. Rinpoche, p. 259.

21. One avenue to great deaths is through literature. Gavin, pp. 147–65, treats the deaths of Plato's Socrates, Tolstoy's Ivan Ilych, and Nietzsche's Zarathustra. There is a much larger and more recent literature, even a new genre, on "great griefs." These typically are first-person accounts of one's terminal illness and anticipatory grief or are mid- and postdying accounts by bereaved family members, usually a parent or a spouse. A few examples: Lucy Bregman and Sara Thiermann, *First Person Mortal* (1995); Simone de Beauvoir, *A Very Easy Death* (1965); Virginia Hine, *Last Letter to the Pebble People* (1977); Nicholas Wolterstorff, *Lament for a Son* (1987); John Gunther, *Death Be Not Proud* (1949); Jerry Irish, *A Boy Thirteen* (1975); Ted Rosenthal, *How Could I Not Be Among You?* (1973); Stewart Alsop, *Stay of Execution* (1973); C. S. Lewis, *A Grief Observed* (1976); Gilda Radner, *It's Always Something* (1989); Jill Ireland, *Life Wish* (1987); Doris Lund, *Eric* (1989); Norman Cousins, *Anatomy of an Illness* (1979); Edwin Schneidman, *Voices of Death* (1995); Gerda Lerner, *A Death of Our Own* (1978). Any good urban bookstore will carry many such books, especially these days on cancer deaths.

Bregman and Thiermann (1995) study the significance of these autobiographies in contemporary culture and provide an extensive bibliographical sample. They note several types into which these many accounts fit: (1) How I came close to death and recovered; (2) how I grew closer to death; (3) how I tended and cared for my dying loved one; (4) how I mourned and learned to live again; (5) journalists' accounts.

Literature from the East, above all from Buddhism, is full of accounts of the deaths of great spiritual masters. The serene enlightenment they attained and the inspiring peacefulness of their deaths are held up as an example and encouragement for all.

22. Bregman and Thiermann (1995), in the preface to their collection of first-person narratives on grieving, try to account for why such narratives are currently flourishing. Following a diagnosis of the public sphere as the realm of statism and bureaucratic rationality, they see the private sphere as the place where somewhat lonely and isolated individuals must craft their own meanings, including religious meanings. (This is similar to my analysis of individualism in chapter 1 and elsewhere in this book.) "If personal meaning is a private-sphere matter, a process of 'identity construction,' then the fascination with autobiographical narratives may lie in their revelations of others' attempts to construct and reconstruct identities in the light of threatening new realities. What many authors of these stories of suffering, illness, and dying manage to do is continue the same process of personal meaning-making that all of us . . . are inevitably forced into by the peculiar structure of modern industrial society and its bifurcated worldview" (p. 8). They remark on the "do-it-yourself" quality of private-sphere identity formation, in which people invent their own patterns and formulae. These new manuals provide recipes for the rest of us.

23. In her book *Deathing* (1984), Anya Foos-Graber calls for Lamaze-style coaching of the dying and wonders whether the Gallup-identified eight million Americans who have had a near-death experience might become a cohort that will change our age's thinking about death.

24. In "Social Dramas in Brazilian Umbanda: The Dialectics of Meaning," in *The Anthropology of Performance* (1987), Victor Turner argued that such social dramas exhibit a regular course of events which can be grouped in successive phases of public action. These are (1) a breach of regular norm-governed social relations, (2) a crisis when people take sides over a threshold of more or less stable social process, (3) redressive or remedial procedures, and (4) reintegration of the disturbed social group or the recognition and legitimation of irreparable schism between the contending parties. It is in stage three that performance rituals play their crucial role. Turner takes up these same issues in his article "Are There Universals of Performance in Myth, Ritual, and Drama?" in Richard Schechner and Willa Appel, eds., *By Means of Performance* (1990).

25. Turner (1990), p. 9.

26. Turner (1990), p. 11.

27. Christopher Justice, *Dying the Good Death* (1997), provides an ethnography that introduces a number of individuals and their families who pilgrimage to Banares to die. Jonathan Parry, *Death in Banares* (1994), sets this act in the larger context of Hindu thought and in the immediate and often unedifying context of the Banares cremation industry.

28. I am following the summary account in David Kertzer, *Ritual, Politics, and Power* (1988), pp. 57–61.

29. This account is set into the discussion of conflict and crisis in political ritual in Kertzer, pp. 140–44.

30. Bregman and Thiermann, p. 185, analyze many such narratives.

31. Lyn Lofland, *The Craft of Dying* (1978).

32. This is the bitter claim of Ivan Illlich, *Medical Nemesis* (1976), p. 206.

33. Harry R. Moody in Marc Kaminsky, ed., *The Uses of Reminiscence* (1984), p. 13.

34. Moody, p. 13.

35. This is called for in Victor Kestenbaum, ed., *The Humanity of the Ill* (1982).

36. The Alcor Life Extension Foundation in California, and later Arizona, became the center of the movement, which prefers the term *de-animated* to *dead.* Movement enthusiasts see themselves as freezing the living, not the dead. The newly de-animated body is attached to a heart-lung machine, blood is replaced with glycerol, the body is cooled to –110°F, and then, a few days later, to a liquid nitrogen temperature of –210°F. Four bodies are installed per "dewar," which looks like a ten-foot-tall stainless steel thermos bottle. In *Death* (1993), Gary Palmer, pp. 123–28, tells a touching and bizarre story of one cryonics enthusiast who has already frozen his wife's head, her body having been riddled with cancer, and is planning on cryonics for himself as well. They plan to be reunited again. Though the cryonics movement was widely pronounced dead, a fad that didn't take, an article in London's *Sunday Times* of July 7, 1996, "The Big Chill," reported there are sixty-seven bodies or heads in four cryonics institutes across the United States. A further 380 people are signed up as members. Typically, a special life insurance policy provides for the initial freezing and care henceforth. The typical cryonicist is highly educated, technically sophisticated, financially secure, individualistic, optimistic, male, and Caucasian. Cryonics was invented in 1964 when Robert Ettinger, a physics professor, wrote *The Prospect of Immortality.*

37. Robert Veatch, *Death, Dying, and the Biological Revolution* (1976).

38. Rinpoche, p. 17.

39. Rinpoche, p. 19.

40. Rinpoche, p. 20.

41. Rinpoche, p. 26.

42. Gilbert Greshake, "Towards a Theology of Dying," in Norbert Greinacher and Alois Muller, eds., *The Experience of Dying* (1974), p. 82.

43. Camille, p. 117.

44. Camille, p. 118.

45. Camille, p. 120, discusses the use of the deaths of saints in books used for public liturgy and private devotion: "What the text of the missal calls the *supplices* or tortures of the saints were recited aloud as part of a performative structure of death very different from the silently scanned simulacra of torment that fill the vernacular *Miroir.* Yet both the public and the private, the spiritual and sensational, function of the saints was still grounded on the idea of their deaths."

46. Vanderlyne Pine, ed., *Acute Grief and the Funeral* (1976), pp. 207–8, quotes a

poem, received from the League of Hospital Friends in England, reportedly left in the locker of a patient when she died. It is the "Cry From a Crabbit Old Woman," who demands that nurses see beyond appearances.

47. Lisl Goodman, *Death and the Creative Life* (1981), p. 17.

CHAPTER 4: THE LAST CAREER

1. Anya Foos-Graber, *Deathing* (1984).

2. This paragraph is indebted to the lovely and evocative introduction by Thomas R. Cole to *The Oxford Book of Aging* (1994), pp. 3–12.

3. A good example may be the fourth of John Updike's Rabbit novels. After *Rabbit Run* (1960), *Rabbit Redux* (1971), and *Rabbit Is Rich* (1981) came *Rabbit at Rest* (1990). Rabbit comes to rest in a cardiac intensive care unit in a Florida hospital. The novel's theme is the blossoming and fruition of the seed of death carried inside us. Here Updike explores the human body as Thanatos, after the sex saturation of earlier works. Unfortunately, Rabbit has learned little or nothing, his career having peaked at age eighteen when he was a high-school basketball star. Perhaps Updike's quartet is meant to be the story of America. This is the conclusion of Joyce Carol Oates, in her review of the last Rabbit novel in the *New York Times Book Review* (September 30, 1990).

4. John Weston, "Aging the Last Stage? or, the Dream Continued," in *Second Opinion* (March 1991), p. 126, thinks Erikson's stage theory has remained popular as much because "he hit upon counselors' needs for life to be meaningful as because he correctly identified the choice presented by late life." Weston is not satisfied with Erikson's theory as a full and sufficient account of the human condition in the face of aging and dying. Missing from Erikson's theory are the religious sensitivities to obligation and covenant. There is little ethical concern in stage theory. One's obligations extend only to oneself. Weston offers as an alternative the paradigm of "tragic responsibility," which emphasizes right relationships above all. He believes Erikson's approach does not successfully deal with guilt, always a human dilemma (p. 134): "I am generative not insofar as I fulfill my generative needs but insofar as I respond rightly to the various ways in which I am called upon; I attain to integrity not insofar as my experience of myself conveys some world order and spiritual sense but insofar as my response to others and to the world contributes to order and meaning of the kind I value."

5. Erik Erikson, *Childhood and Society* (1963), p. 140.

6. This is the translation of Walter Kaufmann, in his *Existentialism, Religion, and Death* (1976), p. 231.

7. Lisl Goodman, *Death and the Creative Life* (1981), p. xi.

8. Carl Jung, "The Soul and Death," in Herman Feifel, ed., *The Meaning of Death* (1959), p. 10.

9. James Hillman, *Re-Visioning Psychology* (1975), pp. 165–228.

10. Kaufmann, p. 228.

11. Stanley Keleman, *Living Your Dying* (1974), pp. 16–17.

12. Keleman, pp. 16–17.

13. Marjorie Casebear McCoy, *To Die with Style* (1974).

14. Robert Kastenbaum and Ruth Aisenberg, *The Psychology of Death* (1972), pp. 104–5.

15. James Empereur, *Prophetic Anointing* (1982), pp. 199–200.

16. Harry Moody, "The Meaning of Life and the Meaning of Old Age," in Thomas Cole and Sally Gadow, eds., *What Does It Mean to Grow Old* (1986), p. 32.

17. Moody (1986), p. 32, is quoting Jean-Pierre Dupuy.

18. Moody (1986), p. 33.

19. Quoted in Virginia Sloyan, ed., *Death* (1990), p. 61.

20. W. B. Yeats, "The Tower," in *The Collected Poems of W. B. Yeats* (1996), p.194.

21. Yeats, "Sailing to Byzantium," in *The Collected Poems of W. B. Yeats* (1996), p. 193.

22. Quoted in Robert Jay Lifton, *The Broken Connection* (1979), pp. 105–6. Translated by J. M. Cohen, *London Times Literary Supplement*, December 12, 1963.

23. Robert Butler, "The Life Review: An Interpretation of Reminiscence in the Aged," *Psychiatry* (February 1963).

24. Lars Tornstam, "Gero-Transcendence: A Theoretical and Empirical Exploration," in Eugene Thomas and Susan Eisenhandler, eds., *Aging and the Religious Dimension* (1994), pp. 203–25.

25. Tornstam, p. 203.

26. Tornstam, p. 210, notes: "Everyone in Western culture 'knows' that it is social activity, ego-strength and a realistic view of the world that counts. By claiming this as 'fact,' we are making a moral judgment; as a result, we may impede the process toward gero-transcendence by making the individual feel guilty about his or her new view of life. Supported by well-meaning gerontologists, staff and relatives of old people obstruct the natural progression toward gero-transcendence. The attitude is that old people who are 'turning inward,' withdrawing to something we don't understand, must be activated. Old people themselves participate in this obstruction. Like everyone else, the elderly recognize that it is activity and engagement that count in our society."

Tornstam, pp. 211–12, suggests seven empirical questions raised by the concept of gero-transcendence and proposes future research.

27. Alexander and Margarete Mitscherlich have argued in their book *The Inability to Mourn* (1975) that German culture has unfinished grief work that can lead to disorientation, self-hate, or even violence. Commenting on this thesis, Neil Postman, *Amusing Ourselves to Death* (1988), p. 48, suggests: "Germany has tried to provide itself with a future by adopting America's present." But American public discourse has been changed by the electronic media from serious exposition into a form of entertainment. Following Aldous Huxley, Postman finds people being controlled by inflicting pleasure on them rather than pain. He writes, p. 51:

"As Germans flee from the first terror—a culture without a past—they recoil from the second—an American culture that offers them intimations and shadows of that which ruined them." The Germans "sense that they have imported a culture with little intellectual coherence, uninterested in its own traditions, and preoccupied with the creation of spectacle."

28. Butler, p. 75.

29. Wallace Stevens, *Opus Posthumous* (1957), p. 257.

30. William Carlos Williams, *The Desert Music and Other Poems* (1954).

31. Moody, p. 28.

32. William Dunning, *The Roots of Postmodernism* (1995), p. 196.

33. Deena Metzger, *Writing for Your Life* (1992), p. 71.

34. Moody, p. 24.

35. Carol Zaleski, *The Life of the World to Come* (1996), p. 74.

36. Bonnie Miller-McLemore, *Death, Sin and the Moral Life* (1988), calls for a recovery of the moral dimension in modern discussions of death and dying.

37. Frederick Paxton, *Christianizing Death* (1990), p. 51.

38. Such public penance is almost unimaginable today. Paxton, pp. 74–76, describes a three-stage ritual: a rite of separation, involving tonsure, communion, the laying on of sackcloth, and signing with ashes; a ritual of transition, suspending the penitent between his former and future states (this depended on the intercessory prayers of the community and the mercy of God); and a rite of incorporation, involving reclothing in a clean garment and communion.

Paxton, p. 203, says the rites of deathbed penance focused on the state of the dying, who were taken by the community through a set of ritual moments that prepared them for their death. "Separated from the community, absolved, reclothed, and brought back into the fold as new persons, they received a second baptism." The ritual process paralleled the experience of death and created bonds between the living and the dead. "Before they could meet death with any equanimity, they had to be ritually 'passed on' while they still lived."

CHAPTER 5: FINISHING THE STORY

1. Paul Ricoeur and Stephen Crites especially emphasized this in their work.

2. Linda J. Vogel, *Rituals for Resurrection* (1996), p. 24.

3. The significance of storytelling has recently come even to legal studies. In the anthology *Law's Stories* (1996), Peter Brooks and Paul Gewirtz offer essays that argue for the significant role of storytelling in legal practice and thinking. The stories of the oppressed figure particularly in this new movement. In *Doctors' Stories* (1991), Kathryn Montgomery Hunter argues that medical knowledge and medical practice are fundamentally and intrinsically the stuff of narratives.

4. One example among many is Clifford Geertz's *After the Fact* (1995). See also his *Works and Lives* (1988). An influential anthology is James Clifford and George

Marcus, eds., *Writing Culture* (1986). See also the collection of James Clifford's articles in his *The Predicament of Culture* (1988).

5. Carolyn Ellis, *Final Negotiations* (1995).

6. It sometimes seems this admirable but not entirely likable couple struggle as much with monogamy as with mortality. Reflecting on her work, Ellis considers calling it an ethnographic novel, experimental ethnography, autoethnography, self-ethnography, introspective ethnography, interpretive ethnography, and impressionistic tale—citing the relevant literature on each.

7. Larry Churchill, "The Human Experience of Dying: The Moral Primacy of Stories Over Stages," *Soundings* (Spring 1979).

8. Lucy Bregman and Sara Thiermann, *First Person Mortal* (1995), discuss them in chapter 3 of their study.

9. In his Nobel Peace Prize acceptance speech Elie Wiesel said: "And now the boy is turning to me. 'Tell me,' he asks, 'what have you done with my future? What have you done with your life?' And I tell him that I have tried. That I have tried to keep memory alive, that I have tried to fight those who would forget."

10. Deena Metzger, *Writing for Your Life* (1992), p. 65, offers these and many other useful exercises.

11. Marc Kaminsky, ed., *The Uses of Reminiscence* (1984).

12. Kaminsky, p. 18.

13. Kaminsky, p. 12.

14. Harry Moody, "The Meaning of Life and the Meaning of Old Age," in Thomas Cole and Sally Gadow, eds., *What Does It Mean to Grow Old* (1986), pp. 27–28.

15. Moody, pp. 27–28.

16. Moody (1986), p. 29.

17. Harry Moody, "Reminiscence and the Recovery of the Public World," in Kaminsky, p. 158.

18. Moody (1984), p. 161.

19. Grace Worth, "At the Center of the Story," in Kaminsky, p. 56.

20. Janet Bloom, "Minerva's Doll," in Kaminsky, p. 117.

21. Arthur Frank, *The Wounded Storyteller: Body, Illness, and Ethics* (1995).

22. Loren Eiseley, *All the Strange Hours* (1975), p. 217.

23. Eiseley, p. 222.

24. James Hillman, *Re-Visioning Psychology* (1975), p. xi.

25. Eiseley, pp. 227–28.

26. Hillman (1975), p. 42.

27. Hillman (1975), p. 57.

28. Hillman (1975), p. 71.

29. Hillman (1975), p. 65.

30. Hillman (1975), p. 107.

31. In *The Soul's Code* (1996), James Hillman develops an "acorn theory," which proposes that each life is formed by a particular image that is the essence of that

life and calls it to a destiny. There is much more to life, he argues, than can be explained by the categories nature or environment.

32. Hillman (1975), p. 181.

33. Isaiah: 6:1–7.

34. I take up some of these issues again in the final section of the last chapter of this book. There I allude to such writers as Jürgen Moltmann, who has dealt extensively with eschatological themes, both in his early *Theology of Hope* and in his culminating work, *The Coming of God.*

35. At the end of a study of flourishing first-person narratives of dying and grieving, Lucy Bregman (in Bregman and Thiermann [1995], p. 186) allows herself a personal note, in which she laments the complete absence of eschatological themes in both Christian and other autobiographical accounts. Even Christian writers seem to reject any otherworldly focus to their faith as anachronistic, escapist, and immature. Rival eschatologies are also completely lacking—no reincarnation stories, no near-death experiences. Dante and John Bunyan would find the landscape incomprehensible. Hymnody from another time, still sung by contemporary congregations, registers that lost world of eschatology.

36. Jürgen Moltmann, *The Coming of God* (1996), p. 35. Moltmann devotes pp. 29–46 to "The Rebirth of Messianic Thinking in Judaism."

37. Juan Luis Ruiz de la Peña, "The Element of Projection and Belief in Heaven," in Bas van Iersel and Edward Schillebeeckx, eds., *Heaven* (1979), p. 73.

38. Ruiz de la Peña, p. 74.

39. Virginia Sloyan, ed., *Death* (1990), p. 16.

40. In the critique of Feuerbach and in setting forth the thought of Ernst Bloch as a counterargument, I am indebted to Juan Luis Ruiz de la Peña's article on projection and heaven (1979).

41. Ernst Bloch, quoted in de la Peña, p. 77.

42. Ruiz de la Peña, p. 78.

43. Ruiz de la Peña, p. 78, summarizing Ernst Bloch.

44. Carol Zaleski, *The Life of the World to Come* (1996).

45. Zaleski (1996), p. 15.

46. Sogyal Rinpoche, *The Tibetan Book of Living and Dying* (1993), pp. 319–36, compares near-death experiences to the teachings of the Tibetan Book of the Dead, especially the so-called *bardo* of becoming, the state which immediately follows death. Rinpoche decries any "facile optimism" to which typically positive near-death experiences might lead and instead invokes them to call for a spiritual discipline in dying.

47. In *Otherworld Journeys* (1987) Zaleski traced return-from-death stories in medieval Christian narratives, especially in their heyday in the twelfth century, and in modern accounts. She analyzes their implications in *The Life of the World to Come* (1996).

48. Quoted in Zaleski (1996), pp. 41–42.

49. *Resurrection Reconsidered* (1996), edited by Gavin D'Costa, is an international collection of essays that take up anew questions about the resurrection of Christ, both in contemporary Christian theology and as viewed from the standpoint of other religious traditions.

50. Zaleski (1996), p. 45. On the same page she notes: "There is both a time-bound and a timeless aspect to this transformation—it is a mystery present eternally to the triune will of God, present temporally as the kingdom already active in our midst, present in the Eucharist as the 'medicine of immortality,' and present in the person of the Holy Spirit, who from the time of Christ's rising from death to glory has been poured out into the world. Nonetheless, this eschatological transformation is said to be still unfolding through time for humankind. The alchemy is at work now, but its final distillation is reserved for the world to come."

51. Zaleski (1996), p. 93.

52. Zaleski (1996), p. 47.

53. Once one is committed to reflecting on an afterlife, problems of the "soul" and its demythologization or remythologization are not far behind. Zaleski (1996), pp. 51–64, discusses the role of the soul at some length because she believes it is necessary in order to dramatize the experience of death.

54. Paul Ricoeur developed this concept in order to chart a possible journey for an intellectual who needs to move beyond the simple, literal faith of childhood without simply abandoning or renouncing all faith. In second naivete one sees and understands that religion and theology are symbolic enterprises and still arrives at a full and ripe believing.

55. Zaleski (1996), p. 63.

56. Zaleski (1996), p. 66.

57. Zaleski (1996), pp. 81–82.

58. Moltmann (1996), pp. x–xi.

59. Moody (1984), p. 165.

60. Cole and Gadow, p. xii.

61. Moody (1984), p. 165.

62. Worth, p. 58.

63. Bloom, p. 118.

64. Bloom, pp. 122–23.

65. Bloom, p. 127.

66. Bloom, p. 129.

67. Bloom, p. 129.

68. Barbara Myerhoff, "A Symbol Perfected in Death: Continuity and Ritual in the Life and Death of an Elderly Jew," in Barbara Myerhoff and Andrei Simic, eds., *Life's Career—Aging* (1978), p. 164.

69. Myerhoff, p. 198.

70. Myerhoff, p. 201.

71. Hillman (1975), p. 217.

72. Boris Pasternak, "The Passing Storm," in Pasternak, *Poems*, translated from the Russian by Eugene M. Kayden (1959), p. 185.

73. So notes Robert Jones in a *Commonweal* (May 17, 1985), p. 305, review of Richard Kieckhefer's *Unquiet Souls* (1984).

74. Jones, p. 305.

75. William Carlos Williams, *Paterson* (1963).

76. Gilbert Meilander, "Theology in Stories: C. S. Lewis and the Narrative Quality of Experience," *Word and World* (1981), pp. 222–29. Meilander builds on Stephen Crites's work on narrative.

77. Meilander, p. 226.

78. Meilander, p. 227.

79. Meilander, p. 228.

80. Meilander, p. 229.

81. John Dominic Crossan, *The Dark Interval* (1975), p. 124.

CHAPTER 6: ALONG THE RITUAL WAY

1. Michael J. Behe's recent book *Darwin's Black Box* (1996) is a conspicuous exception. He contends that the molecular machinery of living things works too well to have been produced by chance alone. Life must have been designed by some intelligent being.

2. Maurice Bloch and Jonathan Parry, in *Death and the Regeneration of Life* (1982), have argued that rites of passage, serving the ends of society and its masters, seek to drive a conceptual wedge between biological and social reproduction, in order to privilege the latter. I am not arguing this extreme view, at least as attributed to them by Peter Metcalf and Richard Huntington in *Celebrations of Death* (1991), pp. 6–7. In any case, to me, the opposite seems true in contemporary society. That is, a raw biologism, aided by a medical model of dying, is far more pervasive than the notion of death as a cultural or societal construction. Yet if one sees the domination of nature as the legacy of recent centuries, then one could argue that medicine belongs to the cultural side of the equation and that in the medical model of death we see the attempt to dominate nature by the culture of science and medicine.

3. Clifford Geertz, "Religion as a Cultural System," in his *The Interpretation of Cultures* (1973b), p. 112.

4. Michael Camille, *Master of Death* (1996), p. 196.

5. R. S. Solecki, *Shanidar* (1971).

6. Richard Rutherford, *The Death of a Christian* (1980), provides an extremely useful brief history of the evolution of Christian (Catholic) funeral rites, from the early church to the reforms following the Roman Catholic Second Vatican Council.

7. Metcalf and Huntington, p. 24.

8. Roger Grainger, *The Unburied* (1988), p. 78.

9. E. M. Broner, *Mornings and Mourning* (1994).

10. Anne Brener, *Mourning and Mitzvah* (1993).

11. T. Rodabough, "Funeral Roles: Ritualized Expectations," *Omega* (1981–82).

12. In 1954 Paul Irion, *The Funeral and the Mourners,* pp. 86–87, was admonishing the clergy how to evaluate "the effectiveness of the personal function of the funeral":

1. The funeral must deal with death realistically.

2. The funeral must present a vision of God which will be of comfort and help to the mourners in their suffering. This includes the understanding of the love of God, the nearness of God, and his concern for his people.

3. The funeral must see man as an individual of worth, turning man's attention to the importance of his personal integration and the resources which God offers for the strengthening and stabilizing of the self.

4. The funeral must demonstrate that the Christian faith is a resource which enables the individual to mourn, rather than a substitute for mourning.

5. The funeral must recognize and accept deep feelings, rather than cover them up by a superficial aestheticism.

6. The funeral must provide a sense of finality.

7. The funeral must be an aid in recalling memories of the deceased.

8. The funeral is to establish a climate of mourning.

9. The funeral must be sensitive to the individual needs of the bereaved, dynamic, variable in both form and content.

13. William May, "The Sacred Power of Death in Contemporary Experience," *Social Research* (1972), p. 469.

14. Robert Blauner, "Death and Social Structure," in Charles Jackson, ed., *Passing* (1977), p. 189.

15. Patricia Hannaford, "The Social Meaning of the Funeral to the Elderly," in Otto Margolis et al., eds., *Grief and the Meaning of the Funeral* (1975), p. 74.

16. H. C. Raether and R. C. Slater, "Immediate Postdeath Activities in the US," in Herman Feifel, ed., *New Meanings of Death* (1977), p. 237.

17. In his newsletter *Context,* Martin Marty quotes Princeton Theological Seminary professor Thomas G. Long, researching a book on Christian funerals and writing in the Easter 1996 issue of *Journal for Preachers.* Long wryly notes that the kitsch and commercialism of the funeral industry is not unlike what one finds in the typical Christian bookstore. What is troubling about funeral directors is what is troubling about many clergy: "They saunter casually and nonchalantly around a reality that the rest of us find mysterious and frightening. They seem as comfortable at the edge of death's abyss as clergy do in the face of the awe-full holiness of God." The business of the funeral industry, Long suggests, is not unlike the bureaucracy of organized religion. "Such mundane matters seem to be intrusions of human structuring onto what is essentially wild, untameable, and seared with holy dread." What impressed Long was the sense of calling that many funeral directors seem

to evidence—a vocation of human compassion amidst swirling cultural changes.

18. Gordon Geddes, *Welcome Joy* (1981), offers in chapters 5 and 6 a very useful history of the funeral in Puritan New England.

19. Philippe Ariès, "The Reversal of Death," in David Stannard, ed., *Death in America* (1975), pp. 154–55.

20. Metcalf and Huntington, pp. 191–214.

21. Talcott Parsons and Victor Lidz, "Death in American Society," in Edwin Schneidman, ed., *Essays in Self-Destruction* (1967).

22. May, p. 474.

23. May, p. 477.

24. Paul Irion, "Changing Patterns of Ritual Response to Death," *Omega* (1990–91).

25. Roland Delattre, "Ritual Retrospective and Cultural Pluralism," *Soundings* (Fall 1978), pp. 281–82.

26. Delattre, p. 282.

27. Susanne Langer, *Philosophy in a New Key* (1957), p. 153.

28. Langer, p. 290.

29. Delattre, p. 286.

30. Delattre, pp. 299–300, note 14, writes: "Ritual is involved in negotiating, healing, celebrating, purifying, transforming, overcoming, obscuring, intensifying, sublimating and otherwise articulating these and like relationships with their different and sometimes competing and conflicting demands and attractions. Ritual is commonly central to both the maintenance and the inversion of natural and cultural forms of order, and also to such contrasting changes of cultural geography as people's periodic return to their beginnings and their venturing across forbidding (and forbidden) frontiers into new and unexplored regions. Ritual negotiations may be transacted with whatever beings and objects we imagine ourselves to be engaged with or by which we experience ourselves addressed—divine beings and powers, social and psychological and cultural pressures, personal desires and judgments, forces and energies of nature or natural elements, legal systems and institutionalized versions of the healing arts."

31. Delattre, p. 288, emphasis added.

32. Jonathan Smith, *To Take Place* (1987), p. 103.

33. Smith, p. 105.

34. Smith, p. 109.

35. Tom Driver, *The Magic of Ritual* (1991), p. 133, is building on the work of Roy Rappaport, "The Obvious Aspects of Ritual," in his *Ecology, Meaning, and Religion* (1979), p. 197.

36. Driver, p. 136.

37. Rappaport, p. 206.

38. Rappaport, p. 214.

39. Driver, p. 156.

40. Driver, p. 173.

41. Driver, p. 173.

42. Driver quotes these lines from Shakespeare's *A Midsummer Night's Dream* V, 1, 16–17.

43. Geertz (1973b), p. 114.

44. Geertz (1973b), p. 112.

45. Geertz (1973b), p. 119.

46. Geertz, "The Impact of the Concept of Culture on the Concept of Man," in his *The Interpretation of Cultures* (1973a).

47. Daniel Rudman, "Nursing Home Medicine," in *Second Opinion* (March 1991), pp. 110–11.

48. James Empereur, *Prophetic Anointing* (1982).

49. Driver, p. 16.

50. Edmund Leach, *Culture and Communication* (1976), p. 45, emphasis added.

51. Max Weber, *Essays in Sociology,* ed. by H. H. Gerth and C. Wright Mills (1946).

52. Driver, p. 165.

53. Richard Sennett, *The Fall of Public Man* (1977), pp. 266–67.

54. Sennett, p. 267.

55. In *The Archaeology of Ritual and Magic* (1987), Ralph Merrifield, who specializes in Roman Britain, claims that even modern archaeology is afflicted with "ritual phobia." He decries how archaeologists are reluctant to recognize evidence of behavior that has no obvious material purpose. He suspects ritual hypothesizing may also not go well with archaeology's strong desire to be a real science.

56. Richard Payne, "Realizing Inherent Enlightenment: Ritual and Self-Transformation in Shingon Buddhism," in Aune and DeMarinis, p. 71.

57. Mark Searl, "Ritual," in Cheslyn Jones et al., eds., *The Study of Liturgy* (1992), pp. 56–57.

58. Ronald Grimes, *Beginnings in Ritual Studies* (1982), p. 4.

59. Driver, p. 203.

60. Clare Gittings, *Death, Burial and the Individual in Early Modern England* (1984), p. 40.

61. Driver, p. 79.

62. Michael Harner, *The Way of the Shaman* (1990).

63. Ronald Grimes, *Ritual Criticism* (1990), p. 122, contrasts shamanism and parashamanism.

Shamanism: (1) a revelatory call, usually in the form of illness; (2) a visionary experience of descent, death, dismemberment; (3) replacement of normal bones or organs with special ones; (4) helper spirits or animals derived from socially sanctioned myths or rites; (5) use of a special spirit language; (6) a multileveled cosmology with narrow passages, mountains, or trees connecting the levels; (7) use of ritual or hunting instruments, typically bow, arrow, and drum; (8) use of herbs and/or hallucinogens for healing. Parashamanism: (1) call by self-selection;

(2) workshop experience of togetherness; (3) special reverence for the body, coupled with social alienation; (4) helper spirits or animals derived from art, dreams, or books about other cultures; (5) use of psychological or aesthetic language; (6) interiorization of cosmos, mythologized as "the unconscious" and populated with archetypes; (7) use of musical instruments, especially drums and bells; (8) use of herbs, "health" food, and/or crystals for healing.

64. Driver, p. 241, endnote 48, quotes Urban Holmes, *The Priest in Community* (1978), p. 80: "It is customary in anthropology to distinguish between the shaman and the priest. The shaman is typical of tribal cultures, he gets his power direction from the spirits, he is independent and part-time, he focuses on the individual, and he uses spirit possession, trance, and frenzy. The priest is typical of structural role definition. He receives his credentials as a result of special training, he is the member of an organization and works full-time, he leads groups, and he participates in routine acts of adoration, prayer, and offering."

65. James Lewis, ed., *Magical Religion and Modern Witchcraft* (1996). This anthology also has an interesting account, "Where Christian Liturgy and Neo-Pagan Ritual Meet," in which a United Church of Christ minister, Richard E. Kuykendall, describes his attempts to open his church to New Age people and open Christian liturgy to "liturgies of the earth."

66. Ritual evolution can also be a product of very careful, even bureaucratic planning. The epochal Second Vatican Council of the Roman Catholic Church promulgated as its first document "The Constitution on the Sacred Liturgy." The bishops of this council saw liturgical reform (I am content with the term *evolution*, though I recognize my book is really a call for radical reform) as a two-stage process. First, a complete revision of the rites of the church is based on thorough theological, historical, and pastoral studies. Second, the liturgy is adapted to various cultures and peoples. In *The Changing Face of Jewish and Christian Worship in North America* (1991), ed. by Paul Bradshaw and Lawrence Hoffman, Kathleen Hughes, pp. 71–87, describes this process and its products.

67. William Roberts, *Initiation to Adulthood* (1982), p. 22, a minister who attempted, single-handedly, to create new rituals of adult initiation, saw clearly that "societies rely upon recurring experiences of liminality to nurture religious and aesthetic sensitivities. The poet, the artist, the religious genius all develop their special gifts by departing from the norms that prove restrictive and by entering the wasteland to recover the symbols that all societies need in order to flourish. If and when they return, these aesthetes are more likely to be rejected than accepted, but somehow the culture will take the gift of their labors."

68. Margaret Thompson Drewal, *Yoruba Ritual* (1992), p. xvi.

69. Drewal, p. xiv. She sees the recovery of this emphasis as resonating with poststructuralist theories of performance and social process. To such an approach, ritual again becomes visible as transformational process, as improvisation. "There are no predictable or verifiable constants endlessly repeated. . . . Performance is

a multilayered discourse employing multiple voices and perspectives," p. 11.

70. Eric Hobsbawm and Terence Ranger, *The Invention of Tradition* (1983).

71. Hobsbawm and Ranger, p. 1.

72. Hobsbawm and Ranger, p. 13.

73. Victor Turner, "Images and Reflections: Ritual, Drama, Carnival, Film and Spectacle in Cultural Performance," in his *The Anthropology of Performance* (1987), p. 21.

74. John Kelly and Martha Kaplan, "History, Structure, and Ritual," *Annual Review of Anthropology* (1990), pp. 139–41.

75. Victor Turner, "Social Dramas in Brazilian Umbanda: The Dialectics of Meaning," in his *The Anthropology of Performance* (1987), pp. 33–71.

76. Lawrence Taylor, "Cultural Constructions of Death in Ireland," *Anthropological Quarterly* (1989), p. 182.

77. Ronald Grimes, *Beginnings in Ritual Studies* (1982), p. 57.

78. Grimes (1982), p. 53.

79. Grimes (1982), p. 62.

80. May, p. 464.

81. Ronald Grimes, *Ritual Criticism* (1990), pp. 109–44.

82. Driver, p. 200.

83. Driver, p. 202.

84. Hannah Ward and Jennifer Wild, eds., *Human Rites* (1995).

85. D. H. Tripp, "Liturgy and Pastoral Service," in Cheslyn Jones et al., eds., *The Study of Liturgy* (1992).

86. Ritual evolution evokes and requires theological reflection, as Rutherford, pp. 120–25, shows. Following reforms in Catholic funeral rites after the Second Vatican Council of the 1960s, new questions emerged: Is the Mass for the Dead an act of worship celebrated as an end in itself, or is it a channel of grace applicable to other ends? Is the Eucharist celebrated as a sign of the person's personal passover, with Christ, now, or are the "fruits of the mass" applied to the amelioration of purgatory? Is the mass proclamation or petition?

87. Rutherford, pp. 128–35, discusses the dialog that should be occurring between the Church and the funeral industry. Rejecting a gospel of cosmetic restoration, the Christian funeral proclaims life through death—above all, the death of Christ—and not through the appearance of life. Above all, the Christian funeral should be characterized by community, prayerfulness, and simplicity.

88. Rutherford, p. 141, notes that the Catholic funeral rite set in motion by the Second Vatican Council recognizes "the legitimacy of different cultural patterns and is primarily interested in their ability to be a context for paschal faith and Christian consolation."

89. Aiden Kavanagh, *Elements of Rite* (1990), p. 10.

90. Kavanagh, p. 89.

91. Kavanagh, p. 46.

92. Kavanagh, pp. 93–94.

93. Kavanagh, p. 104.

94. Drewal, p. 7.

95. In "The Maid Is not Dead but Sleepeth': Death and Revival in Writing by Women," in Jon Davies, ed., *Ritual and Remembrance* (1994), Maria Lisboa writes a bitter and angry chapter.

96. Bradshaw and Hoffman (1991), p. 199.

97. Kay Turner, "Contemporary Feminist Rituals," in Charlene Spretnak, ed., *The Politics of Women's Spirituality* (1982), p. 220.

98. Kay Turner, p. 221.

99. Kay Turner, p. 226.

100. Louis Chauvet and François Kabasele Lumbala, eds., *Liturgy and the Body* (1995), pp. 116–17.

101. Religious women have been working on many kinds of rituals. Rosemary Radford Reuther's *Women-Church* and Marcia Falk's *The Book of Blessings* are examples. Jewish women have created popular feminist Passover Haggadahs to be used at women's seders. Neopagan religions and goddess religions have been the most self-conscious about creating and developing new rituals. Margot Adler's *Drawing Down the Moon* and Starhawk's *The Spiral Dance* document this. Such a feminist critique does not limit itself to traditional rituals. A feminist methodology and insight can deliver a ritual critique of the social order and structures of meaning in a male-dominated society. In *The Last Word* (1991), Seremetakis turns Durkheimian and other anthropological approaches to death on their head. Death becomes the lens, she sees, through which the women of Maniat society in southern Greece defamiliarize the social order and see it in radically different ways. Death does not tamely reinforce social structure, but radically subverts it.

102. Robert Kastenbaum and Ruth Aisenberg, *The Psychology of Death* (1972).

CHAPTER 7: RITUAL QUARRYING: BODIES IN MOTION

1. Victor Turner, in "Social Drama in Brazilian Umbanda: The Dialectics of Meaning," in his *The Anthropology of Performance* (1987), pp. 54–55, has used categories of frame, flow, and reflexivity to analyze performance rituals. "Ritual is multi-dimensional; any given performance is shaped by the experiences poured into it as much as by its conventional framing structures. Experiences make the structures 'glow,' the structures focus and channel the experiences" (p. 56).

2. Victor Turner, in Richard Schechner and Willa Appel, eds., *By Means of Performance* (1990), p. 1.

3. Sharon Strocchia, *Death and Ritual in Renaissance Florence* (1992), p. 30, comments on symbols, objects, and bodies in funerals in Renaissance Florence and sees in the body, mirror and maker of its historical and natural environment, the most densely packed symbol of all.

4. Thomas Berry, *The Dream of the Earth* (1988); Matthew Fox, *Creation Spirituality* (1991).

5. Sallie McFague, *The Body of God* (1993).

6. Sallie McFague, *Metaphorical Theology* (1982); Sallie McFague, *Models of God* (1987).

7. Michel Ragon, *The Space of Death* (1983), p. 4.

8. Peter Metcalf and Richard Huntington, *Celebrations of Death* (1991), p. 34.

9. In her study of funerals in southern, rural Greece, Seremetakis, p. 74, notes: "Women represent the violence of death through their own bodies. Their postures, gestures, and general facial expressions function as corporeal texts which reaudit the experience of death as passage and disorder on behalf of the now silent and immobile dead. It is through this imagery of bodily disorder and movement that women not only establish their shared substance with the dead but also establish themselves as the iconic representatives of the dead in the world of the living. For women, the corporeal mimesis of death, the transformation of their bodies into a text of disorder, is part of an incremental process of desocialization—a process of leaving society, as symbolized in the stripping off and disarray of clothing and the scarring of flesh."

10. Frederick Paxton, *Christianizing Death* (1990), p. 66.

11. In *The Unburied* (1988), Roger Grainger provides an extensive and very useful discussion of ghosts and their significance as evidence of our unfinished business with the dead.

12. Metcalf and Huntington, p. 134.

13. Metcalf and Huntington, p. 169, quote the studies of Ernst Kantorowicz.

14. Ragon, p. 9.

15. Mary Douglas, *Natural Symbols* (1973).

16. Lindsay Prior, *The Social Organization of Death* (1989), p. 17.

17. Prior, p. 18.

18. Prior, p. 18.

19. Prior, p. 20.

20. Prior, pp. 20–21.

21. Ruth Richardson, *Death, Dissection, and the Destitute* (1987), p. 14.

22. Richardson, p. 15.

23. Prior, p. 197.

24. R. C. Finucane, "Sacred Corpse, Profane Carrion: Social Ideals and Death Rituals in the Later Middle Ages," in Joachim Whaley, ed., *Mirrors of Mortality* (1981), p. 41.

25. Finucane, p. 42.

26. Thomas Kselman, *Death and the Afterlife in Modern France* (1993), p. 51.

27. Finucane, pp. 44–45.

28. Ragon, p. 199.

29. Ragon, p. 7.

30. Maurice Bloch and Jonathan Parry, eds., *Death and the Regeneration of Life* (1982), p. 14.

31. Robert Jay Lifton, *The Broken Connection* (1979), p. 94.

32. In "Death in the People's Republic of China," in James Watson and Evelyn Rawski, eds., *Death Ritual in Late Imperial and Modern China* (1988), Martin K. Whyte documents the radical attempts and the various successes of the Communist Party in revolutionizing the Chinese way of dying. They rejected the religious beliefs, the superstitions (as they saw it) connected to the death system, ancestral worship, *feng shui* siting of graves, etc.

33. James Farrell, *Inventing the American Way of Death* (1980), p. 164.

34. Otto Margolis et al., eds., *Grief and the Meaning of the Funeral* (1975), p. 28.

35. Joseph Matthews, "The Time My Father Died," in Nathan Scott, ed., *The Modern Vision of Death* (1967), pp. 111–12.

36. Richard Lattimore, *Themes in Greek and Latin Epitaphs* (1962), p. 329.

37. Farrell, p. 103.

38. Ragon, p. 98.

39. Ragon, p. 221.

40. Ragon, p. 234.

41 Bruce Lincoln, *Discourse and the Construction of Society* (1989), p. 112.

42. In "Mao's Remains," in James Watson and Evelyn Rawski, eds., *Death Ritual in Late Imperial and Modern China* (1988), Frederic Wakeman Jr. describes in detail Mao's funeral and the subsequent and ongoing display of his body for public veneration. He also compares this to the funeral of Chiang Kai-shek.

43. Interestingly, in the memorial services that take place in southern Greece three days, nine days, forty days, and one year from the day of death, the corpse is of course absent, but deliberate provisions are made so that it can continue to speak. Seremetakis, p. 97, notes: "When the corpse is absent, an imaginary center is created. In the memorial service, there is no pretense that the body is present. The mourners are conscious of its absence. They ask the dead, 'Are you coming back? For this is the last trial.' The mourners play with presence and absence by standing in as doubles and surrogates of the dead. In the memorial, as in other later stages of the mourning cycle such as exhumation, there is a symbolic reassemblage of the body and persona of the dead. In both the original *klama* when the corpse is present and later memorial services, the voice of the mourner supplements the silence of the corpse. Positioning the voice and body next to the corpse and in place of the corpse expressed shared substance."

44. *Lutheran Book of Worship* (1978), p. 211.

45. Ronald Grimes, *Ritual Criticism* (1990), p. 153.

46. An extremely useful overview of the body in twentieth-century social theory is the chapter "Body in Social Theory" by Wimal Dissanayake in Thomas P. Kasulis, ed., *Self as Body in Asian Theory and Practice* (1993). Dissanayake suggests that the deficiencies in understanding of the body everywhere evident in Western social theory can profitably be remedied by turning to Asian theory and practice.

47. Grimes (1990), p. 155.

48. Paxton, p. 44.

49. To be sure, this one-sidedness in liturgical studies is beginning to be corrected. Lawrence A. Hoffman's *Beyond the Text* (1987) signals, in its title, this new direction. It is a move beyond the text to the people who use the text. This move has carried liturgical studies into new neighborhoods—the sociology of knowledge, philosophy of language, anthropology of ritual, psychology of belief, theory of action.

50. Grimes (1990), p. 151.

51. Mark Searl, "Ritual," in Cheslyn Jones et al, eds., *The Study of Liturgy* (1992), p. 57.

52. Hugh Wybrew, "Ceremonial," in Cheslyn Jones et al., eds., *The Study of Liturgy* (1992), pp. 485–89.

53. Louis Chauvet and Francois Kabasele Lumbala, eds., *Liturgy and the Body* (1995), p. 73.

54. Chauvet and Lumbala, p. 73.

55. Chauvet and Lumbala, p. 73.

56. Melanie May, *A Theopoetics of Death and Resurrection* (1995).

57. Tom Driver, *The Magic of Ritual* (1991), p. 87.

58. Grimes (1990), p. 148. Grimes (p. 150) concludes from his philosophy of embodiment that illness or the sickness career is itself a ritualized process; that symptoms ought to be seen as ultimate gestures and the transitions back and forth between illness and health as rites of passage; and that the distance between interaction rites in health centers, ecclesiastic rites in churches and synagogues, and domestic rites in homes is itself a source of illness. He goes on (p. 152): "Ritually considered, an illness is a heightened state of receptivity in which a patient calls not only for medical procedures such as injections but for another style of knowing, one that leads to embodiment and receptivity in a context not segregated from a person's community and ultimate values."

59. David Feinstein and Peg Mayo, *Mortal Acts* (1993). This is a shortened and revised version of their earlier book, *Rituals for Living and Dying* (1990).

60. Alfred Killilea, *The Politics of Being Mortal* (1988), p. 152.

61. Killilea, p. 148.

62. Paxton, p. 126.

63. Paxton, p. 127.

64. Richard Rutherford, *The Death of a Christian* (1990).

65. Seremetakis, pp. 99–100.

66. Seremetakis, p. 213, notes the dialectic between the living and the dead: "The iconic construction of status is bidirectional. By 'appearing' for the dead, the kin makes visual claims concerning its own status. The dead ornament the living as much as the living ornament the dead. This reversibility of adornment and endowment is linked to shared substance, which always involves reciprocity, the exchange of artifacts, emotions, and presences."

67. Lawrence Taylor, "Introduction: The Uses of Death in Europe," *Anthropological Quarterly* (1989), p. 150.

68. Ellen Badone, *The Appointed Hour* (1989), p. 245, quotes the folklorist LeBraz.

69. W. Lloyd Warner, *The Living and the Dead* (1975).

70. Lifton.

71. Nigel Llewellyn, *The Art of Death* (1991), p. 10, describes an English painting from 1560, "The Judd Marriage." A newly married husband and wife each rest a hand on a skull, making their vows. Beneath them lies a corpse. In the upper picture we see a social body, a couple united by marriage. In the lower picture the natural body is represented in allegory by a corpse. Beneath the skull, engraved on the altar, are the words: "The word of God / Hathe knit us twain / And Death shall us / Divide again." "The unfamiliar juxtaposition of portraits and a corpse is rather unsettling. In our culture the states of life and death are twinned, yet invariably opposed. The two words tend to be used with connotations of a strong contrast, as between the positive and negative of an electrical current, between black and white or good and evil. Post-Reformation emblematic images such as 'The Judd Marriage' are, however, intended to present life and death as part of a single cultural process, not as opposing values in a crude binary model of the human condition."

72. This is the argument of Berthold Von Schenk, reprinted in *The Lutheran* (November 1996), p. 3.

73. Dermot A. Lane, *Keeping Hope Alive* (1996), pp. 119–21, discusses the famous postwar debate between Max Horkheimer and Walter Benjamin of the Frankfurt School. Benjamin argued that even for the historical materialist the past was not necessarily closed. Horkheimer replied this was mere idealism—or theology. For Benjamin, history could be a form of empathetic memory that identifies not with the victor but with the sufferers. Jürgen Moltmann, in *The Coming of God* (1996), also discusses this debate in his chapter on Jewish contributions to eschatological thought.

74. Moltmann (1996), p. 106.

75. Moltmann (1996), p. 108.

76. Roy Rappaport, "The Obvious Aspects of Ritual," in Rappaport, *Ecology, Meaning, and Religion* (1979), p. 177.

77. Richard Schechner and Willa Appel, eds., in their anthology *By Means of Performance* (1990), take audience-performer interaction as one of six issues in modern performance studies.

78. Marvin Carlson, *Places of Performance* (1989), pp. 129–30.

79. Carlson, p. 129, is following the anthropologist David Cole.

80. Driver, p. 112.

81. Driver, p. 114.

82. William May, "The Sacred Power of Death in Contemporary Experience," *Social Research* (1972), pp. 487–88.

83. Philip Williams, "Who Is the Funeral For?" *Dialog* (Summer 1993), p. 174.

84. Peter Berger, *The Sacred Canopy* (1965), p. 45.

85. Berger, p. 46.

86. Ralph Houlbrooke, *Death, Ritual and Bereavement* (1989), p. 170.

87. Harry Moody, "Foreword: The Owl of Minerva," in Eugene Thomas and Susan Eisenhandler, *Aging and the Religious Dimension* (1994), p. xiii.

88. Christopher Lasch, *The Minimal Self* (1984), p. 32.

89 Evelyn Elsaesser Valarino, *On the Other Side of Life* (1997), is an excellent recent study. She mentions estimates ranging from eight to thirteen million Americans who have had near-death experiences.

90. In many cultures, food would be one of the central elements of material culture to play a role in death rituals. While American funerals are often followed by a potluck or light buffet, I have not included food as an ingredient for ritual quarrying in the discussion below. In China, for example, that omission would be unthinkable. In his article "Death, Food, and Fertility," in James Watson and Evelyn Rawski, eds., *Death Ritual in Late Imperial and Modern China* (1988), p. 71, Stuart E. Thompson asserts: "Food is intrinsic to most Chinese ritual activity." He focuses on the semantics of food in Chinese death rituals, where the role of food is integral. "Food prestations have been a perennial and indispensable feature of Chinese death ritual for at least seven millennia." Thompson shows how food offerings, especially rice and pork, play key roles in the transformation of a corpse into an ancestor. Exchanges between the living and the dead convert death into fertility and regeneration. Rice (male) and pork (female) express Chinese conceptions of duality in the cosmic and social universe.

Sometimes material culture is all that is left of a tradition, the religious or other ideation having been forgotten. So, before she died, one of the few surviving Shakers commented: "I almost expect to be remembered as a chair or a table" (Aune and DeMarinis, p. 106).

91. Rutherford, p. 25, notes that for a period in the early church, the eucharistic bread was given to the corpse.

92. Lane, pp. 189, 194.

93. Marvin Carlson, in *Places of Performance* (1989), devotes himself to the space in which theater takes place and its contributions to the meaning structure of the theater event as a whole. In his conclusion he notes that such "matrices" as time, place, and character help us position and consider a particular event as a "happening" or as a more conventional theatrical scene. "Happenings" were self-chosen descriptions of some experimental theater of the 1960s. In the experimental theater in which rites of last passage are rehearsed or improvised, space will be one matrix that helps us position what kind of ritual we wish to stage.

94. Aiden Kavanagh, *Elements of Rite* (1990), p. 14.

95. Ragon, pp. 19–21.

96. Neither in this section nor in the later section on ritual movement do I discuss specific uses of space within a particular site. But this can be an important

dimension of ritual action, as Seremetakis shows in her study of funerals in southern Greece (p. 97): "The mourners themselves are very conscious of the value connotations and power of space in the ceremony. They play with the dynamics of center/periphery. One technique is to call to women in the audience, to name them, and ask them to draw closer to the dead—a rhetorical strategy that intensifies the emotions of the ceremony. . . . The center of the ceremony is amplified by the loss and pains of others present."

97. W. Jardine Grisbrooke, "Vestments," in Cheslyn Jones et al., eds., *The Study of Liturgy* (1994), p. 543.

98. Carlson, p. 14.

99. Carlson, p. 15.

100. Carlson, p. 19.

101. Driver, p. 213.

102. Julian Litten, *The English Way of Death* (1991), p. 3.

103. Kavanagh, p. 15.

104. Victor Turner, "The Anthropology of Performance," in Turner, *The Anthropology of Performance* (1987b), p. 76.

105. In *The Coming of God*, Jürgen Moltmann offers a very extensive treatment of time and history and their place in eschatology.

106. Johann Baptist Metz, however, warns against absolutizing time as "the last remaining monarch after all the metaphysical thrones have been overthrown" and time becomes "the only post-metaphysical fascination." The result is that always more time is demanded, and the new fascination in the West with reincarnation is one way of getting it. This discussion is in Lane, p. 169.

107. Kavanagh, p. 24.

108. Kavanagh, p. 25, makes this point about every Sunday Eucharist in the Christian tradition, when the ritual meal is called "a foretaste of the feast to come." Thus Sunday is not a little Easter; Easter is a big Sunday.

109. Moltmann, p. 138.

110. Driver, p. 91. Driver, pp. 91–92, disagrees with Edmund Leach's assertion that "myth is a charter for ritual performance and . . . we can only understand what is being symbolized in the ritual if we take note of what is being 'said' in the mythology." Viewing ritual as enacting a myth is looking at it from the rear. Rituals acquire mythical interpretations only in the course of time. To look at ritual from the front is to see it laying out ways to act, prompted by felt needs, fears, joys, and aspirations.

111. Margaret Thompson Drewal, *Yoruba Ritual* (1992), pp. 29–47, in a chapter on "the ontological journey," sees *journey* as an important organizing metaphor in Yoruba thought, a world emanating from southwestern Nigeria to Cuba, Brazil, and black America. She describes a seven-day funeral passage. "Ritual journeys have a synecdochic relationship to the greater ontological journey of the human spirit in that they are nested in 'life's journey.' Not conceived as cyclical in the

sense of beginning time over or returning to the world the same each time, journeying is always a progression, a transformation" (p. 46).

112. Ivan Illich, *Medical Nemesis* (1976), pp. 176–81, traces the evolution of the "dance of death" and offers an extensive bibliography. From the fourth century on, crowds of naked and frenzied people, often brandishing swords, danced on tombs. There were frequent ecclesiastical prohibitions. Death occasioned rituals for the renewal of life, affirmations of the joy of being alive, and many erotic songs. By the fourteenth century the dance of death was more meditative. The first dance of the dead painted on a Paris cemetery wall in 1424 depicted all classes of people dancing with the one mirror image they had in common—a corpse. This contributed to the macabre self-consciousness in which Everyman is constantly aware of the gaping grave. By the fifteenth century death had become autonomous and coexisted as a separate agent. In the sixteenth century death assumed the leading role among the four great apocalyptic terrors. In the art of Holbein naked skeletons are the dance partners, not putrefied flesh. Death remains the egalitarian executioner.

113. Kavanagh, p. 37.

114. Lane, pp. 112–17, offers a good discussion.

115. Rutherford, p. ix.

116. Grimes (1990), p. 163.

117. Mumford, quoted in Carlson, p. 19.

118. Philippe Rouillard, "The Liturgy of the Dead as a Rite of Passage," in David Power and Luis Maldonado, eds., *Liturgy and Human Passage* (1979), p. 74.

119. Rouillard, p. 77.

120. Rouillard, p. 77.

121. Rouillard, pp. 77–78.

122. Rouillard, p. 80.

123. Yorick Spiegel, *The Grief Process* (1977), p. 114.

124. Spiegel, p. 112.

125. Alexander and Margarete Mitscherlich argue in their book *The Inability to Mourn* (1975) that German culture and society is rife with unresolved conflicts over an intense love of Hitler and the collapse of German society and the rejection of guilt. How to mourn a loss in which evil is discovered is the question. Intensive guilt and shame led to an inability to mourn and a struggle with breaking affective bridges to the past. They discuss how a politically dominant father who enforces renunciation then evokes aggression, how the aggression is diverted to outside enemies, and how a blind patriotism then flourishes. After 1945 the foundering paternal authority became everyone's culprit.

126. Paxton, p. 18.

127. Sogyal Rinpoche, *The Tibetan Book of Living and Dying* (1993), p. 299, emphasis added.

128. Linda J. Vogel, *Rituals for Resurrection* (1996), p. 40, describes such a funeral, where participants in the ritual brought forward many such symbols and objects.

CHAPTER 8: RITUAL QUARRYING: THE ARTS AND LETTERS OF HOPE

1. J. Gelineau, "Music and Singing in the Liturgy," in Cheslyn Jones et al., eds., *The Study of Liturgy* (1992).

2. An extraordinarily fine compendium of spirituals, hymn texts, poetry, and prose is *Death* (1990), edited by Virginia Sloyan with art by Linda Ekstrom. It is a Liturgy Training Publication, produced by the Roman Catholic Archdiocese of Chicago. I know of no other collection as useful as this for those who are looking for resources to use in the construction of funeral rituals.

3. *Opera to Die For,* Philips 106539 (1994), program notes by James Chater. This CD includes great death scenes/arias from the following operas: Verdi's *Un ballo in maschera;* Wagner's *Tristan und Isolde;* Purcell's *Dido and Aeneas;* Mozart's *Don Giovanni;* Donizetti's *Maria Stuarda;* Verdi's *La Traviata;* Verdi's *Don Carlo;* Leoncavallos's *Pagliacci;* Verdi's *Rigoletto;* both Verdi's and Rossini's *Otello;* Puccini's *Tosca;* and Gounod's *Faust.*

4. Michael Aune and Valerie DeMarinis, eds., *Religious and Social Ritual* (1996), p. 188.

5. In "Let Every Tongue, by Art Refined, Mingle Its Softest Notes with Mine," in Michael Aune and Valerie DeMarinis, eds., *Religious and Social Ritual* (1996), Rebecca J. Slough provides an exploration of hymn-singing events and the musical dimensions of knowing through ritual.

6. Therese Schroeder-Sheker, "Music for the Dying: Using Prescriptive Music in the Death-Bed Vigil," *Noetic Sciences Review* (Autumn 1994), p. 34. A videotape on her work produced in 1997, "Chalice of Repose: A Contemplative Musician's Approach to Death and Dying," is available from Sounds True, PO Box 8010, Boulder, CO 80306.

7. Schroeder-Sheker, p. 33.

8. Schroeder-Sheker, pp. 33–34.

9. James Pruett, "Requiem," *The New Grove Dictionary of Music and Musicians* (1980).

10. The Dies Irae is divided into the following parts: *Tuba mirum* (Hark, the trumpet), *Liber scriptus* (A book is written), *Quid sum miser* (How wretched I am), *Rex tremendae* (King of Glory), *Recordare* (Remember), *Ingemisco* (Sadly groaning), *Confutatis* (From the accursed), and *Lacrimosa* (Lamentation).

11. Eric Cross, "Death in War: Britten and the War Requiem," in Jon Davies, ed., *Ritual and Remembrance* (1994), discusses the commissioning of Britten's *Requiem* to celebrate the consecration of the new Coventry Cathedral, the powerful effect of its first performance on May 30, 1962, and its continuing popularity since. It is to be expected that music, including the requiem mass, should become connected to war death, above all in the twentieth century. Such music raises another problem: Should such art be viewed as commemorative or as a protest? This led to the concept of the "antimonument." An example is Wilfred Owen's

poetry, taken up by Britten: "My subject is War, and the pity of War / The Poetry is in the pity / All a poet can do today is warn."

12. Robert Jay Lifton, *The Broken Connection* (1979), p. 8.

13. Peter Sacks, *The English Elegy* (1985), p. xi.

14. In his biography *Mozart* (1995), p. 11, Maynard Solomon notes, however: "Whatever the partial validity of theories of art as restoration of the past, it seems clear that they are forms of piety to tradition and to ancestry, and often they are unmindful that recollection and forgetfulness are always intertwined, that creativity involves destruction as well as restoration, erasing and undoing as well as making and preserving. Surely, some part of the creative impulse aims to accomplish a separation from the dead, or at least from the paralysis of tradition."

One thinks of Britten turning his commission to produce a great requiem for the rededication of Coventry Cathedral into an antiwar protest.

15. Sacks, p. 2.

16. Michael Camille, *Master of Death* (1996), p. 1.

17. Gary Palmer, *Death* (1993), pp. 214–18.

18. In *Medical Nemesis* (1976), pp. 174–94, Ivan Illich discusses death and the arts and provides a bibliography.

19. Faubion Bowers, "Arts, Crafts, and Religion," *The Encyclopedia of Religion* (1987), pp. 426–27.

20. Auden is quoted in Nathan Scott, *The Poetry of Civic Virtue* (1976), p. 108.

21. Camille, p. 237.

22. Camille, p. 239.

23. Camille, p. 245.

24. Arlene Croce discussed the issues surrounding her decision not to review Bill T. Jones's "Still/Here" in "Discussing the Undiscussable," *The New Yorker* (December 26, 1994), pp. 54–60. Her article provoked an outpouring of letters, printed in a later issue of *The New Yorker* (January 30, 1995).

25. Michel Ragon, *The Space of Death* (1983), p. 45.

26. Quoted in Ragon, p. 220.

27. Ragon, p. 107.

28. Ragon, p. 110.

29. Nigel Llewellyn, *The Art of Death* (1991), p. 7, has written of the visual culture that grew up around post-Reformation English death practices.

30. Ragon, p. 78.

31. Gary Palmer, *Death* (1993), p. 77.

32. Lou Taylor, *Mourning Dress* (1983); Barbara Jones, *Design for Death* (1967).

33. Carla Gottlieb, "Modern Art and Death," in Herman Feifel, ed., *The Meaning of Death* (1959), p. 160.

34. Ragon, p. 109.

35. Ragon, p. 97.

36. Ragon, p. 215.

37. In the Christian liturgical churches the funeral pall accomplishes two important functions. It mantles the deceased in a linen embroidered with Christian symbols, a reminder of the believer being clothed with the righteousness of Christ.
Also, the use of the pall to cover all caskets, whether of mahogany or copper or
cardboard, strongly lends itself to theological assertions and minimizes status
assertions rooted in wealth. Unfortunately, most churches have the custom of
removing the pall before the casket is sent on its way to the cemetery. In some cases,
this provides the opportunity for the American flag to reassert itself as the final
symbolic statement.

38. There are good treatments in Judith Strupp Green, "The Days of the Dead
in Oaxaca, Mexico," in Richard Kalish, ed., *Death and Dying* (1980); David Stannard, ed., *Death in America* (1975).

39. J. Coleman, *Kentucky* (1971), p. 164.

40. After leading a march in memory of one thousand San Franciscans who
had died of AIDS, Cleve Jones and Mike Smith created the Names Project in 1985,
which in turn created the quilt to celebrate the lives of those killed by AIDS. Six
million people on five continents had seen parts of the quilt by 1996.

41. Gottlieb, p. 185.

42. Llewellyn, p. 48.

43. Llewellyn, pp. 50–51, relates the visual depiction of the two bodies to the
semiotic theory of Saussure and to structuralism.

44. *The Quest for Eternity* (1987), p. 41.

45. Once important moral distinctions were also made through visual culture,
as Llewellyn notes (p. 59): "In Hampshire and elsewhere parishioners made
crowns from wood and paper to be carried before the coffins of local virgins.
These were made to hang in the church as a challenge to any imputation against
the purity of the deceased. Once the proper period had elapsed, they were hung
from the rafters to act as a continuing symbol of virtue."

46. Llewellyn, p. 60. Julian Litten provides an elaborate account of the heraldic
funeral in chapter 7 of his book *The English Way of Death* (1991).

47. Llewellyn, p. 101.

48. Llewellyn, p. 104.

49. Llewellyn, p. 105.

50. "The Builder's Creed" of Forest Lawn is widely disseminated. Because the
builder believes in a happy eternal life and that those left behind should be glad in
their beliefs, he says:

> I therefore know the cemeteries of today are wrong because they depict
> an end, not a beginning. They have consequently become unsightly
> stoneyards full of inartistic symbols and depressing customs; places that
> do nothing for humanity save a practical act, and that not well.
>
> I therefore prayerfully resolve on this New Year's Day, 1917, that I shall
> endeavor to build Forest Lawn as different, as unlike other cemeteries as
> sunshine is unlike darkness, as eternal life is unlike death.

51. Faubion Bowers, "Arts, Crafts, and Religion," *The Encyclopedia of Religion* (1987), I, p. 428.

52. Camille, p. 159.

53. Sung to the tune of the Shaker song Aaron Copland set in his *Appalachian Spring,* this popular text was written by Sydney Carter. It is reprinted, among many other places, in *Hymnal Supplement* (1991). The chorus with each of five verses is the following:

> *Dance then wherever you may be;*
> *I am the Lord of the Dance, said he,*
> *And I'll lead you all, wherever you may be,*
> *And I'll lead you all in the dance, said he.*

54. Susan A. Blain, *Imaging the Word* (1995), p. 203.

55. Driver, p. 31.

56. Richard Schechner and Willa Appel, *By Means of Performance: Intercultural Studies of Theater and Ritual* (1990), p. 12.

57. Schechner and Appel, p. 13.

58. Victor Turner's book *The Anthropology of Performance* (1987) is the fourth volume of the Performance Studies Series, edited by Richard Schechner. The series includes another work by Turner, *From Ritual to Theater.*

59. The "Cambridge anthropologists" (Jane Ellen Harrison, Gilbert Murray, Francis Cornford, and others), actually classical scholars, believed that a primal ritual, a *sacer ludus,* was the root of Greek theater. They thought they saw vestiges of this primal ritual in existing Greek plays.

60. It is perhaps not to be expected, as we come to the end of this call for the recovery of a death of our own, that even the most eloquent, spiritually deep words will speak for the public. Lucy Bregman and Sara Thiermann, *First Person Mortal* (1995), p. 180, conclude their study of first-person narratives of dying and grieving with the opinion that we may not soon achieve any shared, publicly articulated vision of death. "American society may not ever replace a lost religiously based vision of death with one equally public and firmly accepted. The situation where autobiography is the favored and appropriate vehicle may be here to stay. This implies that the very hope for a shared society-wide vision about death and illness is misguided." They go on: "Saying something is necessary, but no one yet feels authorized to speak for all" (p. 181).

61. Edgar Jackson, *Understanding Grief* (1957), p. 156.

62. David Switzer, *The Dynamics of Grief* (1978), p. 195.

63. It is well to remind ourselves that the unlocked heart that speaks on the occasion of death does not restrict itself to mourning the deceased. The Chinese have a proverb: "We use the occasions of other people's funerals to release personal sorrows." In "Grieving for the Dead, Grieving for the Living: Funeral Laments of Hakka Women," in James Watson and Evelyn Rawski, eds., *Death Ritual in the Late Imperial and Modern China* (1988), Elizabeth L. Johnson describes

how funeral laments function also to lament the fate of the living. In particular, the laments of women may disclose the grief of the marginalized over their estate in life. A "ritual of reversal" allows the normally dumb to speak.

64. Aiden Kavanagh, *Elements of Rite: A Handbook of Liturgical Style* (1990), p. 86.

65. Kavanagh, p. 102.

66. Thucydides, *History*, IV. 23, 2–3.

67. Alexander Solzhenitsyn, *The Cancer Ward* (1972), p. 483.

68. Roy Rappaport, "The Obvious Aspects of Ritual," in Rappaport, *Ecology, Meaning, and Religion* (1979), p. 206.

69. *Funeral Orations* by St. Gregory Nazianzus and St. Ambrose, intro. by Martin R. P. McGuire, (1953), pp. viii–ix.

70. Richard Lattimore, *Themes in Greek and Latin Epitaphs* (1962), p. 327.

71. Lattimore, p. 340.

72. There are excellent collections of the literature of death. Among them are the following: Mary Jane Moffat, ed., *In the Midst of Winter* (1982); Robert F. Weir, ed., *Death in Literature* (1980); D. J. Enright, ed., *The Oxford Book of Death* (1983). In addition, there are dozens of books that are first-person accounts of dying, death, and mourning; several new ones appear every year. Sara Goodwin and Elisabeth Bronfen, eds., *Death and Representation* (1993), provide excellent bibliographies on the representation of death in literature and history.

73. John Sawyer, "Isaiah as a Source Book for Scriptural Texts about Death and Mourning," in Jon Davies, ed., *Ritual and Remembrance* (1994), studies just texts from the prophet Isaiah. The Tibetan Book of the Dead has gone through repeated printings, versions, and editions in recent years, as Westerners look to enlightenment from the East. Martin Marty's *A Cry of Absence* (1983) is a meditation on mourning, using verses from the Psalms as illustration and inspiration. He writes: "To my surprise I noticed that more than half of the psalms had as their major burden or context life on the wintry landscape of the heart. Many more contained extensive reference to the spiritual terrain of winter, even if it did not predominate. Only about a third of the psalms were, indeed, the simple property of those for whom the summery style would exhaust Christian spirituality" (p. 39). All Christian funeral manuals are replete with stipulated and optional selections from the Bible that are suitable for rites of last passage; see the next endnote.

74. In *Dying We Live* (1990) Edward S. Gleason provides a series of concrete meditations and stories to accompany and illustrate the various sections of the funeral liturgy: hymns, collects, scripture readings, creed, confession, Eucharist, commendation, committal.

The following are manuals or liturgies from various Christian traditions. The *Abingdon Funeral Manual* (1976) offers selections and guidance for the working pastor and includes Methodist, Episcopal, Presbyterian, United Church of Christ, Baptist, Church of South India, and Free Church services. J. B. Bernardin's *Burial Services* (1980) offers Episcopal services from the *Book of Common Prayer* (1979). *The Burial of the Dead* (1976) is the Lutheran order used in *Lutheran Book of Worship* (1978). *The*

Funeral (1986) is a Presbyterian order. *Funeral Services of the Christian Churches in England* (1986) provides ecumenical Protestant, Anglican, and Roman Catholic services for use at cemeteries and crematoria. Edward Searl's *In Memoriam* (1993) offers free-form services recommended for Unitarian usage. *A Service of Death and Resurrection* (1979) offers Methodist services. It offers unusually helpful essays on the ministry of the Church at death, the significance of the Christian funeral, and a commentary on the service, rubrics, etc. *Order of Christian Funerals* (1989) is a beautifully printed and elaborate collection of all Roman Catholic services approved for use in the United States. Almost every one of these manuals provides very ample Bible texts, liturgical texts, and hymn selections and recommendations.

75. Jack Riemer and Nathaniel Stampfer, *Ethical Wills* (1983). The "ethical will" is primarily a Jewish custom whose aim is to bequeath a spiritual legacy. People, often parents writing to children, try to sum up what they have learned in life and to express what they want most for and from their loved ones. Ethical wills are windows into the souls of those who write them, left behind in the belief that the wisdom acquired in a lifetime is as much a part of a family's legacy as are its material possessions. Such wills, when collected from a particular period or people, give a unique insight into the values and preoccupations of a period.

76. Peter Sacks, *The English Elegy* (1985).

77. Among them are Thomas Parnell's "Night Piece on Death," Edward Young's "Night Thoughts," Robert Blair's "The Grave," and Thomas Gray's "Elegy in a Country Churchyard." The American poets John Trumbull and Philip Frenean wrote elegies. This tradition culminated in Bryant's "Thanatopsis." Sacks offers an extensive bibliography.

78. Sacks, p. 18.

79. Sacks, p. 7.

80. Sacks, p. 4.

81. Sacks, p. 6.

82. Sacks, p. 7.

83. Sacks, p. 8.

84. Sacks, p. 22, discusses how the elegy frees the affective energies from being locked inside the mourner. Anger and guilt, for example, are carried away from the self through incantatory elegiac questioning that acts almost like a ritual exorcism. Catharsis occurs. Gradually the mourner "brings his loss into language, testing how it feels to speak *and hear* of it in words" (p. 25).

85. Sacks, p. 19.

86. Jack Goody, *Death, Property, and the Ancestors* (1962), p. 129.

87. Richard Stamelman, quoted in Goodwin and Bronfen, p. 21.

88. Jahan Ramazani, quoted in Goodwin and Bronfen, p. 21.

89. Bregman and Thiermann, p. 188.

90. Ira Progoff created and taught through innumerable workshops his Intensive Journal Method, which has achieved tremendous popularity since the late 1960s. He proposed the journal method, which watches-waits-nurtures, instead of

psychoanalysis, which cuts up. The journal provides a written record that is the best guide to who you are and where you are going. Progoff's method emphasizes active self-transforming involvement rather than literary creation or religious soul-searching. Progoff's best-known journal-related work is *At a Journal Workshop* (1975). Progoff's proposed journal entry categories include: period log and daily log; dialog with persons, works, society, events, body; dream log and enlargements; twilight log and extensions; inner wisdom dialog; life history log; stepping stones; roads taken and not taken; and now—the open moment.

In general, all proponents of journal keeping emphasize the act of writing as an impetus to formulate and clarify thoughts and feelings; to choose what we attend to; and to define, work through, and resolve problems. All this produces a document that can be mined again and again. Journal keeping can also stimulate creativity, become a technique of catharsis, and help to explore causes behind the events and patterns of life.

91. Deena Metzger, *Writing for Your Life* (1992).

92. Metzger, p. 3.

93. Metzger, p. 71.

94. Mary Jane Moffat, *In the Midst of Winter* (1982), p. xxiii.

95. Moffat, p. xxiv.

96. Carol Zaleski, *The Life of the World to Come* (1996), p. 76.

97. It may be that the end of the millennium will stimulate many new constructions and evocations of hope. I mention some of the most important theological treatises at the end of this section. A new work by Dermot A. Lane, *Keeping Hope Alive* (1996), notes that more and more people are asking about human, social, and cosmic destiny as they move toward the third millennium. Does the universe have a purpose? What happens at death? What can we hope for? Is it possible to talk meaningfully about another world? I applaud the setting of hope in larger social and cultural movements, while also noting that for each individual the coming of death may be experienced as an eschatological—and, yes, millennial, event.

98. This phrase is the premise of Dermot Lane's *Keeping Hope Alive.*

99. Consider, however, the unexpected return to contemplative spiritualities at the end of the millennium. The lure of monasticism in particular is well caught in the best-seller of the late 1990s, Kathleen Norris's *The Cloister Walk* (1996). Her earlier best-seller, *Dakota* (1993), connected such a spirituality to a certain landscape.

100. I take the distinction of a "model of" and a "model for" from Clifford Geertz, "Religion as a Cultural System," in Geertz, *The Interpretation of Cultures* (1973), pp. 93–94.

101. Jane Wynne Wilson has compiled a booklet, *Funerals Without God* (1990), on behalf of the British Humanist Association. Unfortunately, it takes a minimalist approach. It knows it does not want in any way to be religious, but it does not really plow any promising alternative ground. It assumes cremation will be the context of the ritual. There are three sample rituals, all following the same outline: opening words,

thoughts on life and death, the tribute, the committal, closing words. The booklet closes with selections of poetry and prose that might be useful. As I have argued that religious communities must much more radically take the lead in ritual evolution but mostly have not, it should not be surprising that nonreligious or postreligious communities have made scarcely any attempts at all. The attempts of East European Marxist or Chinese Communist regimes have been mostly dismal—hostile to religion but offering little in its place and driven by economic rationalization.

102. Rappaport, p. 214.

103. Antonin Artaud, *The Theater and Its Double* (1958), p. 91.

104. Artaud, p. 99.

105. William May, "The Sacred Power of Death in Contemporary Experience," *Social Research* (1972).

106. Dionisio Borobio, "The 'Four Sacraments' of Popular Religiosity: A Critique," in David Power and Luis Maldonado, eds., *Liturgy and Human Passage* (1979), pp. 86–87.

107. John Weston, "Aging the Last Stage? or, the Dream Continued," *Second Opinion* (March 1991).

108. Lars Tornstam, "Gero-Transcendence: A Theoretical and Empirical Exploration," in Eugene Thomas and Susan Eisenhandler, eds., *Aging and the Religious Dimension* (1994).

109. Catherine Gunsalus Gonzalez, "Culture, the Church, and Funerals," *Reformed Liturgy and Music* (Fall 1986), p. 197.

110. George Stroup, "Death, Resurrection and the Communion of the Saints," *Reformed Liturgy and Music* (Fall 1986), p. 189.

111. Borobio, p. 97.

112. Borobio, p. 92, writes: "Man's whole life is marked by a sacramental structure or 'complexity,' a religious dimension, a call to the transcendent; this structure, dimension and call come forth with all their necessitating force, all their mysterious power, principally at the great, decisive moments of the life-cycle. At these moments, man finds himself needing and impelled to express his deeper reality, his basic sacramentality. In them, he finds himself at the 'threshold' through which he has to pass in order to meet the sacred, the mystery he discovers in himself and surpassing him. These are the moments of religious experience, of encounter with a totally other, unconditional, definitive and ultimate truth. On the frontiers of his life, which partly correspond to his vital transitions, man obtains a more clearsighted perception of the nearness and presence of God. If plunging deeper into his own immanence makes his own mystery transparent, this transparency calls him to transcendence in the mystery of God."

113. Monika Hellwig, *What Are They Saying About Death and Christian Hope* (1978), p. 40. Hellwig, p. 21, notes, regarding the evolution of hope: "Later images expressing the hope of Christians for the future became much more individualistic and certainly more unearthly. The resurrection from the dead, which had a

very strong communal character for Jews at the time of Jesus and for Jesus and his early followers, began to fade into the background and give way to the teaching of the immortality of the soul." When the question asked implied the spirit or consciousness of the essential self in the accidental body, the answer was an image of the soul being released from the imprisoning body and then continuing its existence without being much changed.

114. Quoted in Lane, *Keeping Hope Alive,* p. 69.

115. Hellwig, pp. 24–28.

116. Whitehead is quoted in Lane, pp. 15 and 57.

117. Lane, p. 18.

118. Hellwig, p. 23.

119. Hellwig, p. 24.

120. Thomas O'Gorman, *An Advent Sourcebook* (1988), p. 84.

121. O'Gorman, p. 95.

EPILOGUE

1. My remarks on Paul Tillich and Søren Kierkegaard are indebted to the argument developed in chapter 5 of *Death, Sin and the Moral Life* by Miller-McLemore.

2. Miller-McLemore, p. 136.

3. Miller-McLemore, p. 138.

4. Paul Tillich, quoted in Miller-McLemore, p. 140.

5. Paul Tillich, *The Courage To Be* (1952).

6. Miller-McLemore, pp. 155–73.

7. There are many worship aids prepared for the enrichment of the Advent season, but the most notable is *An Advent Sourcebook,* ed. by Thomas J. O'Gorman (1988). Three of the greatest Advent hymns ever written are the Lutheran chorales "Wake, Awake, for Night Is Flying" and "O Lord, How Shall I Meet You" and the hymn attributed to St. Ambrose in the fourth century, "Savior of the Nations, Come," all occuring in the Advent section of the *Lutheran Book of Worship* (1978). It is widely remarked and lamented that the four-week liturgical season of Advent is completely overwhelmed by the commercialization of Christmas. While Advent, commencing in early December, is intended to prepare the community for a proper celebration of Christmas, American stores begin doing so well before Halloween. A neocapitalist culture specializing in instant and maximum material gratification is not likely to do well with death and will approach rituals of hope with no rehearsal.

8. O'Gorman, p. 57.

9. In *The Coming of God* (1996), pp. 25–29, Jürgen Moltmann strongly emphasizes the difference between *futurum* and *adventus,* and develops the latter with reference to the category of *novum,* while the former is more likely to be seen as an extension of the present.

Bibliography

Amore, R. C. "The Heterodox Philosophical Systems." In *Death and Eastern Thought,* ed. Frederick H. Holck. Nashville: Abingdon, 1974.

Ariès, Philippe. *The Hour of Our Death.* New York: Vintage, 1982.

———. "The Reversal of Death." In *Death in America,* ed. David Stannard. Philadelphia: University of Pennsylvania Press, 1975.

Artaud, Antonin. *The Theatre and Its Double.* New York: Grove, 1958.

Aune, Michael B., and Valerie DeMarinis, eds. *Religious and Social Ritual: Interdisciplinary Explorations.* Albany: SUNY Press, 1996.

Backer, Barbara A., Natalie Hannon, and Noreen A. Russell. *Death and Dying: Individuals and Institutions.* New York: John Wiley and Sons, 1982.

Badone, Ellen. *The Appointed Hour: Death, Worldview, and Social Change in Brittany.* Berkeley: University of California Press, 1989.

Bailey, Lloyd R., Sr. *Biblical Perspectives on Death.* Philadelphia: Fortress, 1979.

Bakan, David. *Disease, Pain, and Suffering: Toward a Psychology of Suffering.* Chicago: University of Chicago Press, 1968.

Baldwin, Frank. "Chrysanthemum and Sword." *Christianity and Crisis,* March 20, 1989: 82–84.

Barber, Paul. *Vampires, Burial and Death.* New Haven: Yale University Press, 1988.

Bassett, Steven, ed. *Death in Towns: Urban Responses to the Dying and the Dead, 100–1600.* Leicester: Leicester University Press, 1992.

Battin, Margaret Pabst. *Least Worst Death: Essays in Bioethics on the End of Life.* New York: Oxford University Press, 1994.

Beauchamp, Tom L. *Intending Death: The Ethics of Assisted Suicide and Euthanasia.* Upper Saddle River, NJ: Prentice Hall, 1996.

Becker, Ernst. *The Denial of Death.* New York: Free Press, 1973.

Bedford, Gary. "Notes on Mythological Psychology: Reimagining the Historical Psyche." *Journal of the American Academy of Religion,* 49, 2 (June 1981): 231–48.

Behe, Michael J. *Darwin's Black Box.* New York: Free Press, 1996.

Bell, Catherine. *Ritual Theory, Ritual Practice.* New York: Oxford University Press, 1992.

Bellah, Robert. *The Broken Covenant.* New York: Seabury, 1975.

———. *Habits of the Heart.* Berkeley: University of California Press, 1985.

———. *Habits of the Heart: Individualism and Commitment in American Life,* updated edition. Berkeley: University of California Press, 1996.

———, et al. *The Good Society.* New York: Vintage, 1992.

Berger, Peter L. *The Sacred Canopy.* Garden City, NY: Doubleday, 1965.

————, and Thomas Luckman. *The Social Construction of Reality.* Garden City, NY: Doubleday, 1966.

Berry, Thomas. *The Dream of the Earth.* San Francisco: Sierra Club Books, 1988.

Bianchi, Eugene. *Aging as a Spiritual Journey.* New York: Crossroad, 1984.

Biddle, Perry H., Jr. *Abingdon Funeral Manual.* Nashville: Abingdon, 1976.

Blain, Susan A., ed. *Imaging the Word: An Arts and Lectionary Resource,* vol. 2. Cleveland: United Church Press, 1995.

Blaud, Olivia. *The Royal Way of Death.* London: Constable, 1986.

Blauner, Robert. "Death and Social Structure." In *Passing: The Vision of Death in America,* ed. Charles O. Jackson. Westport, CT: Greenwood, 1977.

Bloch, Maurice, and Jonathan Parry, eds. *Death and the Regeneration of Life.* Cambridge: Cambridge University Press, 1982.

Bloom, Janet. "Minerva's Doll." In *The Uses of Reminiscence: New Ways of Working with Older Adults,* ed. Marc Kaminsky. New York: Haworth, 1984.

Boase, T. S. R. *Death in the Middle Ages.* New York: McGraw-Hill, 1972.

Borobio, Dionisio. "The 'Four Sacraments' of Popular Religiosity: A Critique." In *Liturgy and Human Passage,* ed. David Power and Luis Maldonado. New York: Seabury, 1979.

Boros, Ladislaus. *The Mystery of Death.* New York: Herder and Herder, 1965.

Bowers, Faubion. "Arts, Crafts, and Religion." In *The Encyclopedia of Religion,* ed. Mircea Eliade. New York: Macmillan, 1987.

Bowman, Leroy. *The American Funeral: A Study in Guilt, Extravagance, and Sublimity.* Washington, DC: Public Affairs Press, 1959.

Bradshaw, Paul F., and Lawrence A. Hoffman. *The Changing Face of Jewish and Christian Worship in North America.* Notre Dame: University of Notre Dame Press, 1991.

Bram, Robert, and Adam Pollock. *Bangwa Funerary Sculpture.* Toronto: University of Toronto Press, 1971.

Brandon, S. G. F. *The Judgement of the Dead: The Idea of Life After Death in the Major Religions.* New York: Scribner, 1967.

Bregman, Lucy. *Death in the Midst of Life.* Grand Rapids: Baker, 1992.

————, and Sara Thiermann. *First Person Mortal.* New York: Paragon House, 1995.

Brener, Anne. *Mourning and Mitzvah: A Guided Journal for Walking the Mourner's Path Through Grief to Healing.* Woodstock, VT: Jewish Lights, 1993.

Briner, Lewis A. "The New Funeral Rite." *Reformed Liturgy and Music* 20 (Fall 1986): 198–203.

Brody, Howard. *Stories of Sickness.* New Haven: Yale University Press, 1987.

Broner, E. M. *Mornings and Mourning.* San Francisco: Harper San Francisco, 1994.

Bronfen, Elisabeth. *Over Her Dead Body: Death, Femininity, and the Aesthetic.* New York: Routledge, 1992.

Brown, Peter. *The Cult of the Saints: Its Rise and Function in Latin Christianity.* Chicago: University of Chicago Press, 1981.

Brueggemann, Walter. *The Prophetic Imagination.* Philadelphia: Fortress, 1978.

Burial of the Dead. Minneapolis: Augsburg, 1976.

Butler, Robert N. "The Life Review: An Interpretation of Reminiscence in the Aged." *Psychiatry* 26 (February 1963): 65–76

Camille, Michael. *Master of Death: The Lifeless Art of Pierre Reniet, Illuminator*. New Haven: Yale University Press, 1996.

Cantor, Robert Chernin. *And a Time to Live: Toward Emotional Well-Being During the Crisis of Cancer*. New York: Harper and Row, 1980.

Carlson, Lisa. *Caring for Your Own Dead: A Complete Guide for Those Who Wish to Handle Funeral Arrangements Themselves*. Hinesburg, VT: Upper Access, 1987.

Carlson, Marvin. *Places of Performance: The Semiotics of Theatre Architecture*. Ithaca: Cornell University Press, 1989.

Carroll, David. *Living With Dying: Consumers Union Guide*. Mt. Vernon, NY: Consumers Union, 1985.

Cátedra, Maria. *This World, Other Worlds: Sickness, Suicide, Death and the Afterlife Among the Vaqueiros de Alzada of Spain*. Trans. William A. Christian Jr. Chicago: University of Chicago Press, 1992.

Chapman, John. "The Living, the Dead, and the Ancestors: Time, Life Cycles, and the Mortuary Domain in Later European Prehistory." In *Ritual and Remembrance: Responses to Death in Human Societies*, ed. Jon Davies. Sheffield: Sheffield Academic Press, 1994.

Charme, Stuart. "Sartre's Existential Psychoanalysis." *Journal of the American Academy of Religion* 50, no. 4 (December 1982): 557–75.

Chauvet, Louis, and Francois Kabasele Lumbala, eds. *Liturgy and the Body*. Maryknoll, NY: Orbis Books, 1995.

Chidester, David. *Patterns of Transcendence: Religion, Death and Dying*. Belmont, CA: Wadsworth, 1990.

Choron, Jacques. *Death and Western Thought*. New York: Collier, 1963.

Churchill, Larry. "The Human Experience of Dying: The Moral Primacy of Stories Over Stages." *Soundings* 62 (Spring 1979): 24–37.

Clifford, James. *The Predicament of Culture: Twentieth-Century Ethnography, Literature, and Art*. Cambridge: Harvard University Press, 1988.

———, and George Marcus, eds. *Writing Culture: The Poetics and Politics of Ethnography*. Berkeley: University of California Press, 1986.

Coffin, Margaret M. *Death in Early America*. Nashville: Thomas Nelson, 1976.

Cole, Thomas R., and Sally A. Gadow, eds. *What Does It Mean to Grow Old? Reflections from the Humanities*. Durham: Duke University Press, 1986.

Cole, Thomas R., and Mary G. Winkler, eds. *The Oxford Book of Aging: Reflections on the Journey of Life*. Oxford: Oxford University Press, 1994.

Coleman, J. *Kentucky: A Pictorial History*. Lexington: University Press of Kentucky, 1971.

Coult, Tony, and Baz Kershaw, eds. *Engineers of the Imagination: The Welfare State Handbook*. London: Methuen, 1983.

Covell, Mara Brand. *The House Alternatives to Hospitals and Nursing Homes.* New York: Rawson, 1983.

Crenshaw, David A. *Bereavement: Counseling the Grieving Throughout the Life Cycle.* New York: Continuum, 1990.

Crissman, James K. *Death and Dying in Central Appalachia.* Urbana: University of Illinois Press, 1994.

Crites, Stephen. "The Narrative Quality of Experience." *Journal of the American Academy of Religion* 39 (1971): 291–311.

Cross, Eric. "Death in War: Britten and the War Requiem." In *Ritual and Remembrance: Responses to Death in Human Societies,* ed. Jon Davies. Sheffield: Sheffield Academic Press, 1994.

Crossan, John Dominic. *The Dark Interval: Towards a Theology of Story.* Niles, IL: Argus, 1975.

Cullmann, Oscar. *Immortality of the Soul or Resurrection of the Dead: The Witness of the New Testament.* London: Epworth, 1958.

Curl, James Stevens. *A Celebration of Death: An Introduction to Some of the Buildings, Monuments, and Settings of Funerary Architecture in the Western European Tradition.* New York: Scribner, 1980.

Danforth, Loring M. *The Death Rituals of Rural Greece.* Princeton: Princeton University Press, 1982.

Davies, Jon. "One Hundred Billion Dead: A General Theology of Death." In *Ritual and Remembrance: Responses to Death in Human Societies,* ed. Jon Davies. Sheffield: Sheffield Academic Press, 1994.

D'Costa, Gavin, ed. *Resurrection Reconsidered.* Oxford: Oneworld, 1996.

Delattre, Roland A. "Ritual Retrospective and Cultural Pluralism." *Soundings* 61 (Fall 1978): 281–301.

Dempsey, David. *The Way We Die.* New York: McGraw-Hill, 1975.

Dickinson, Emily. *Collected Poems of Emily Dickinson.* Ed. Mabel Loomis Todd and T. W. Higginson. New York: Gramercy, 1982.

Dissanayake, Wimal. "Body in Social Theory." In *Self as Body in Asian Theory and Practice,* ed. Thomas P. Kasulis. Albany: SUNY Press, 1993.

Donnelly, John, ed. *Language, Metaphysics, and Death.* New York: Fordham University Press, 1978.

Douglas, Mary. *Natural Symbols.* New York: Vintage, 1973.

Drewal, Margaret Thompson. *Yoruba Ritual.* Bloomington: Indiana University Press, 1992.

Driver, Tom F. *The Magic of Ritual.* San Francisco: Harper, 1991.

Droege, Thomas A. *Guided Grief Imagery: A Resource for Grief Ministry and Death Education.* New York: Paulist, 1987.

Dumont, Louis. "Religion, Politics, and Society in the Individualistic Universe." *Proceedings of the Royal Anthropological Institute for 1970,* 1971.

Dumont, Richard G., and Dennis C. Foss. *The American View of Death: Acceptance or Denial.* Cambridge: Schenkman, 1972.

Dunning, William V. *The Roots of Postmodernism.* Englewood Cliffs, NJ: Prentice Hall, 1995.

Durkheim, Emile. *The Elementary Forms of the Religious Life.* New York: Free Press, 1915.

———. *Suicide: A Study in Sociology.* New York: Free Press, 1951.

"Funerals" [editorial]. *Dialog* 32 (Summer 1993): 162.

Eiseley, Loren. *All the Strange Hours: The Excavation of a Life.* New York: Scribner, 1975.

Eliade, Mircea. *Death, Afterlife and Eschatology.* New York: Harper and Row, 1974.

Eliot, T. S. "Little Gidding." *Collected Poems 1909–1962.* New York: Harcourt Brace, 1963.

Elliot, Gil. *Twentieth Century Book of the Dead.* New York: Scribner, 1972.

Ellis, Carolyn. *Final Negotiations: A Story of Love, Loss and Chronic Illness.* Philadelphia: Temple University Press, 1995.

Empereur, James. *Prophetic Anointing: God's Call to the Sick, the Elderly, and the Dying.* Wilmington, Delaware: Michael Glazier, 1982.

Enright, D. J., ed. *The Oxford Book of Death.* New York: Oxford University Press, 1983.

Episcopal Church. *Burial Services,* comp. J. B. Bernardin. Wilton, CT: Morehouse-Barlow, 1980.

Erikson, Erik. *Childhood and Society.* New York: Norton, 1963.

Evans, Jocelyn. *Living with a Man Who Is Dying.* New York: Taplinger, 1971.

Fabian, Johannes. "How Others Die—Reflections on the Anthropology of Death." *Social Research,* 39, 3 (Autumn 1972): 543–67.

Farrell, James J. *Inventing the American Way of Death.* Philadelphia: Temple University Press, 1980.

Feinstein, David, and Peg Elliot Mayo. *Mortal Acts: Eighteen Empowering Rituals for Confronting Death.* San Francisco: Harper, 1993.

———. *Rituals for Living and Dying.* San Francisco: Harper, 1990.

Feldman, Fred. *Confrontations with the Reaper.* New York: Oxford University Press, 1992.

Feldman, Marvin J., et al. *Fears Related to Death and Suicide.* New York: MSS Information Corporation, 1974.

Fenn, Richard K. *Liturgies and Trials: The Secularization of Religious Language.* New York: Pilgrim, 1982.

Fiedler, Leslie A. *Love and Death in the American Novel.* New York: Criterion, 1960.

Finucane, R. C. "Sacred Corpse, Profane Carrion: Social Ideals and Death Rituals in the Later Middle Ages." In *Mirrors of Mortality,* ed. Joachim Whaley. New York: St. Martin's, 1981.

Fitzgerald, William. *Speaking About Death: Poetic Resources for Ministers of Consolation.* Chicago: Publications, 1990.

Flanagan, Teresa M. *Mourning on the Pejepscot (Maine).* Lanham, MD: University Press of America, 1992.

Foos-Graber, Anya. *Deathing: An Intelligent Alternative to the Final Moments of Life*. Reading: Addison-Wesley, 1984.

Fox, Matthew. *Creation Spirituality*. New York: HarperCollins, 1991.

Frank, Arthur W. *The Wounded Storyteller: Body, Illness, and Ethics*. Chicago: University of Chicago Press, 1995.

Fulton, Robert. "The Funeral in Contemporary Society." In *Death: Facing the Facts*, ed. Hannelore Wass, Felix M. Berardo, and Robert A. Neimeyer. Washington, DC: Hemisphere, 1988.

———. "The Traditional Funeral and Contemporary Society." In *Acute Grief and the Funeral*, ed. Vanderlyn R. Pine et al. Springfield, IL: Charles C. Thomas, 1976.

———, ed. *Death and Identity*, revised edition. Bowie, MD: Charles, 1976.

Funeral Services of the Christian Churches in England. Norwich, England: Canterbury, 1986.

Garland, Robert. *The Greek Way of Death*. Ithaca, NY: Cornell University Press, 1985.

Gavin, William Joseph. *Cuttin' the Body Loose*. Philadelphia: Temple University Press, 1995.

Gay, Volney P. "Ritual and Psychotherapy." In *Religious and Social Ritual: Interdisciplinary Explorations*, ed. Michael B. Aune and Valerie DeMarinis. Albany: SUNY Press, 1996.

Geddes, Gordon E. *Welcome Joy: Death in Puritan New England, 1630–1730*. Ann Arbor: University Microfilms International, 1981.

Geertz, Clifford. *After the Fact: Two Countries, Four Decades, One Anthropologist*. Cambridge: Harvard University Press, 1995.

———. "The Impact of the Concept of Culture on the Concept of Man." In *The Interpretation of Cultures*. New York: Basic Books, 1973.

———. "Religion as a Cultural System." In *The Interpretation of Cultures*. New York: Basic Books, 1973.

———. *Works and Lives: The Anthropologist as Author*. Stanford: Stanford University Press, 1988.

Gelineau, J. "Music and Singing in the Liturgy." In *The Study of Liturgy*, ed. Cheslyn Jones et al. New York: Oxford University Press, 1992.

Gibbs, C. Earl. *Caring for the Grieving*. Corte Madera, CA: Omega, 1976.

Gittings, Clare. *Death, Burial and the Individual in Early Modern England*. London: Croom Helm, 1984.

Gleason, Edward S. *Dying We Live*. Cambridge: Cowley, 1990.

Gonda, Thomas Andrew, and John Edward Ruark. *Dying Dignified: The Health Professional's Guide to Care*. Menlo Park, CA: Addison-Wesley, 1984.

Gonzalez, Catherine Gunsalus. "Culture, the Church, and Funerals." In *Reformed Liturgy and Music* 20 (Fall 1986): 194–97.

Goodman, Lisl Marburg. *Death and the Creative Life: Conversations with Prominent Artists and Scientists*. New York: Springer, 1981.

Goodwin, Sarah, and Elisabeth Bronfen, eds. *Death and Representation*. Baltimore: John Hopkins University Press, 1993.

Goody, Jack. *Death, Property, and the Ancestors*. Stanford: Stanford University Press, 1962.

Gorer, Geoffrey. *Death, Grief, and Mourning*. Garden City, NY: Doubleday, 1965.

Gott, Ted. *Don't Leave Me this Way: Art in the Age of AIDS*. Melbourne: National Gallery of Australia, 1994.

Gottlieb, Carla. "Modern Art and Death." In *The Meaning of Death*, ed. Herman Feifel. New York: McGraw-Hill, 1959.

Grainger, Roger. *The Unburied*. Worthing, West Sussex, UK: Churchman, 1988.

Greaves, Richard L. *Society and Religion in Elizabethan England*. Minneapolis: University of Minnesota Press, 1981.

Green, Judith Strupp. "The Days of the Dead in Oaxaca, Mexico." In *Death and Dying: Views from Many Cultures*, ed. Richard Kalish. San Francisco: Baywood, 1980.

Gregory, of Nazianzus and Ambrose of Milan. *Funeral Orations by St. Gregory Nazianzus and St. Ambrose*, tr. by Leo P. McCauley, intro. by Martin R. P. McGuire. Washington: Catholic University of America Press, 1968, c1953.

Greinacher, Norbert, and Alois Muller, eds. *The Experience of Dying*. New York: Herder and Herder, 1974.

Greshake, Gilbert. "Towards a Theology of Dying." In *The Experience of Dying*, ed. Norbert Greinacher and Alois Muller. New York: Herder and Herder, 1974.

Grimes, Ronald L. *Beginnings in Ritual Studies*. Lanham, MD: University Press of America, 1982.

———. *Marrying and Burying: Rites of Passage in a Man's Life*. Boulder: Westview, 1995.

———. *Research in Ritual Studies: A Programmatic Essay and Bibliography*. ATLA Bibliography Series no. 14. Metuchen, NJ: Scarecrow, 1985.

———. *Ritual Criticism: Case Studies in Its Practice, Essays on Its Theory*. Columbia: University of South Carolina Press, 1990.

———. "Sources for the Study of Ritual." *Religious Studies Review* 10 (April 1984): 134–45.

Grisbrooke, W. Jardine. "Vestments." In *The Study of Liturgy*, ed. Cheslyn Jones et al. New York: Oxford University Press, 1994.

Grof, Stanislav, and Christina Grof. *Beyond Death: The Gates of Consciousness*. London: Thames and Hudson, 1980.

Grof, Stanislav, and Joan Halifax. *The Human Encounter with Death*. New York: Dutton, 1977.

Gula, Richard M. *What Are They Saying About Euthanasia*. New York: Paulist, 1986.

Gutierrez, Ramon A., and Genevieve Fabre. *Feasts and Celebrations in North American Ethnic Communities*. Albuquerque: University of New Mexico Press, 1995.

Habenstein, Robert W., and William M. Lamers. *Funeral Customs the World Over*, second edition. Milwaukee: Buffin, 1963.

Hampe, Johann Christoph. *To Die Is Gain: The Experience of One's Own Death.* Atlanta: John Knox, 1979.

Hannaford, Patricia P. "The Social Meaning of the Funeral to the Elderly." In *Grief and the Meaning of the Funeral*, ed. Otto S. Margolis et al. New York: MSS Information Corporation, 1975.

Harding, Rachael, and Mary Dison, eds. *A Book of Condolences: From the Private Letters of Illustrious People.* New York: Continuum, 1981.

Harmer, Ruth Mulvey. *The High Cost of Dying.* New York: Collier, 1963.

Harner, Michael. *The Way of the Shaman.* San Francisco: Harper and Row, 1990.

Harrington, Michael. *The Politics at God's Funeral: The Spiritual Crisis of Western Civilization.* New York: Holt, Rinehart, and Winston, 1983.

Hateley, B. J. *Telling Your Story, Exploring Your Faith: Writing Your Life Story for Personal Insight and Spiritual Growth.* St. Louis: CBP Press, 1985.

Hauerwas, Stanley. *A Community of Character.* Notre Dame, IN: University of Notre Dame Press, 1981.

Hellwig, Monika K. *What Are They Saying About Death and Christian Hope.* New York: Paulist, 1978.

Hertz, Robert. *Death and the Right Hand.* London: Cohen and West, 1960.

Heschel, Abraham J. *Who Is Man?* Stanford: Stanford University Press, 1965.

Hill, T. Patrick, and David Shirley. *A Good Death: Taking More Control at the End of Your Life.* Reading, Mass.: Addison-Wesley, 1996.

Hillman, James. *Re-Visioning Psychology.* New York: Harper, 1975.

———. *The Soul's Code: In Search of Character and Calling.* New York: Random House, 1996.

Hine, Virginia. *Last Letter to the Pebble People.* Santa Cruz, CA: Unity Press, 1979.

Hobsbawm, Eric, and Terence Ranger, eds. *The Invention of Tradition.* Cambridge: Cambridge University Press, 1983.

Hoffman, Lawrence, A. *Beyond the Text: A Holistic Approach to Liturgy.* Bloomington: Indiana University Press, 1987.

Holbein, Hans. *Dance of Death and Bible Woodcuts.* New York: Sylvan, 1947.

———. *The Dance of Death.* Boston: Cygnet, 1974.

Holmes, Urban T. *The Priest in Community: Exploring the Roots of Ministry.* New York: Seabury, 1978.

Holper, J. Frederick. "From Amnesia to Anamnesis: Sacraments and the Presbyterian Funeral Rite." *Reformed Liturgy and Music* 20 (Fall 1986): 204–7.

Hopkins, Gerard Manley. *The Poetical Works of Gerard Manley Hopkins.* Ed. Norman H. MacKenzie. Oxford: Clarendon Press, 1990.

Houlbrooke, Ralph. *Death, Ritual and Bereavement.* London: Routledge, 1989.

Humann, Harvey. *Death Without Fear.* Lawrence, KS: Penthe, 1992.

Humphreys, S. C., and Helen King, eds. *Mortality and Immortality: The Anthropology and Archaeology of Death.* London: Academic, 1981.

Humphry, Derek. *Final Exit.* New York: Dell, 1991.

Hunter, Kathryn Montgomery. *Doctors' Stories: The Narrative Structure of Medical Knowledge*. Princeton: Princeton University Press, 1996.

Hymnal Supplement. Chicago: GIA, 1991.

Illich, Ivan. *Medical Nemesis: The Expropriation of Health*. New York: Pantheon, 1976.

Immaculate, Sr. M. *The Cry of Rachel: An Anthology of Elegies on Children*. New York: Random House, 1966.

Ionesco, Eugène. *Exit the King*. New York: Grove, 1963.

Irion, Paul E. "Changing Patterns of Ritual Response to Death." *Omega* 22, no.3 (1990–91): 159–72.

———. *Cremation*. Philadelphia: Fortress, 1968.

———. *The Funeral and the Mourners: Pastoral Care of the Bereaved*. New York: Abingdon, 1954.

———. *The Funeral: An Explanation of Value*. Milwaukee: National Funeral Directors Association, 1956.

———. *The Funeral: Vestige or Value?* Nashville: Abingdon, 1966.

Irish, Donald P., Kathleen F. Lundquist, and Vivian Jenkins Nelsen, eds. *Ethnic Variations in Dying, Death, and Grief*. Washington, DC: Taylor and Francis, 1993.

Jackson, Charles O., ed. *Passing: The Vision of Death in America*. Westport, CT: Greenwood, 1977.

Jackson, Edgar N. *Understanding Grief*. Nashville: Abingdon, 1957.

James, Alice. *Death and Letters*. Ed. Ruth Yeazell. Berkeley: University of California Press, 1981.

Jones, Barbara. *Design for Death*. London: Andre Deutsch, 1967.

Jordahn, Bruno. *Das Kirchliche Begräbnis*. Göttingen: Vandenhoeck and Ruprecht, 1949.

Judd, Dorothy. *Give Sorrow Words: Working with a Dying Child*. London: Free Association, 1989.

Jung, Carl. "The Soul and Death." In *The Meaning of Death,* ed. Herman Feifel. New York: McGraw-Hill, 1959.

Jungel, Eberhard. *Death: The Riddle and the Mystery*. Philadelphia: Westminster, 1974.

Justice, Christopher. *Dying the Good Death: The Pilgrimage to Die in India's Holy City*. Albany: SUNY Press, 1997.

Kaiser, Otto, and Eduard Lohse. *Death and Life*. Nashville: Abingdon, 1981.

Kalish, Richard A., ed. *Death and Dying: Views from Many Cultures*. San Francisco: Baywood, 1980.

———, and David K. Reynolds. *Death and Ethnicity*. Los Angeles: University of Southern California Press, 1976.

Kaminsky, Marc, ed. *The Uses of Reminiscence: New Ways of Working with Older Adults*. New York: Haworth, 1984.

Kaplan, Edward K., trans. and ed. *Mother Death: The Journal of Jules Michelet*. Amherst: University of Massachusetts Press, 1984.

Kapleau, Philip. *The Wheel of Death.* New York: Harper and Row, 1971.

———. *The Wheel of Life and Death: A Practical and Spiritual Guide.* New York: Doubleday, 1989.

Karo, Nancy. *Adventure in Dying.* Chicago: Moody, 1976.

Kastenbaum, Robert. "Do We Die in Stages?" In *Understanding Death and Dying,* ed. Sandra Wilcox and Marilyn Sutton. Palo Alto, CA: Mayfield, 1981.

———, and Ruth Aisenberg. *The Psychology of Death.* New York: Springer, 1972.

Kastenbaum, Victor, ed. *The Humanity of the Ill.* Knoxville: University of Tennessee Press, 1982.

Kaufmann, Walter. *Existentialism, Religion, and Death.* New York: New American Library, 1976.

Kavanagh, Aidan. *Elements of Rite: A Handbook of Liturgical Style.* Collegeville, MN: Liturgical Press, 1990.

Keleman, Stanley. *Living Your Dying.* New York: Random House, 1974.

Kelly, John D., and Martha Kaplan. "History, Structure, and Ritual." *Annual Review of Anthropology* 19 (1990): 119–50.

Kertzer, David I. *Ritual, Politics, and Power.* New Haven: Yale University Press, 1988.

Kieckhefer, Richard. *Unquiet Souls: Fourteenth Century Saints and Their Religious Milieu.* Chicago: University of Chicago Press, 1984.

Killilea, Alfred. *The Politics of Being Mortal.* Lexington: University Press of Kentucky, 1988.

———. "Some Political Origins of the Denial of Death." *Omega* 8, no. 3 (1977): 205–14.

Kinast, Robert L. *When a Person Dies: Pastoral Theology in Death Experiences.* New York: Crossroad, 1984.

Kinnell, Galway. *Mortal Arts, Mortal Words.* Boston: Houghton Mifflin, 1980.

———. *Selected Poems.* Boston: Houghton Mifflin, 1982.

Klass, Dennis, Phyllis R. Silverman, and Steven L. Nickman, eds. *Continuing Bonds: New Understandings of Grief.* Washington, DC: Taylor and Francis, 1996.

Kleinman, Arthur. *The Illness Narratives: Suffering, Healing, and the Human Condition.* New York: Basic Books, 1988.

Kligman, Gail. *The Wedding of the Dead: Ritual, Poetics, and Popular Culture in Transylvania.* Berkeley: University of California Press, 1988.

Kramer, Kenneth. *The Sacred Art of Dying: How World Religions Understand Death.* New York: Paulist, 1988.

Kreeft, Peter J. *Heaven: The Heart's Deepest Longing.* San Francisco: Harper and Row, 1980.

Kselman, Thomas A. *Death and the Afterlife in Modern France.* Princeton: Princeton University Press, 1993.

Kübler-Ross, Elisabeth. *Death: The Final Stage of Growth.* Englewood Cliffs, NJ: Prentice Hall, 1975.

———. *On Death and Dying.* New York: Macmillan, 1969.

Kumin, Maxine. *Our Ground Time Here Will Be Brief.* New York: Penguin, 1982.

Kushner, Harold S. *When Bad Things Happen to Good People.* New York: Avon, 1981.

La Fleur, W. R. "Japan." In *Death and Eastern Thought,* ed. Frederick H. Holck. Nashville: Abingdon, 1974.

Lair, George S. *Counseling the Terminally Ill: Sharing the Journey.* Washington, DC: Taylor and Francis, 1996.

Lane, Dermot A. *Keeping Hope Alive: Stirrings in Christian Theology.* New York: Paulist, 1996.

Langer, Susanne K. *Philosophy in a New Key.* Cambridge: Harvard University Press, 1957.

Lasch, Christopher. *The Culture of Narcissism.* New York: Norton, 1991.

———. *The Minimal Self: Psychic Survival in Troubled Times.* New York: Norton, 1984.

Lati, Rinbochay, and Jeffrey Hopkins. *Death, Intermediate State and Rebirth in Tibetan Buddhism.* Ithaca, NY: Snow Lion Publications, 1979.

Lattimore, Richmond. *Themes in Greek and Latin Epitaphs.* Urbana: University of Illinois Press, 1962.

Leach, Edmund. *Culture and Communication.* New York: Cambridge University Press, 1976.

Lee, Jung Young. *Death Overcome: Towards a Convergence of Eastern and Western Views.* Washington, DC: University Press of America, 1983.

Le Goff, Jacques. *The Birth of Purgatory.* Chicago: University of Chicago Press, 1986.

Lerner, Gerda. *A Death of One's Own.* New York: Simon and Schuster, 1978.

Lesy, Michael. *Wisconsin Death Trip.* New York: Pantheon, 1973.

Lévi-Strauss, Claude. *The Savage Mind.* Chicago: University of Chicago Press, 1966.

———. *Tristes Tropiques.* Chicago: University of Chicago Press, 1955.

Levine, Philip. *One for the Rose.* New York: Atheneum, 1981.

Levinson, Daniel J. *The Seasons of a Man's Life.* New York: Alfred A. Knopf, 1978.

Leviton, D. "Death Education." In *New Meanings of Death,* ed. Herman Feifel. New York: McGraw-Hill, 1977.

Lewis, James R., ed. *Magical Religion and Modern Witchcraft.* Albany: SUNY Press, 1996.

Libby, Anthony. *Mythologies of Nothing: Mystical Death in American Poetry, 1940–1970.* Urbana: University of Illinois Press, 1984.

Lifton, Robert Jay. *The Broken Connection: On Death and the Continuity of Life.* New York: Simon and Schuster, 1979.

Lisboa, Maria Manuel. "'The Maid Is Not Dead but Sleepeth': Death and Revival in Writing by Women." In *Ritual and Remembrance: Responses to Death in Human Societies,* ed. Jon Davies. Sheffield: Sheffield Academic Press, 1994.

Litten, Julian. *The English Way of Death: The Common Funeral Since 1450.* London: Robert Hale, 1991.

Llewellyn, Nigel. *The Art of Death: Visual Culture in the English Death Ritual, 1500–1800*. London: Victoria and Albert Museum, 1991.

Lofland, Lyn H. *The Craft of Dying: The Modern Face of Death*. Beverly Hills: Sage Publications, 1978.

Lonetto, Richard, and David I. Templer. *Death Anxiety*. Washington, DC: Hemisphere, 1986.

Loraux, Nicole. *The Invention of Athens: The Funeral Oration in the Classical City*. Trans. Alan Sheridan. Cambridge: Harvard University Press, 1986.

———. *Tragic Ways of Killing a Woman*. Trans. Anthony Forster. Cambridge: Harvard University Press, 1987.

MacAloon, John J., ed. *Rite, Drama, Festival, Spectacle: Rehearsals Toward a Theory of Cultural Performance*. Philadelphia: Institute for the Study of Human Issues, 1984.

Mack, Arien, ed. *Death in American Experience*. New York: Schocken, 1973.

Malinowski, B. "Death and the Reintegration of the Group." In *Magic, Science, Religion, and Other Essays*, ed. B. Malinowski. New York: Doubleday, 1954.

Mandelbaum, D. "Social Uses of Funeral Rites." In *The Meaning of Death*, ed. Herman Feifel. New York: McGraw-Hill, 1959.

Margolis, Otto S., et al, eds. *Grief and the Meaning of the Funeral*. New York: MSS Information Corporation, 1975.

Marks, Amy Seidel, and Bobby J. Calder. *Attitudes Toward Death and Funerals*. Evanston: Center for Marketing Sciences, 1982.

Marshall, Victor W. *Last Chapters: A Society of Aging and Dying*. Monterey, CA: Brooks/Cole Publishing Company, 1980.

———. *Later Life: The Social Psychology of Aging*. Beverly Hills: Sage, 1986.

Marty, Martin E. *A Cry of Absence*. San Francisco: Harper, 1983.

Maschio, Thomas. *To Remember the Faces of the Dead: The Plenitude of Memory in Southwestern New Britain*. Madison: University of Wisconsin Press, 1994.

Mathews, Joseph W. "The Time My Father Died." In *The Modern Vision of Death*, ed. Nathan A. Scott, Jr. Richmond: John Knox Press, 1967.

May, Melanie A. *A Theopoetics of Death and Resurrection*. New York: Continuum, 1995.

May, William F. "The Sacred Power of Death in Contemporary Experience." *Social Research* 39, no.3 (August 1972): 465–74.

———. *The Physician's Covenant: Images of the Healer in Medical Ethics*. Philadelphia: Westminster, 1983.

McClendon, James William, Jr. *Biography as Theology: How Life Stories Can Remake Today's Theology*. Nashville: Abingdon, 1974.

McConn, Barbara A. *The Hospice Project Report*. Chicago: Joint Commision on Accreditation of Hospitals, 1985.

McCoy, Marjorie Casebier. *To Die with Style*. Nashville: Abingdon, 1974.

McFague, Sallie. *The Body of God: An Ecological Theology*. Philadelphia: Fortress, 1993.

————. *Metaphorical Theology*. Philadelphia: Fortress, 1982.

————. *Models of God*. Philadelphia: Fortress, 1987.

McGill, Arthur C. *Suffering: A Test of Theological Method*. Philadelphia: Westminster, 1982.

McManners, John. *Death and the Enlightenment*. Oxford: Oxford University Press, 1981.

Mead, Margaret. "Ritual in Social Crisis." In *Roots of Ritual*, ed. J. Shaughnessy. Grand Rapids: Eerdmans, 1973.

Meilander, Gilbert. "Theology in Stories: C. S. Lewis and the Narrative Quality of Experience." *Word and World* 1 (Spring 1981).

Menten, Ted. *Gentle Closings: How to Say Goodbye to Someone You Love*. Philadelphia: Running Press, 1991.

Merrifield, Ralph. *The Archaelogy of Ritual and Magic*. New York: New Amsterdam, 1987.

Metcalf, Peter, and Richard Huntington. *Celebrations of Death: The Anthropology of Mortuary Ritual*, second edition. Cambridge: Cambridge University Press, 1991.

Metzger, Deena. *Writing for Your Life: A Guide and Companion to the Inner Worlds*. San Francisco: Harper, 1992.

Meyer, Richard E., ed. *Ethnicity and the American Cemetery*. Bowling Green, KY: Bowling Green University University Press, 1993.

Meyers, Jeffrey. *Disease and the Novel, 1880–1960*. New York: St. Martin's, 1985.

Milazzo, G. Tom. *The Protest and the Silence: Suffering, Death, and Biblical Theology*. Minneapolis: Fortress, 1992.

Miller, James H., and Anthony F. Rotatori. *Death Education and the Educator*. Springfield, IL: Charles C. Thomas, 1986.

Miller-McLemore, Bonnie J. *Death, Sin and the Moral Life*. Atlanta: Scholars, 1988.

Milton, Sybil. *In Fitting Memory: The Art and Politics of Holocaust Memorials*. Detroit: Wayne State University Press, 1991.

Mitchell, Kenneth R., and Herbert Anderson. *All Our Losses, All Our Griefs: Resources for Pastoral Care*. Philadelphia: Westminster, 1983.

Mitford, Jessica. *The American Way of Death*. New York: Simon and Schuster, 1963.

Mitscherlich, Alexander, and Margarete Mitscherlich. *The Inability to Mourn: Principles of Collective Behavior*. New York: Grove, 1975.

Moffat, Mary Jane, ed. *In the Midst of Winter: Selections from the Literature of Mourning*. New York: Vintage, 1982.

Mogenson, Greg. *Greeting the Angels: An Imaginal View of the Mourning Process*. Amityville, NY: Baywood, 1992.

Moltmann, Jürgen. *The Coming of God: Christian Eschatology*. Minneapolis: Fortress, 1996.

————. *The Crucified God*. New York: Harper and Row, 1974.

————. *Theology of Hope*. New York: Harper and Row, 1967.

Moody, Harry R. "Foreword: The Owl of Minerva." In *Aging and the Religious*

Dimension, ed. L. Eugene Thomas and Susan A. Eisenhandler. Westport, CT: Auburn House, 1994.

———. "The Meaning of Life and the Meaning of Old Age." In *What Does It Mean to Grow Old? Reflections from the Humanities,* ed. Thomas R. Cole and Sally A. Gadow. Durham, NC: Duke University Press, 1986.

———. "Reminiscence and the Recovery of the Public World." In *The Uses of Reminiscence,* ed. Marc Kaminsky. New York: Haworth, 1984.

Moore, Sally F., and Barbara G. Myerhoff, eds. *Secular Ritual.* Amsterdam: Van Gorcum, 1977.

Morris, Ian. *Death-Ritual and Social Structure in Classical Antiquity.* Cambridge: Cambridge University Press, 1992.

Mullin, Glenn H. *Death and Dying: The Tibetan Tradition.* Boston: Arkana, 1986.

Munn, Nancy D. "Symbolism in a Ritual Context: Aspects of Symbolic Action." In *Handbook of Social and Cultural Anthropology,* ed. John J. Honigmann. Chicago: Rand McNally, 1973.

Myerhoff, Barbara G. "A Death in Due Time: A Construction of Self and Culture in Ritual Drama." In *Rite, Drama, Festival, Spectacle,* ed. John J. MacAloon. Philadelphia: Institutution for Study of Human Issues, 1984.

———. "A Symbol Perfected in Death: Continuity and Ritual in the Life and Death of an Elderly Jew." In *Life's Career—Aging: Cultural Variations on Growing Old,* ed. Barbara G. Myerhoff and Andrei Simic. Beverly Hills: Sage Publications, 1978.

Neale, Robert E. *The Art of Dying.* New York: Harper and Row, 1973.

Neimeyer, Robert A., ed. *Death Anxiety Handbook: Research, Instrumentation, and Application.* Washington, DC: Taylor and Francis, 1994.

Neville, Gwen Kennedy. "The Sacred and the Civic: Representations of Death in the Town Ceremony of Border Scotland." *Anthropological Quarterly* 62 (October 1989): 163–74.

Noren, Carol M. "The Word of God in Worship: Preaching in Relationship to Liturgy." In *The Study of Liturgy,* ed. Cheslyn Jones et al. New York: Oxford University Press, 1992.

Norris, Kathleen. *The Cloister Walk.* New York: Riverhead, 1996.

———. *Dakota: A Spiritual Geography.* New York: Ticknor and Fields, 1993.

North, Michael. *The Final Sculpture: Public Monuments and Modern Poets.* Ithaca, NY: Cornell University Press, 1985.

Nouwen, Henri J. *A Letter of Consolation.* San Francisco: Harper and Row, 1982.

Ochs, Donovan J. *Consolatory Rhetoric: Grief, Symbol, and Ritual in the Greco-Roman Era.* Columbia: University of South Carolina Press, 1993.

Oppenheimer, Helen. *The Hope of Heaven.* Cambridge, MA: Cowley, 1988.

Oraison, Marc. *The Wound of Mortality.* New York: Doubleday, 1971.

Order of Christian Funerals: The Roman Ritual. Chicago: Liturgy Training Publications, 1989.

O'Gorman, Thomas, ed. *An Advent Sourcebook*. Chicago: Liturgy Training Publications, 1988.

Palgi, Phyllis, and Henry Abramovitch. "Death: A Cross-Cultural Perspective." *Annual Review of Anthropology* 13 (1984): 385–417.

Palmer, Gary. *Death: The Trip of a Lifetime*. San Francisco: Harper, 1993.

Palmer, Parker J. *The Company of Strangers: Christians and the Renewal of America's Public Life*. New York: Crossroad, 1981.

Parry, Joan K., and Angela Shen Ryan. *A Cross-Cultural Look at Death, Dying, and Religion*. Chicago: Nelson-Hall, 1995.

Parry, Jonathan P. *Death in Banaras*. Cambridge: Cambridge University Press, 1994.

Parsons, Talcott, and Victor Lidz. "Death in American Society." In *Essays in Self-Destruction*, ed. Edwin S. Shneidman. New York: Science House, 1967.

Pasternak, Boris. *Poems*. Trans. Eugene M. Koyden. Ann Arbor: University of Michigan Press, 1959.

Paxton, Frederick S. *Christianizing Death: The Creation of a Ritual Process in Early Medieval Europe*. Ithaca, NY: Cornell University Press, 1990.

Payne, Richard K. "Realizing Inherent Enlightenment: Ritual and Self-Transformation in Shingon Buddhism." In *Religious and Social Ritual: Interdisciplinary Explorations*, ed. Michael B. Aune and Valerie DeMarinis. Albany: SUNY Press, 1996.

A Pearl of Christian Counsel for the Brokenhearted: Anonymous 14th Century Poem. Trans., ed., and commentary by Vernard Eller. Washington, DC: University Press of America, 1983.

Pfatteicher, Philip H. *Commentary on the Occasional Services*. Philadelphia: Fortress, 1983.

———, and Carlos R. Messerli. *Manual on the Liturgy: Lutheran Book of Worship*. Minneapolis: Augsburg, 1979.

Pine, Vanderlyn R. *Caretaker of the Dead: The American Funeral Director*. New York: Wiley, 1975.

———, et al., eds. *Acute Grief and the Funeral*. Springfield, IL: Charles C. Thomas, 1976.

Postman, Neil. *Amusing Ourselves to Death*. New York: Viking, 1985.

Power, David, and Luis Maldonado, eds. *Liturgy and Human Passage*. New York: Seabury, 1979.

Presbyterian Church, U.S.A. *The Funeral: A Service of Witness to the Resurrection*. Philadelphia: Westminster, 1986.

Prior, Lindsay. *The Social Organization of Death: Medical Discourse and Social Practices in Belfast*. New York: St. Martin's, 1989.

Progoff, Ira. *At a Journal Workshop*. New York: Dialog House, 1975.

Pruett, James. "Requiem." In *The New Grove Dictionary of Music and Musicians*. London: Macmillan, 1980.

Prunkl, Peter R., and Rebecca L. Berry. *Death Week: Exploring the Dying Process*. New York: Hemisphere, 1989.

The Quest for Eternity: Chinese Ceramic Sculptures from the People's Republic of China. Los Angeles: Los Angeles County Museum of Art, 1987.

Raether, H. C., and R. C. Slater. "Immediate Postdeath Activities in the US." In *New Meanings of Death,* ed. Herman Feifel. New York: McGraw-Hill, 1977.

Ragon, Michel. *The Space of Death: A Study of Funerary Architecture, Decoration, and Urbanism.* Trans. Alan Sheridan. Charlottesville: University Press of Virginia, 1983.

Rahner, Karl. *On the Theology of Death.* New York: Seabury, 1973.

Ramsey, Paul. "The Indignity of Death with Dignity." In *Death Inside Out,* ed. Peter Steinfels and Robert M. Veatch. New York: Harper and Row, 1974.

Rappaport, Roy A. "The Obvious Aspects of Ritual." In *Ecology, Meaning, and Religion.* Richmond, CA: North Atlantic Books, 1979.

Richardson, Ruth. *Death, Dissection, and the Destitute.* London: Routledge, 1987.

Ricoeur, Paul. *Freud and Philosophy.* New Haven: Yale University Press, 1970.

Rieff, Philip. *The Triumph of the Therapeutic: Uses of Faith After Freud.* New York: Harper and Row, 1966.

Riemer, Jack, and Nathaniel Stampfer. *Ethical Wills: A Modern Jewish Treasury.* New York: Schocken, 1983.

Rilke, Rainer Maria. *Prose and Poetry.* Ed. Egon Schwarz. New York: Continuum, 1984.

Rinpoche, Sogyal. *The Tibetan Book of Living and Dying.* San Francisco: Harper, 1993.

Roach, Joseph. *Cities of the Dead.* New York: Columbia University Press, 1996.

Roberts, William O. *Initiation to Adulthood: An Ancient Rite of Passage in Contemporary Form.* New York: Pilgrim, 1982.

Robertson, Alec. *Requiem: Music of Mourning and Consolation.* New York: Praeger, 1968.

Rodabough, T. "Funeral Roles: Ritualized Expectations." *Omega* 14 (1981–82): 135–44.

Rosaldo, R. "Grief and the Headhunter's Rage: On the Cultural Force of Emotions." In *Text, Play, and Story: The Construction and Reconstruction of Self and Society,* ed. E. Bruner. Washington, DC: American Ethnological Society, 1984.

Rosenblatt, Paul C., R. Patricia Walsh, and Douglas A. Jackson. *Grief and Mourning in Cross-Cultural Perspective.* New Haven: HRAF Press, 1976.

Rothstein, Edward. [Review of Elemire Zolla's *Archetypes.*] *New York Times Book Review,* May 16, 1982.

Rouillard, Philippe. "The Liturgy of the Dead as a Rite of Passage." In *Liturgy and Human Passage,* ed. David Power and Luis Maldonado. New York: Crossroad, 1979.

Rowell, Geoffrey. *The Liturgy of Christian Burial: An Introductory Survey of the Historical Development of Christian Burial Rites.* London: Alcuin Club/SPCK, 1977.

Rudman, Daniel. "Nursing Home Medicine." *Second Opinion* 16 (March 1991): 109–22.

Ruitenbeek, Hendrik M., ed. *The Interpretation of Death.* New York: Jason Aronson, 1973.

Ruiz de la Peña, Juan Luis. "The Element of Projection and Belief in Heaven." In *Heaven,* ed. Bas van Iersel and Edward Schillebeeckx. New York: Seabury, 1979.

Rutherford, Richard. *The Death of a Christian: The Rite of Funerals.* New York: Pueblo Publishing, 1980.

Sacks, Peter M. *The English Elegy: Studies in the Genre from Spenser to Yeats.* Baltimore: Johns Hopkins University Press, 1985.

Saroyan, Aram. *Last Rites: The Death of William Saroyan.* New York: William Morrow, 1982.

Sawyer, John. "Isaiah as a Source Book for Scriptural Texts About Death and Mourning." In *Ritual and Remembrance: Responses to Death in Human Societies,* ed. Jon Davies. Sheffield: Sheffield Academic Press, 1994.

Schechner, Richard. *The Future of Ritual: Writings on Culture and Performance.* New York: Routledge, 1993.

———, and Willa Appel, eds. *By Means of Performance: Intercultural Studies of Theatre and Ritual.* Cambridge: Cambridge University Press, 1990.

Schleiermacher, Friedrich. *On Religion: Speeches to Its Cultured Despisers.* Trans. John Oman. New York: Harper, 1958.

Schmidt, Herman, ed. *Liturgy in Transition.* New York: Herder and Herder, 1971.

———, and David Power, eds. *Politics and Liturgy.* New York: Herder and Herder, 1974.

Schwarz, Hans. *Beyond the Gates of Death.* Minneapolis: Augsburg, 1981.

Scott, Frances G., and Ruth M. Brewer, eds. *Confrontations of Death: A Book of Readings and a Suggested Method of Instruction.* Corvallis: Continuing Education Books, 1971.

Scott, Nathan A., Jr., ed. *The Modern Vision of Death.* Richmond: John Knox, 1967.

———. *The Poetry of Civic Virtue.* Philadelphia: Fortress, 1976.

Schroeder-Sheker, Therese. "Music for the Dying: Using Prescriptive Music in the Death-Bed Vigil." *Noetic Sciences Review,* Autumn 1994: 32–36.

Searl, Edward. *In Memoriam: A Guide to Modern Funeral and Memorial Services.* Boston: Skinner House, 1993.

Searle, Mark. "Ritual." In *The Study of Liturgy,* ed. Cheslyn Jones et al. New York: Oxford University Press, 1992.

Segundo, Juan. *The Sacraments Today.* Trans. John Drury. Maryknoll, NY: Orbis Books, 1971.

Sennett, Richard. *The Fall of Public Man.* New York: Alfred A. Knopf, 1977.

Seremetakis, C. Nadia. *The Last Word: Women, Death, and Divination in Inner Maui.* Chicago: University of Chicago Press, 1991.

A Service of Death and Resurrection. Nashville: Abingdon, 1979.

Shapiro, Kenneth A. *Dying and Living: One Man's Life with Cancer.* Austin: University of Texas Press, 1985.

Sharkey, Frances. *A Parting Gift.* New York: St. Martin's, 1982.

Simpson, Michael A. *Dying, Death, and Grief: A Critically Annotated Bibliography and Source Book of Thanatology and Terminal Care.* New York: Plenum, 1979.

———. "The Future of Death: Exploration or Exploitation." *Thanatology Today,* October 1980.

Slough, Rebecca J. "Let Every Tongue, by Art Refined." In *Religious and Social Ritual: Interdisciplinary Explorations,* ed. Michael B. Aune and Valerie DeMarinis. Albany: SUNY Press, 1996.

Sloyan, Virginia, ed. *A Sourcebook About Christian Death.* Chicago: Liturgy Training Publications, 1990.

Smith, Jonathan Z. *To Take Place: Toward Theory in Ritual.* Chicago: University of Chicago Press, 1987.

Smith, Roy Steinhoff. "Mourning Becomes Existence: Martin Buber's 'Melancholy' Ontology." *Journal of Religion* 69 (1989): 326–43.

Solecki, R. S. *Shanidar.* New York: Knopf, 1971.

Solomon, Maynard. *Mozart: A Life.* New York: HarperCollins, 1996.

Solzhenitysn, Alexander. *The Cancer Ward.* New York: Bantam, 1972.

Sontag, Susan. *Illness as Metaphor.* New York: Farrar, Straus, and Giroux, 1977.

Southard, Samuel, comp. *Death and Dying: A Bibliographical Survey.* New York: Greenwood Press, 1991.

Spicker, Stuart F., Kathleen M. Woodward, and David D. van Tassel, eds. *Aging and the Elderly: Humanistic Perspectives in Gerontology.* Atlantic Highlands, NJ: Humanities Press, 1978.

Spiegel, Yorick. *The Grief Process.* Nashville: Abingdon, 1977.

Spretnak, Charlene, ed. *The Politics of Women's Spirituality.* Garden City, NY: Doubleday Anchor, 1982.

Stannard, David E., ed. *Death in America.* Philadelphia: University of Pennsylvania Press, 1975.

———. *The Puritan Way of Death: A Study in Religion, Culture and Social Change.* New York: Oxford University Press, 1977.

Starr, Paul. *The Social Transformation of American Medicine.* New York: Basic Books, 1982.

Stein, Arnold. *The House of Death: Messages from the English Renaissance.* Baltimore: Johns Hopkins University Press, 1986.

Sternberg, Franki, and Barbara Sternberg. *If I Die and When I Do: Exploring Death With Young People.* Englewood Cliffs, NJ: Prentice Hall, 1980.

Stevens, Wallace. *Opus Posthumous.* Ed. Samuel French Morse. New York: Knopf, 1957.

Stortz, Martha Ellen. "Ritual Power, Ritual Authority." In *Religious and Social Ritual: Interdisciplinary Explorations,* ed. Michael B. Aune and Valerie DeMarinis. Albany: SUNY Press, 1996.

Stringfellow, William. *Instead of Death.* New York: Seabury, 1976.

Strocchia, Sharon T. *Death and Ritual in Renaissance Florence*. Baltimore: Johns Hopkins University Press, 1992.

Stroup, George W. "Death, Resurrection and the Communion of the Saints." *Reformed Liturgy and Music* 20 (Fall 1986): 189–93.

Sudnow, David. *Passing On: The Social Organization of Dying*. Englewood Cliffs, NJ: Prentice Hall, 1967.

Suilleabhain, Sean O. *Irish Wake Amusements*. Cork: Mercer, 1967.

Sullivan, Lawrence E. *Icanchu's Drum: An Orientation to Meaning in South American Religions*. New York: Macmillan, 1988.

———, ed. *Death, Afterlife, and the Soul: Religion, History, and Cultural Selections from the Encyclopedia of Religion*. New York: Macmillan, 1989.

Switzer, David K. *The Dynamics of Grief*. Nashville: Abingdon, 1978.

Szasz, Thomas. *The Theology of Medicine*. New York: Harper and Row, 1977.

Tashjian, Dickran, and Ann Tashjian. *Memorials for Children of Change: The Art of Early New England Stonecarving*. Middletown, CT: Wesleyan University Press, 1974.

Tatelbaum, Judy. *The Courage to Grieve*. New York: Lippincott and Croinell, 1980.

Taussig, Michael. *Shamanism, Colonialism, and the Wild Man: A Study in Terror and Healing*. Chicago: University of Chicago Press, 1987.

Taylor, Lawrence J. "Cultural Constructions of Death in Ireland." *Anthropological Quarterly* 62 (October 1989): 175–88.

———. "Introduction: The Uses of Death in Europe." *Anthropological Quarterly* 62 (October 1989): 149–54.

Taylor, Lou. *Mourning Dress: A Costume and Social History*. London: George Allen and Unwin, 1983.

Thomas, James L., ed. *Death and Dying in the Classroom: Readings for Reference*. Phoenix: Oryx Press, 1984.

Thomas, L. Eugene, and Susan A. Eisenhandler. *Aging and the Religious Dimension*. Westport, CT: Auburn House, 1994.

Thompson, Stuart. "Death, Food, and Fertility." In *Death Ritual in Late Imperial and Modern China,* ed. James L. Watson and Evelyn S. Rawski. Berkeley: University of California Press, 1988.

Thucydides. *History of the Peloponnesian War*. Trans. Rex Warner. Baltimore: Penguin, 1954.

Tillich, Paul. *The Courage to Be*. New Haven: Yale University Press, 1952.

Tornstam, Lars. "Gero-Transcendence: A Theoretical and Empirical Exploration." In *Aging and the Religious Dimension,* ed. L. Eugene Thomas and Susan A. Eisenhandler. Westport, CT: Auburn House, 1994.

Tripp, D. H. "Liturgy and Pastoral Service." In *The Study of Liturgy,* ed. Cheslyn Jones et al. New York: Oxford University Press, 1992.

Turner, Kay. "Contemporary Feminist Rituals." In *The Politics of Women's Spirituality,* ed. Charlene Spretnak. Garden City, NY: Doubleday, 1982.

Turner, Victor. "The Anthropology of Performance." In *The Anthropology of Performance,* ed. Victor Turner. New York: PAJ, 1987.

———. "Are There Universals of Performance?" In *By Means of Performance,* ed. Richard Schechner and Willa Appel. Cambridge: Cambridge University Press, 1990.

———. "Body, Brain, and Culture." *Zygon* 18, no.3 (1983): 221–45.

———. "Images and Reflections: Ritual, Drama, Carnival, Film and Spectacle in Cultural Performance." In *The Anthropology of Performance,* ed. Victor Turner. New York: PAJ, 1987.

———. *The Ritual Process: Structure and Anti-Structure.* Chicago: Aldine, 1969.

———. "Social Dramas in Brazilian Umbanda: The Dialectics of Meaning." In *The Anthropology of Performance,* ed. Victor Turner. New York: PAJ, 1987.

———. ed. *The Anthropology of Performance.* New York: PAJ, 1987.

van Baaren, Th. P. "Death." In *The Encyclopedia of Religion,* ed. Mircea Eliade. New York: Macmillan, 1987.

van Gennep, Arnold. *The Rites of Passage.* Chicago: University of Chicago Press, 1960.

Veatch, Robert M. *Death, Dying, and the Biological Revolution.* New Haven: Yale University Press, 1976.

Vogel, Linda J. *Rituals for Resurrection: Celebrating Life and Death.* Nashville: Upper Room, 1996.

Wakeman, Frederic Jr. "Mao's Remains." In *Death Ritual in Late Imperial and Modern China,* ed. James L. Watson and Evelyn S. Rawski. Berkeley: University of California Press, 1988.

Ward, Hannah, and Jennifer Wild. *Human Rites: Worship Resources for an Age of Change.* London: Mowbray, 1995.

Ware, James H., Jr. *Not With Words of Wisdom: Performative Language and Liturgy.* Washington, DC: University Press of America, 1981.

Warner, W. Lloyd. *The Living and the Dead: A Study of the Symbolic Life of Americans.* Westport, CT: Greenwood, 1975.

———. "City of the Dead." In *Death and Identity,* ed. Robert Fulton. Revised Edition. Bowie, MD: Charles, 1976.

Wass, Hannelore, ed. *Dying: Facing the Facts.* Washington, DC: Hemisphere, 1979.

———, et al. *Death Education: An Annotated Resource Guide.* Washington, DC: Hemisphere, 1980.

Watson, James L., and Evelyn S. Rawski, eds. *Death Ritual in Late Imperial and Modern China.* Berkeley: University of California Press, 1988.

Weber, Max. *From Max Weber: Essays in Sociology.* Ed. H. H. Gerth and C. Wright Mills. New York: Oxford University Press, 1946.

Weir, Robert, ed. *Death in Literature.* New York: Columbia University Press, 1980.

Weisman, Avery. "Appropriate and Appropriated Death." *Death: Current Perspectives,* third edition, ed. Edwin S. Shneidman. Palo Alto, CA: Mayfield, 1984.

———. *The Realization of Death: A Guide for the Psychological Autopsy.* New York:

Jason Aronson, 1974.

Westberg, Granger E. *Good Grief.* Philadelphia: Fortress, 1962.

Weston, John H. "Aging the Last Stage? or, the Dream Continued." *Second Opinion* 16 (March 1991): 123–38

Whaley, Joachim. *Mirrors of Mortality: Studies in the Social History of Death.* New York: St. Martin's, 1981.

Whitman, Alden. *The Obituary Book.* New York: Stein and Day, 1971.

Whyte, Martin K. "Death in the People's Republic of China." In *Death Ritual in Late Imperial and Modern China,* ed. James L. Watson and Evelyn S. Rawski. Berkeley: University of California Press, 1988.

Williams, Philip W. "Who Is the Funeral For?" *Dialog* 32 (Summer 1993): 171–77.

Williams, William Carlos. *The Desert Music and Other Poems.* New York: Random House, 1954.

———. *Patterson.* New York: New Directions, 1963.

Wilson, Jane Wynne. *Funerals Without God: A Practical Guide to Non-Religious Funerals.* Buffalo, NY: Prometheus, 1990.

Worgul, George S. *From Magic to Metaphor: A Validation of the Christian Sacraments.* New York: Panelist, 1980.

Worth, Grace. "At the Center of the Story." In *The Uses of Reminiscence: New Ways of Working with Older Adults,* ed. Marc Kaminsky. New York: Haworth, 1984.

Wybrew, Hugh. "Ceremonial." In *The Study of Liturgy,* ed. Cheslyn Jones et al. New York: Oxford University Press, 1992.

Wyschograd, Edith. *The Phenomenon of Death: Faces of Mortality.* New York: Harper and Row, 1973.

———. *Spirit in Ashes: Hegel, Heidegger, and Man-Made Mass Death.* New Haven: Yale University Press, 1985.

Yeats, W. B. *The Collected Poems of W. B. Yeats,* revised second edition. Ed. Richard J. Finneran. New York: Scribner, 1996.

Zaleski, Carol. *The Life of the World to Come: Near-Death Experience and Christian Hope.* New York: Oxford University Press, 1996.

———. *Otherworld Journeys: Accounts of Near-Death Experiences in Medieval and Modern Times.* New York: Oxford University Press, 1987.

Index